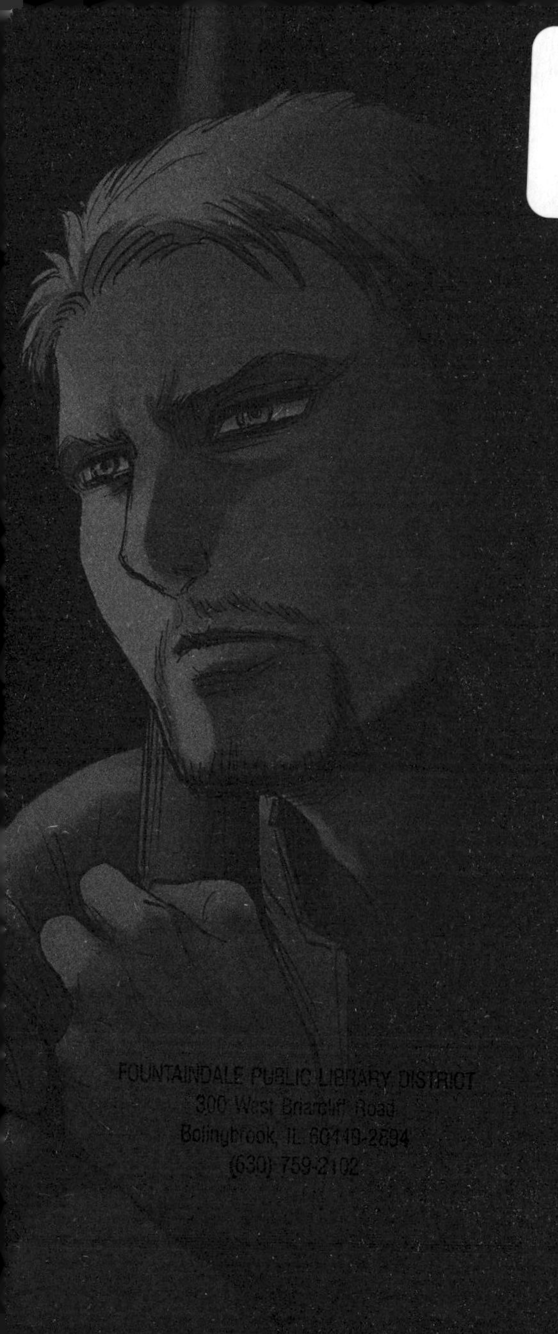



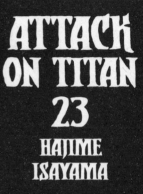

# ATTACK ON TITAN 23

HAJIME ISAYAMA

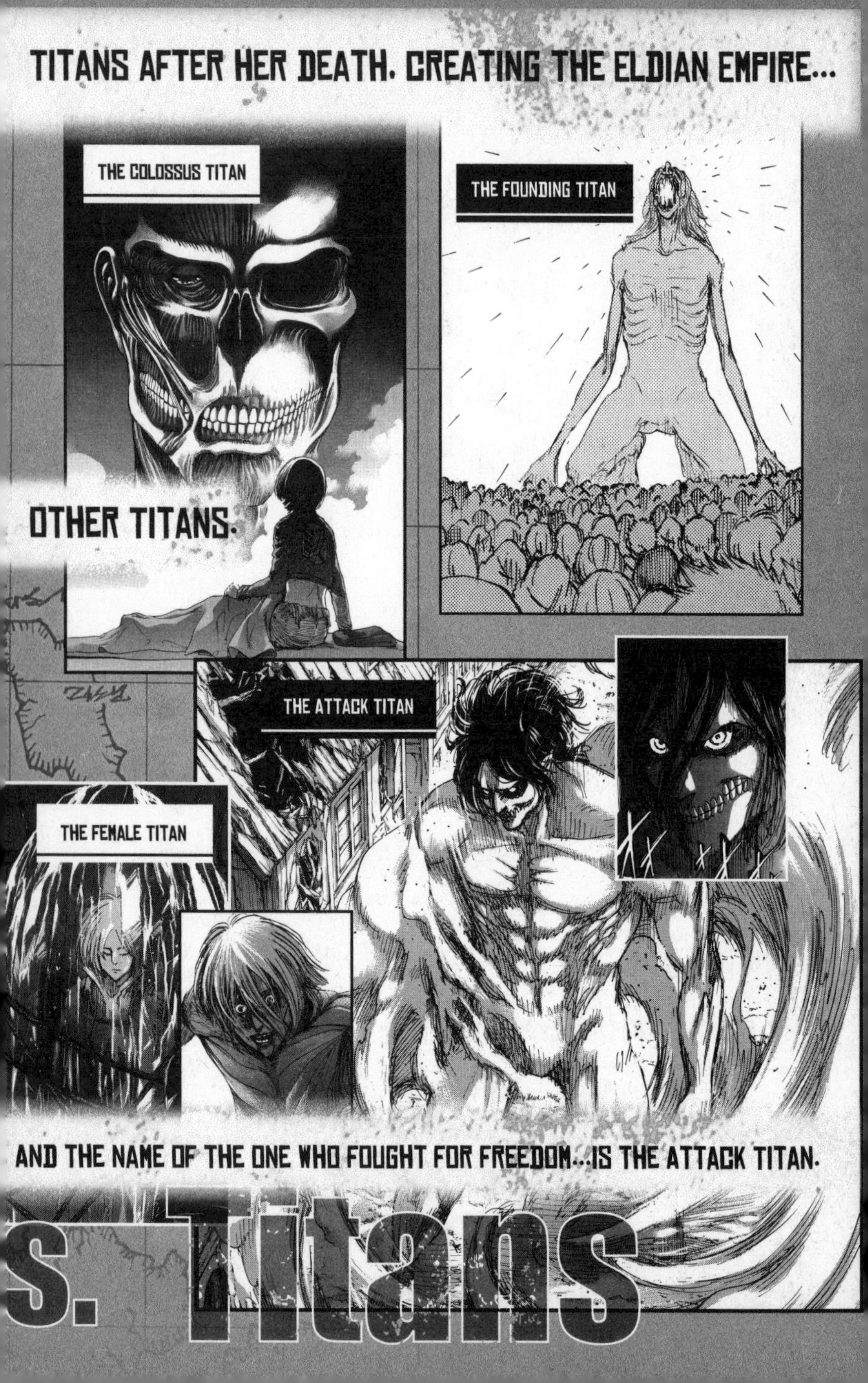
TITANS AFTER HER DEATH, CREATING THE ELDIAN EMPIRE...
THE FOUNDING TITAN
THE COLOSSUS TITAN
OTHER TITANS.
THE ATTACK TITAN
THE FEMALE TITAN
AND THE NAME OF THE ONE WHO FOUGHT FOR FREEDOM...IS THE ATTACK TITAN.
S. Titans

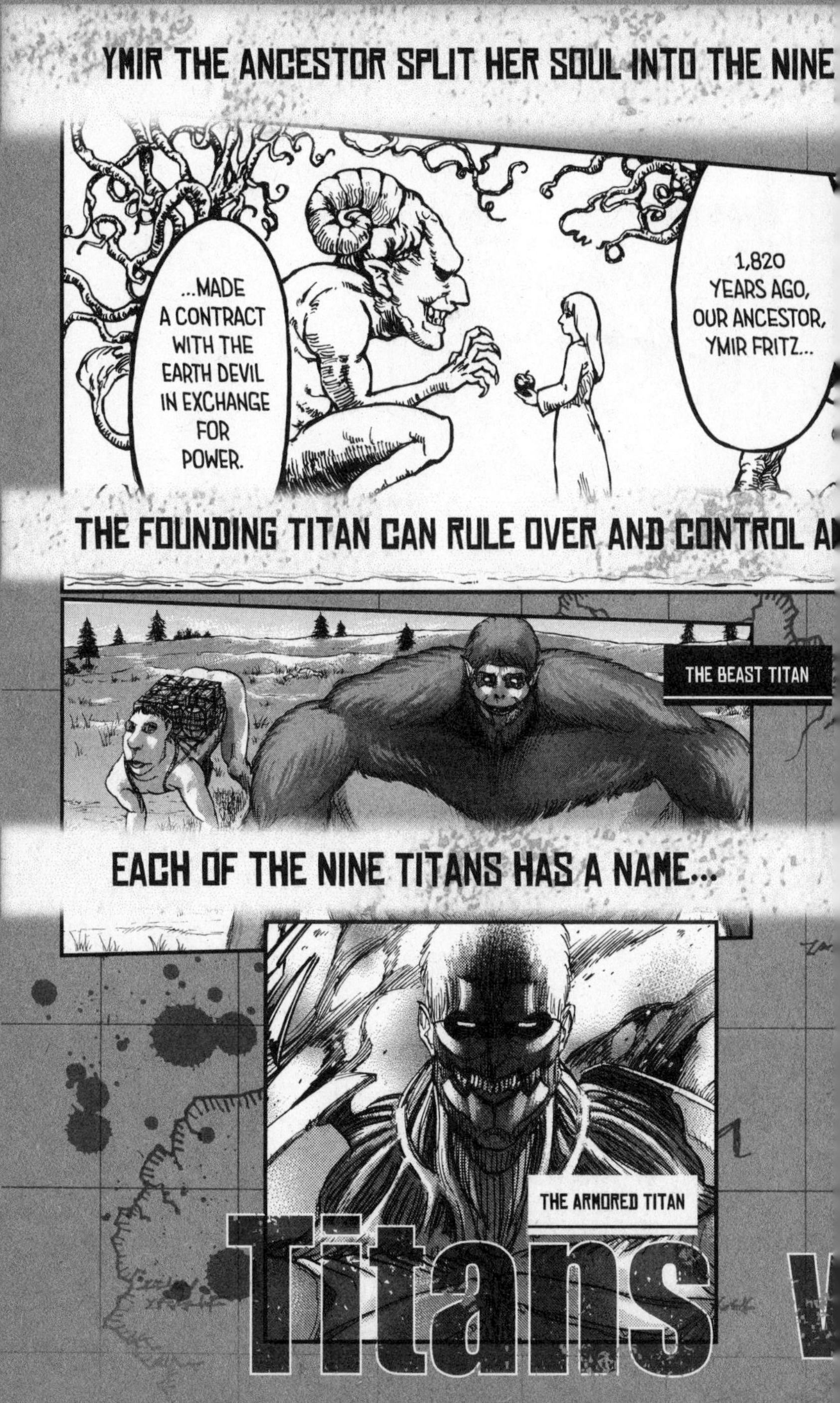
YMIR THE ANCESTOR SPLIT HER SOUL INTO THE NINE
1,820 YEARS AGO, OUR ANCESTOR, YMIR FRITZ...
...MADE A CONTRACT WITH THE EARTH DEVIL IN EXCHANGE FOR POWER.
THE FOUNDING TITAN CAN RULE OVER AND CONTROL
THE BEAST TITAN
EACH OF THE NINE TITANS HAS A NAME...
THE ARMORED TITAN
Titans

# ATTACK on TITAN

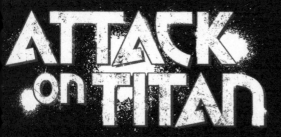

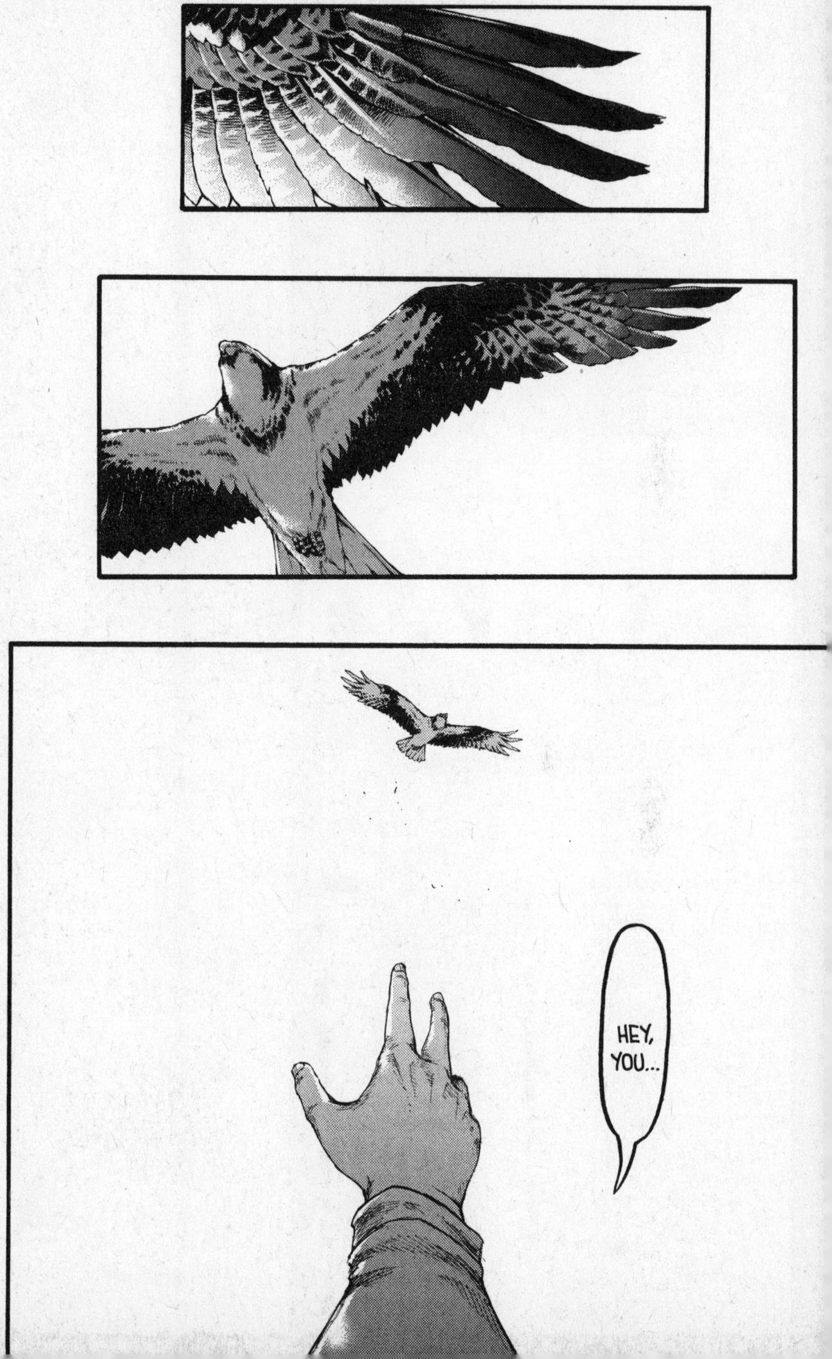
HEY, YOU...

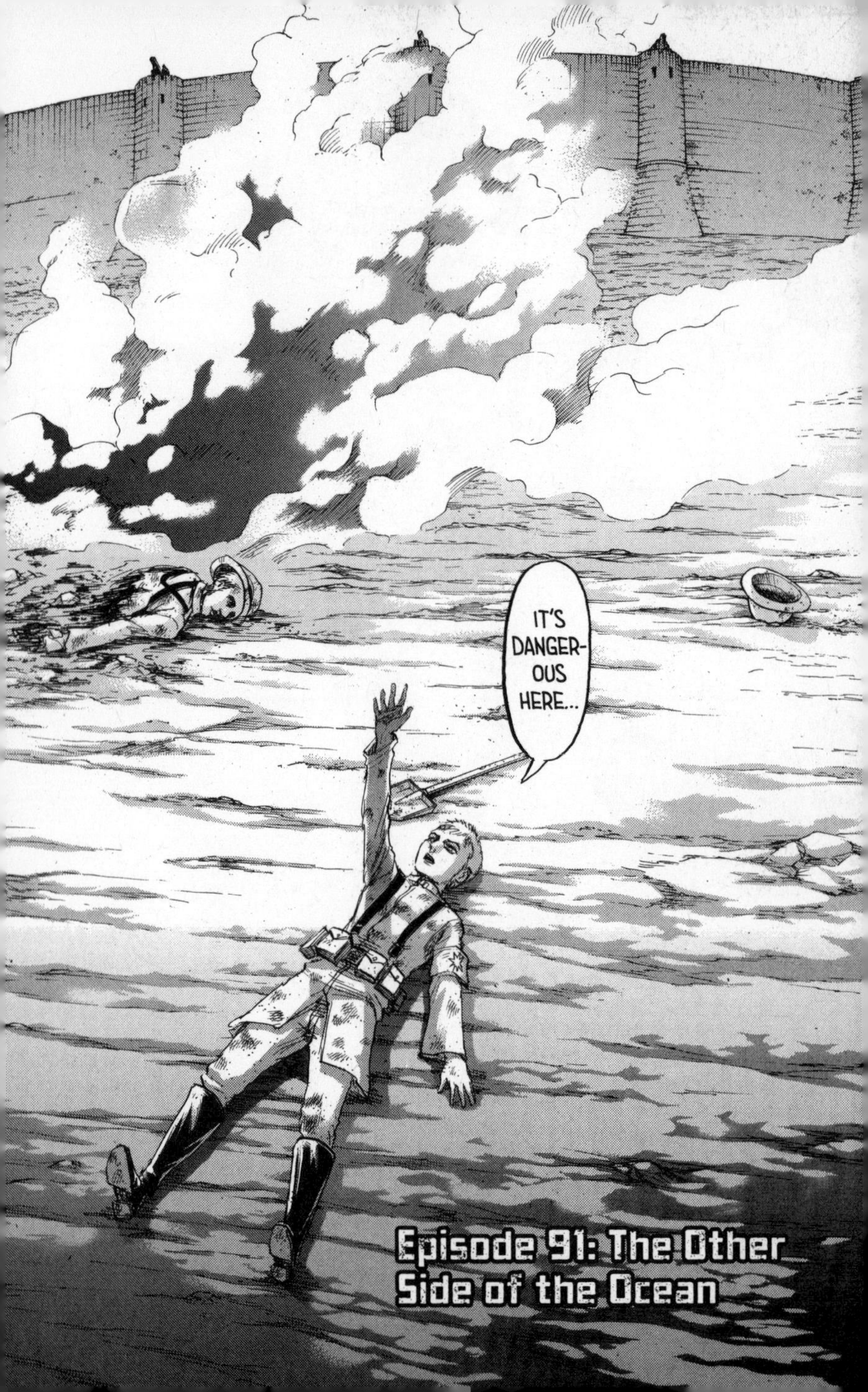
IT'S DANGER-OUS HERE...
Episode 91: The Other Side of the Ocean

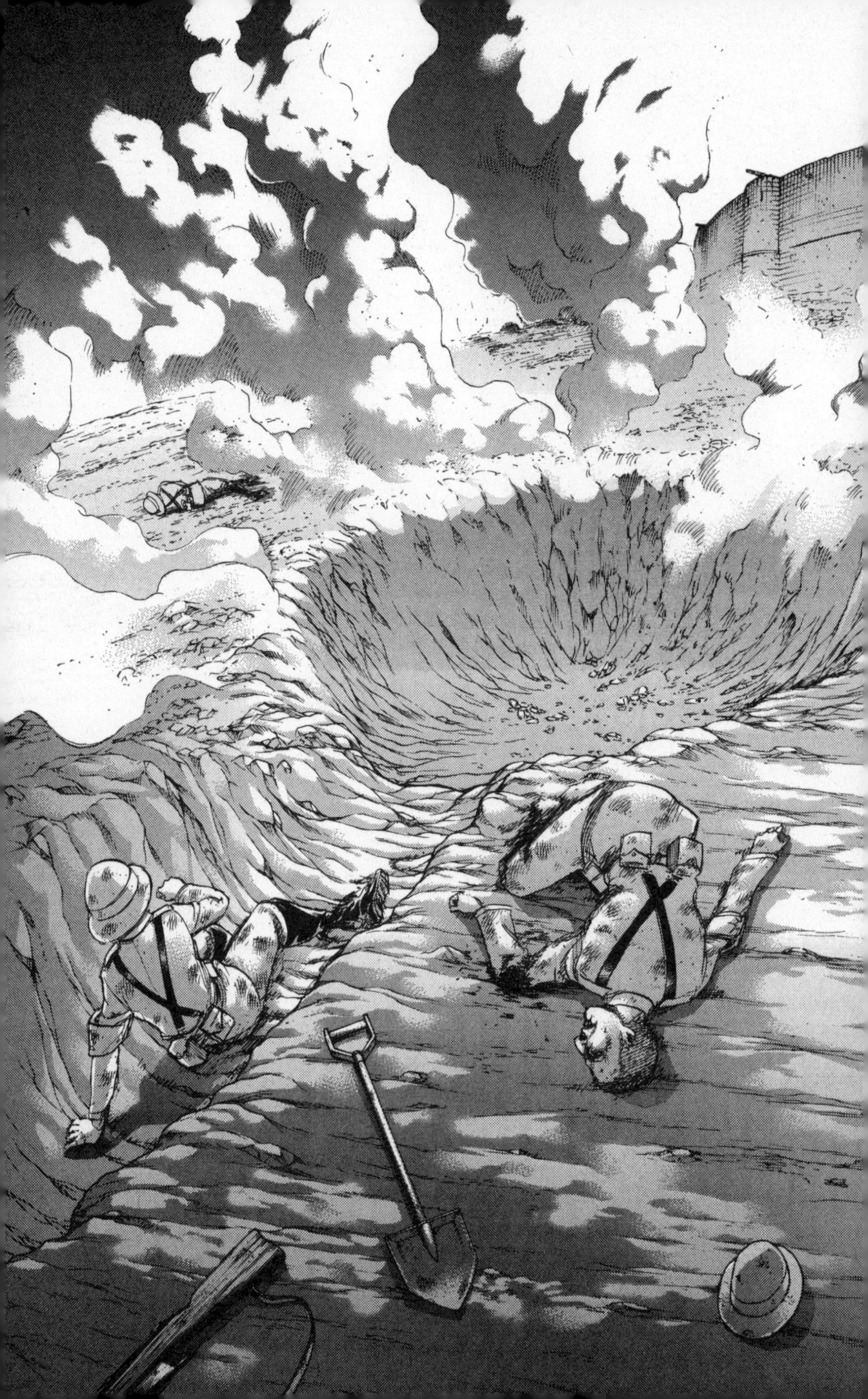

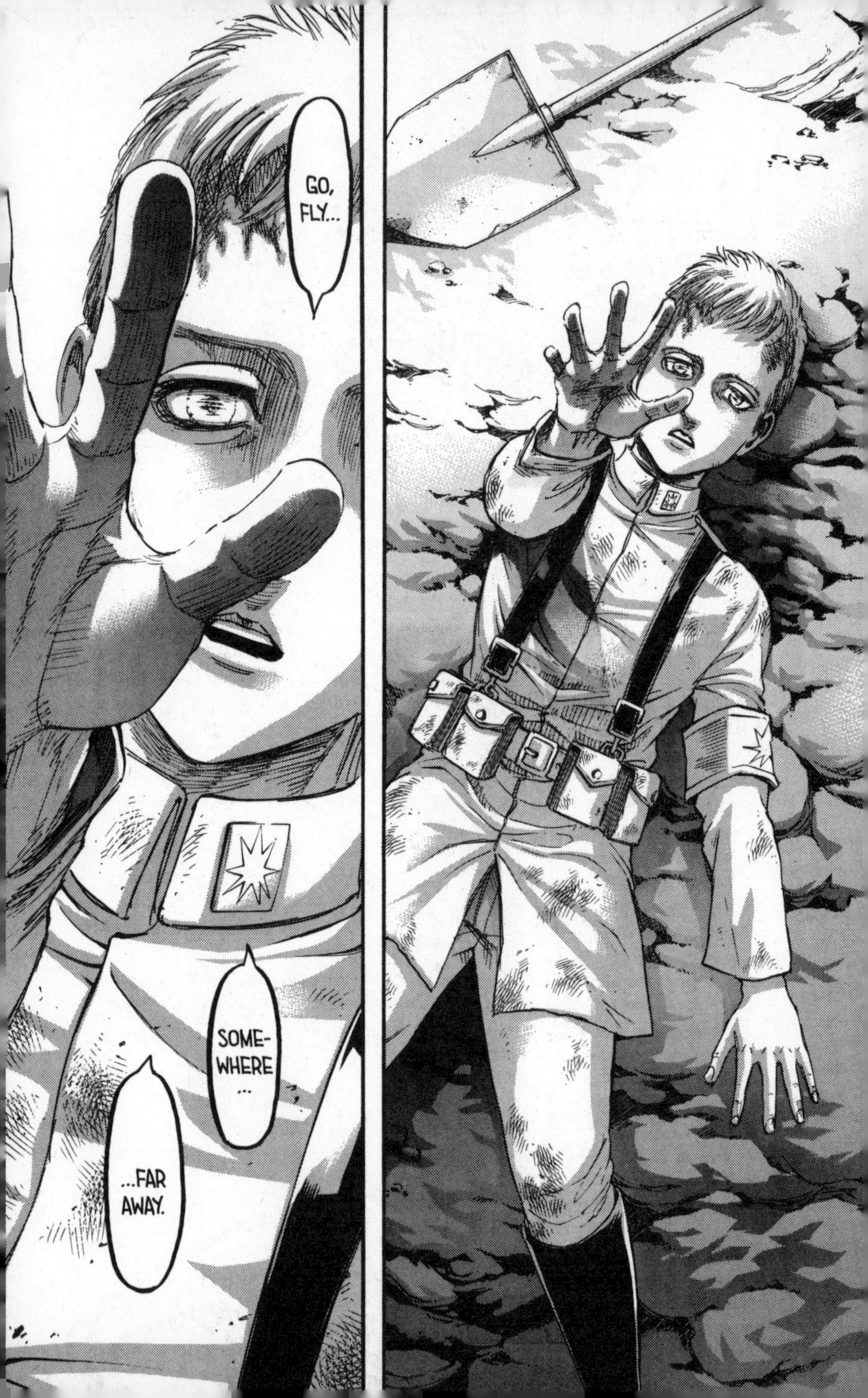
GO, FLY...
SOME-WHERE ...
...FAR AWAY.

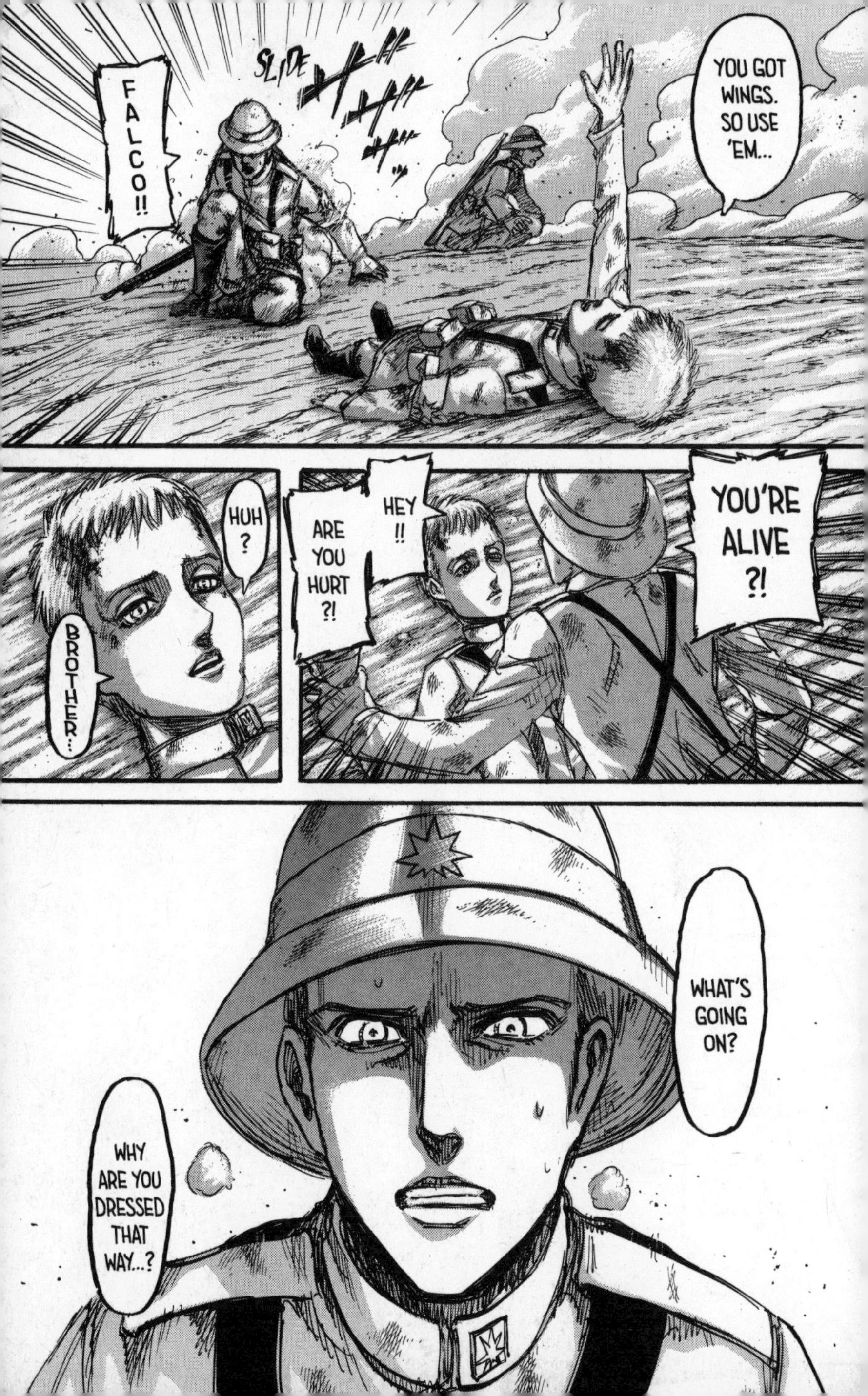
YOU GOT WINGS. SO USE 'EM...
SLIDE
FALCO!!
YOU'RE ALIVE?!
HEY!!
ARE YOU HURT?!
HUH?
BROTHER...
WHAT'S GOING ON?
WHY ARE YOU DRESSED THAT WAY...?

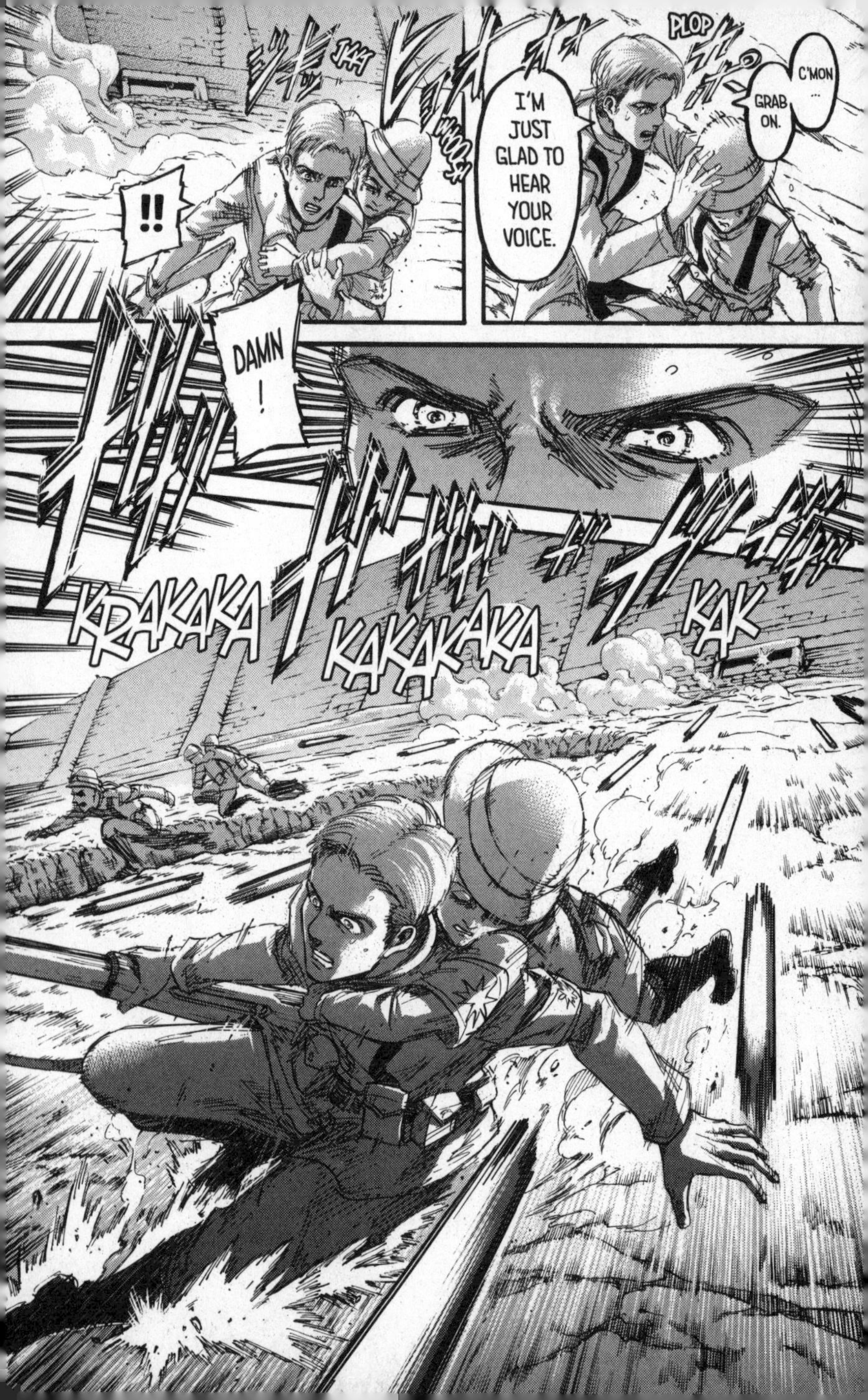
PLOP
C'MON ...
GRAB ON.
I'M JUST GLAD TO HEAR YOUR VOICE.
WHOOSH
JKKT
!!
DAMN !
KAK
KAKAKAKA
KRAKAKA

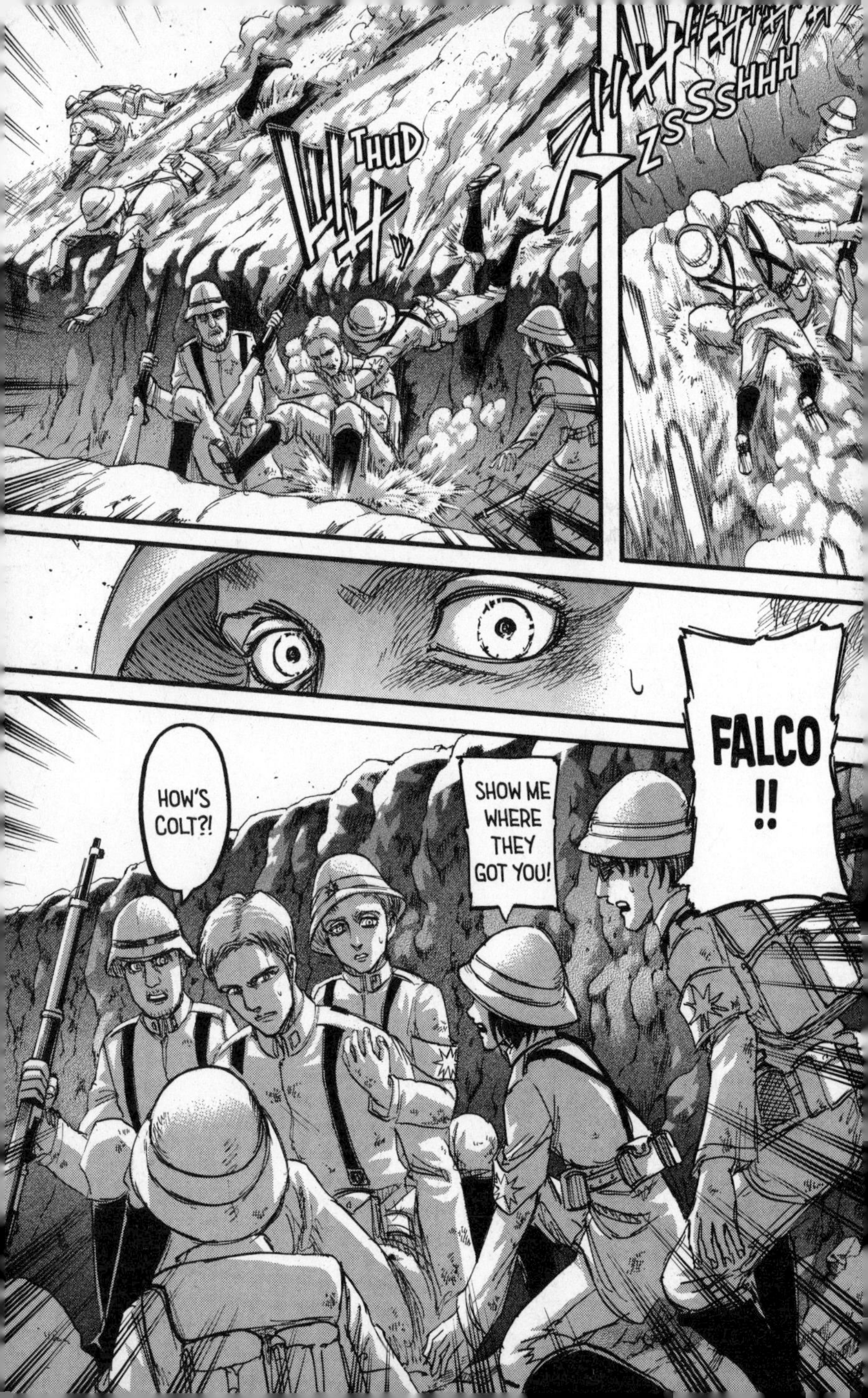
ZSSSHHH
THUD
FALCO !!
SHOW ME WHERE THEY GOT YOU!
HOW'S COLT?!

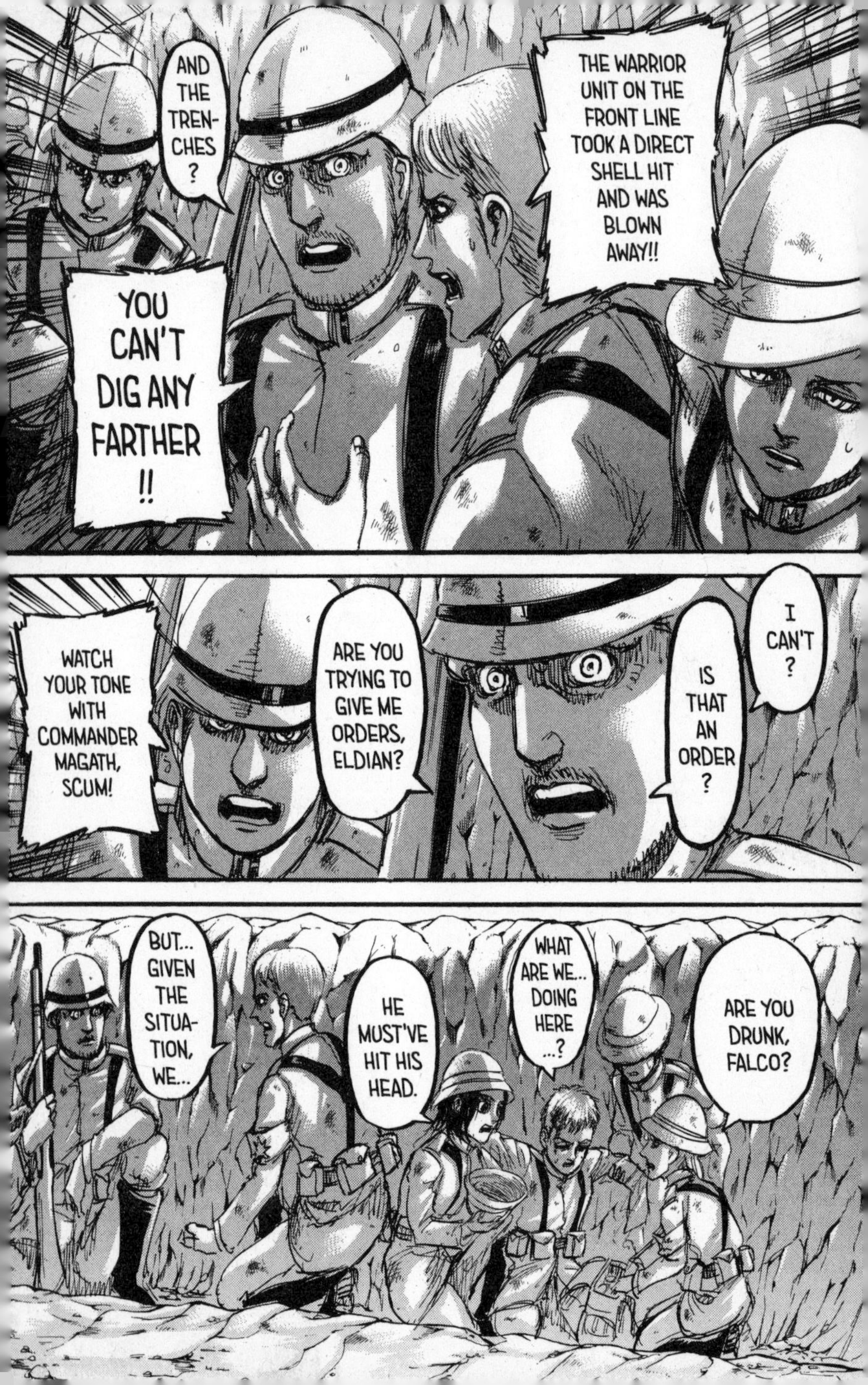
THE WARRIOR UNIT ON THE FRONT LINE TOOK A DIRECT SHELL HIT AND WAS BLOWN AWAY!!
AND THE TRENCHES?
YOU CAN'T DIG ANY FARTHER!!
I CAN'T?
IS THAT AN ORDER?
ARE YOU TRYING TO GIVE ME ORDERS, ELDIAN?
WATCH YOUR TONE WITH COMMANDER MAGATH, SCUM!
ARE YOU DRUNK, FALCO?
WHAT ARE WE... DOING HERE...?
HE MUST'VE HIT HIS HEAD.
BUT... GIVEN THE SITUATION, WE...

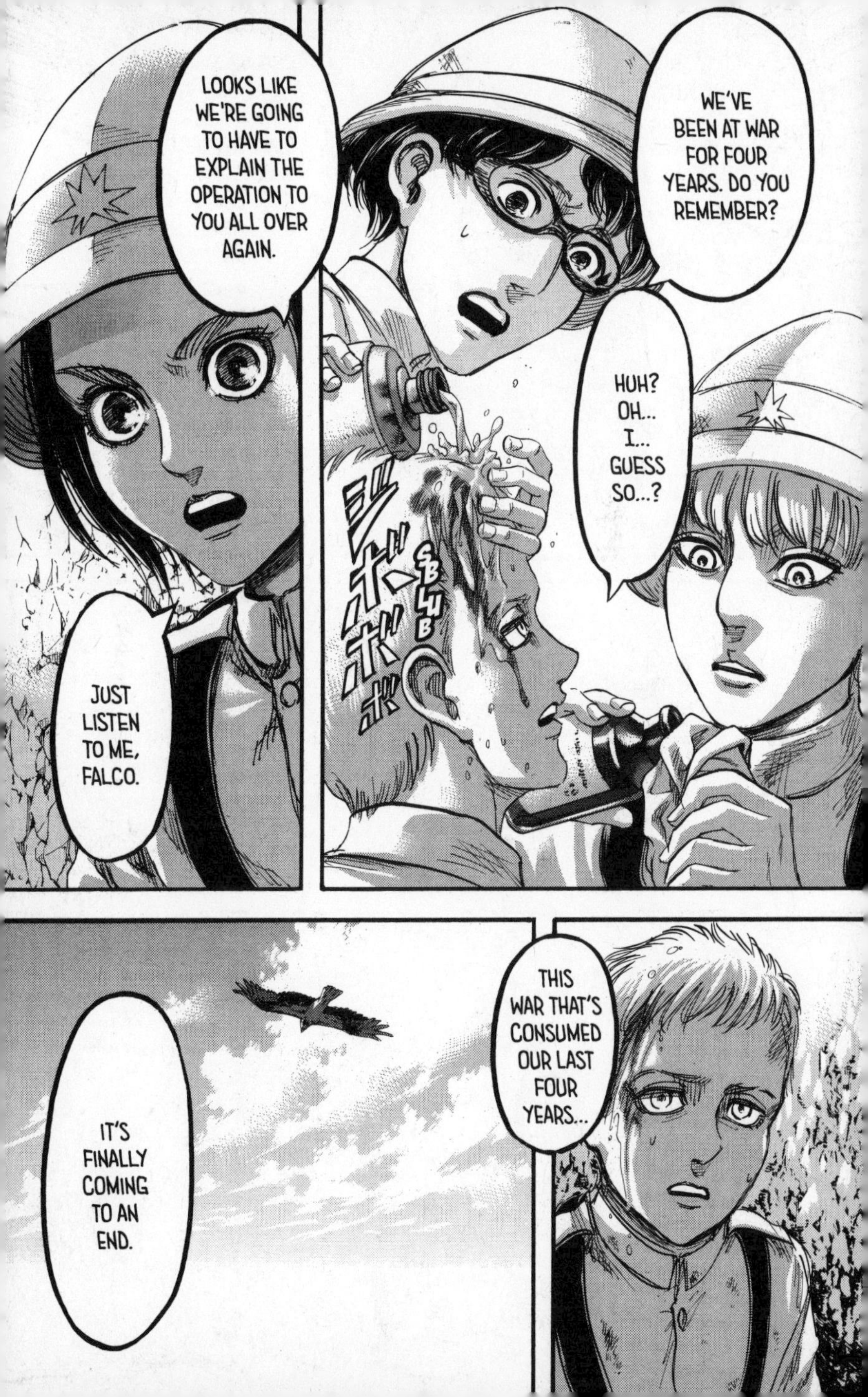
WE'VE BEEN AT WAR FOR FOUR YEARS. DO YOU REMEMBER?
HUH? OH... I... GUESS SO...?
SBLUB
LOOKS LIKE WE'RE GOING TO HAVE TO EXPLAIN THE OPERATION TO YOU ALL OVER AGAIN.
JUST LISTEN TO ME, FALCO.
THIS WAR THAT'S CONSUMED OUR LAST FOUR YEARS...
IT'S FINALLY COMING TO AN END.

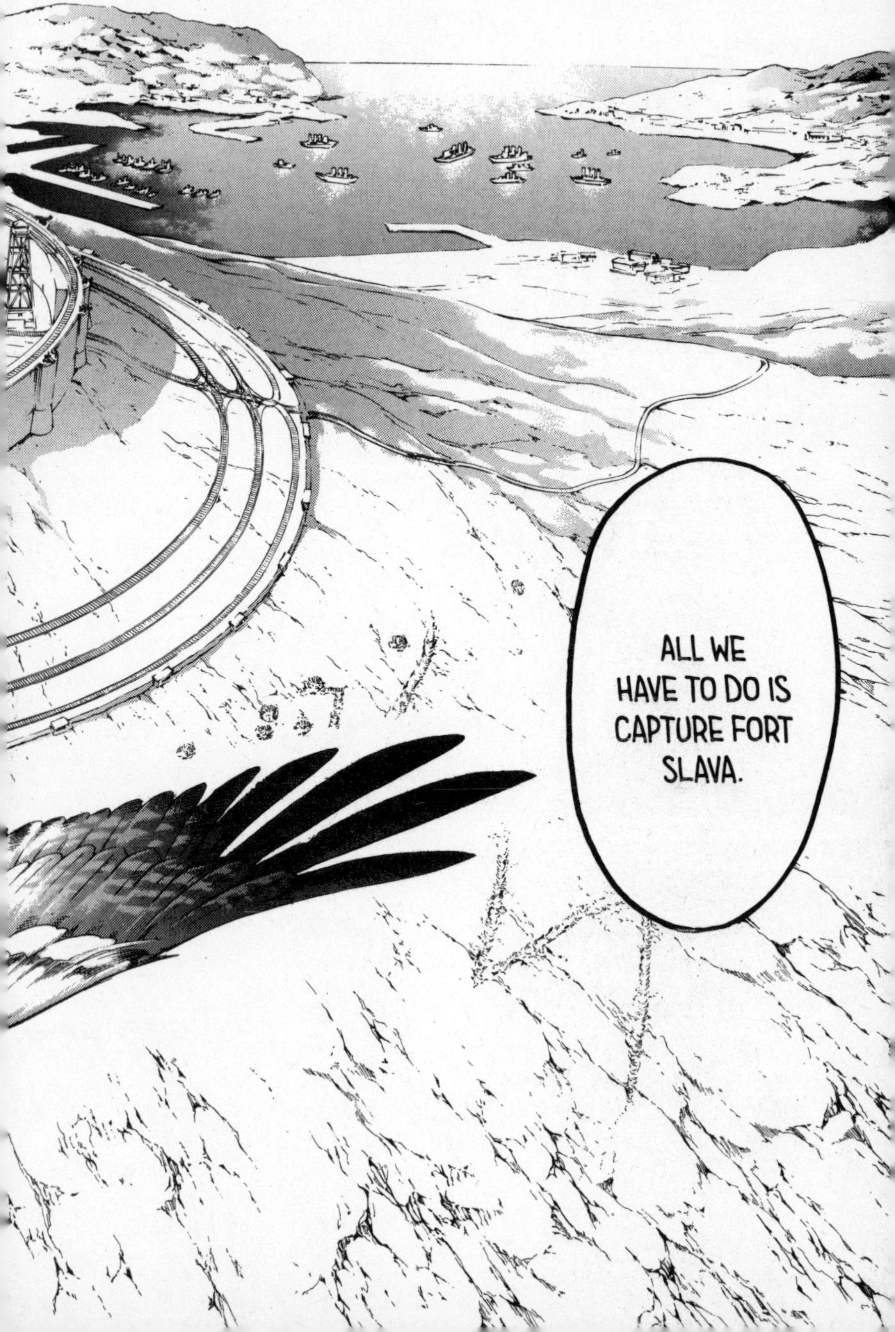
ALL WE HAVE TO DO IS CAPTURE FORT SLAVA.

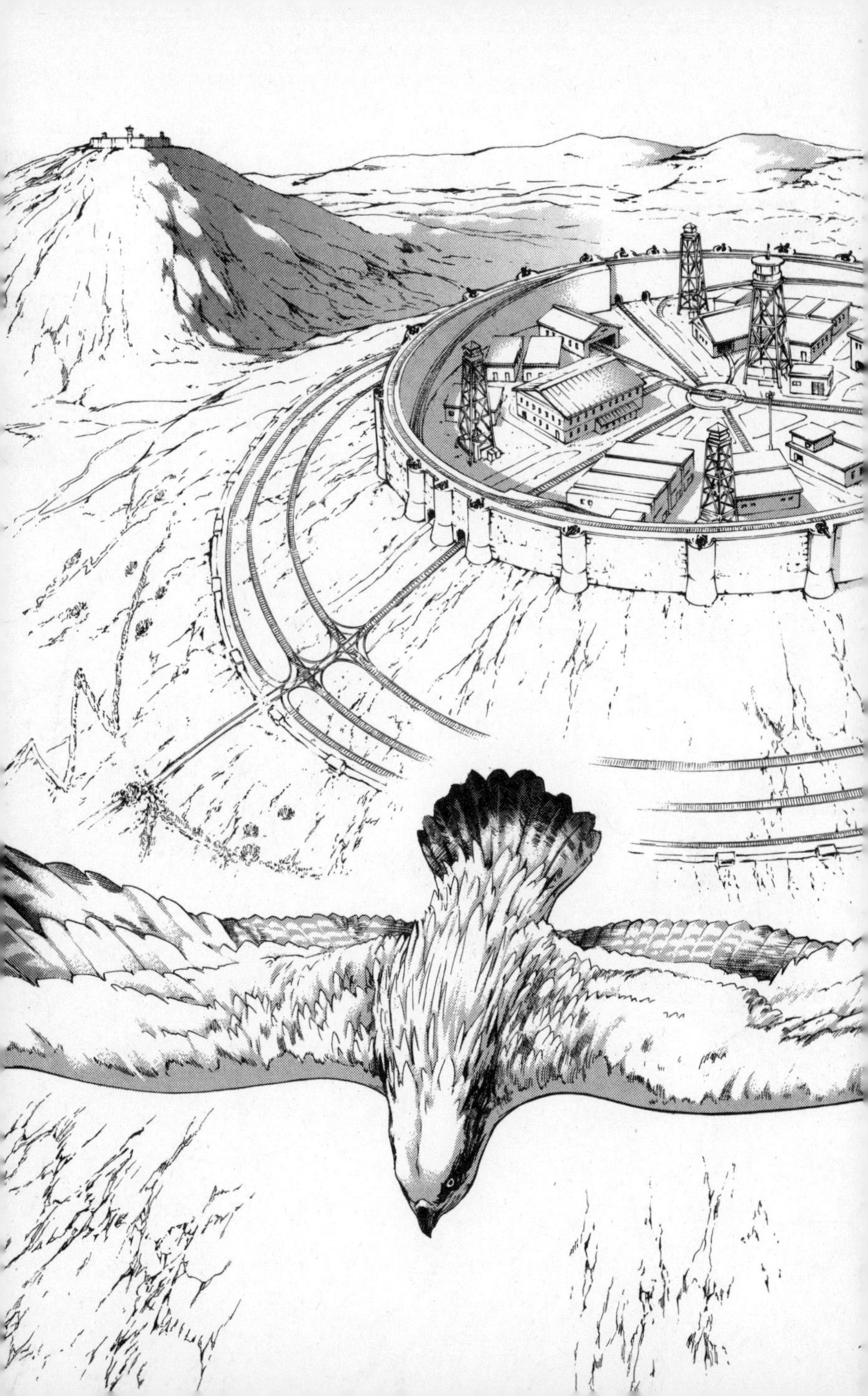

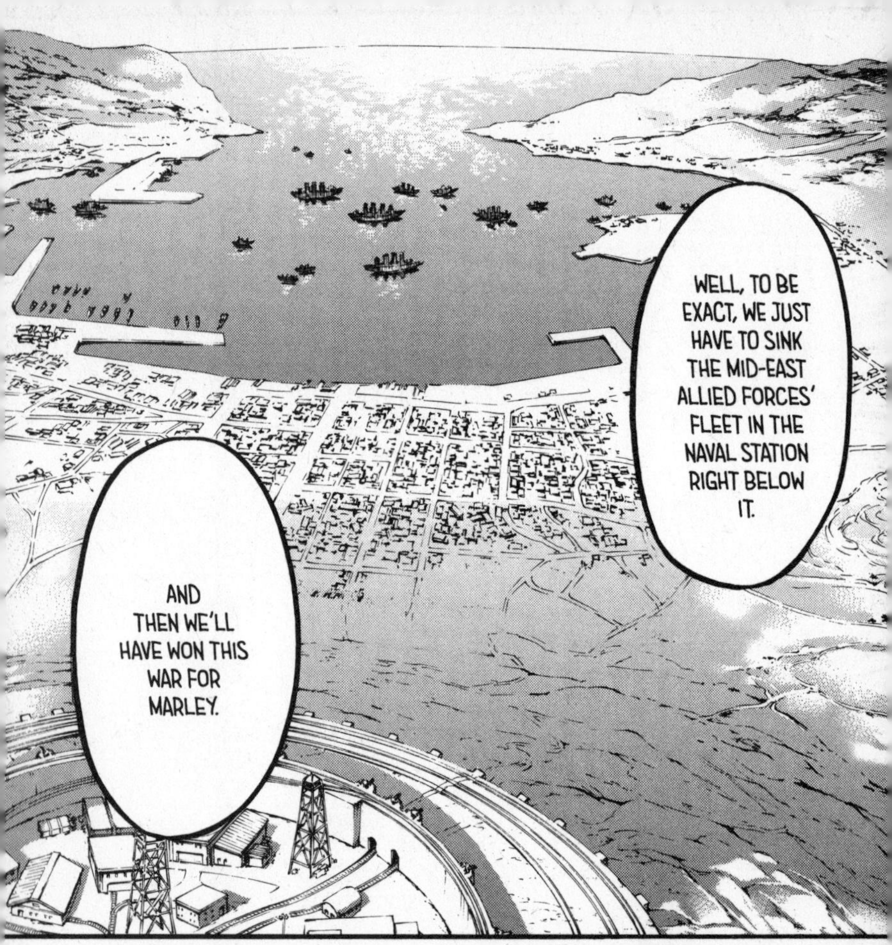
WELL, TO BE EXACT, WE JUST HAVE TO SINK THE MID-EAST ALLIED FORCES' FLEET IN THE NAVAL STATION RIGHT BELOW IT.
AND THEN WE'LL HAVE WON THIS WAR FOR MARLEY.
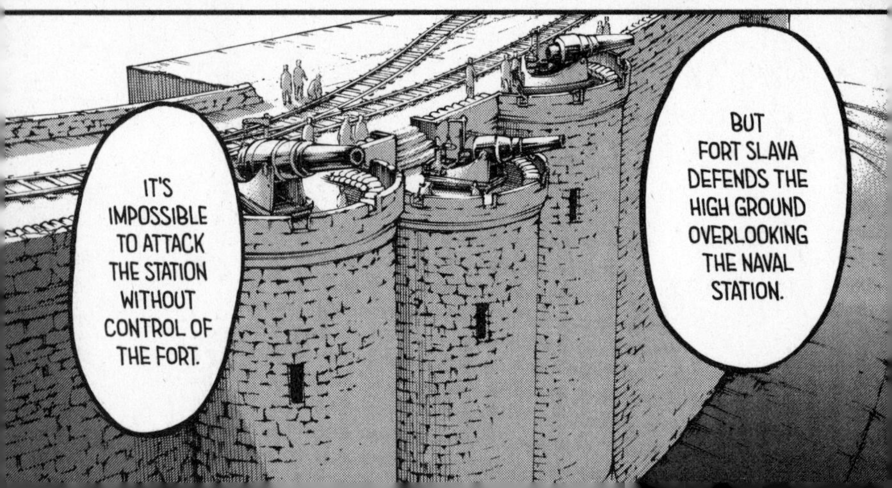
BUT FORT SLAVA DEFENDS THE HIGH GROUND OVERLOOKING THE NAVAL STATION.
IT'S IMPOSSIBLE TO ATTACK THE STATION WITHOUT CONTROL OF THE FORT.

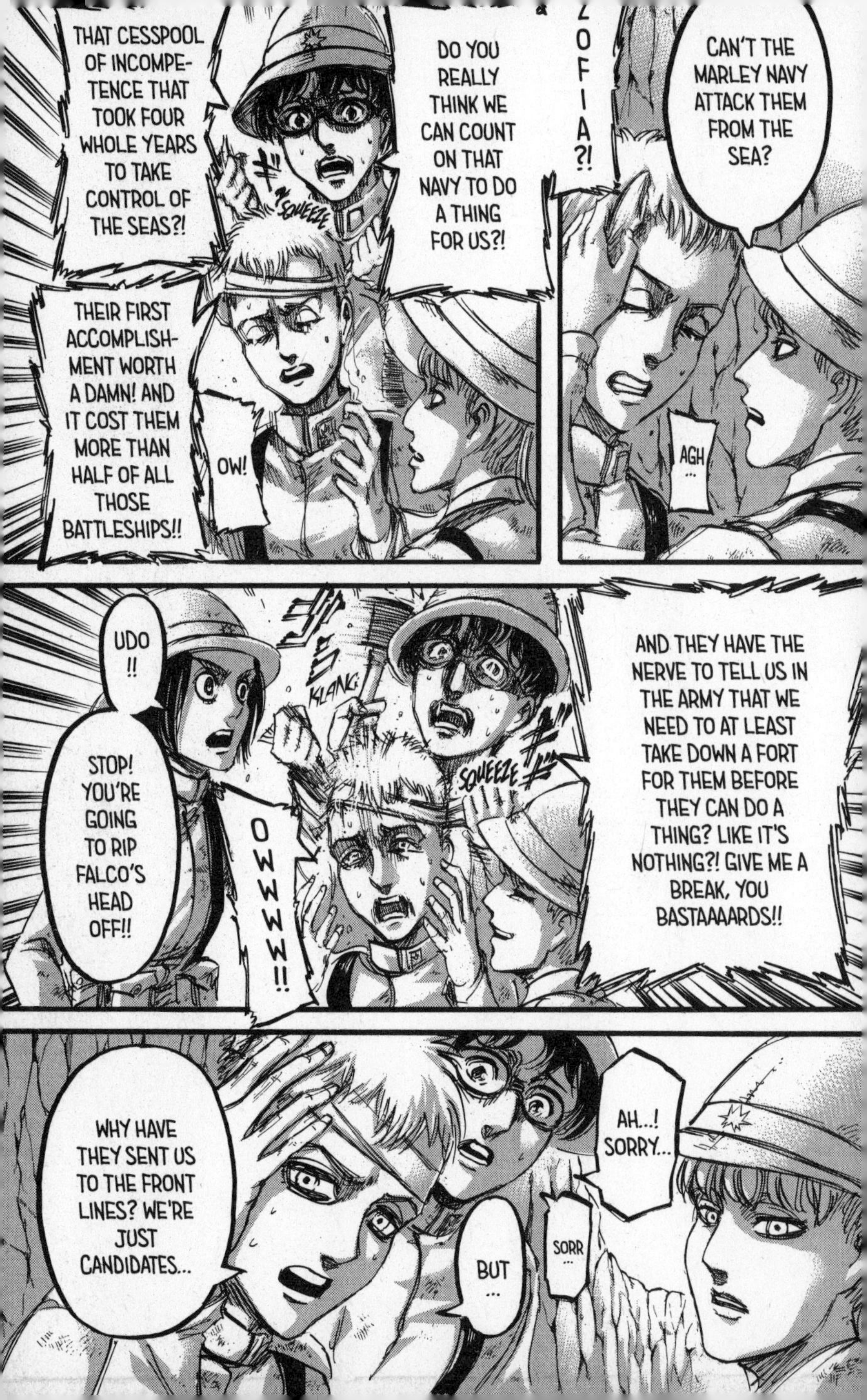
CAN'T THE MARLEY NAVY ATTACK THEM FROM THE SEA?
ZOFIA?!
AGH...
DO YOU REALLY THINK WE CAN COUNT ON THAT NAVY TO DO A THING FOR US?!
THAT CESSPOOL OF INCOMPE-TENCE THAT TOOK FOUR WHOLE YEARS TO TAKE CONTROL OF THE SEAS?!
SQUEEZE
THEIR FIRST ACCOMPLISH-MENT WORTH A DAMN! AND IT COST THEM MORE THAN HALF OF ALL THOSE BATTLESHIPS!!
OW!
AND THEY HAVE THE NERVE TO TELL US IN THE ARMY THAT WE NEED TO AT LEAST TAKE DOWN A FORT FOR THEM BEFORE THEY CAN DO A THING? LIKE IT'S NOTHING?! GIVE ME A BREAK, YOU BASTAAAARDS!!
SQUEEZE
KLANG
UDO!!
STOP! YOU'RE GOING TO RIP FALCO'S HEAD OFF!!
OWWWWW!!
AH...! SORRY...
SORR...
BUT...
WHY HAVE THEY SENT US TO THE FRONT LINES? WE'RE JUST CANDIDATES...

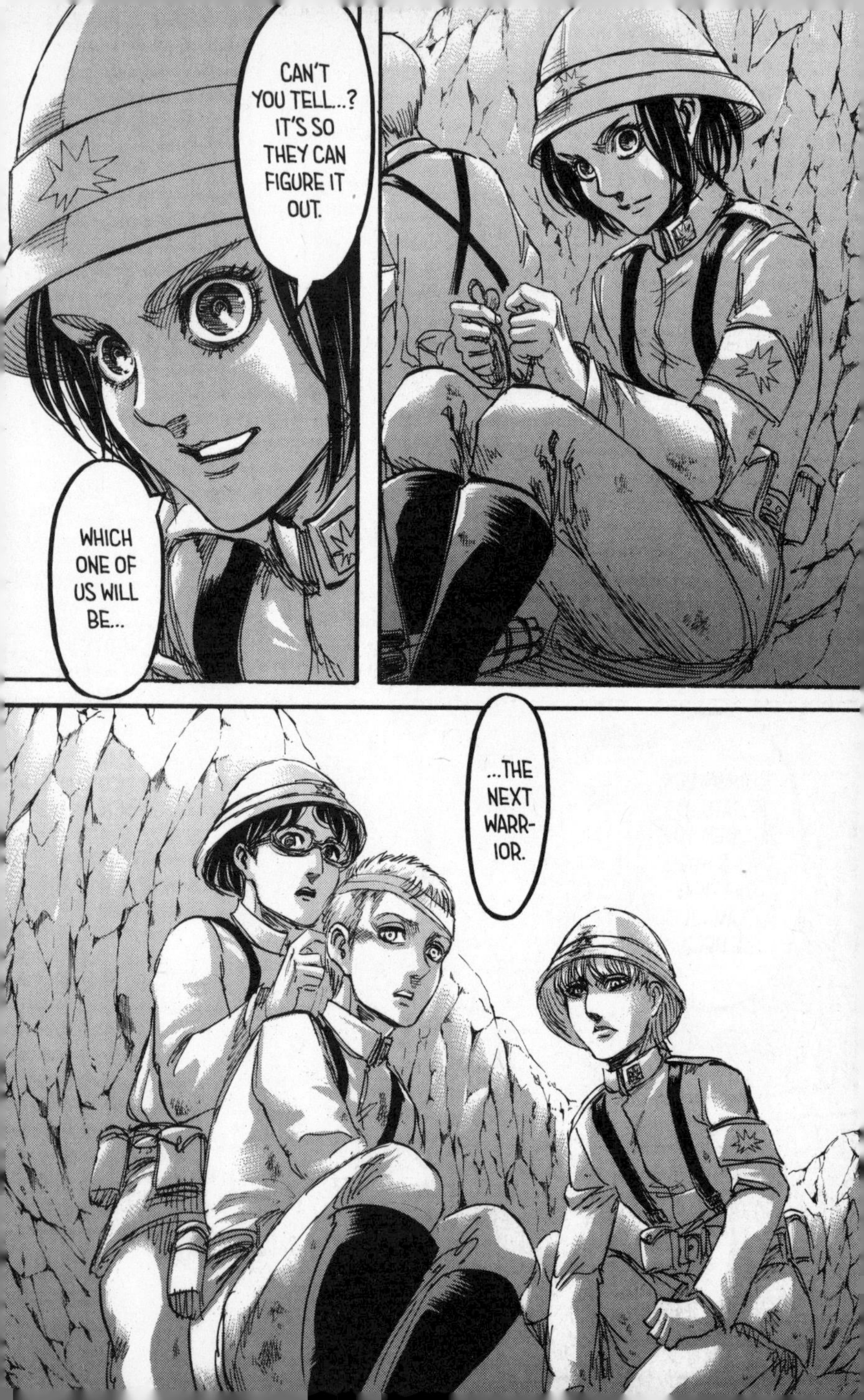
CAN'T YOU TELL...? IT'S SO THEY CAN FIGURE IT OUT.
WHICH ONE OF US WILL BE...
...THE NEXT WARR-IOR.

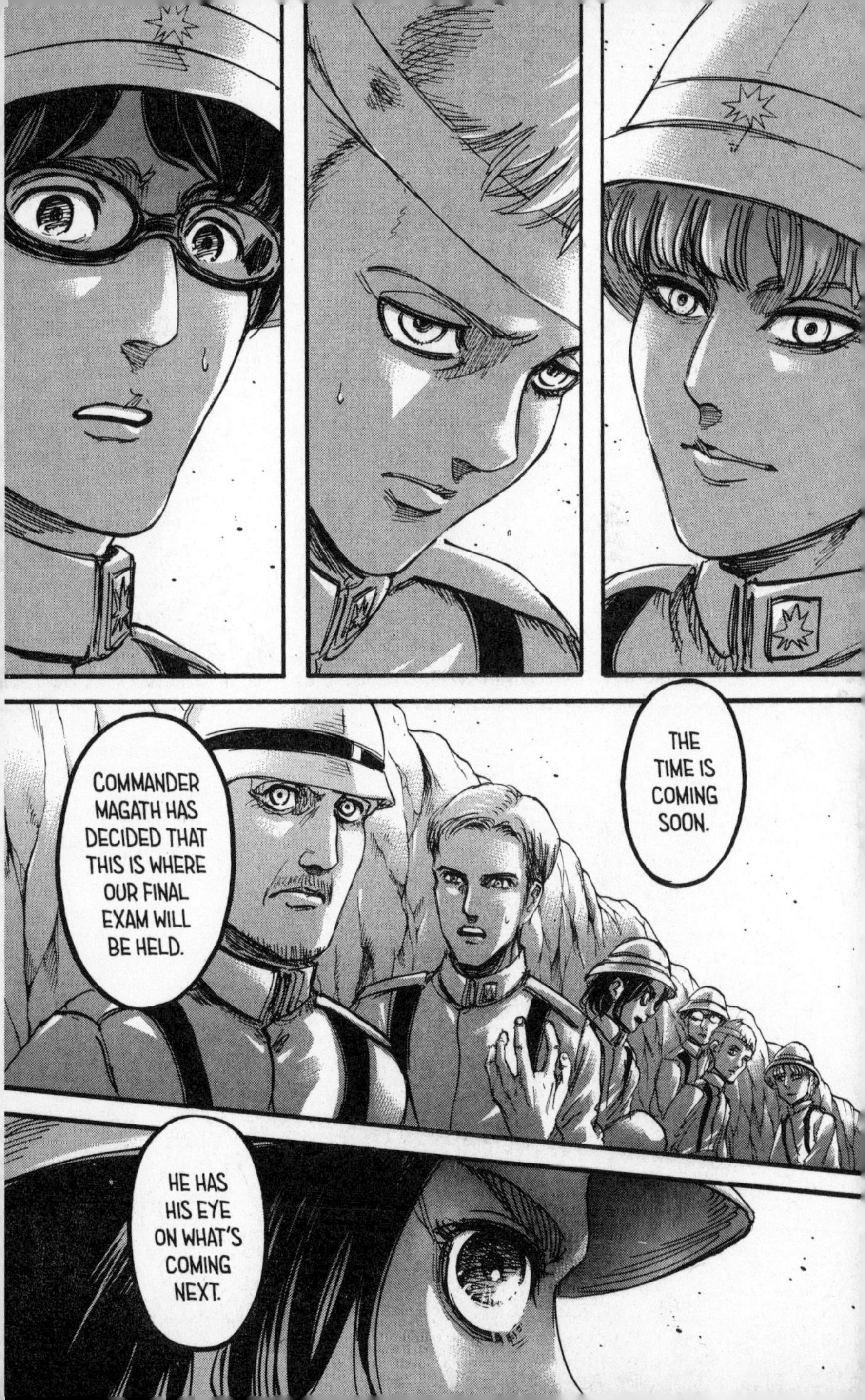
THE TIME IS COMING SOON.
COMMANDER MAGATH HAS DECIDED THAT THIS IS WHERE OUR FINAL EXAM WILL BE HELD.
HE HAS HIS EYE ON WHAT'S COMING NEXT.

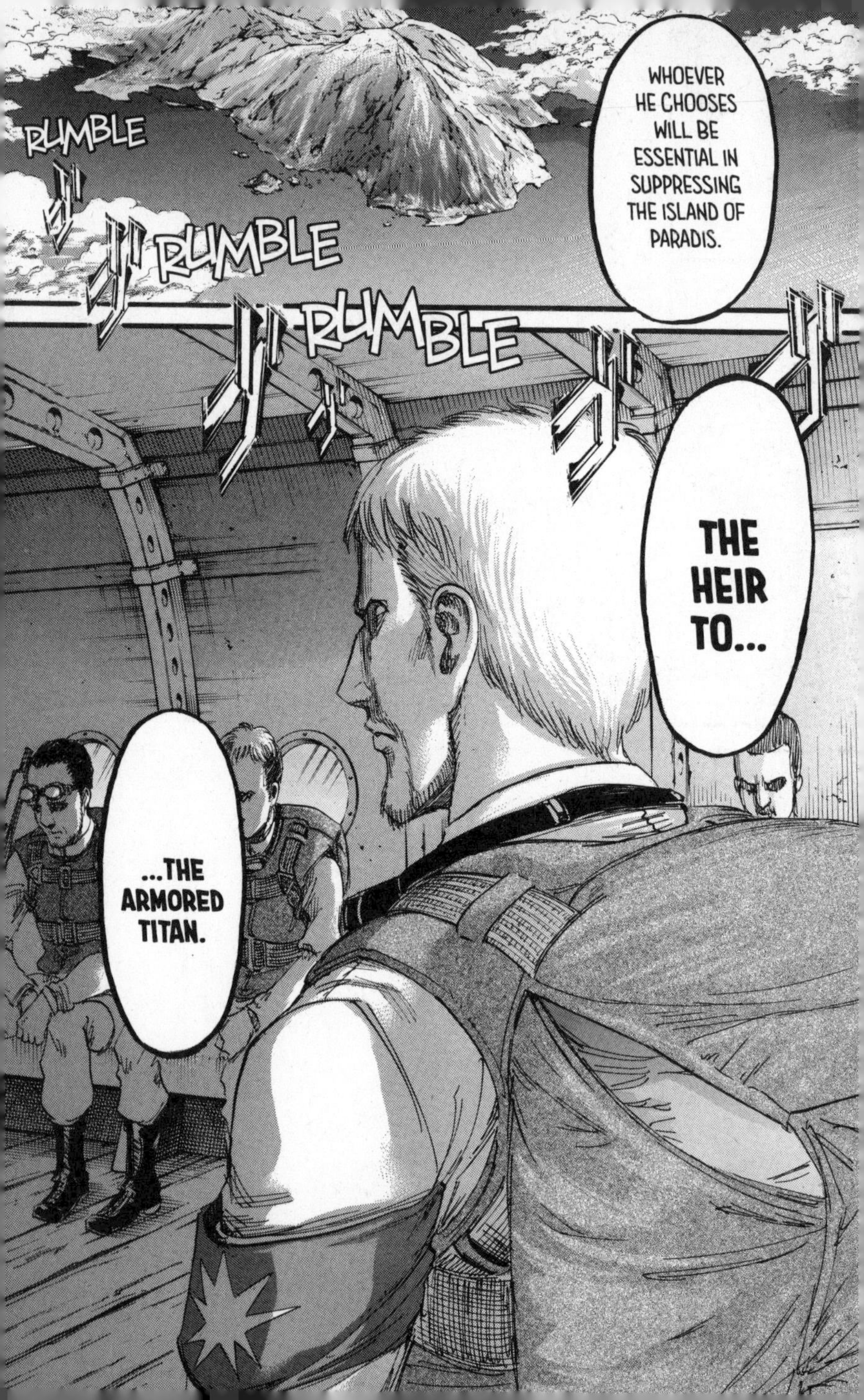
WHOEVER HE CHOOSES WILL BE ESSENTIAL IN SUPPRESSING THE ISLAND OF PARADIS.
RUMBLE
RUMBLE
RUMBLE
THE HEIR TO...
...THE ARMORED TITAN.

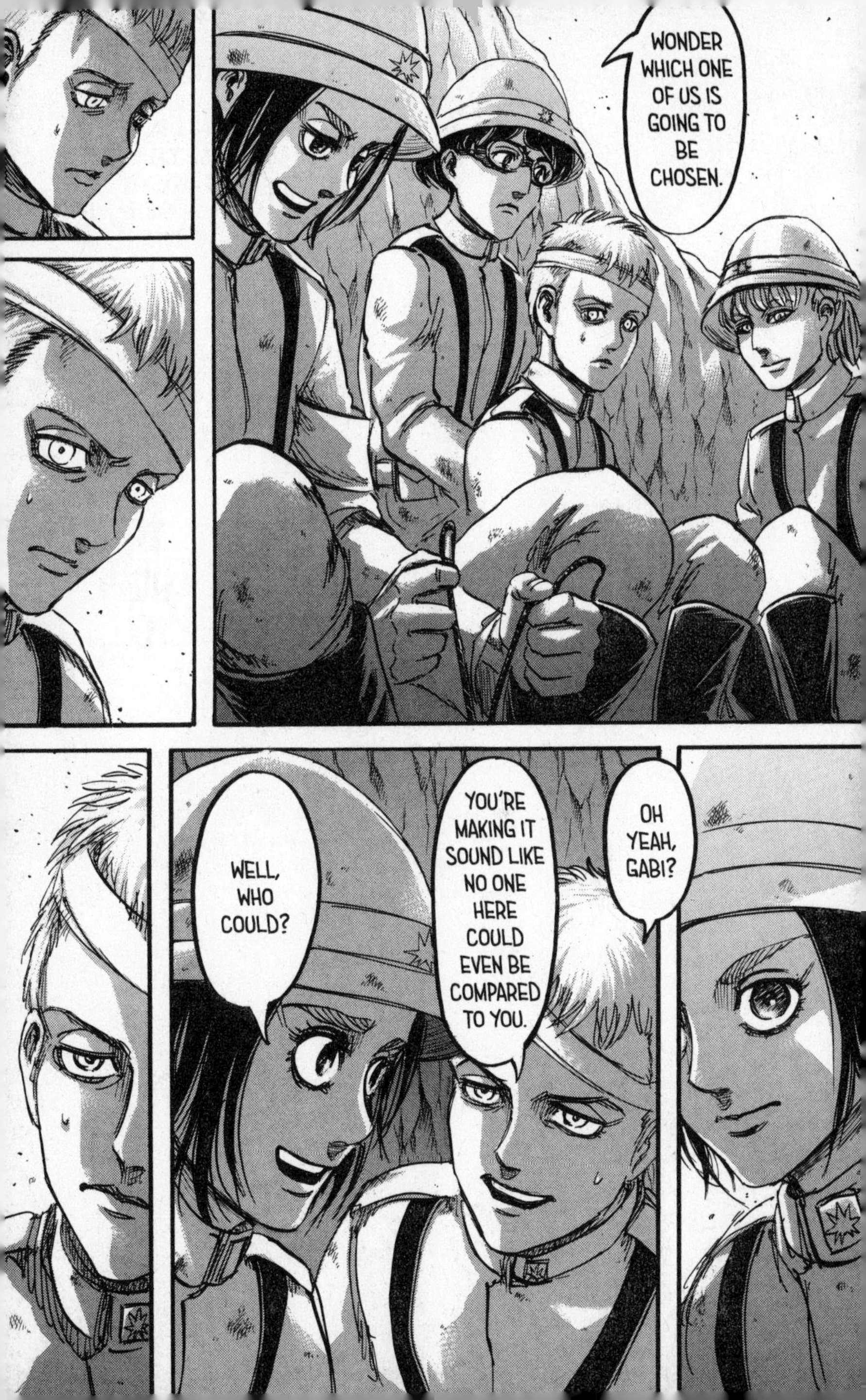
WONDER WHICH ONE OF US IS GOING TO BE CHOSEN.
OH YEAH, GABI?
YOU'RE MAKING IT SOUND LIKE NO ONE HERE COULD EVEN BE COMPARED TO YOU.
WELL, WHO COULD?

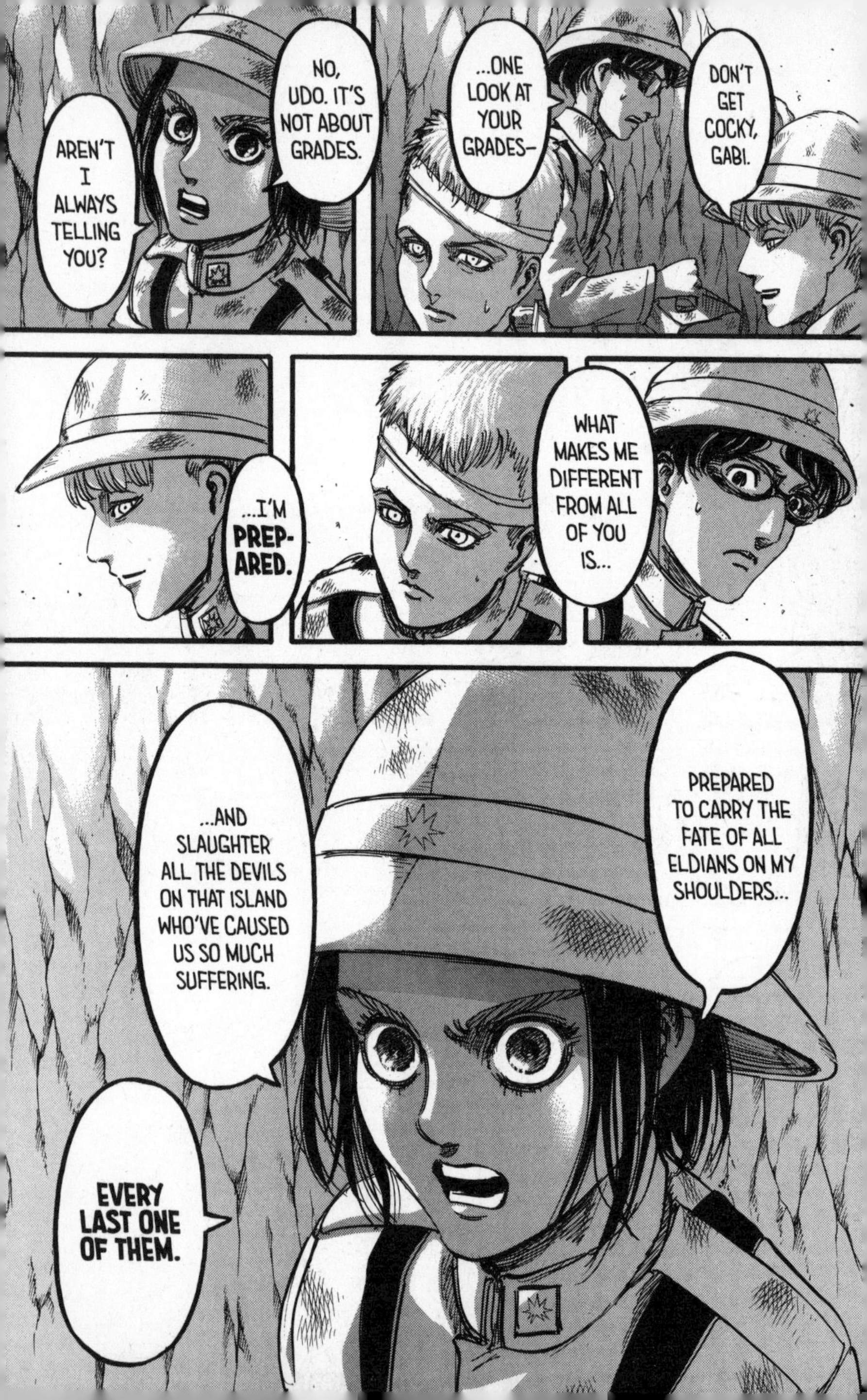
DON'T GET COCKY, GABI.
...ONE LOOK AT YOUR GRADES–
NO, UDO. IT'S NOT ABOUT GRADES.
AREN'T I ALWAYS TELLING YOU?
WHAT MAKES ME DIFFERENT FROM ALL OF YOU IS...
...I'M **PREPARED.**
PREPARED TO CARRY THE FATE OF ALL ELDIANS ON MY SHOULDERS...
...AND SLAUGHTER ALL THE DEVILS ON THAT ISLAND WHO'VE CAUSED US SO MUCH SUFFERING.
**EVERY LAST ONE OF THEM.**

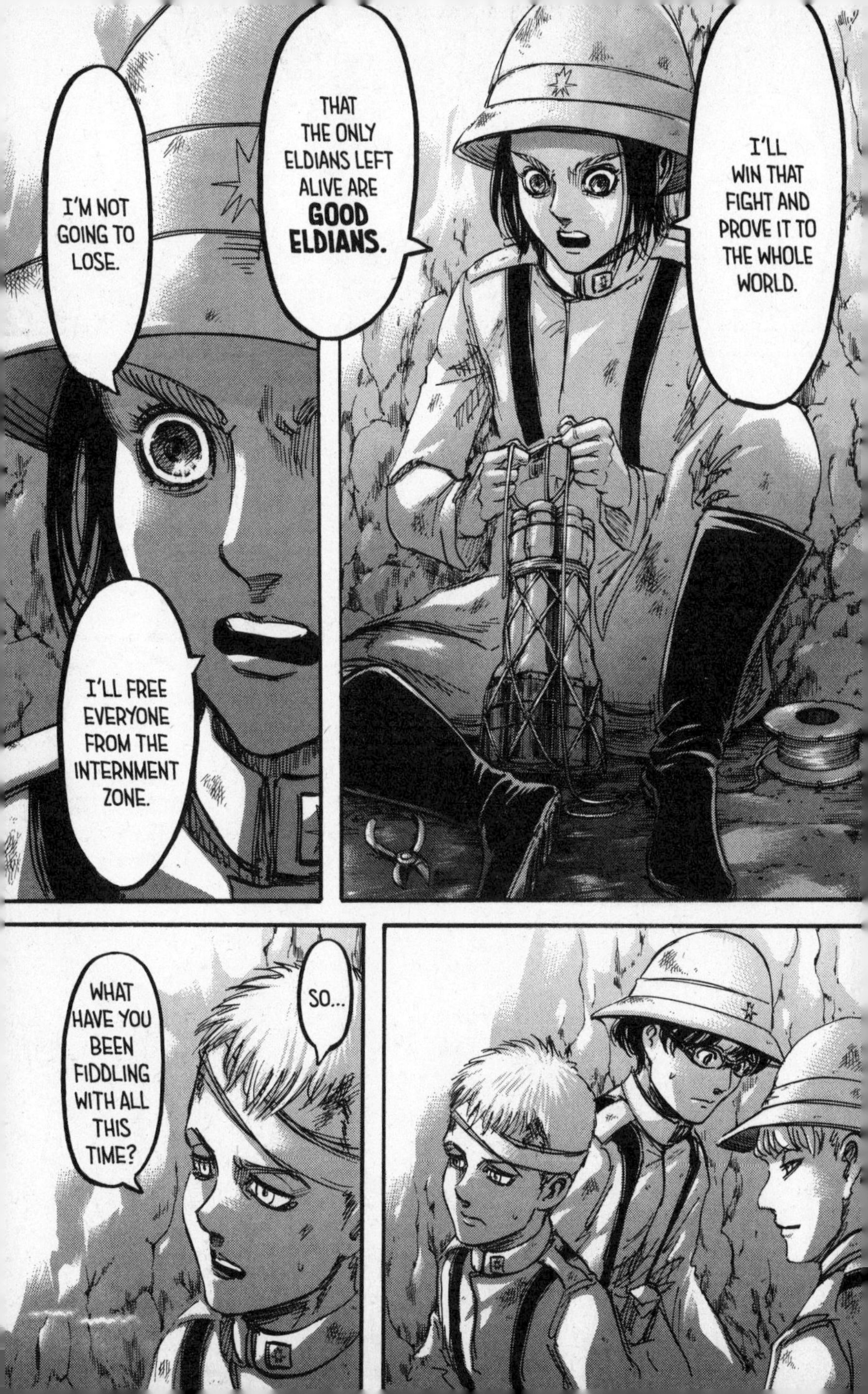
I'LL WIN THAT FIGHT AND PROVE IT TO THE WHOLE WORLD.
THAT THE ONLY ELDIANS LEFT ALIVE ARE **GOOD ELDIANS.**
I'M NOT GOING TO LOSE.
I'LL FREE EVERYONE FROM THE INTERNMENT ZONE.
SO...
WHAT HAVE YOU BEEN FIDDLING WITH ALL THIS TIME?

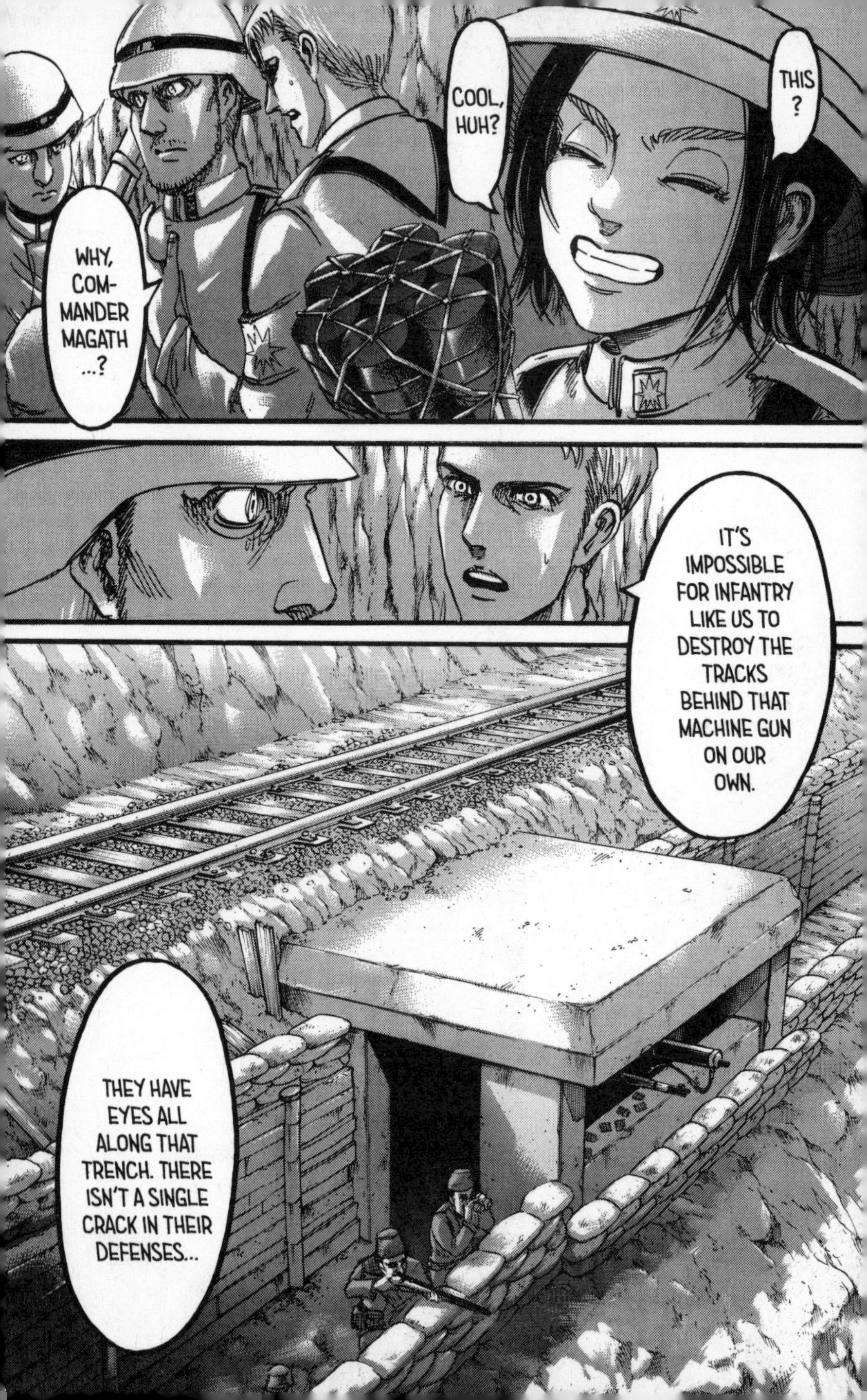
THIS?
COOL, HUH?
WHY, COMMANDER MAGATH...?
IT'S IMPOSSIBLE FOR INFANTRY LIKE US TO DESTROY THE TRACKS BEHIND THAT MACHINE GUN ON OUR OWN.
THEY HAVE EYES ALL ALONG THAT TRENCH. THERE ISN'T A SINGLE CRACK IN THEIR DEFENSES...

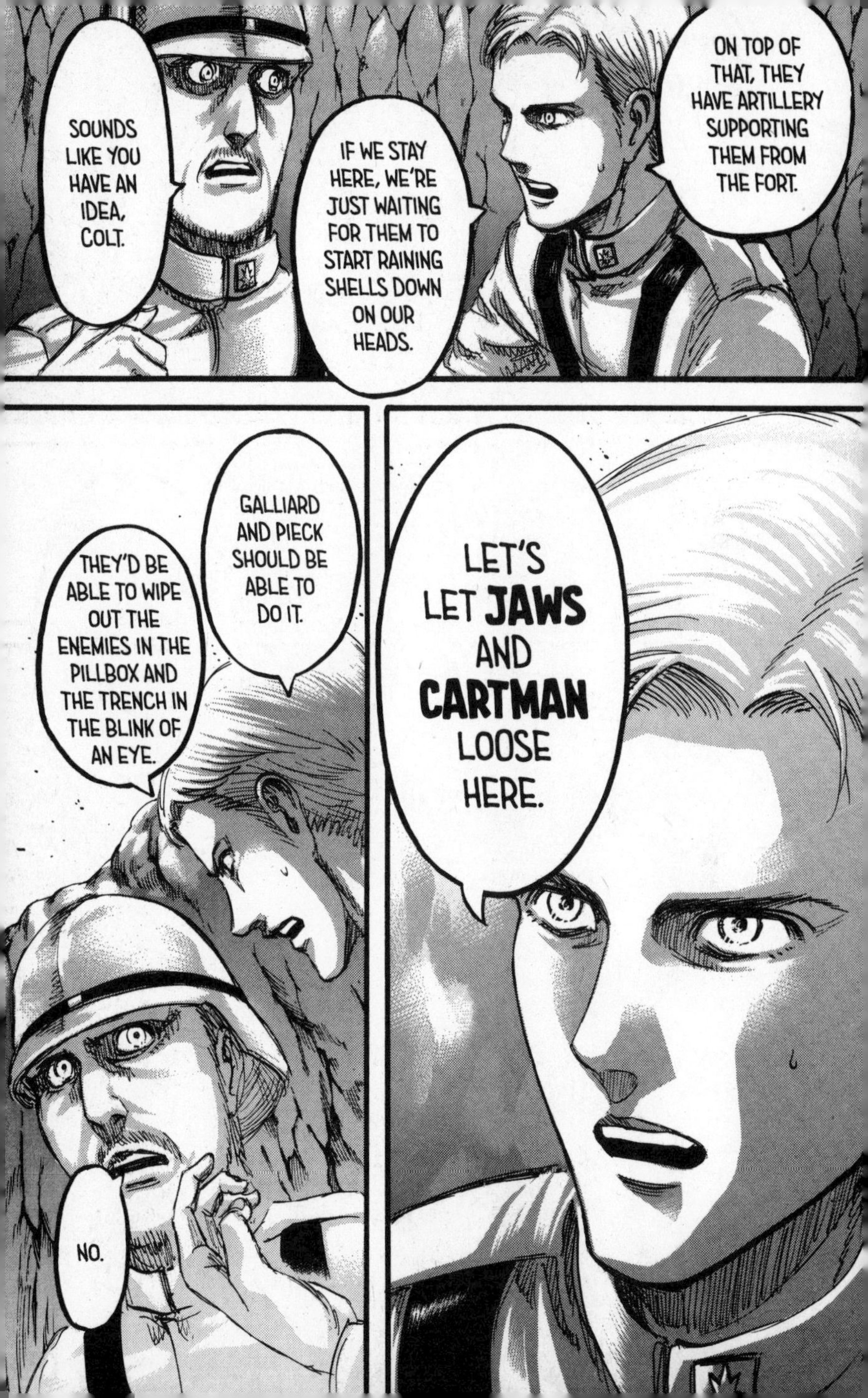
ON TOP OF THAT, THEY HAVE ARTILLERY SUPPORTING THEM FROM THE FORT.
IF WE STAY HERE, WE'RE JUST WAITING FOR THEM TO START RAINING SHELLS DOWN ON OUR HEADS.
SOUNDS LIKE YOU HAVE AN IDEA, COLT.
LET'S LET **JAWS** AND **CARTMAN** LOOSE HERE.
GALLIARD AND PIECK SHOULD BE ABLE TO DO IT.
THEY'D BE ABLE TO WIPE OUT THE ENEMIES IN THE PILLBOX AND THE TRENCH IN THE BLINK OF AN EYE.
NO.

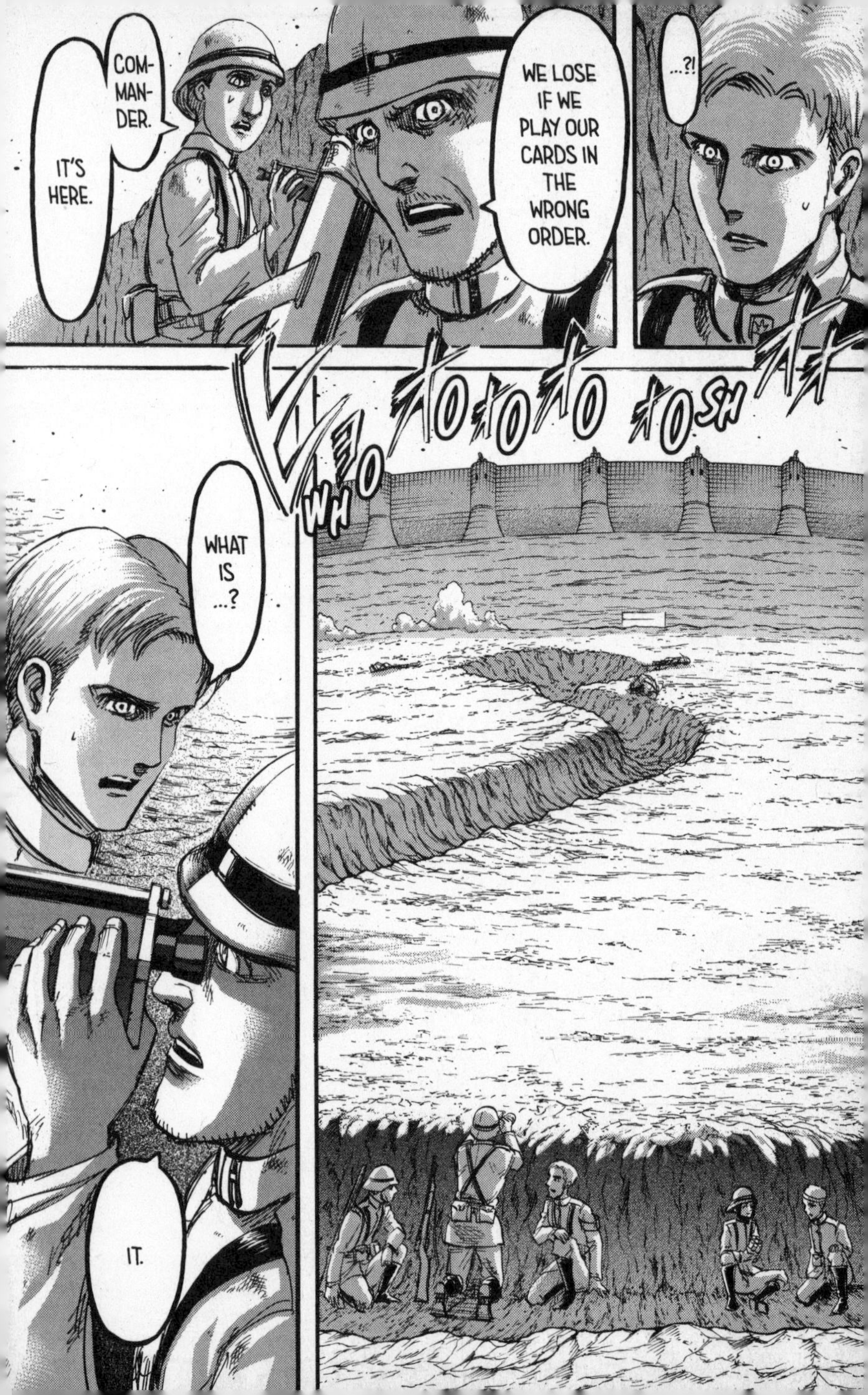
...?!
WE LOSE IF WE PLAY OUR CARDS IN THE WRONG ORDER.
COM-MANDER.
IT'S HERE.
WHOOOOOOSH
WHAT IS ...?
IT.

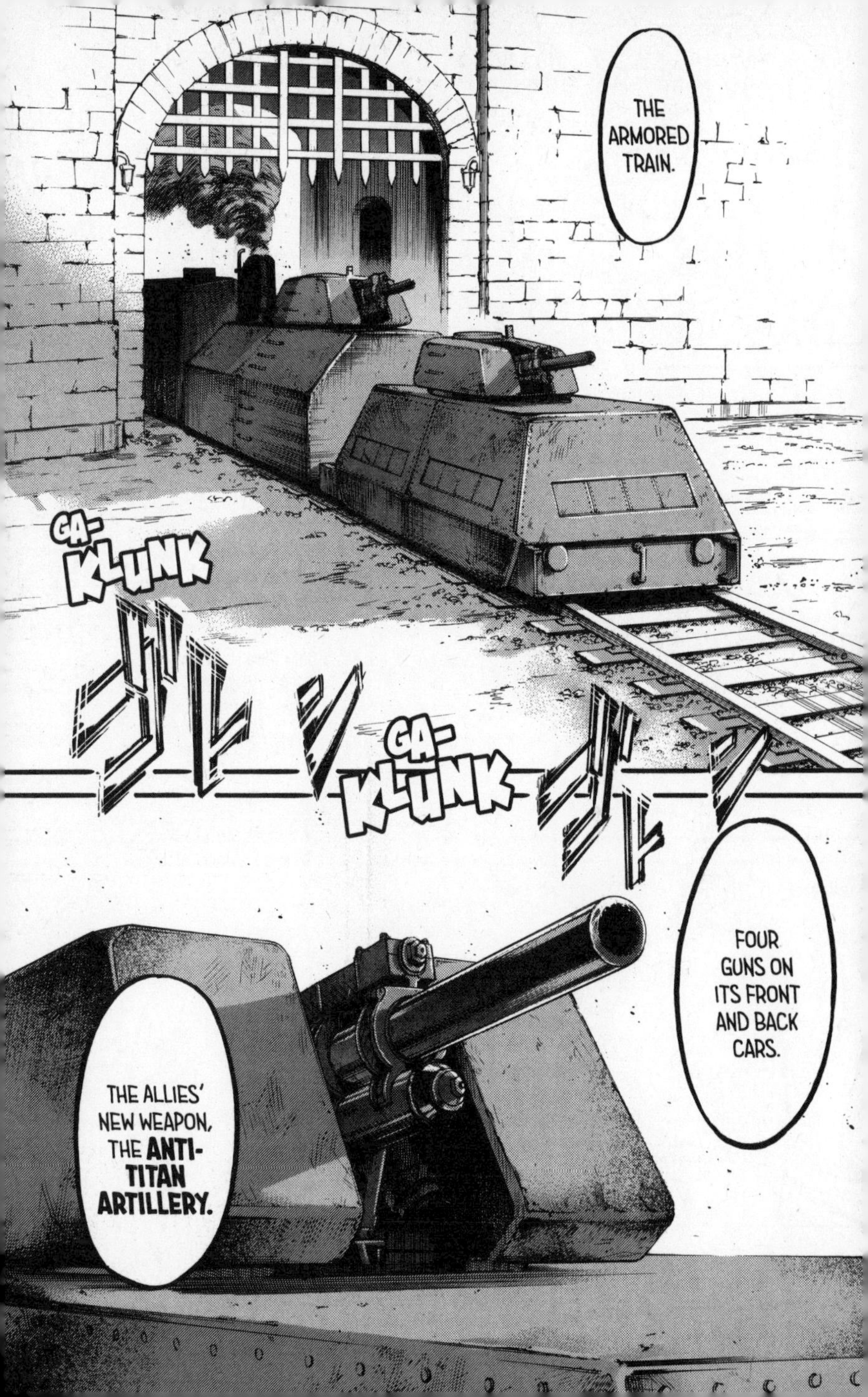
THE ARMORED TRAIN.
GA-KLUNK
GA-KLUNK
FOUR GUNS ON ITS FRONT AND BACK CARS.
THE ALLIES' NEW WEAPON, THE **ANTI-TITAN ARTILLERY.**

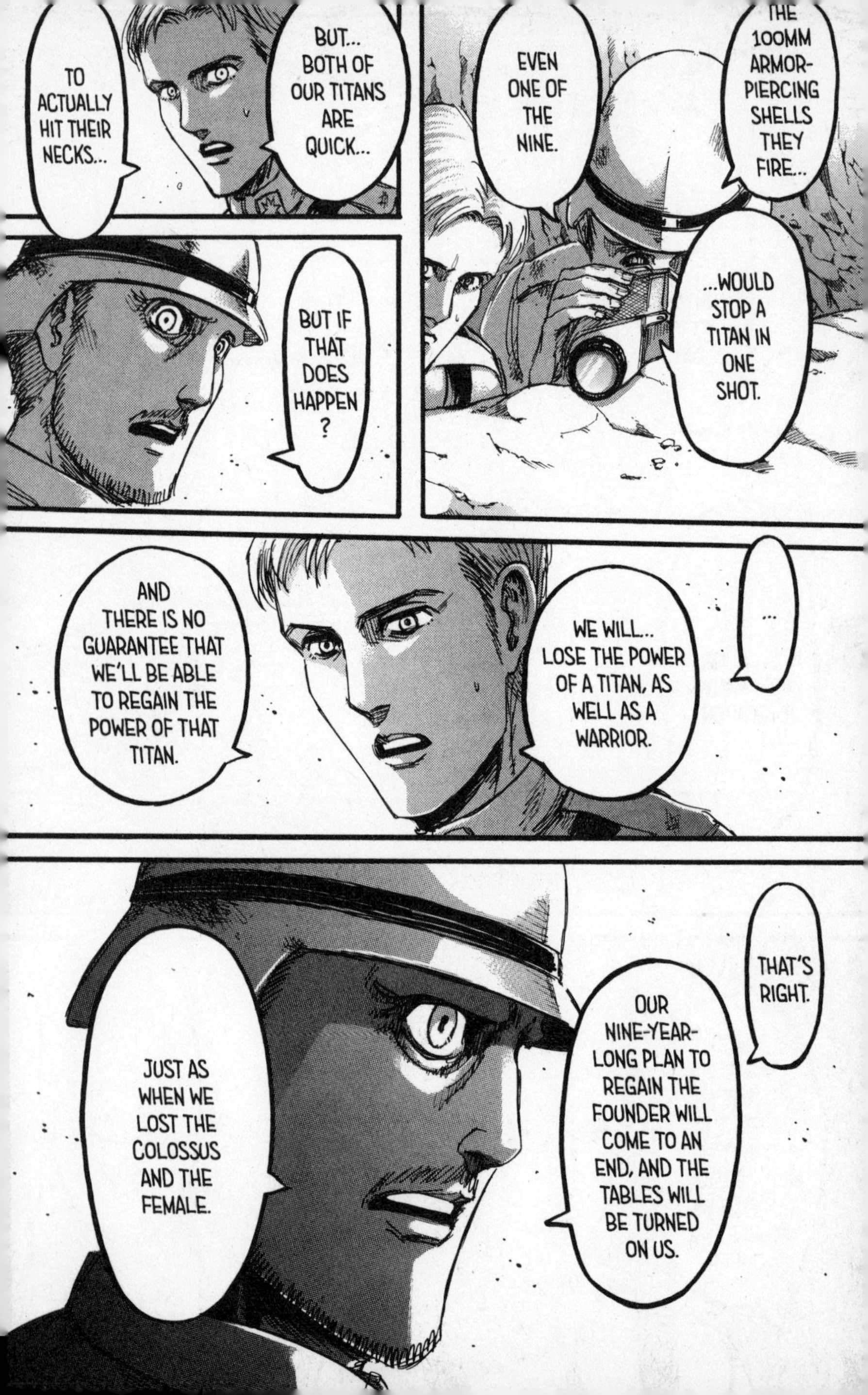
THE 100MM ARMOR-PIERCING SHELLS THEY FIRE...
...WOULD STOP A TITAN IN ONE SHOT.
EVEN ONE OF THE NINE.
BUT... BOTH OF OUR TITANS ARE QUICK...
TO ACTUALLY HIT THEIR NECKS...
BUT IF THAT DOES HAPPEN?
...
WE WILL... LOSE THE POWER OF A TITAN, AS WELL AS A WARRIOR.
AND THERE IS NO GUARANTEE THAT WE'LL BE ABLE TO REGAIN THE POWER OF THAT TITAN.
THAT'S RIGHT.
OUR NINE-YEAR-LONG PLAN TO REGAIN THE FOUNDER WILL COME TO AN END, AND THE TABLES WILL BE TURNED ON US.
JUST AS WHEN WE LOST THE COLOSSUS AND THE FEMALE.

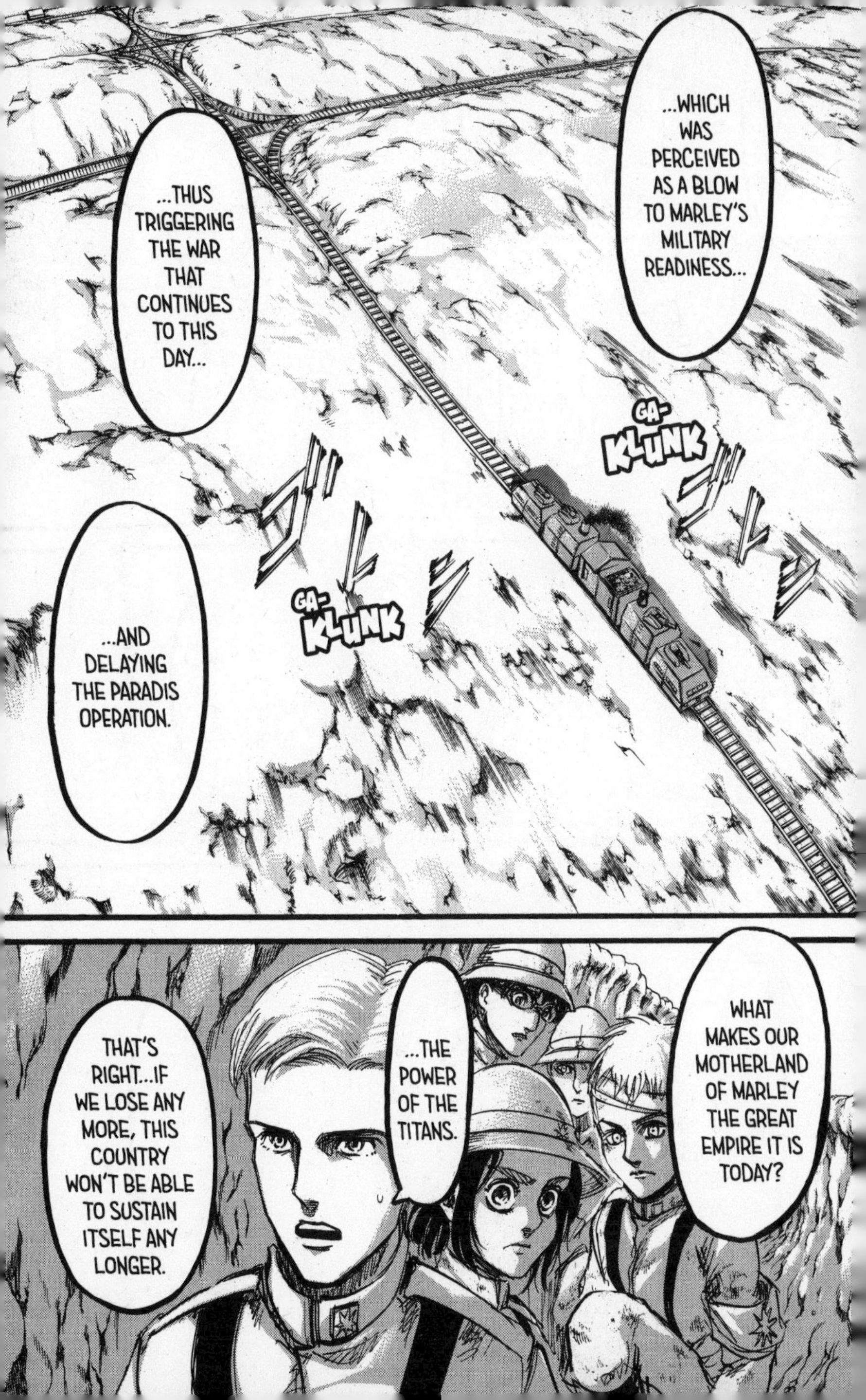
...WHICH WAS PERCEIVED AS A BLOW TO MARLEY'S MILITARY READINESS...
...THUS TRIGGERING THE WAR THAT CONTINUES TO THIS DAY...
GA-KLUNK
GA-KLUNK
...AND DELAYING THE PARADIS OPERATION.
WHAT MAKES OUR MOTHERLAND OF MARLEY THE GREAT EMPIRE IT IS TODAY?
...THE POWER OF THE TITANS.
THAT'S RIGHT...IF WE LOSE ANY MORE, THIS COUNTRY WON'T BE ABLE TO SUSTAIN ITSELF ANY LONGER.

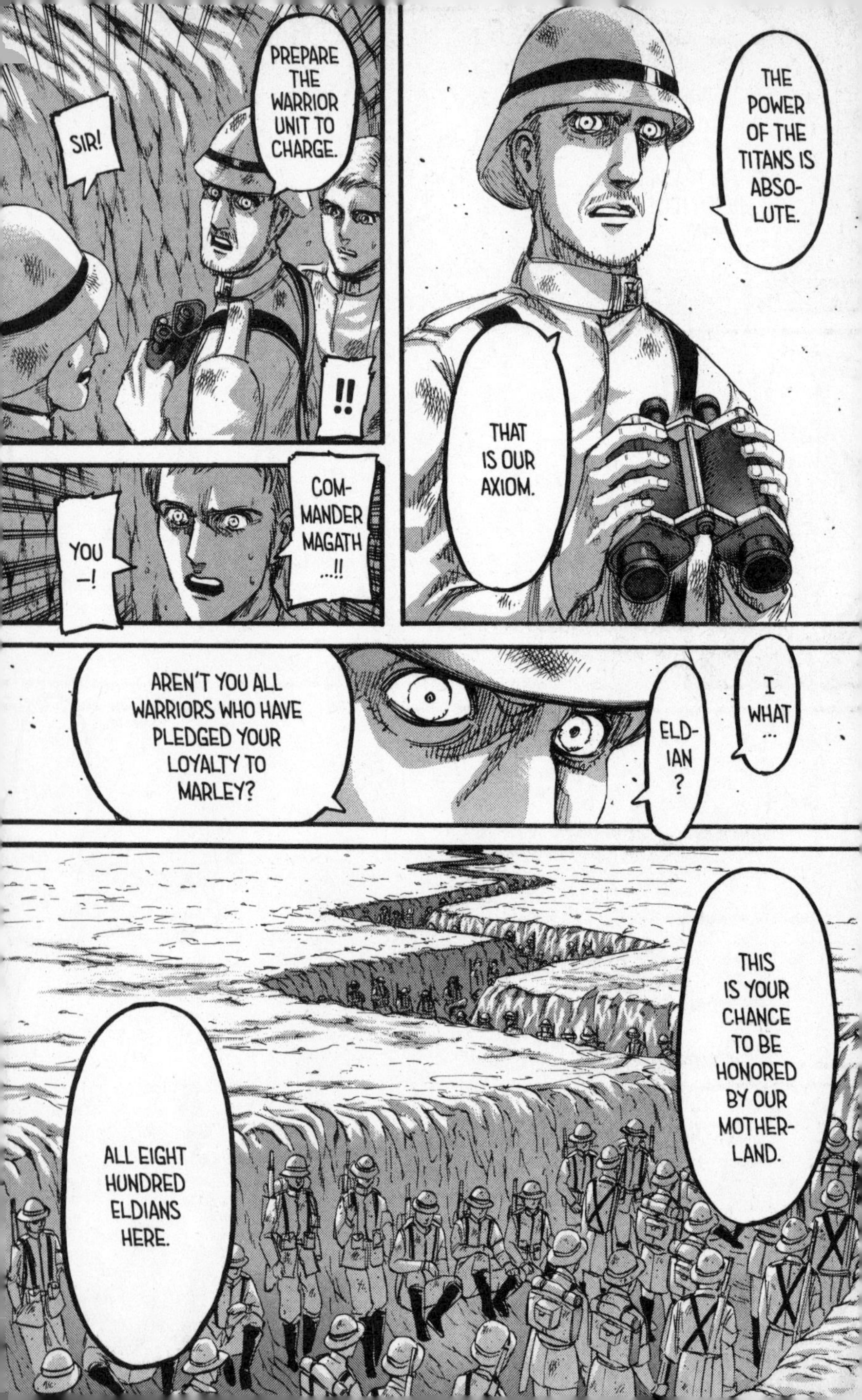
THE POWER OF THE TITANS IS ABSOLUTE.
THAT IS OUR AXIOM.
PREPARE THE WARRIOR UNIT TO CHARGE.
SIR!
!!
COMMANDER MAGATH ...!!
YOU —!
I WHAT ...
ELDIAN ?
AREN'T YOU ALL WARRIORS WHO HAVE PLEDGED YOUR LOYALTY TO MARLEY?
THIS IS YOUR CHANCE TO BE HONORED BY OUR MOTHERLAND.
ALL EIGHT HUNDRED ELDIANS HERE.

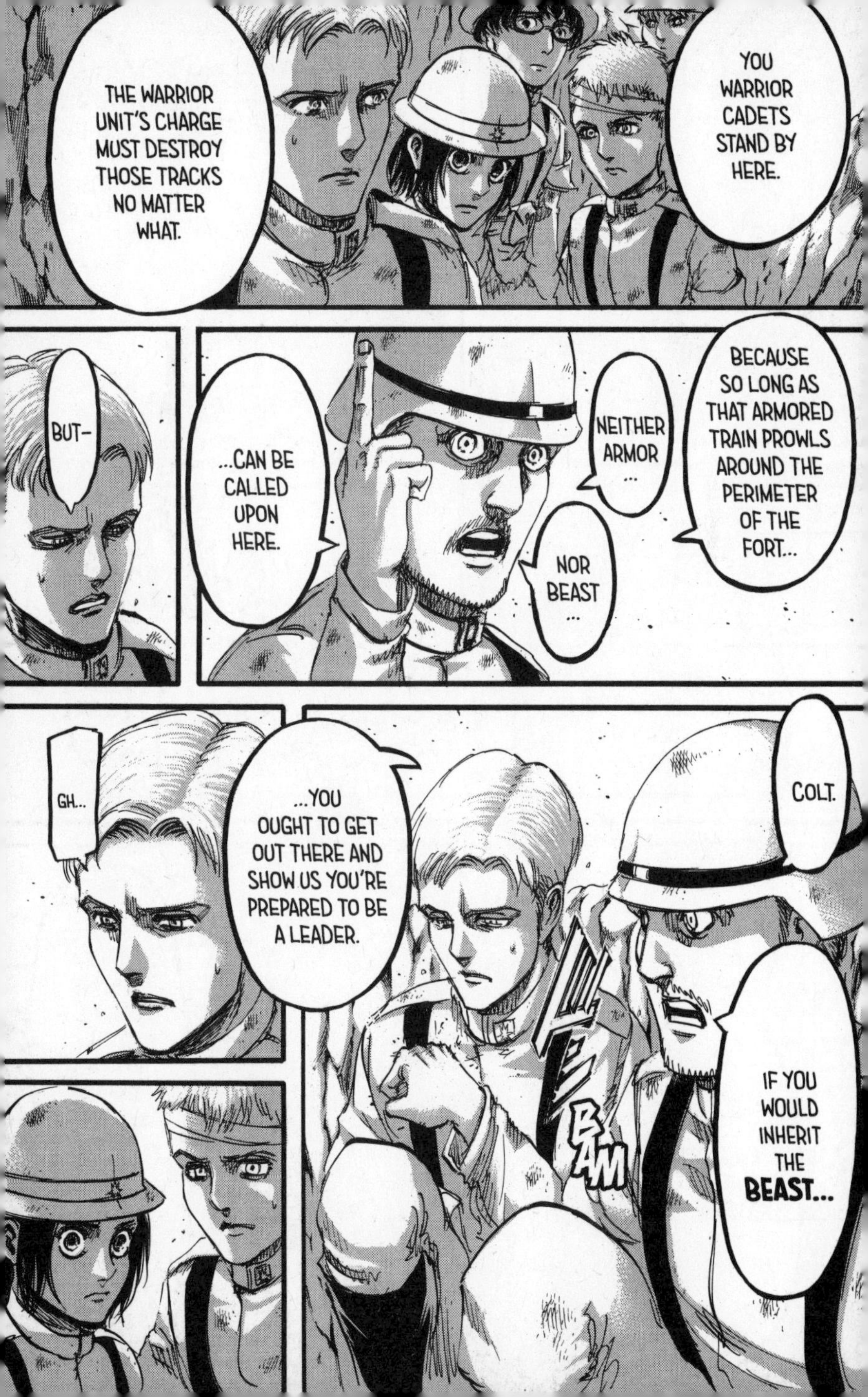
YOU WARRIOR CADETS STAND BY HERE.
THE WARRIOR UNIT'S CHARGE MUST DESTROY THOSE TRACKS NO MATTER WHAT.
BECAUSE SO LONG AS THAT ARMORED TRAIN PROWLS AROUND THE PERIMETER OF THE FORT...
NEITHER ARMOR ...
NOR BEAST ...
...CAN BE CALLED UPON HERE.
BUT-
COLT.
IF YOU WOULD INHERIT THE **BEAST...**
BAM
...YOU OUGHT TO GET OUT THERE AND SHOW US YOU'RE PREPARED TO BE A LEADER.
GH...

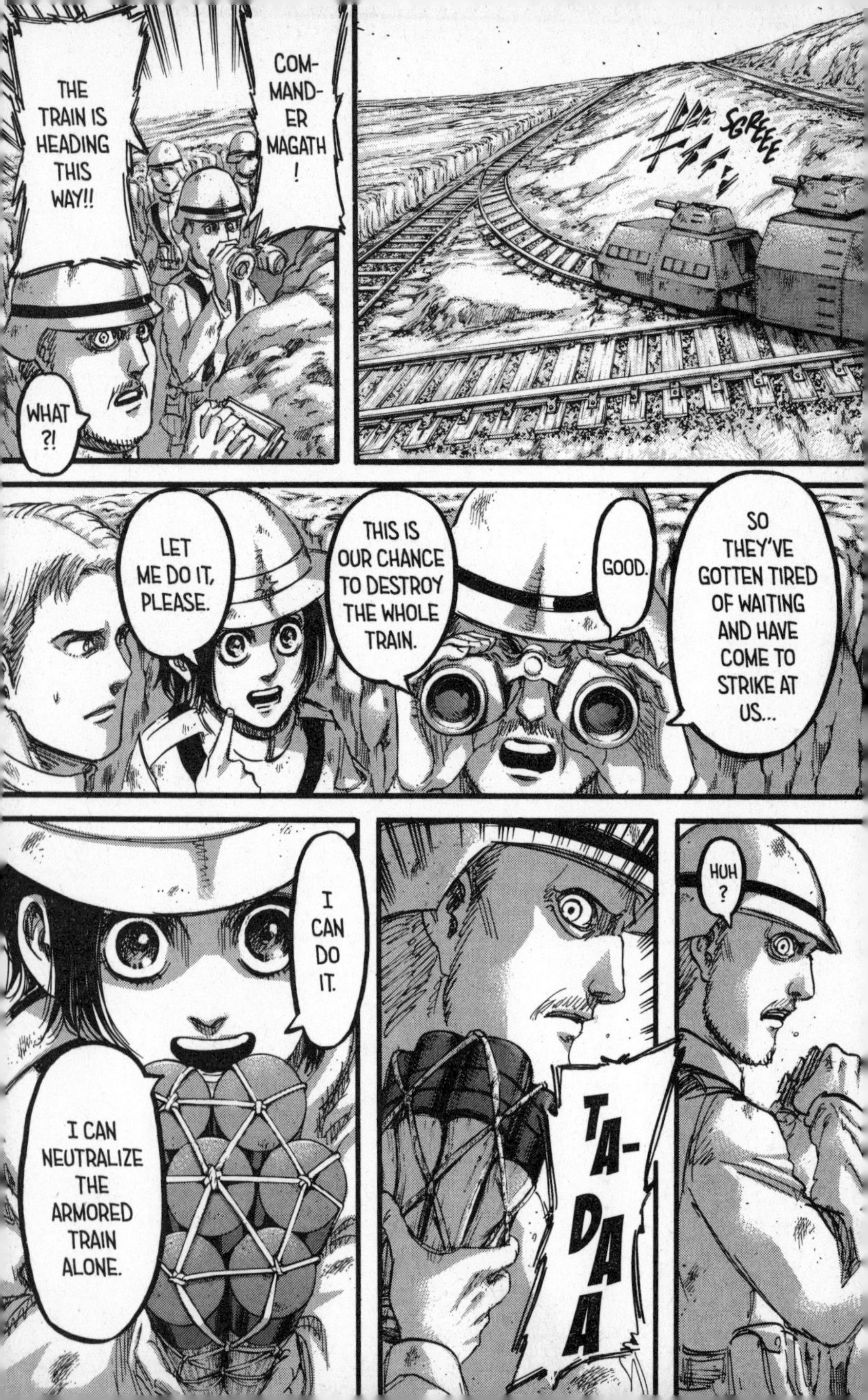
SCREEE
COMMANDER MAGATH!
THE TRAIN IS HEADING THIS WAY!!
WHAT?!
SO THEY'VE GOTTEN TIRED OF WAITING AND HAVE COME TO STRIKE AT US...
GOOD.
THIS IS OUR CHANCE TO DESTROY THE WHOLE TRAIN.
LET ME DO IT, PLEASE.
HUH?
TA-DAA
I CAN DO IT.
I CAN NEUTRALIZE THE ARMORED TRAIN ALONE.

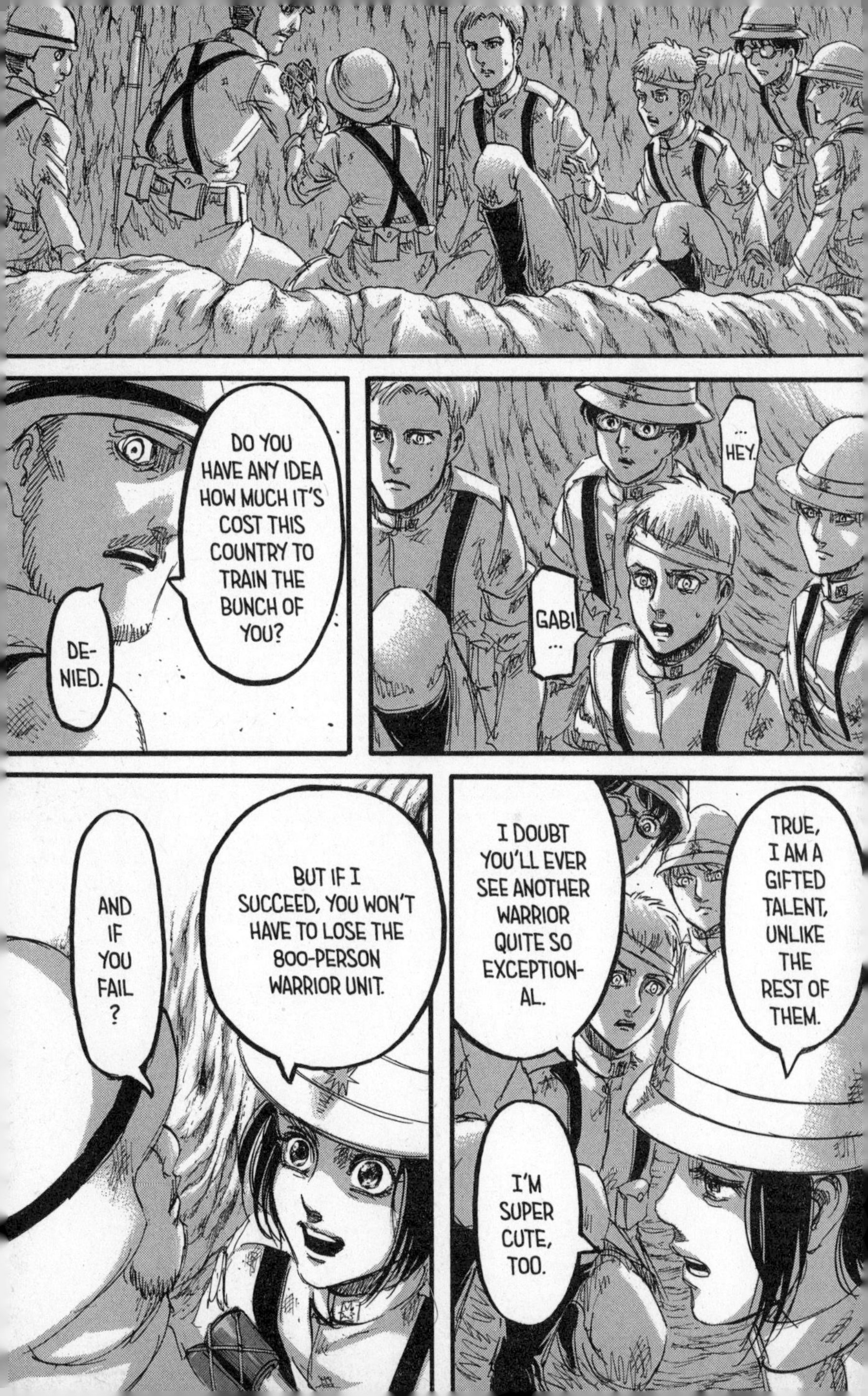
... HEY.
GABI ...
DO YOU HAVE ANY IDEA HOW MUCH IT'S COST THIS COUNTRY TO TRAIN THE BUNCH OF YOU?
DE-NIED.
TRUE, I AM A GIFTED TALENT, UNLIKE THE REST OF THEM.
I DOUBT YOU'LL EVER SEE ANOTHER WARRIOR QUITE SO EXCEPTION-AL.
I'M SUPER CUTE, TOO.
BUT IF I SUCCEED, YOU WON'T HAVE TO LOSE THE 800-PERSON WARRIOR UNIT.
AND IF YOU FAIL ?

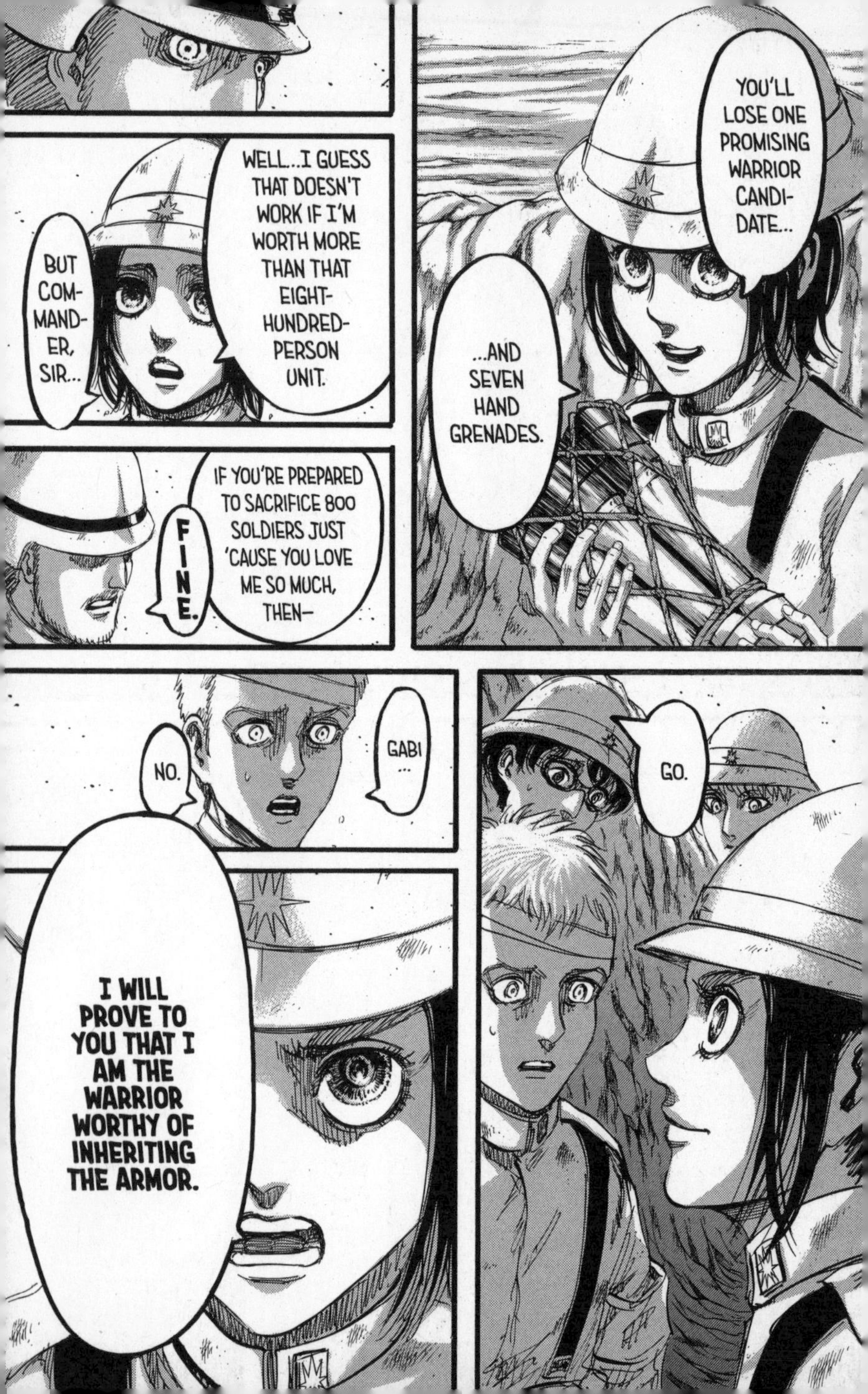
YOU'LL LOSE ONE PROMISING WARRIOR CANDI-DATE...
...AND SEVEN HAND GRENADES.
WELL...I GUESS THAT DOESN'T WORK IF I'M WORTH MORE THAN THAT EIGHT-HUNDRED-PERSON UNIT.
BUT COM-MAND-ER, SIR...
IF YOU'RE PREPARED TO SACRIFICE 800 SOLDIERS JUST 'CAUSE YOU LOVE ME SO MUCH, THEN—
FINE.
GO.
GABI...
NO.
I WILL PROVE TO YOU THAT I AM THE WARRIOR WORTHY OF INHERITING THE ARMOR.

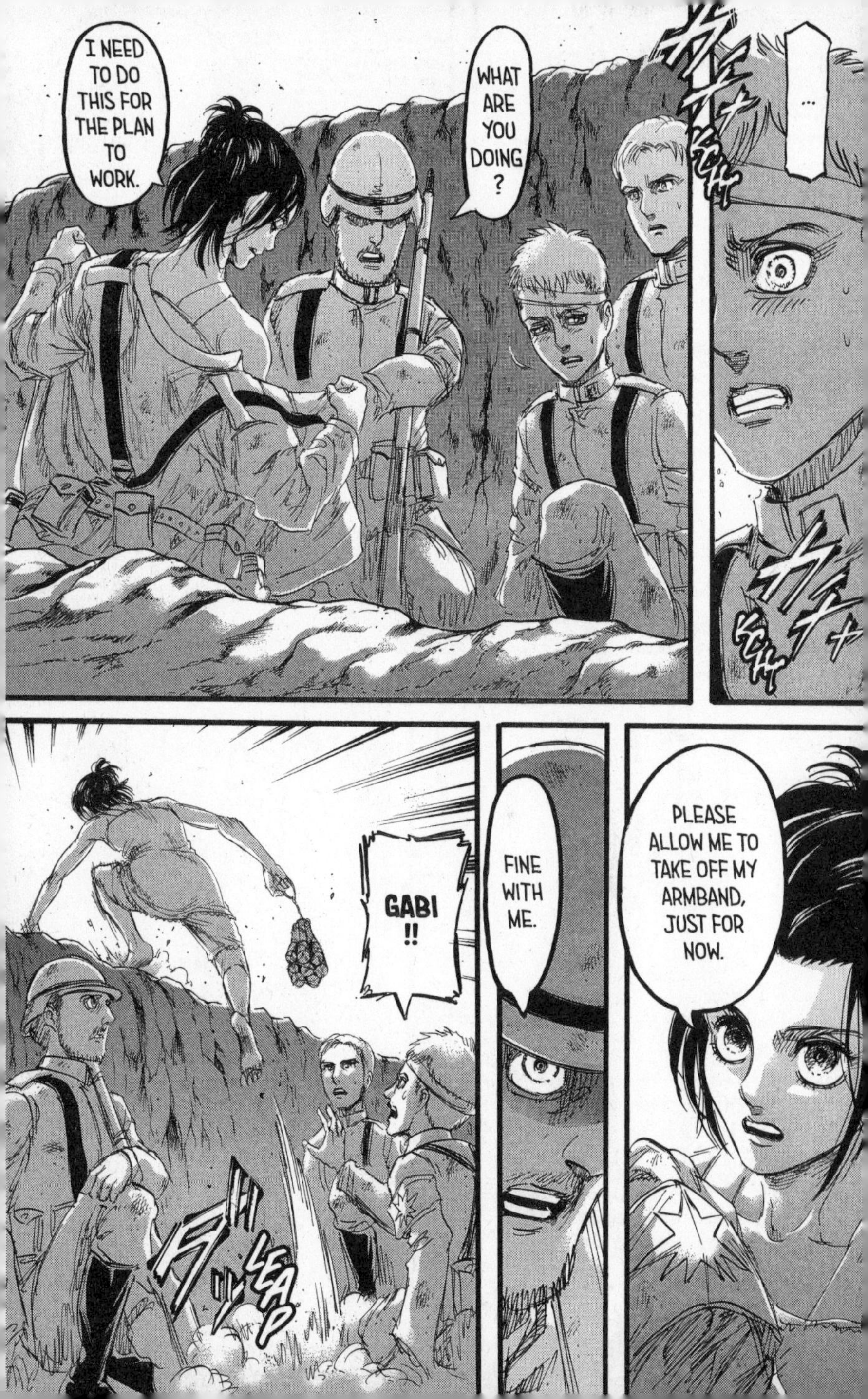
...
KCH
KCH
WHAT ARE YOU DOING?
I NEED TO DO THIS FOR THE PLAN TO WORK.
PLEASE ALLOW ME TO TAKE OFF MY ARMBAND, JUST FOR NOW.
FINE WITH ME.
GABI!!
LEAP

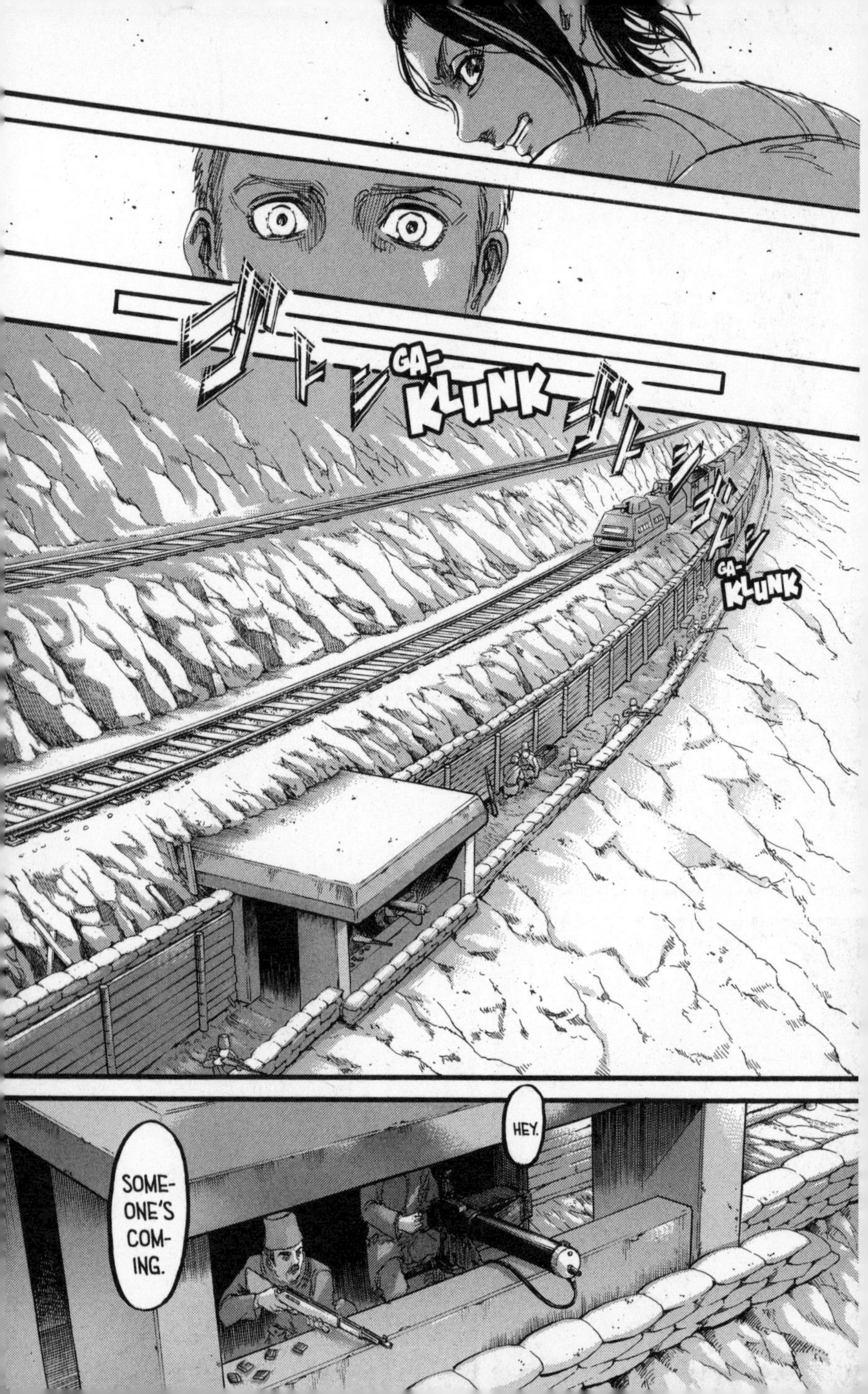
GA-KLUNK
GA-KLUNK
HEY.
SOME-ONE'S COM-ING.

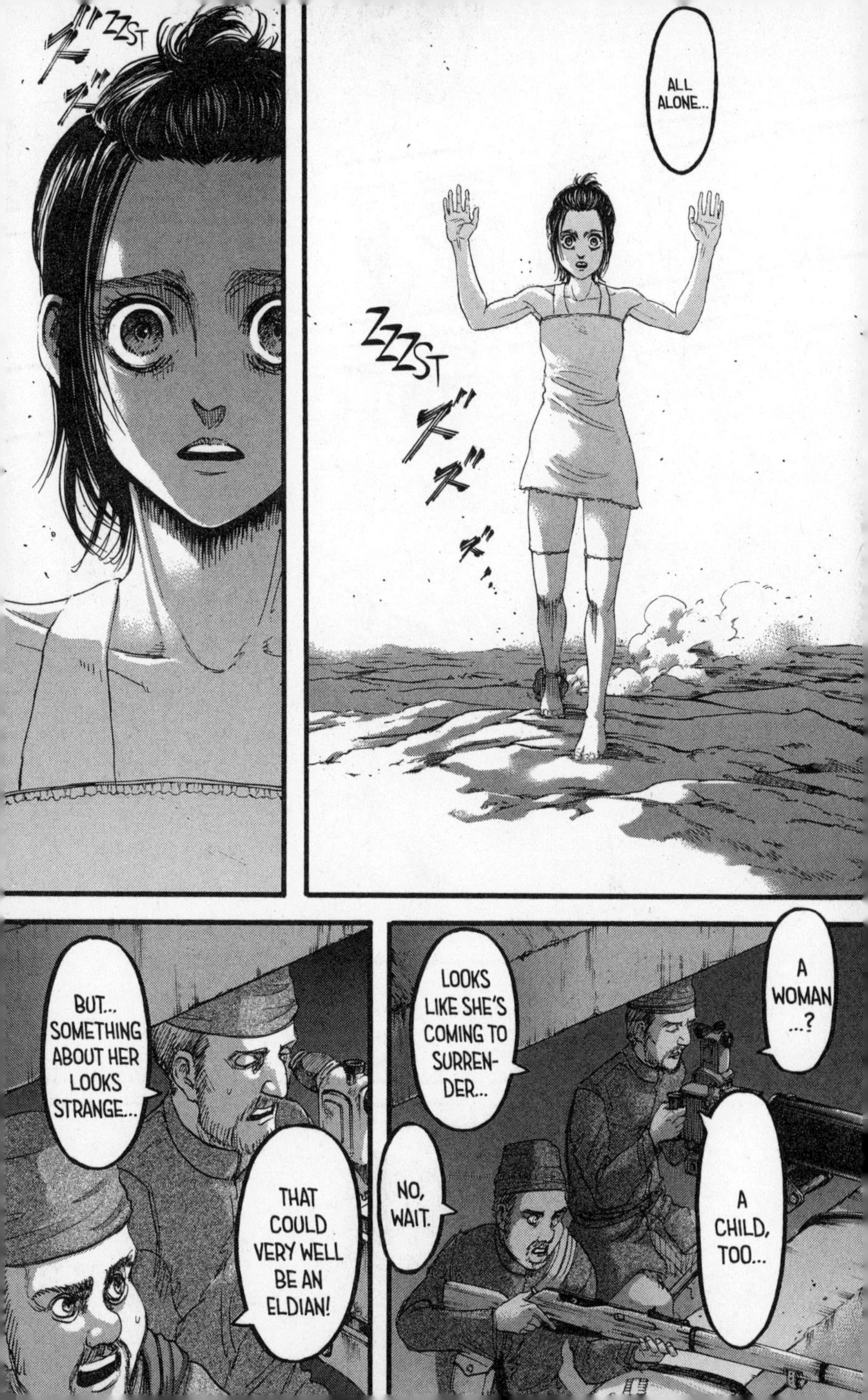

ALL ALONE...
ZZZST
ZZZST
A WOMAN ...?
LOOKS LIKE SHE'S COMING TO SURREN-DER...
A CHILD, TOO...
NO, WAIT.
BUT... SOMETHING ABOUT HER LOOKS STRANGE...
THAT COULD VERY WELL BE AN ELDIAN!

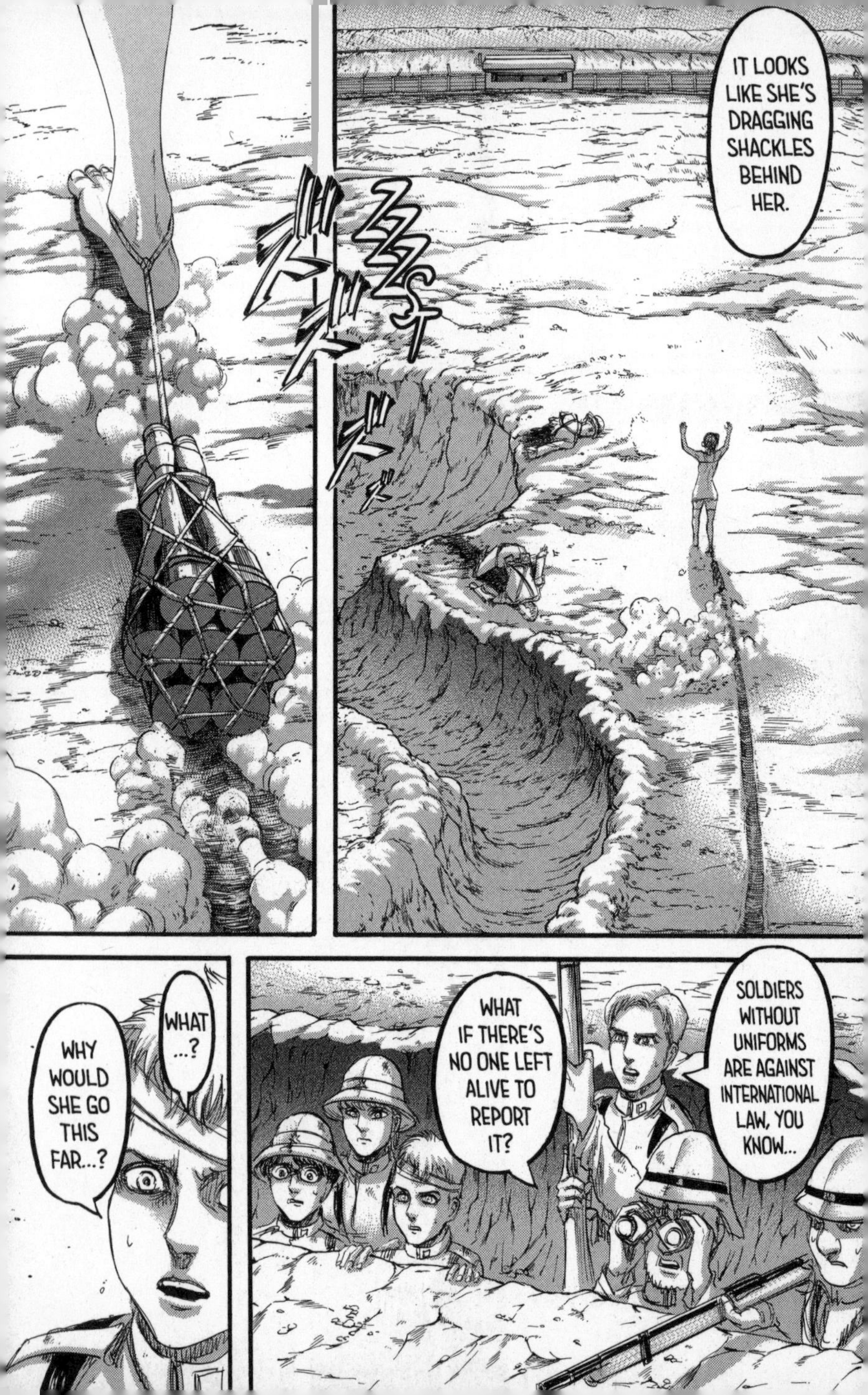
IT LOOKS LIKE SHE'S DRAGGING SHACKLES BEHIND HER.
SOLDIERS WITHOUT UNIFORMS ARE AGAINST INTERNATIONAL LAW, YOU KNOW...
WHAT IF THERE'S NO ONE LEFT ALIVE TO REPORT IT?
WHAT ...?
WHY WOULD SHE GO THIS FAR...?

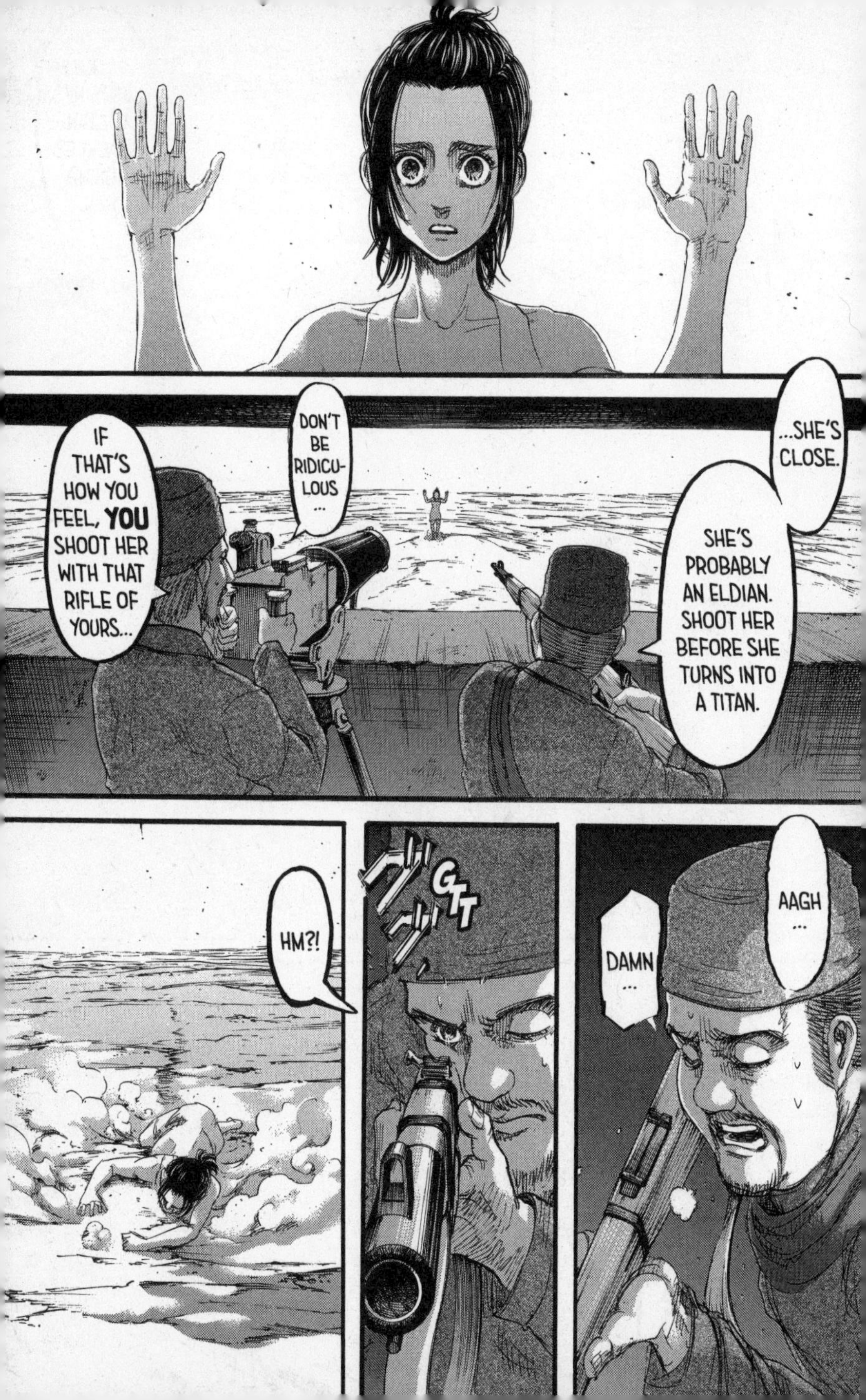
...SHE'S CLOSE.
SHE'S PROBABLY AN ELDIAN. SHOOT HER BEFORE SHE TURNS INTO A TITAN.
DON'T BE RIDICULOUS...
IF THAT'S HOW YOU FEEL, **YOU** SHOOT HER WITH THAT RIFLE OF YOURS...
AAGH...
DAMN...
GTT
HM?!

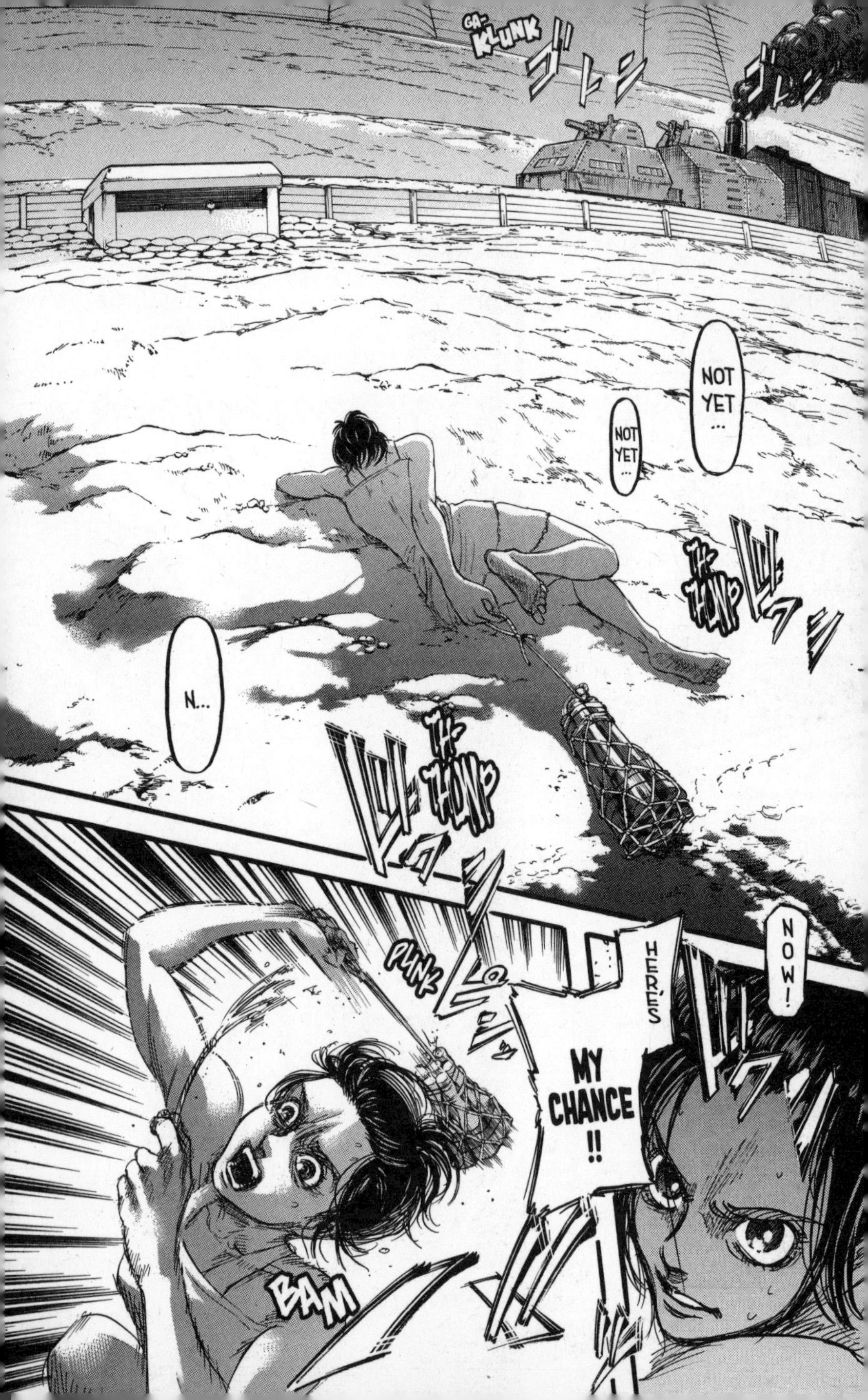
GA-KLUNK
NOT YET...
NOT YET...
TH-THUMP
N...
TH-THUMP
NOW!
HERE'S MY CHANCE!!
PLINK
BAM

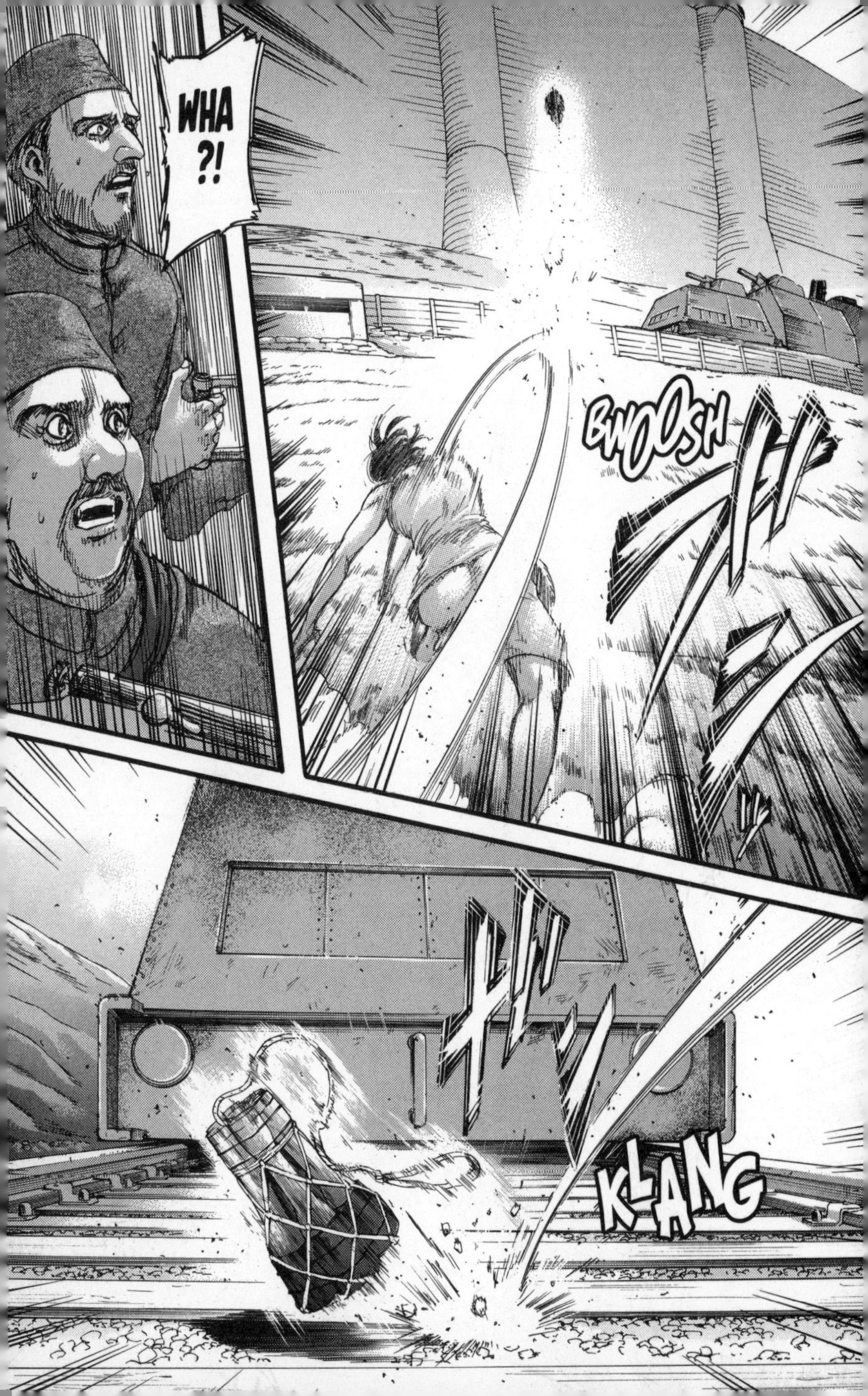
BWOOSH
WHA ?!
KLANG

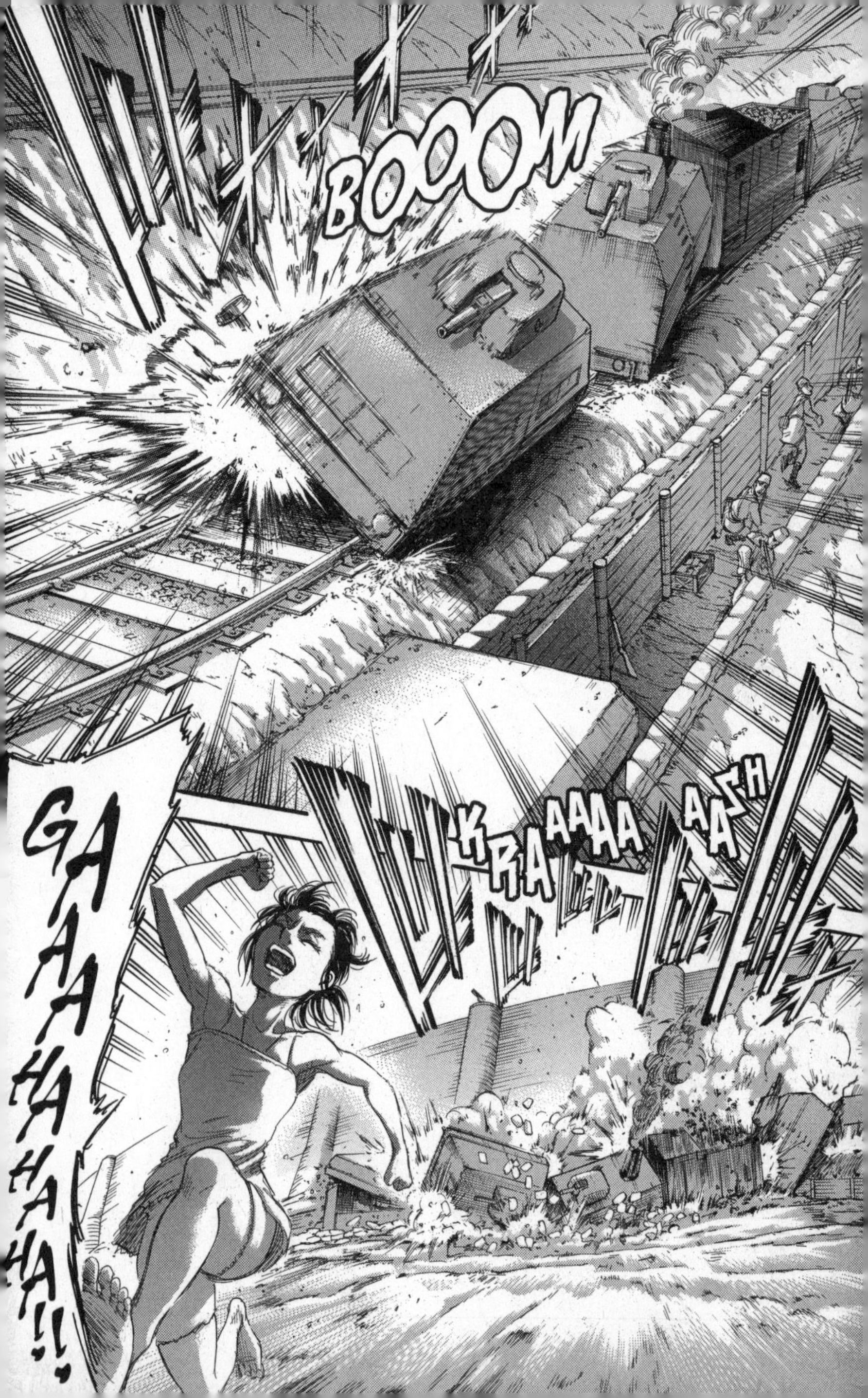
BOOOM
KRAAAAAAASH
GAAAAHAHAHAHA!!!

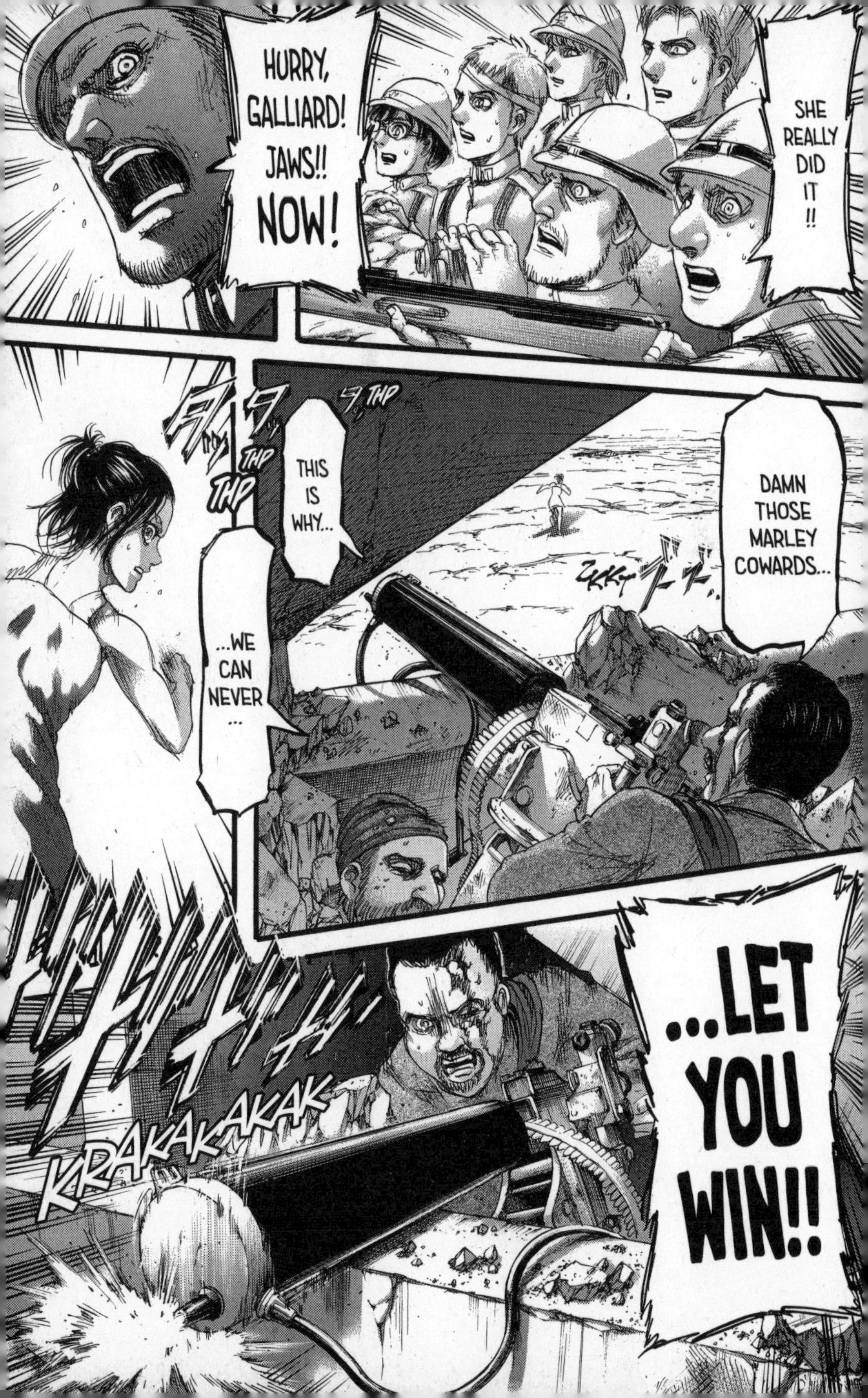
SHE REALLY DID IT !!
HURRY, GALLIARD! JAWS!! NOW!
DAMN THOSE MARLEY COWARDS...
THP
THP
THP
THIS IS WHY...
...WE CAN NEVER ...
...LET YOU WIN!!
KRAKAKAKAK

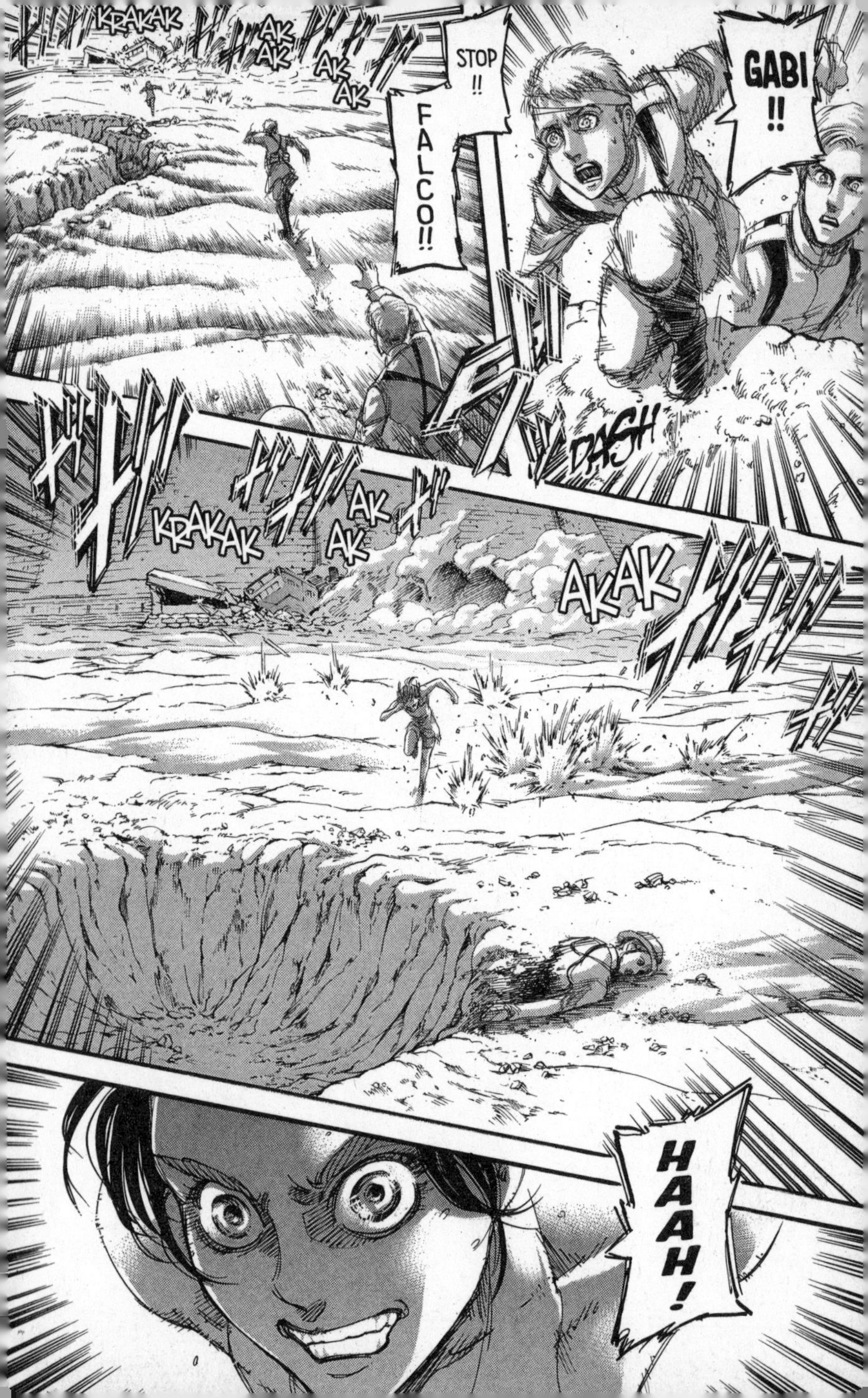

GABI !!
STOP !!
FALCO!!
KRAKAK
AK AK AK AK
DASH
KRAKAK
AK AK
AKAK
HAAAH!

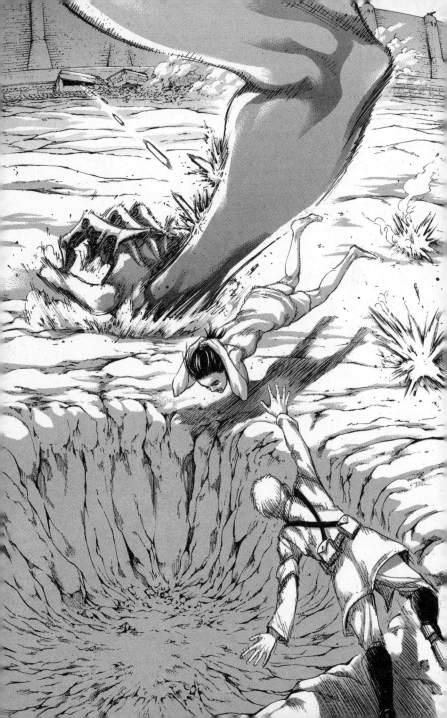

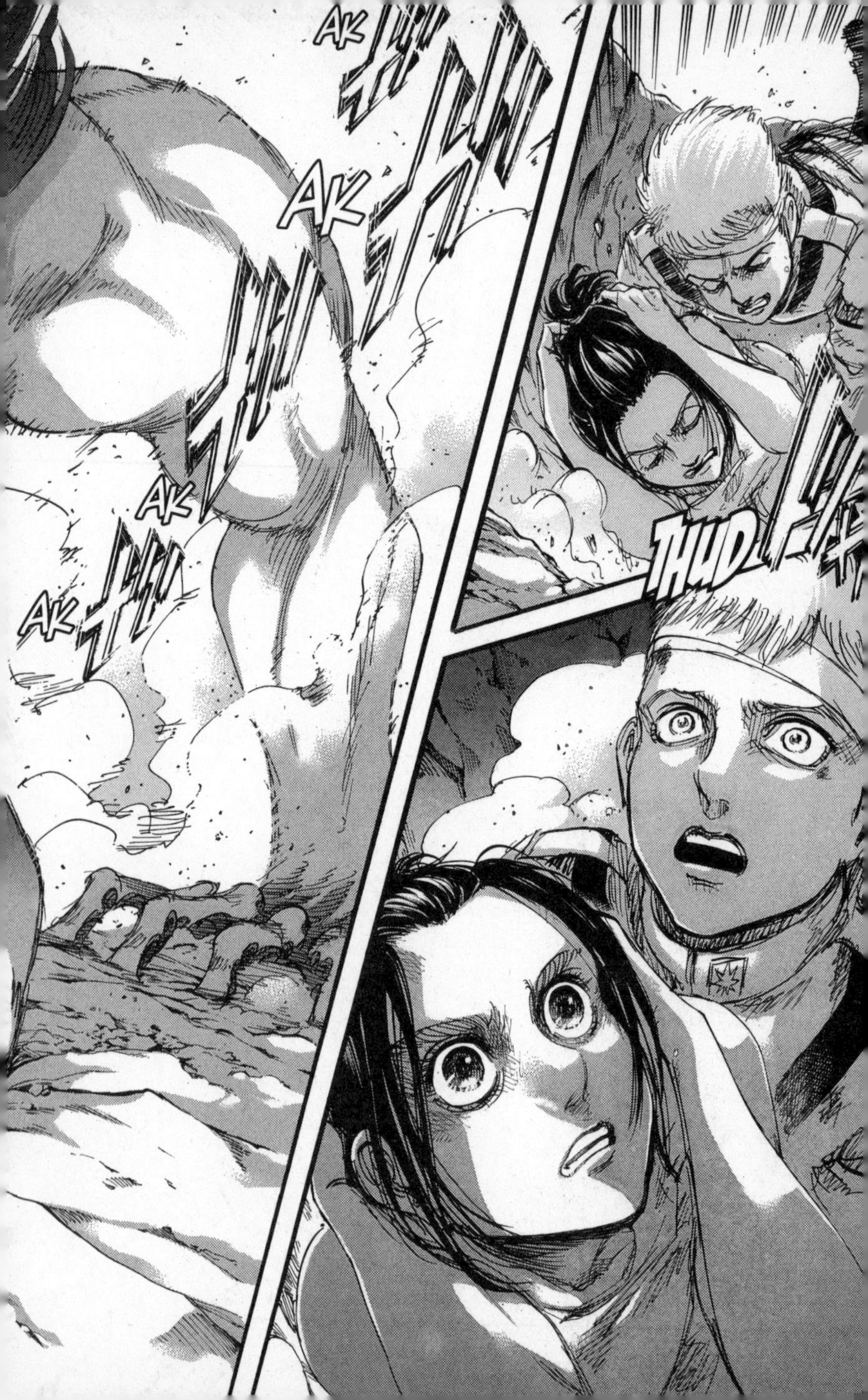
THUD
AK
AK
AK
AK

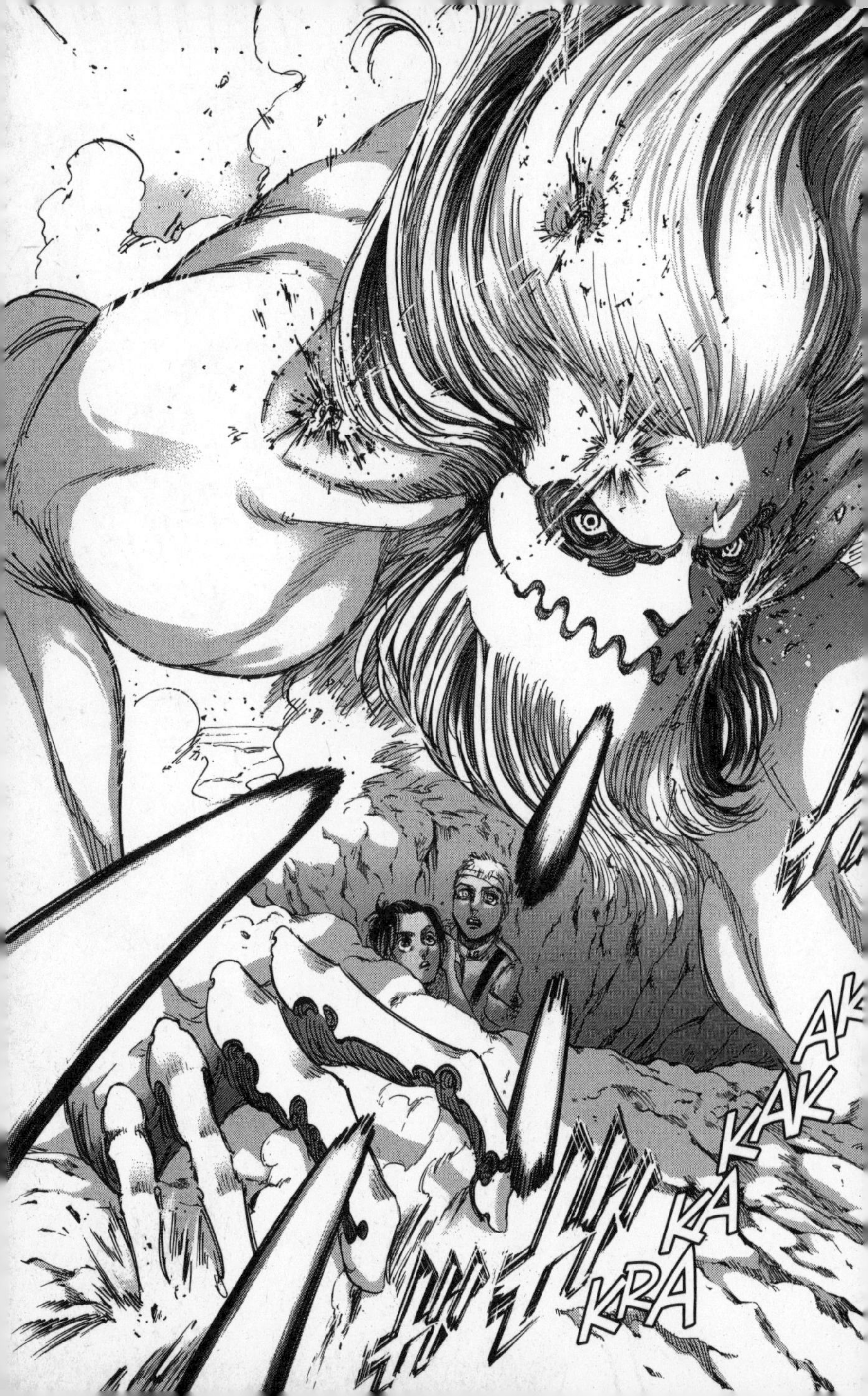
AK
KAK
KA
KRA

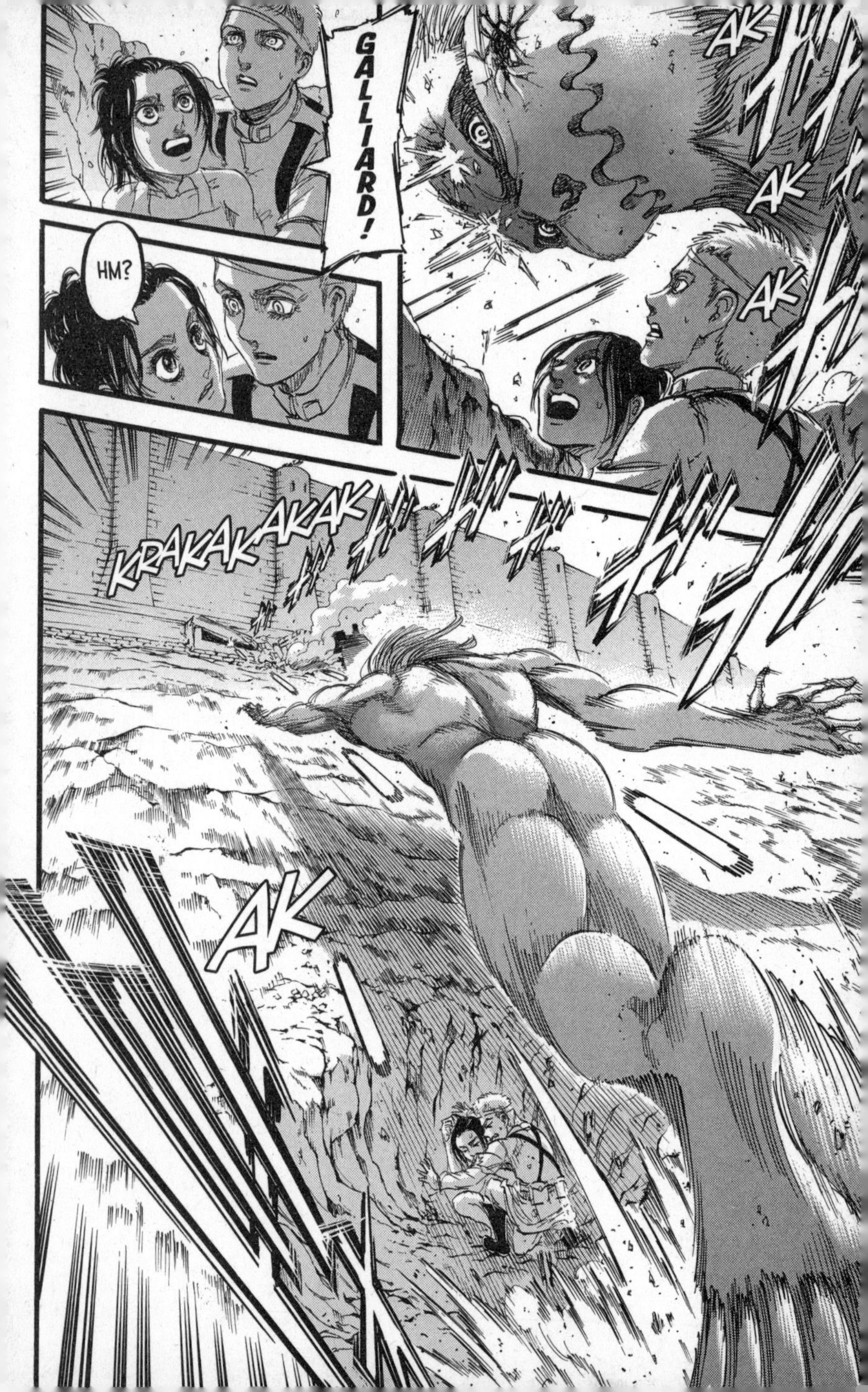
AK
AK
AK
GALLIARD!
HM?
KRAKAKAKAK
AK

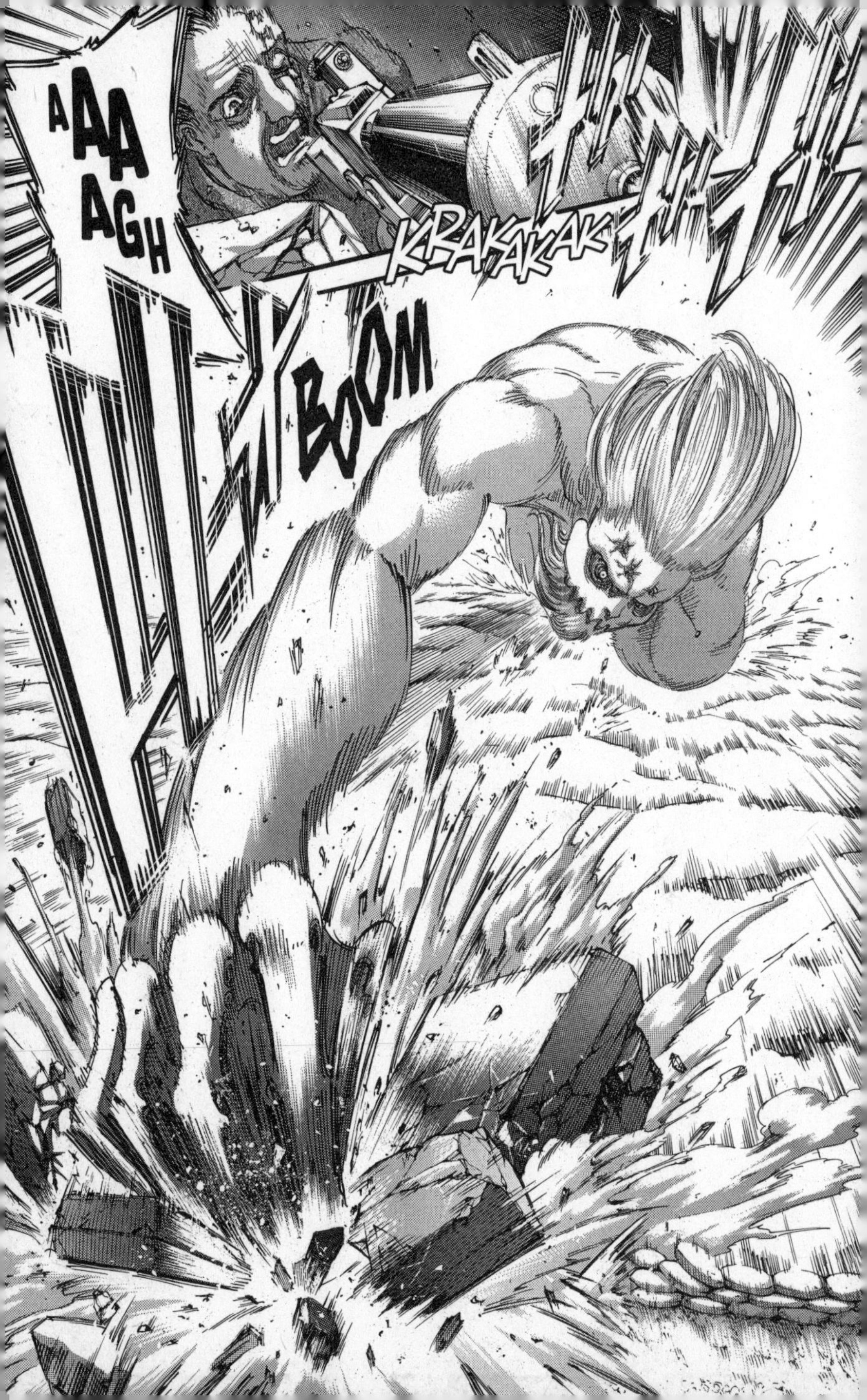
KRAKAKAK
AAAAGH
BOOM

# ATTACK on TITAN

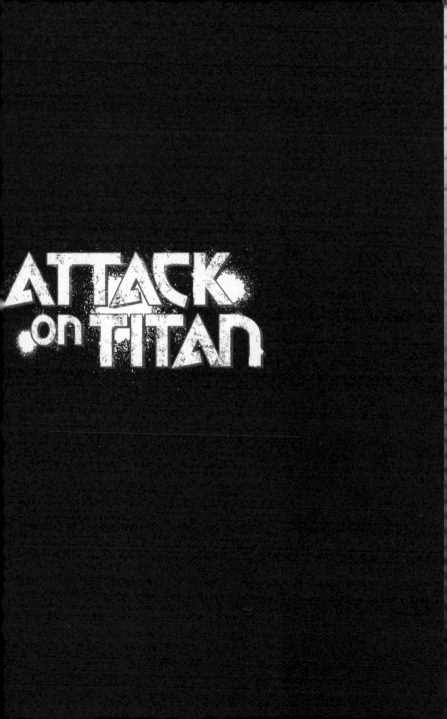

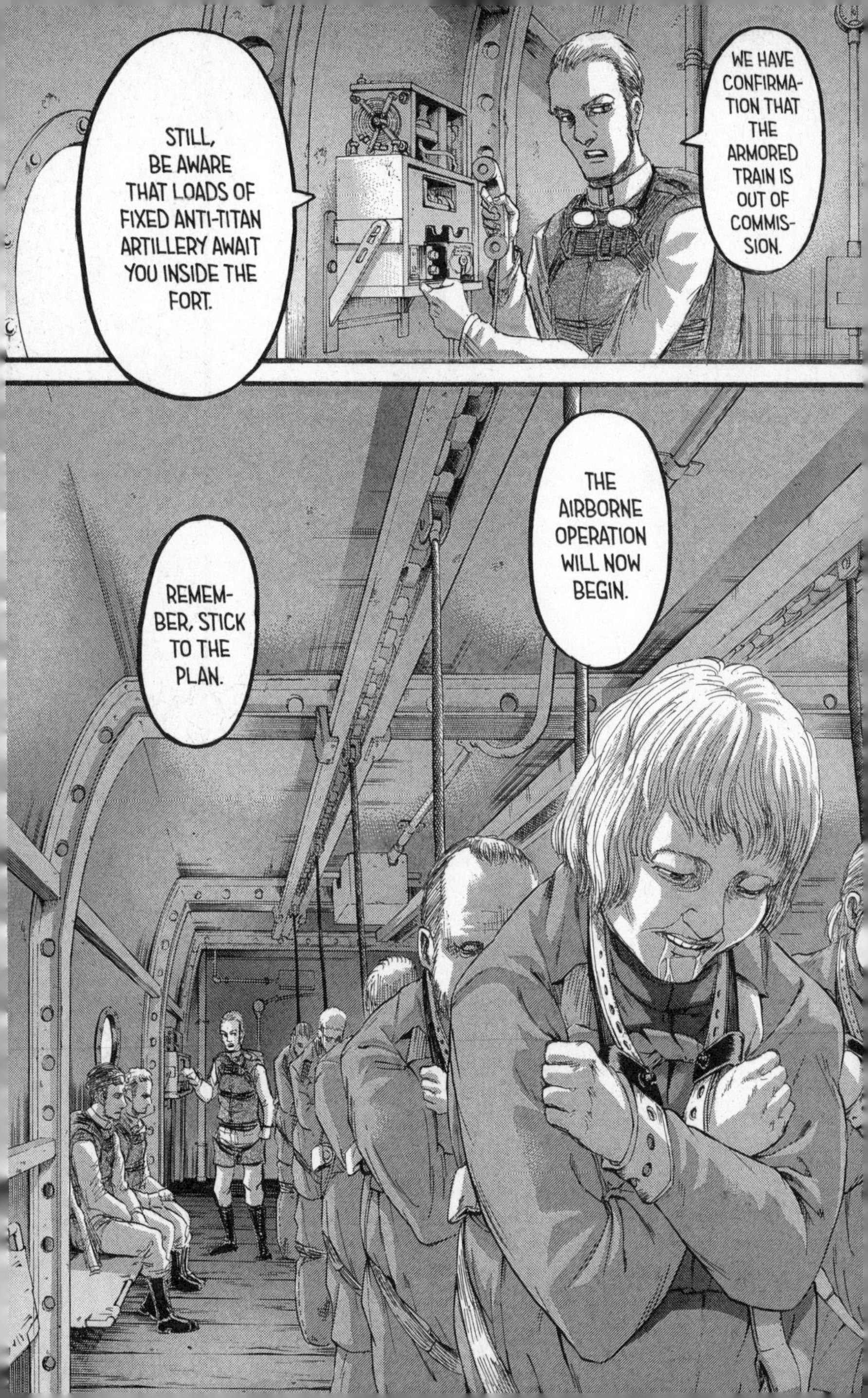
WE HAVE CONFIRMATION THAT THE ARMORED TRAIN IS OUT OF COMMISSION.
STILL, BE AWARE THAT LOADS OF FIXED ANTI-TITAN ARTILLERY AWAIT YOU INSIDE THE FORT.
THE AIRBORNE OPERATION WILL NOW BEGIN.
REMEMBER, STICK TO THE PLAN.

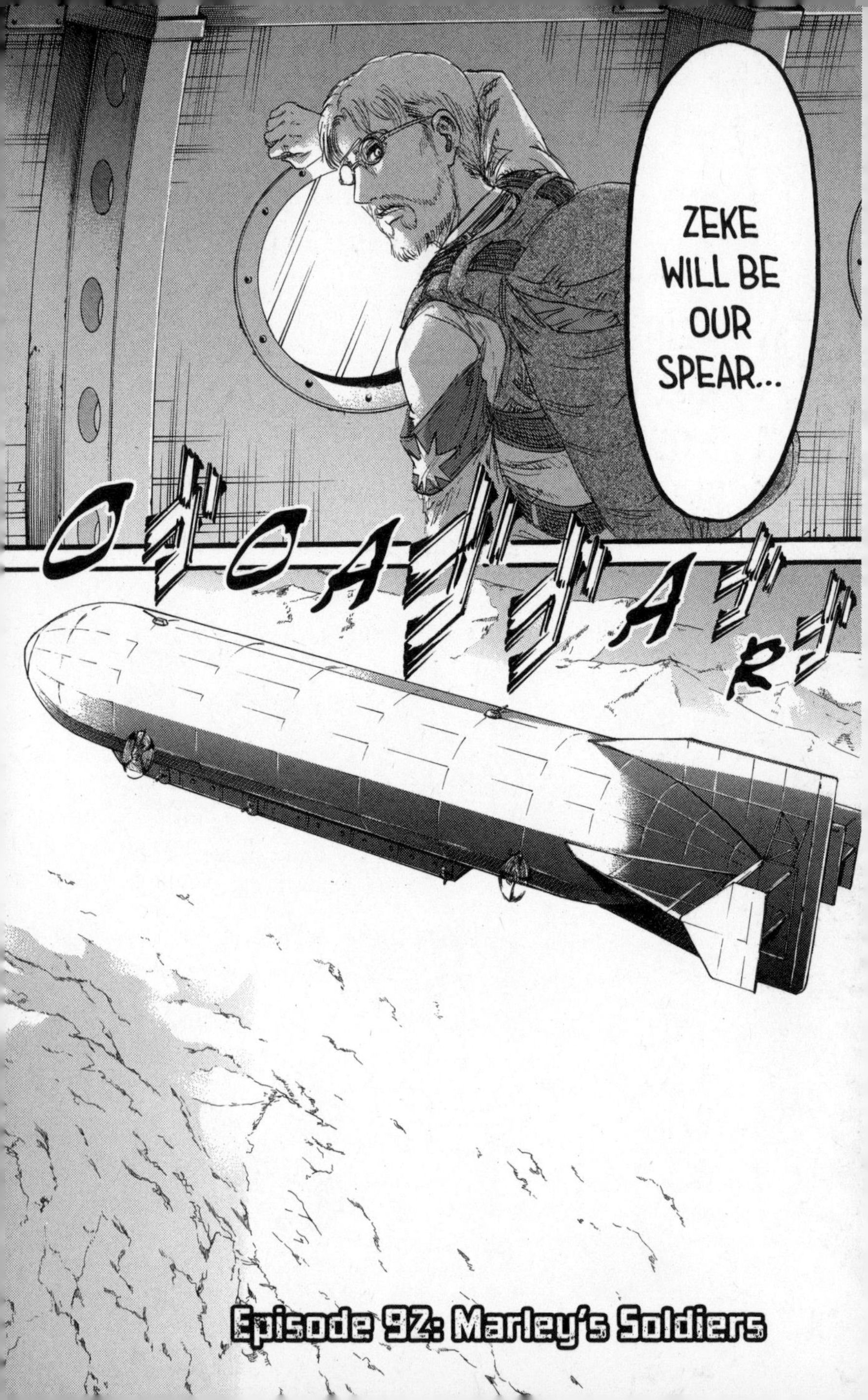
ZEKE WILL BE OUR SPEAR...
Episode 92: Marley's Soldiers

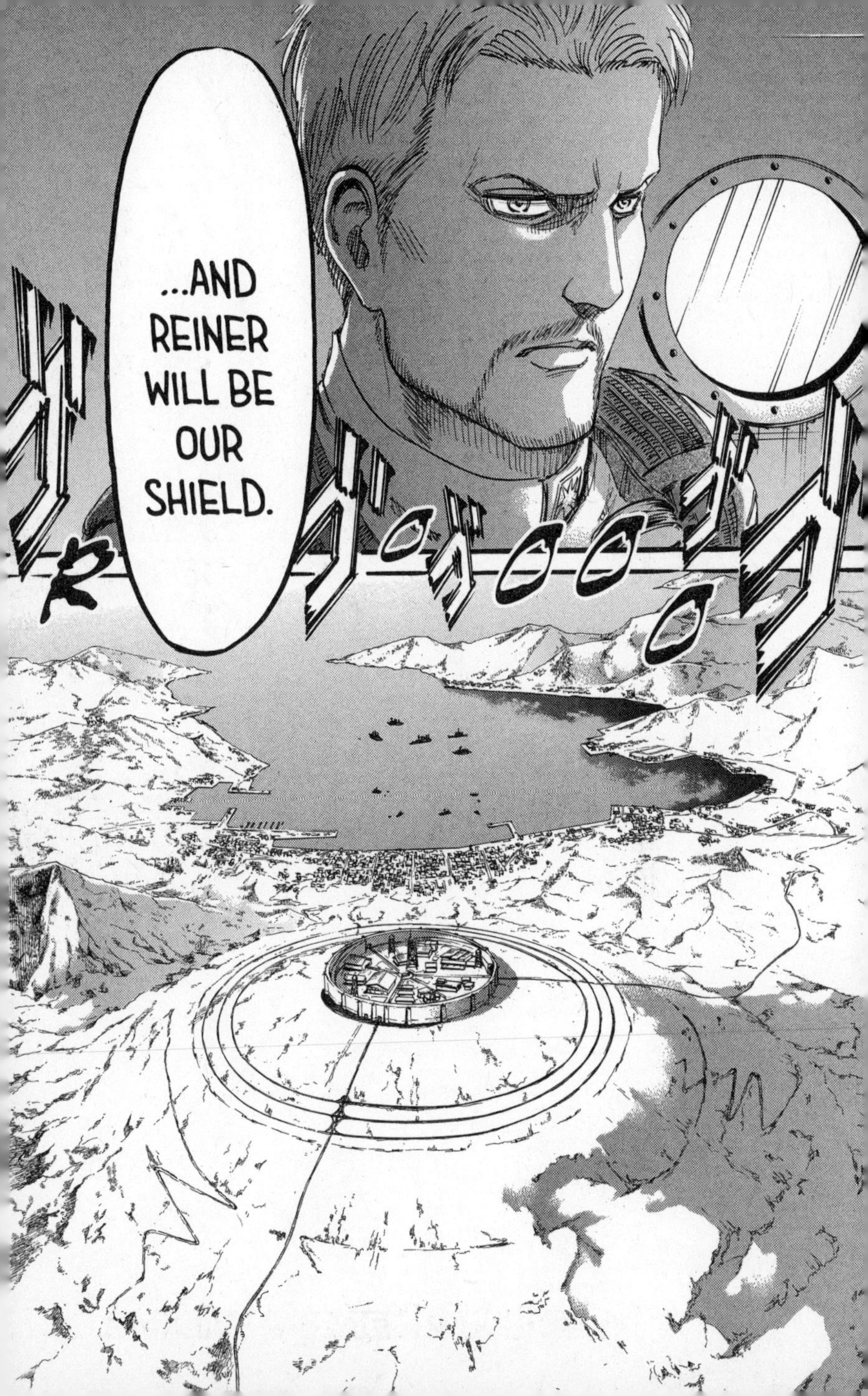
...AND REINER WILL BE OUR SHIELD.

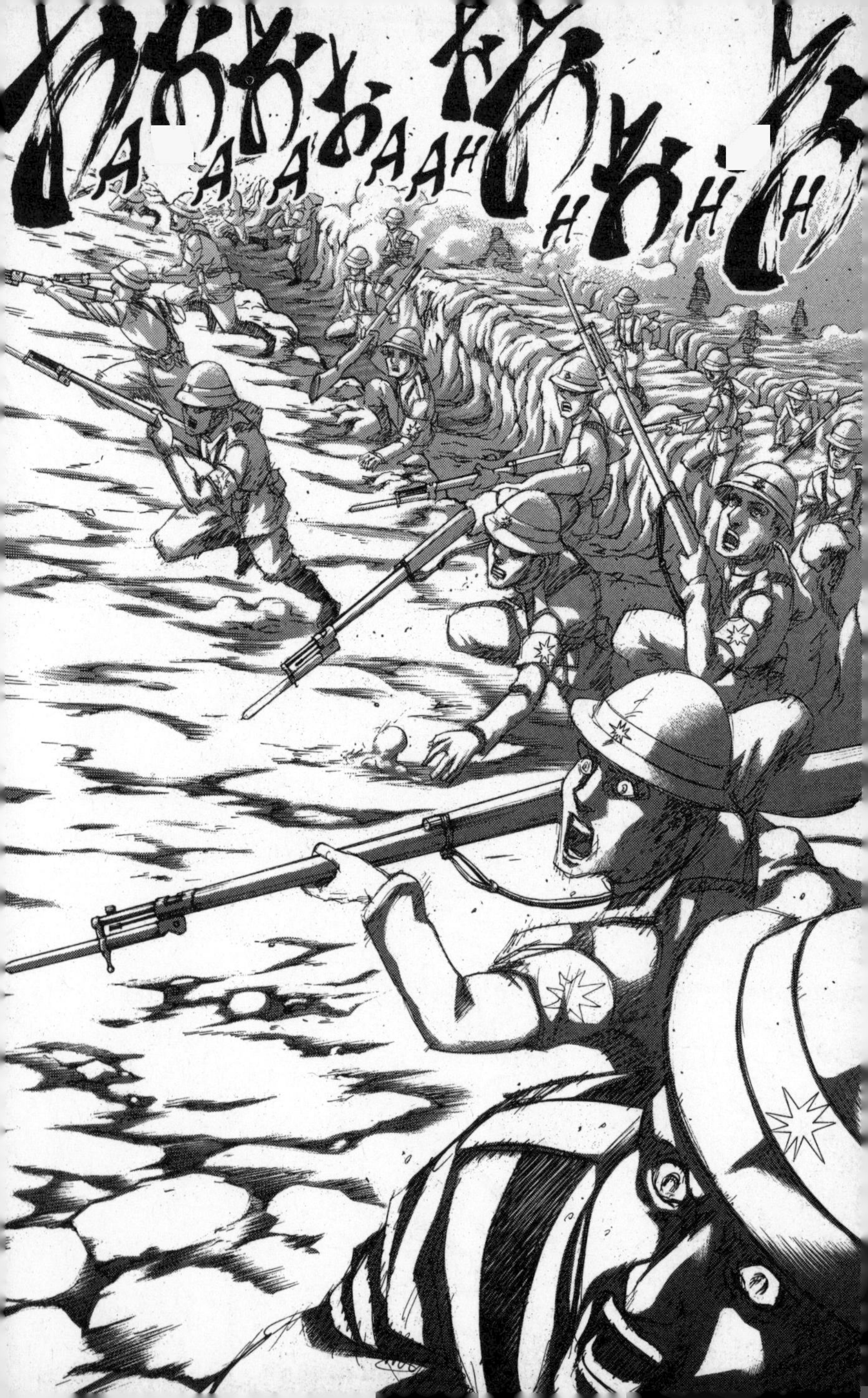
A A A AAH H H H H

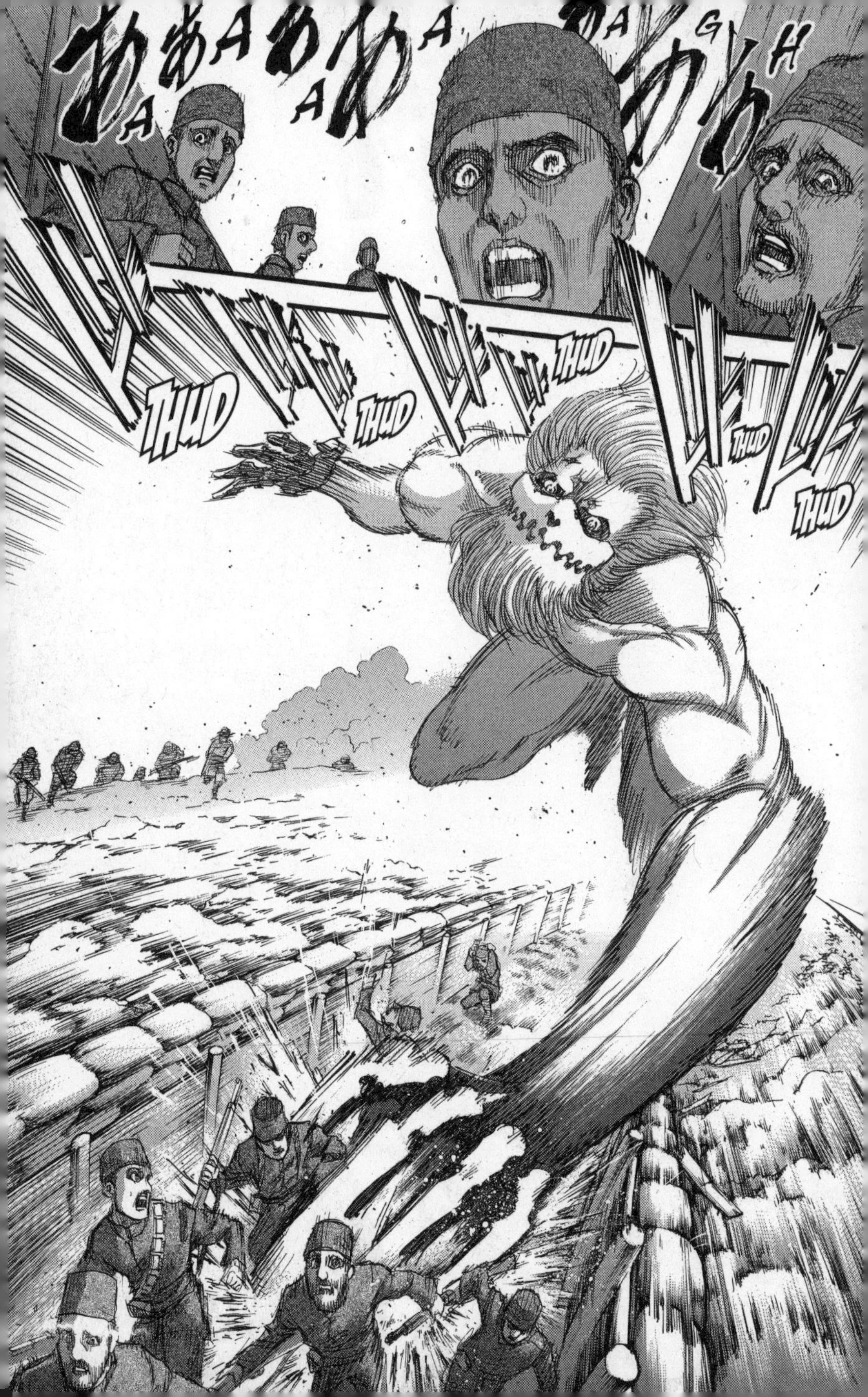
AAAAAGH
THUD
THUD
THUD
THUD
THUD
THUD

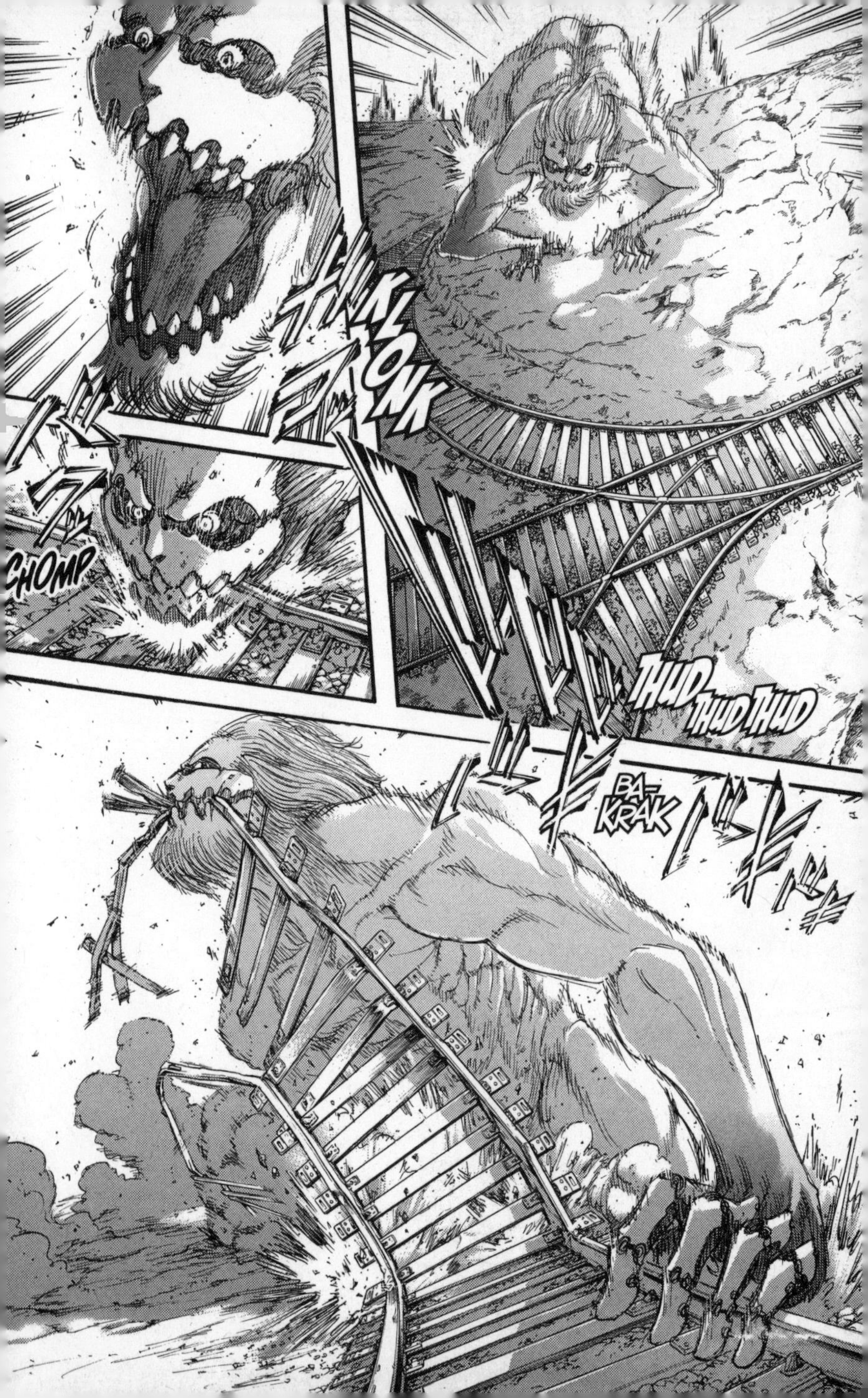
KLONK
THUD THUD THUD
CHOMP
BA-KRAK

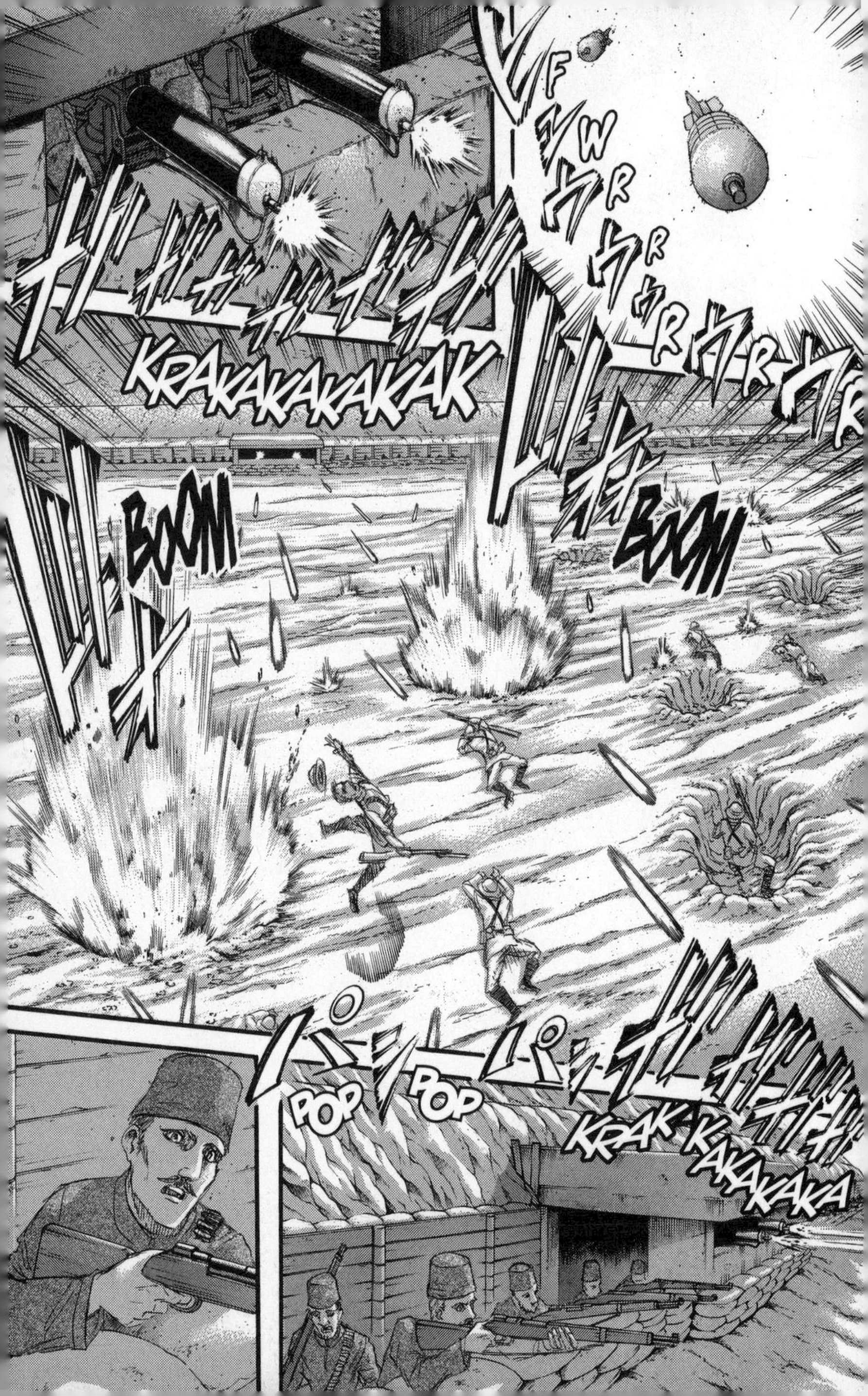
FWRRRRRRR
KRAKAKAKAKAKAK
BOOM
BOOM
KRAK KAKAKAKA
POP POP

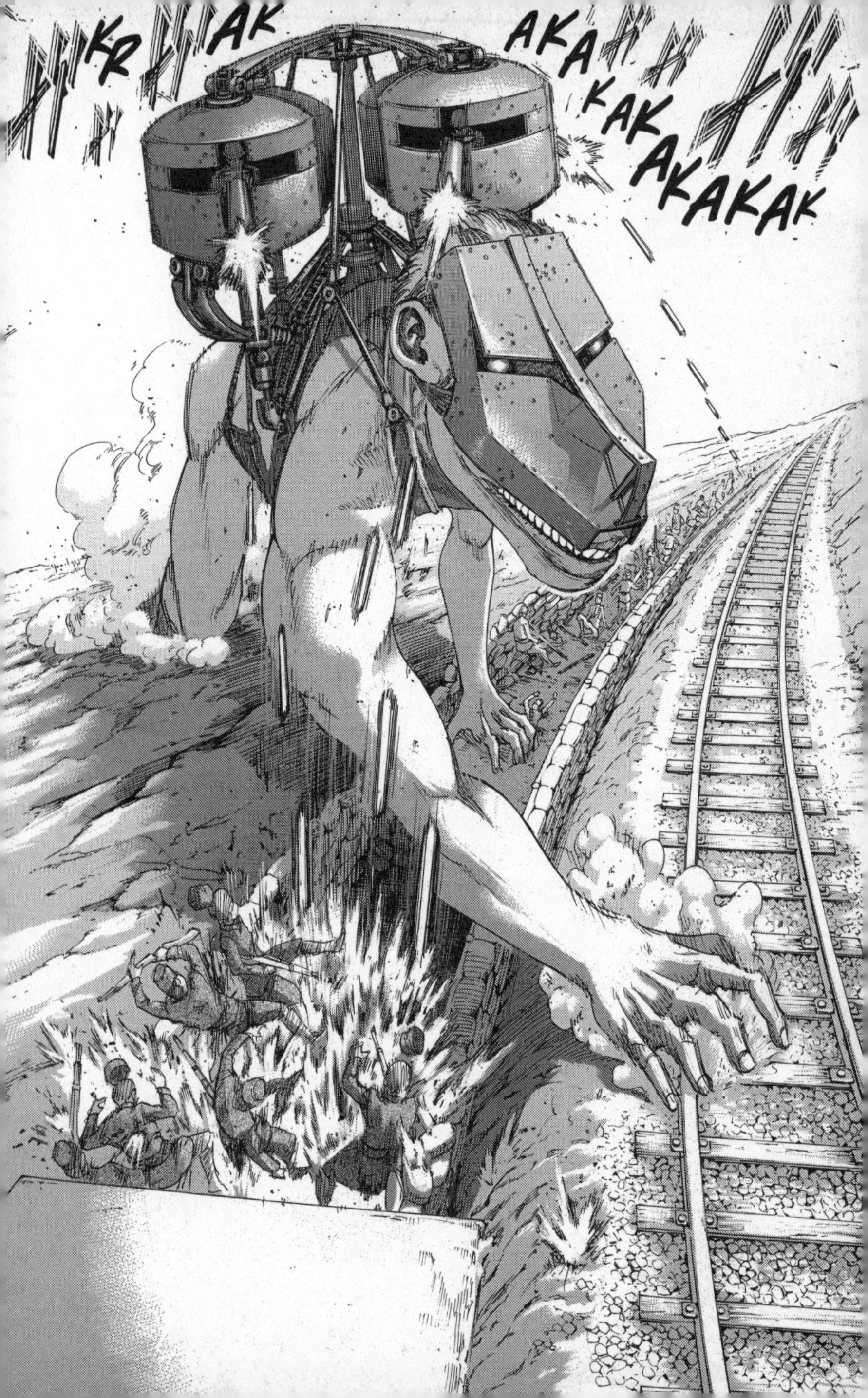
KRAK
AKAKAKAKAKAKAKAK

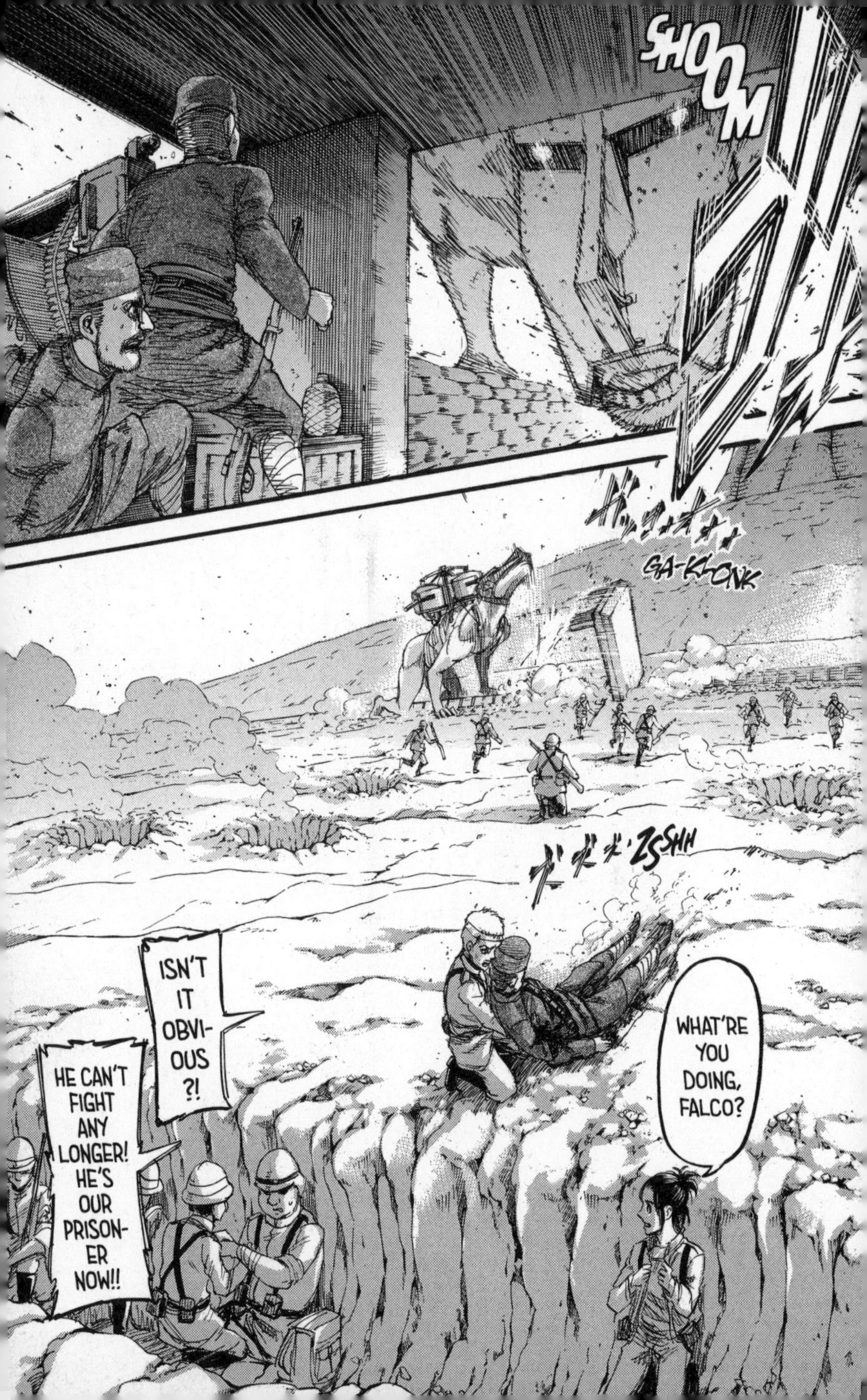
SHOOM
GA-KLONK
ZSSHH
WHAT'RE YOU DOING, FALCO?
ISN'T IT OBVIOUS?!
HE CAN'T FIGHT ANY LONGER! HE'S OUR PRISONER NOW!!

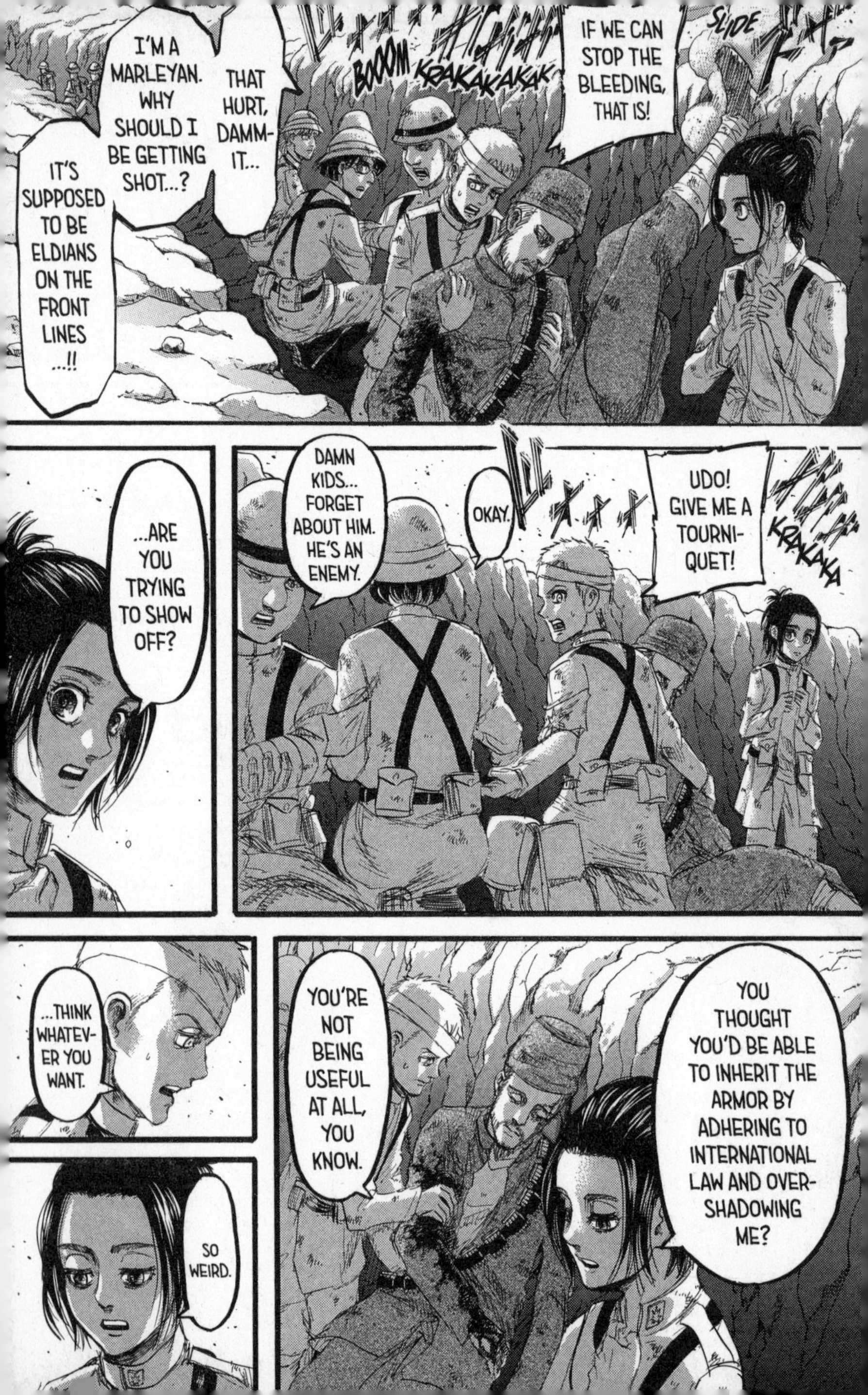

SLIDE
IF WE CAN STOP THE BLEEDING, THAT IS!
BOOOM
KRAKAKAKAKAK
THAT HURT, DAMMIT...
I'M A MARLEYAN. WHY SHOULD I BE GETTING SHOT...?
IT'S SUPPOSED TO BE ELDIANS ON THE FRONT LINES ...!!
KRAKAKA
UDO! GIVE ME A TOURNIQUET!
OKAY.
DAMN KIDS... FORGET ABOUT HIM. HE'S AN ENEMY.
...ARE YOU TRYING TO SHOW OFF?
YOU THOUGHT YOU'D BE ABLE TO INHERIT THE ARMOR BY ADHERING TO INTERNATIONAL LAW AND OVERSHADOWING ME?
YOU'RE NOT BEING USEFUL AT ALL, YOU KNOW.
...THINK WHATEVER YOU WANT.
SO WEIRD.

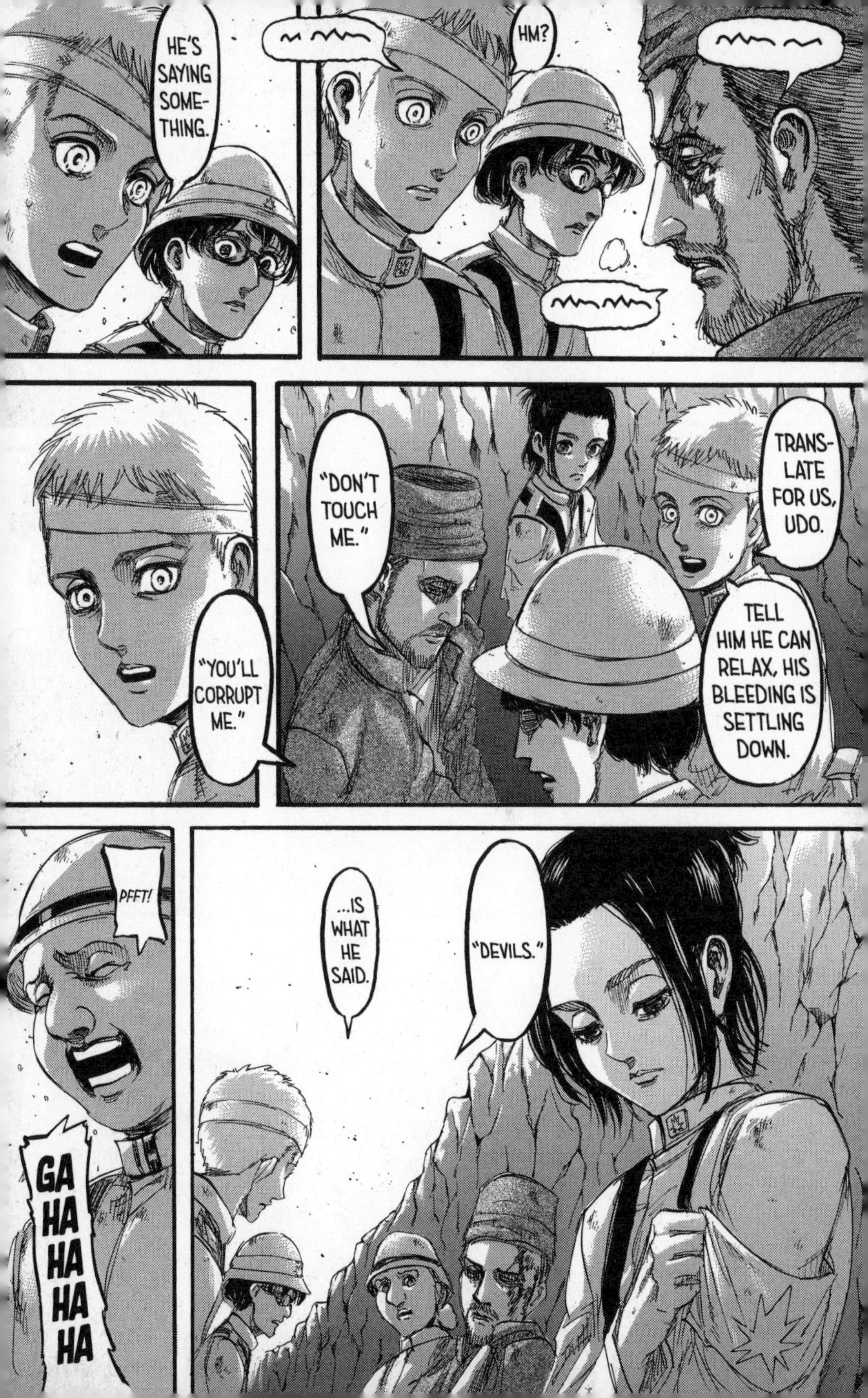
HM?
HE'S SAYING SOMETHING.
TRANSLATE FOR US, UDO.
TELL HIM HE CAN RELAX, HIS BLEEDING IS SETTLING DOWN.
"DON'T TOUCH ME."
"YOU'LL CORRUPT ME."
"DEVILS."
...IS WHAT HE SAID.
PFFT!
GAHAHAHAHAHA

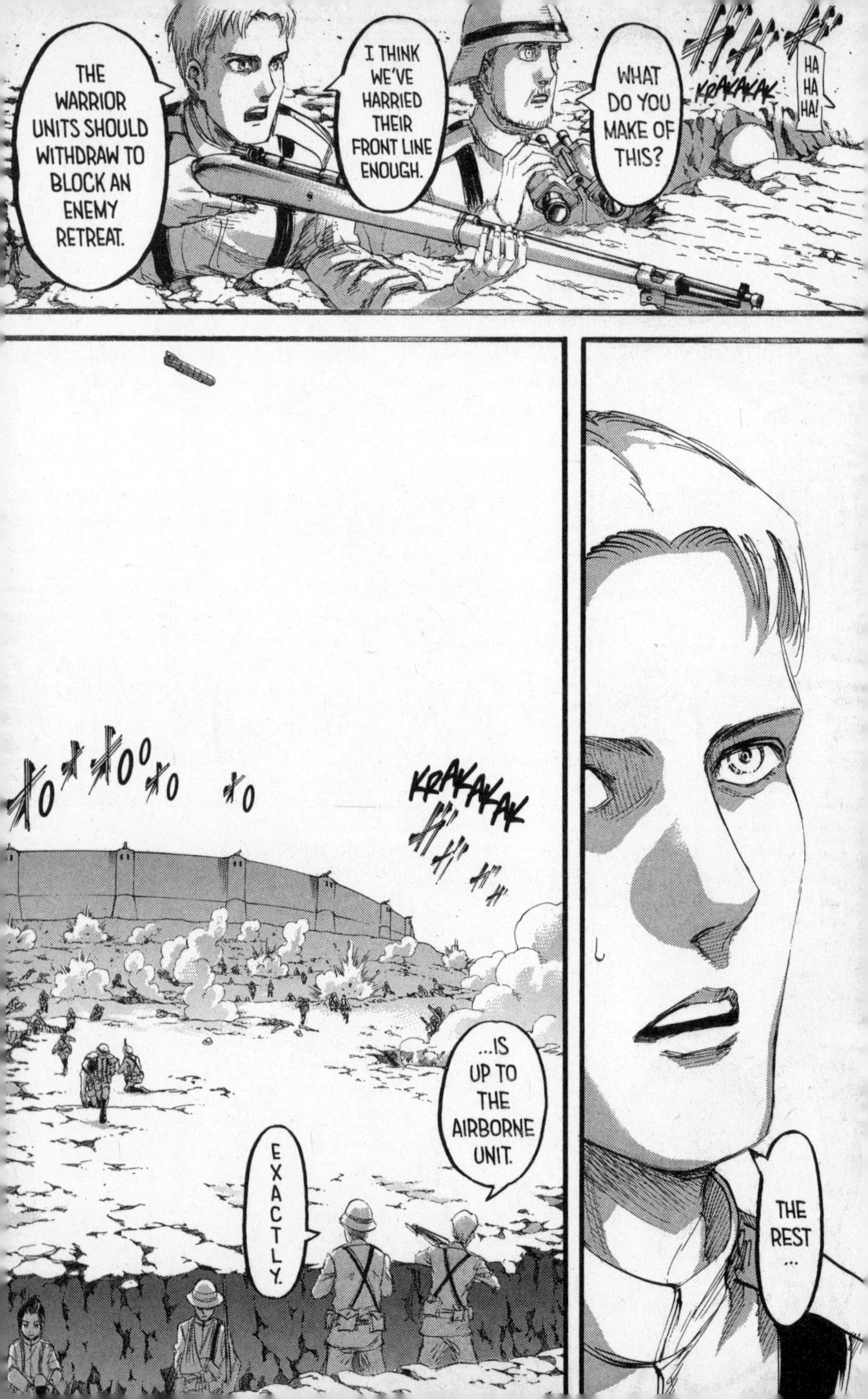
KRAKAKAK
HA HA HA!
WHAT DO YOU MAKE OF THIS?
I THINK WE'VE HARRIED THEIR FRONT LINE ENOUGH.
THE WARRIOR UNITS SHOULD WITHDRAW TO BLOCK AN ENEMY RETREAT.
THE REST ...
KRAKAKAK
...IS UP TO THE AIRBORNE UNIT.
EXACTLY.

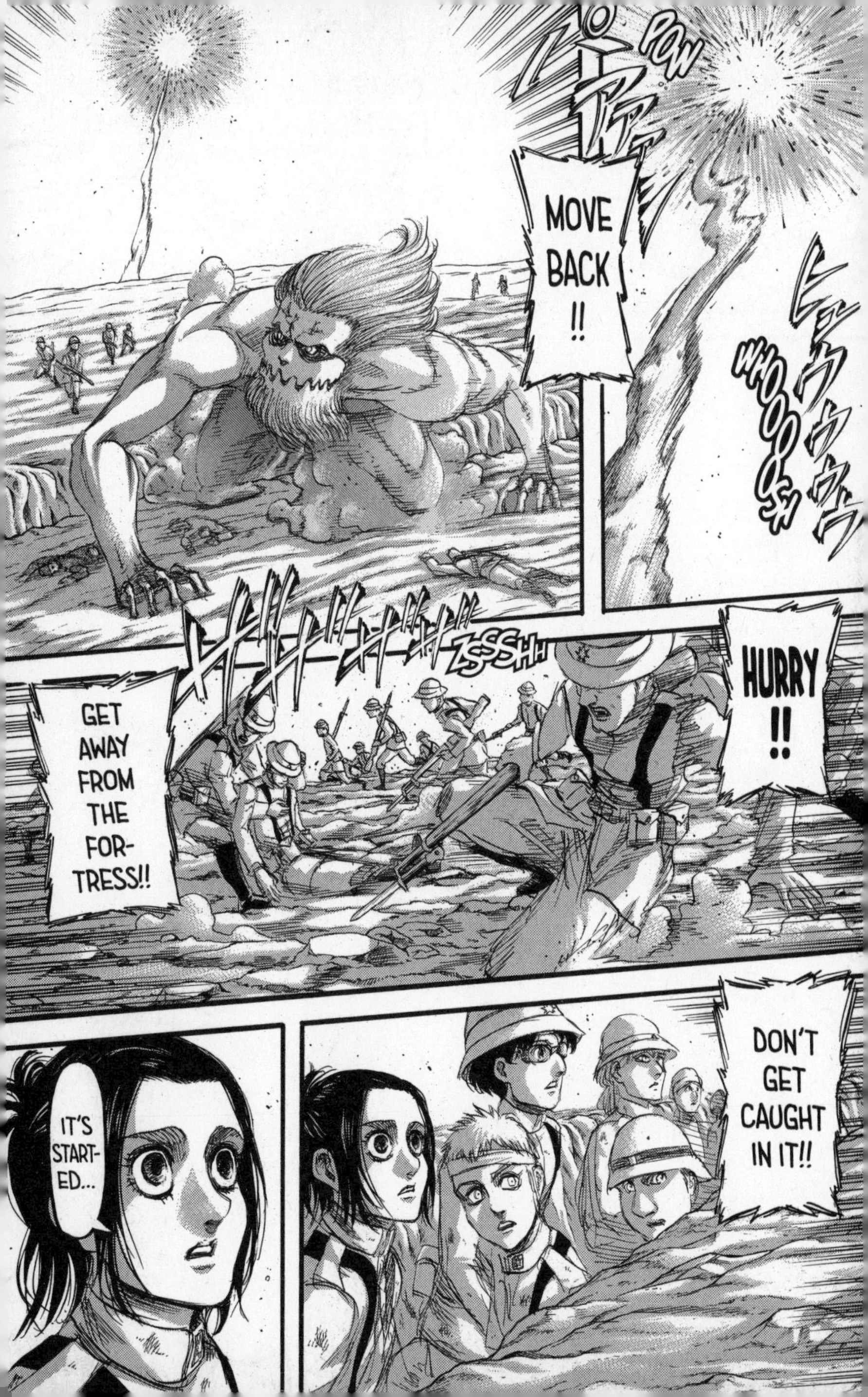
POW
WHOOOOSH
MOVE BACK!!
HURRY!!
TSSHH
GET AWAY FROM THE FOR-TRESS!!
DON'T GET CAUGHT IN IT!!
IT'S START-ED...

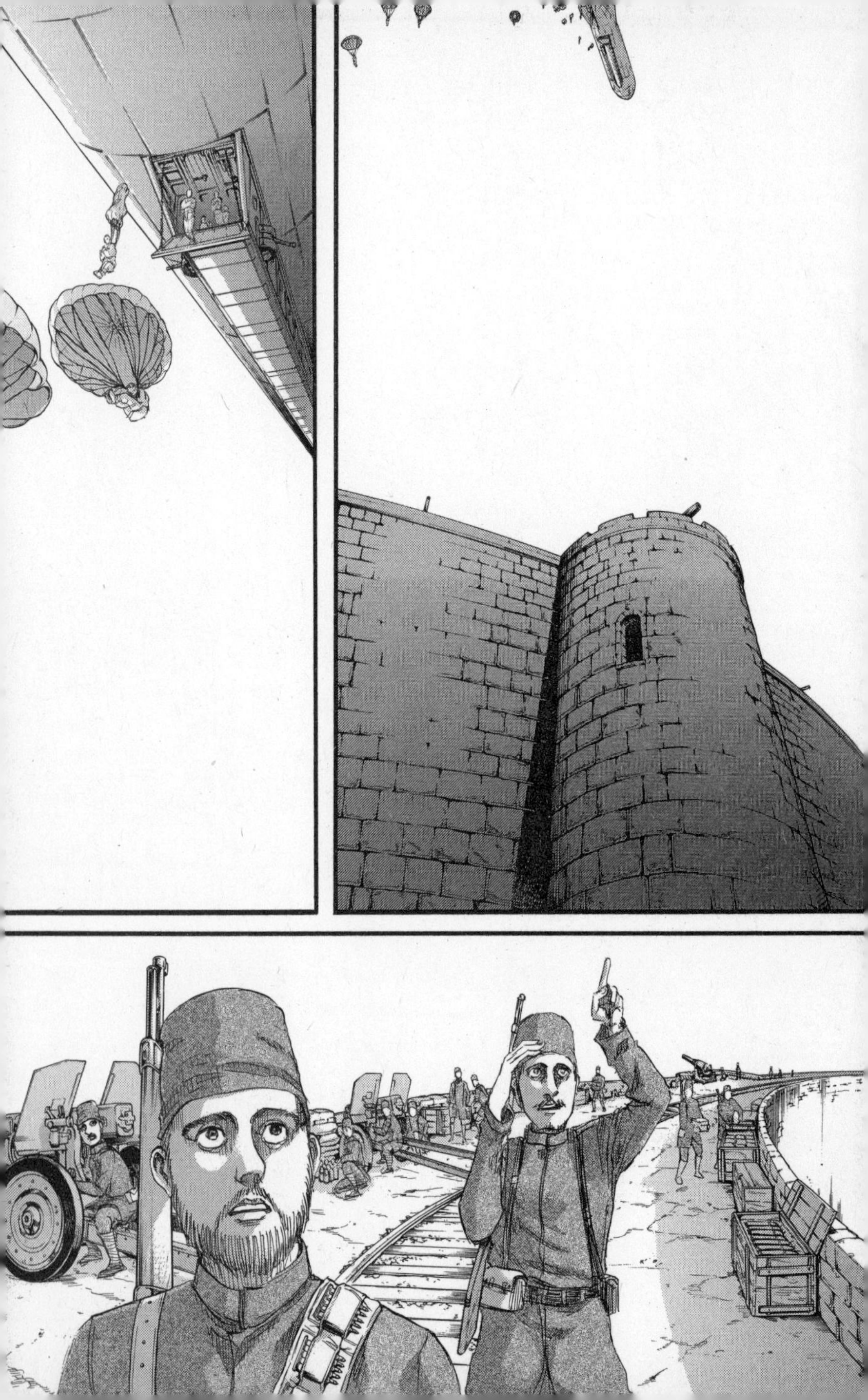

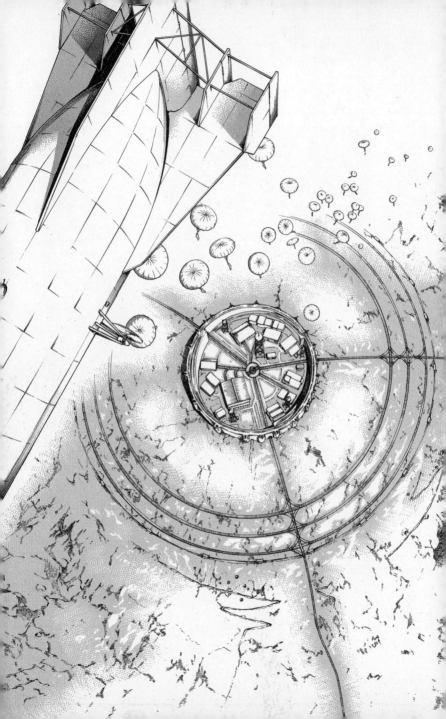

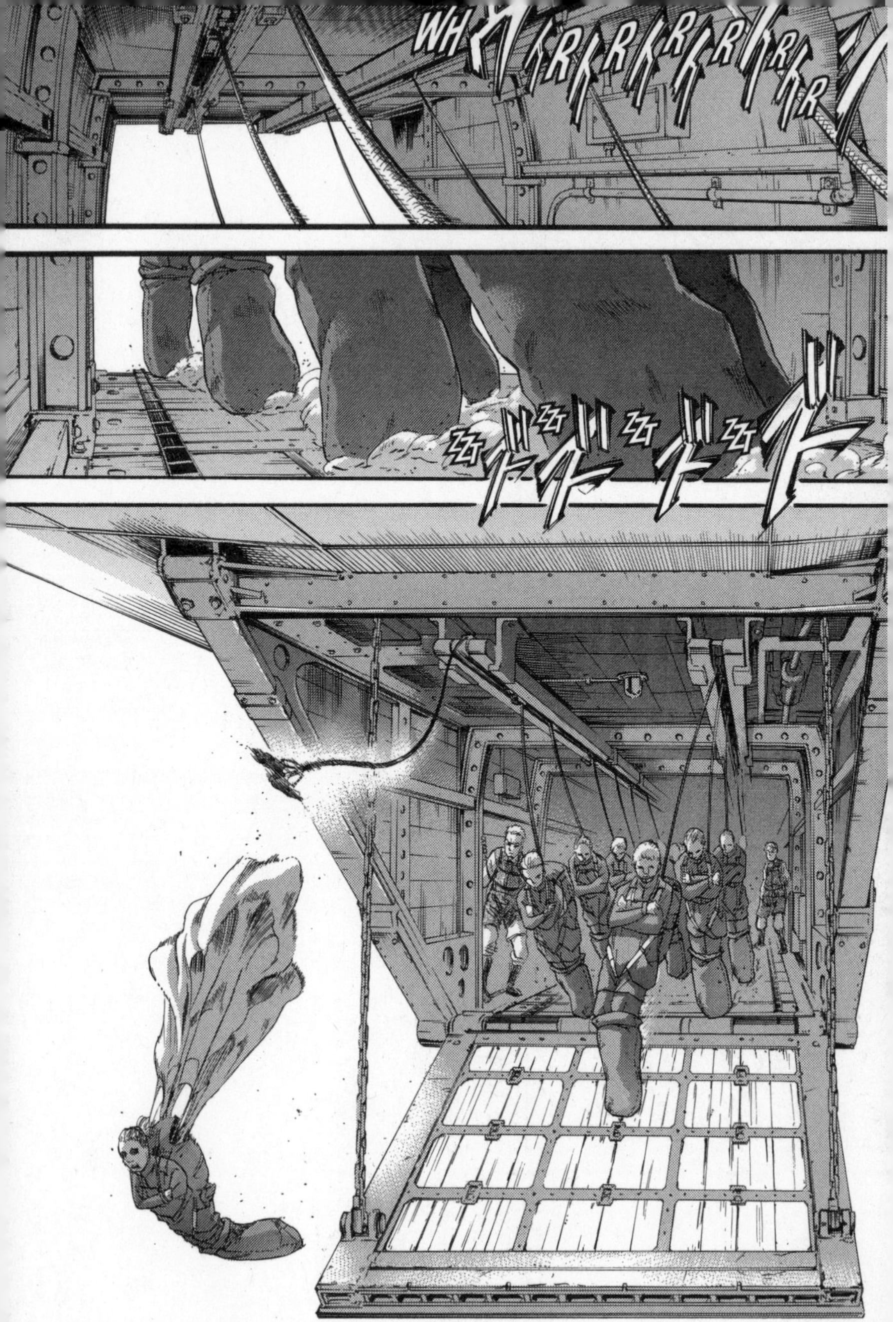
WHRRRRRR
ZZZT ZZZT ZZZT ZZZT

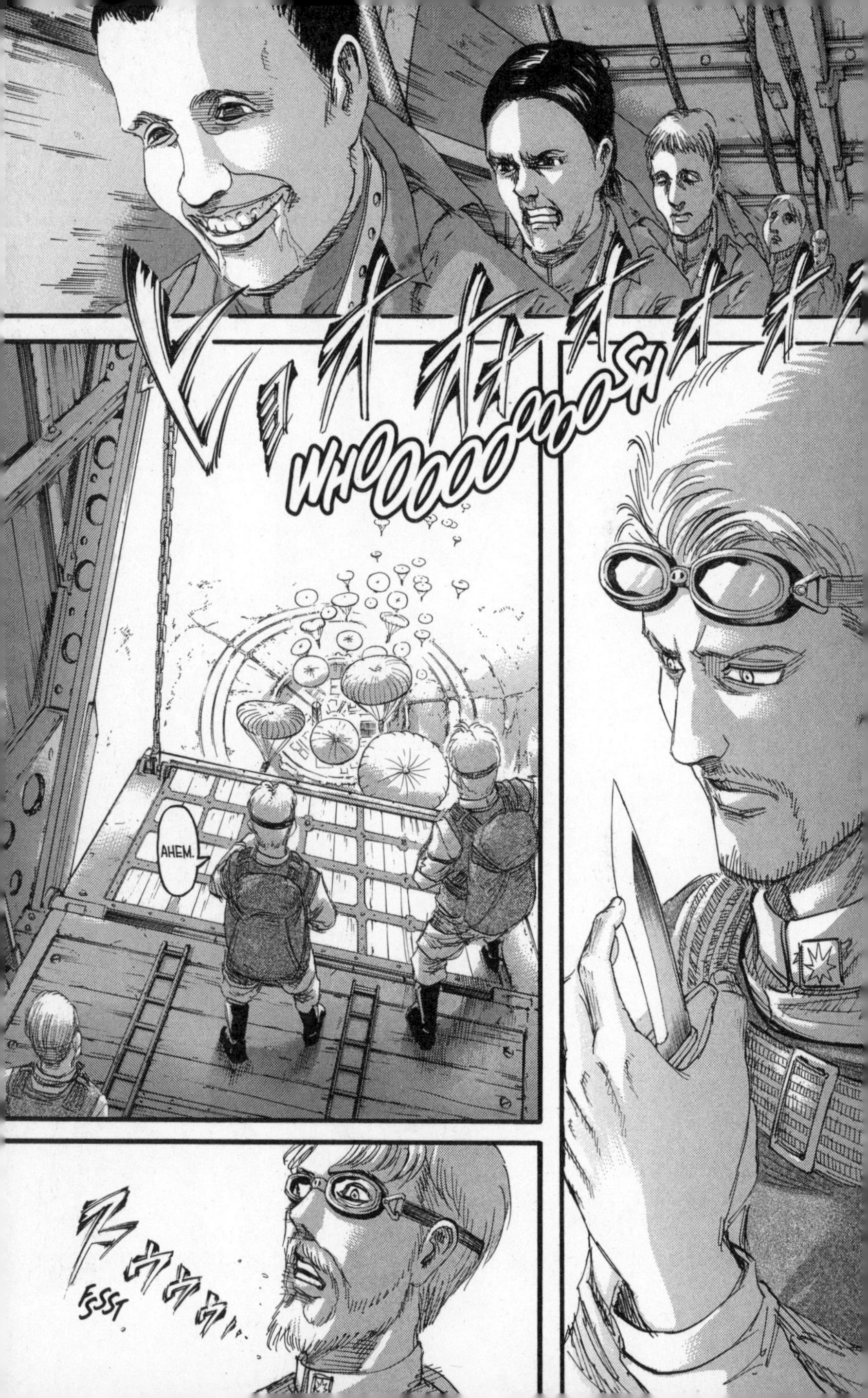
WHOOOOOOOOOOSH
AHEM.
FSSST

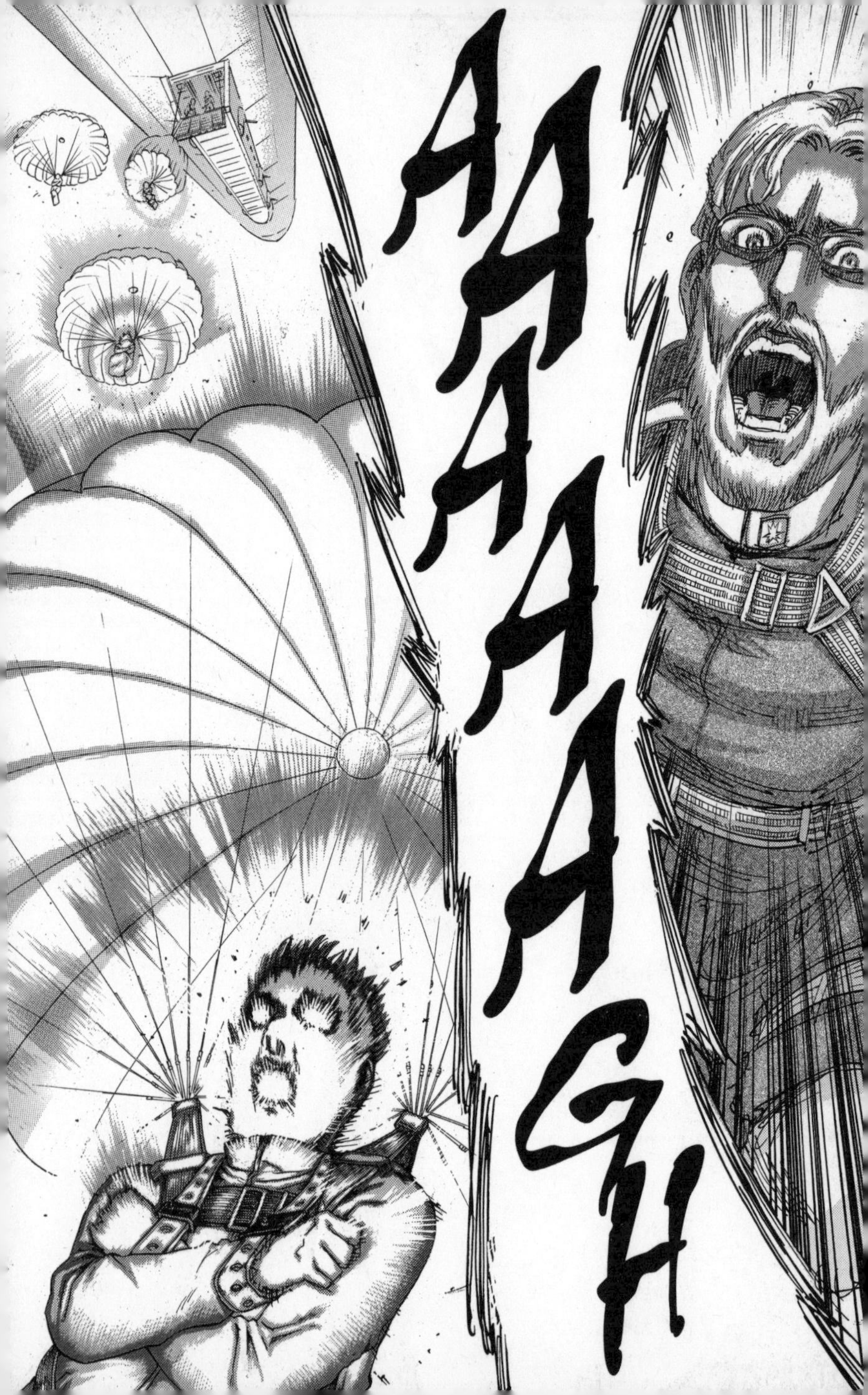
AAAAAAAGH

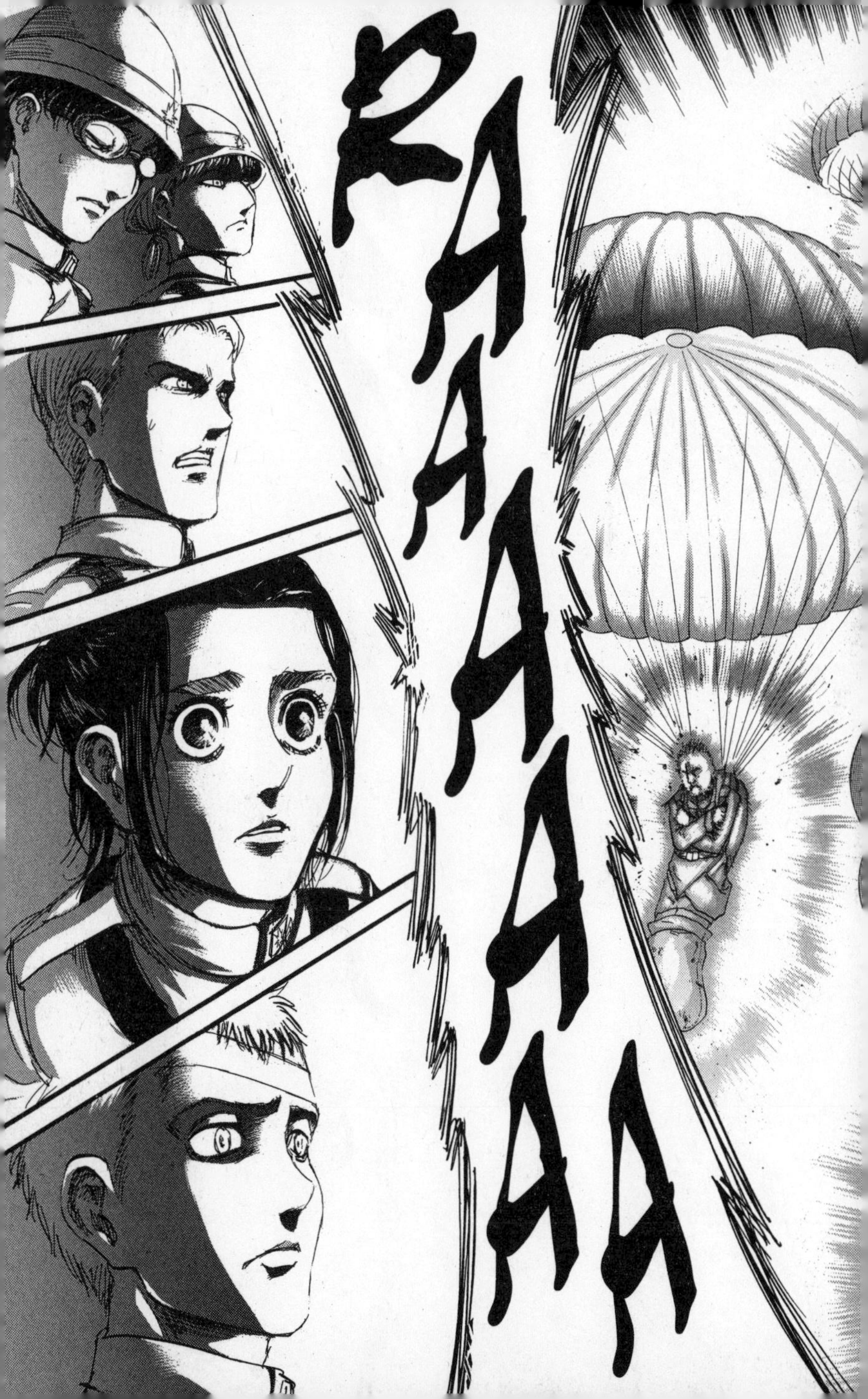
RAAAAAAA

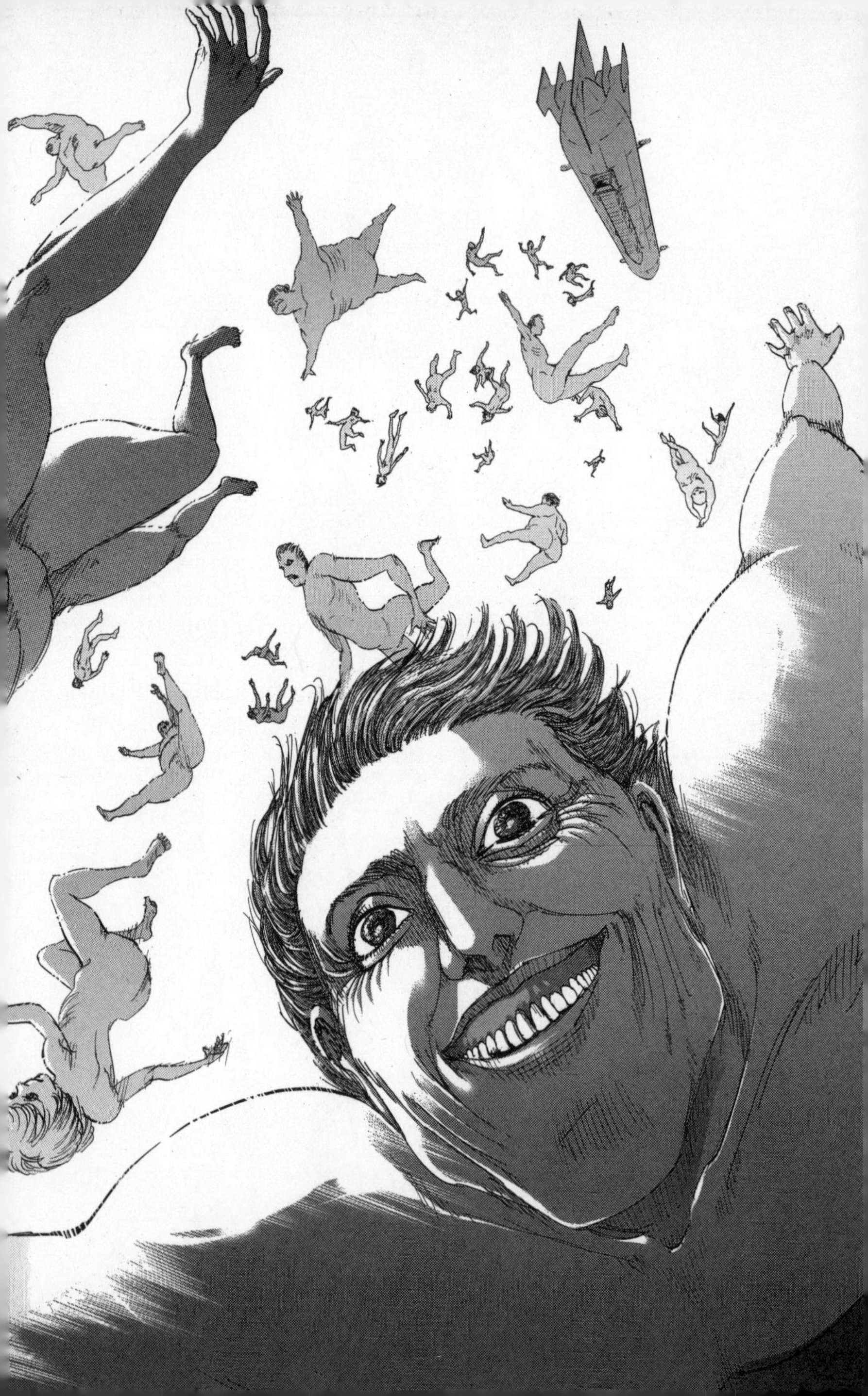

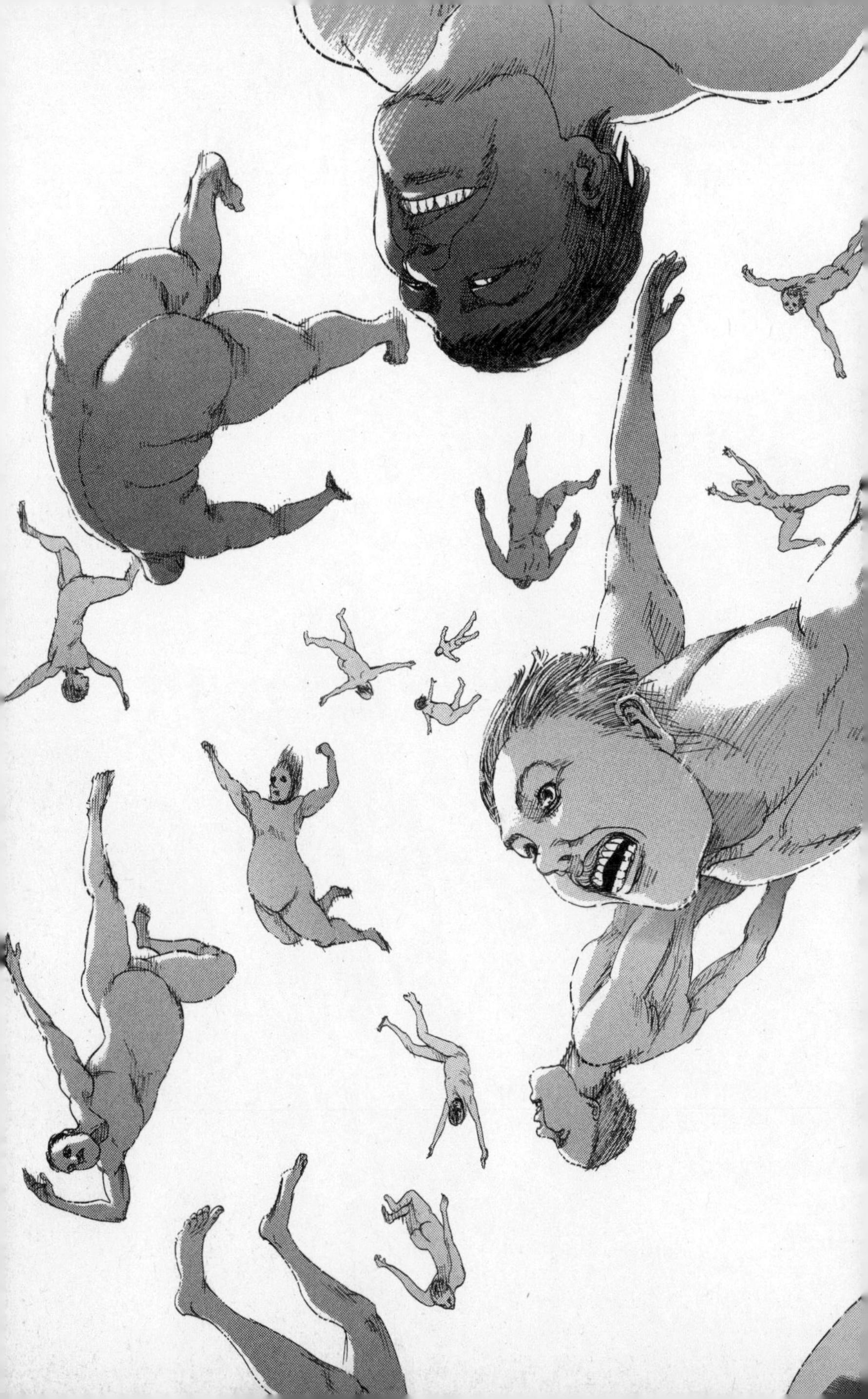

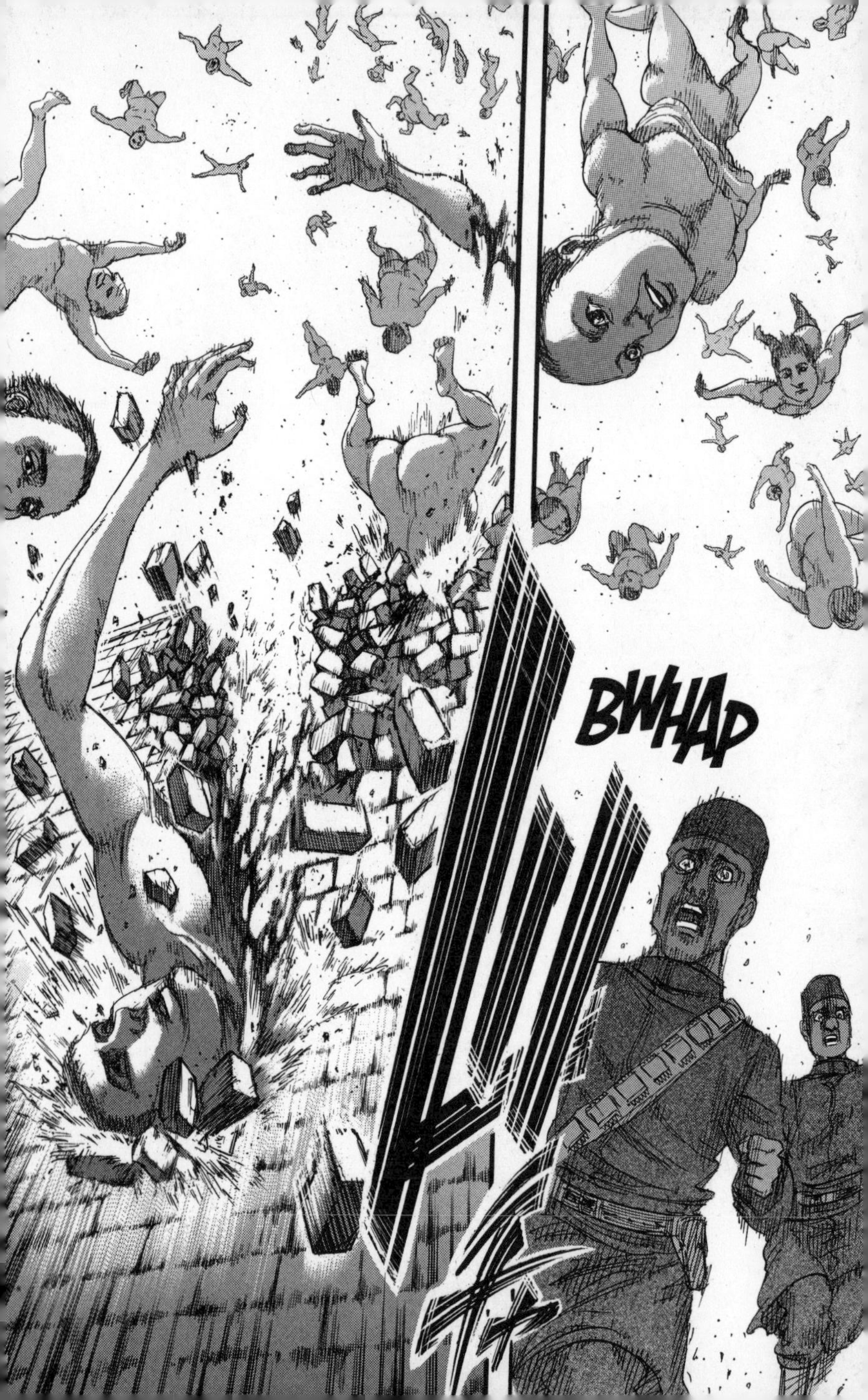
BWHAP

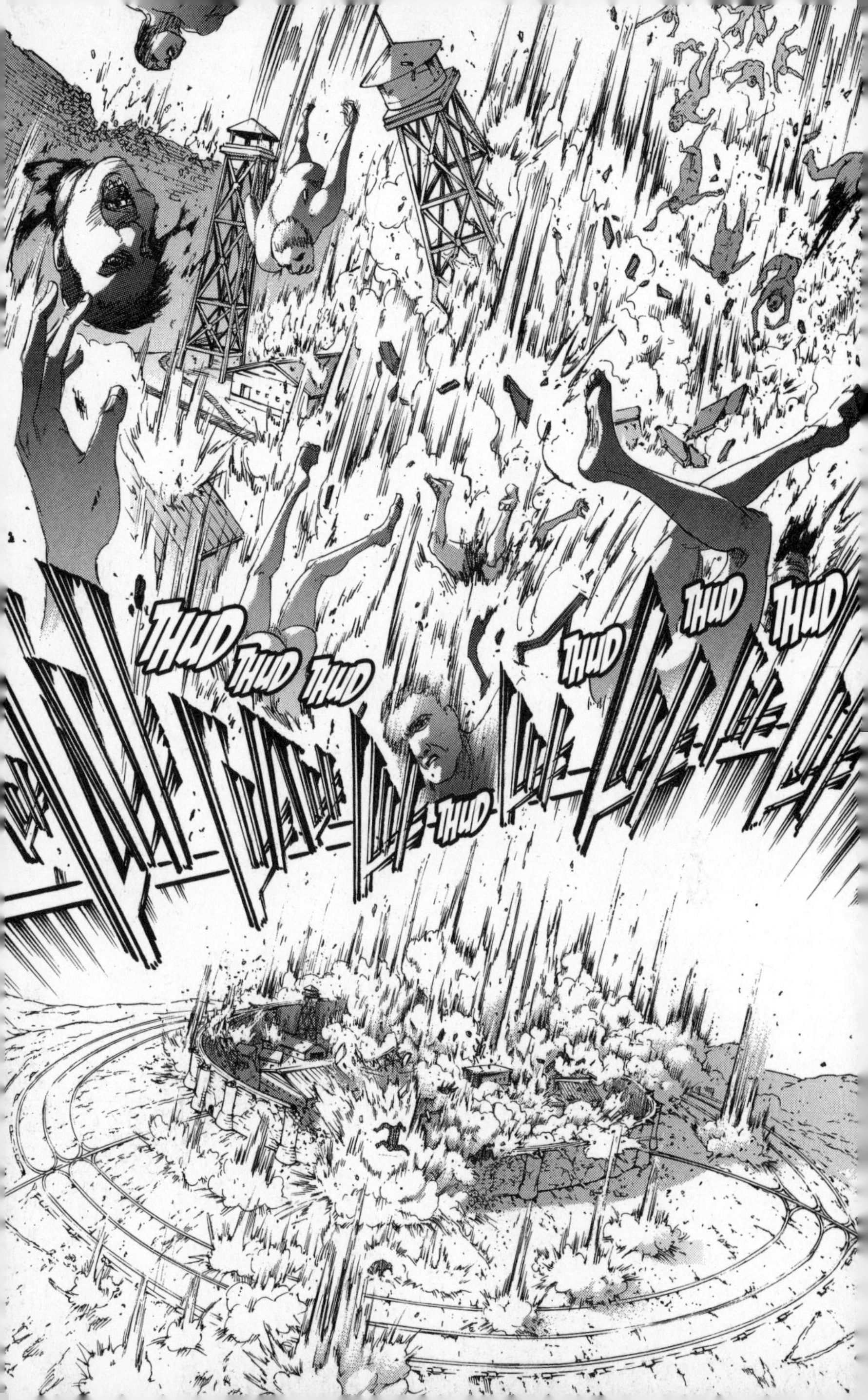
THUD
THUD
THUD
THUD
THUD
THUD
THUD

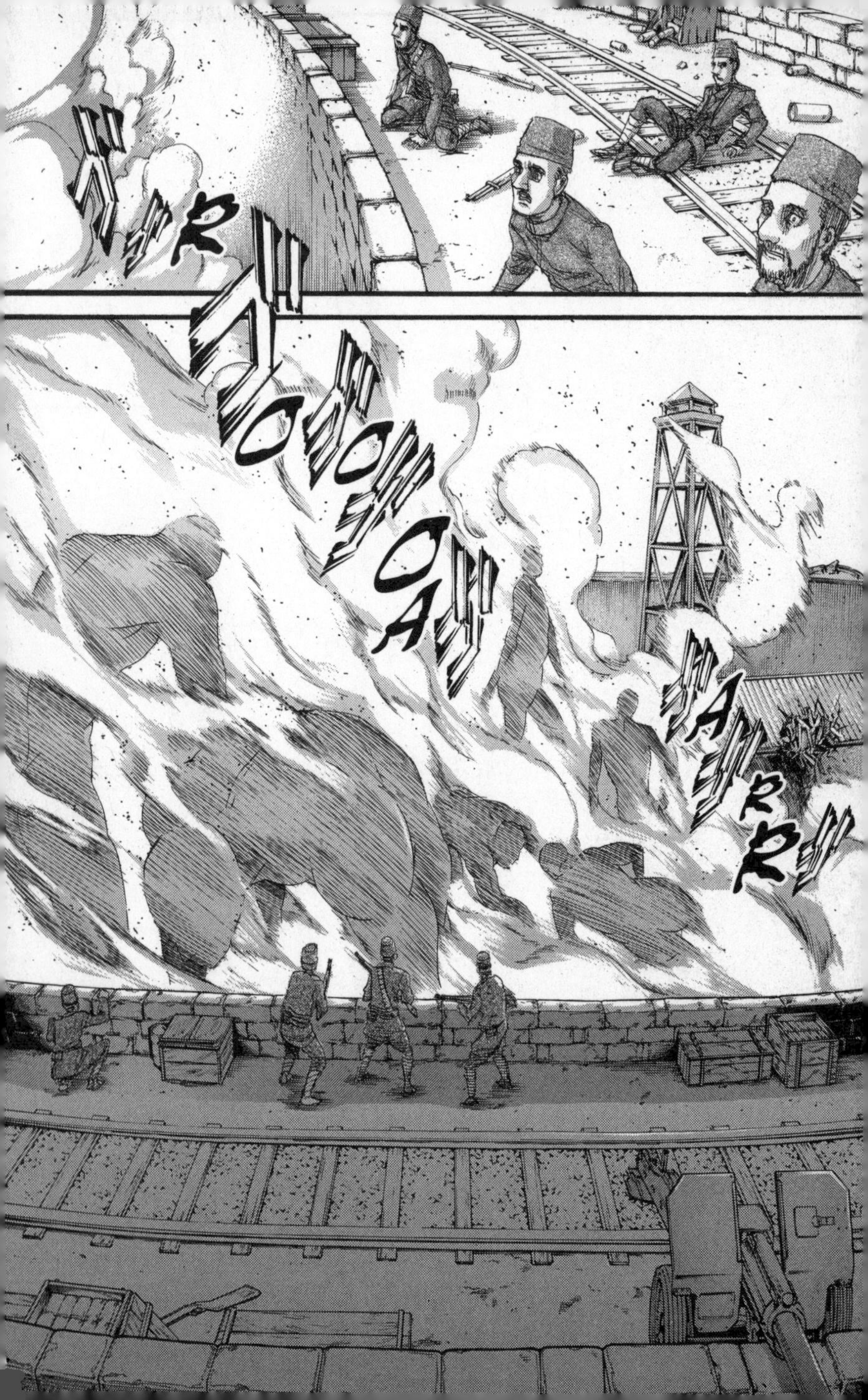
R
OOOOA
ARR

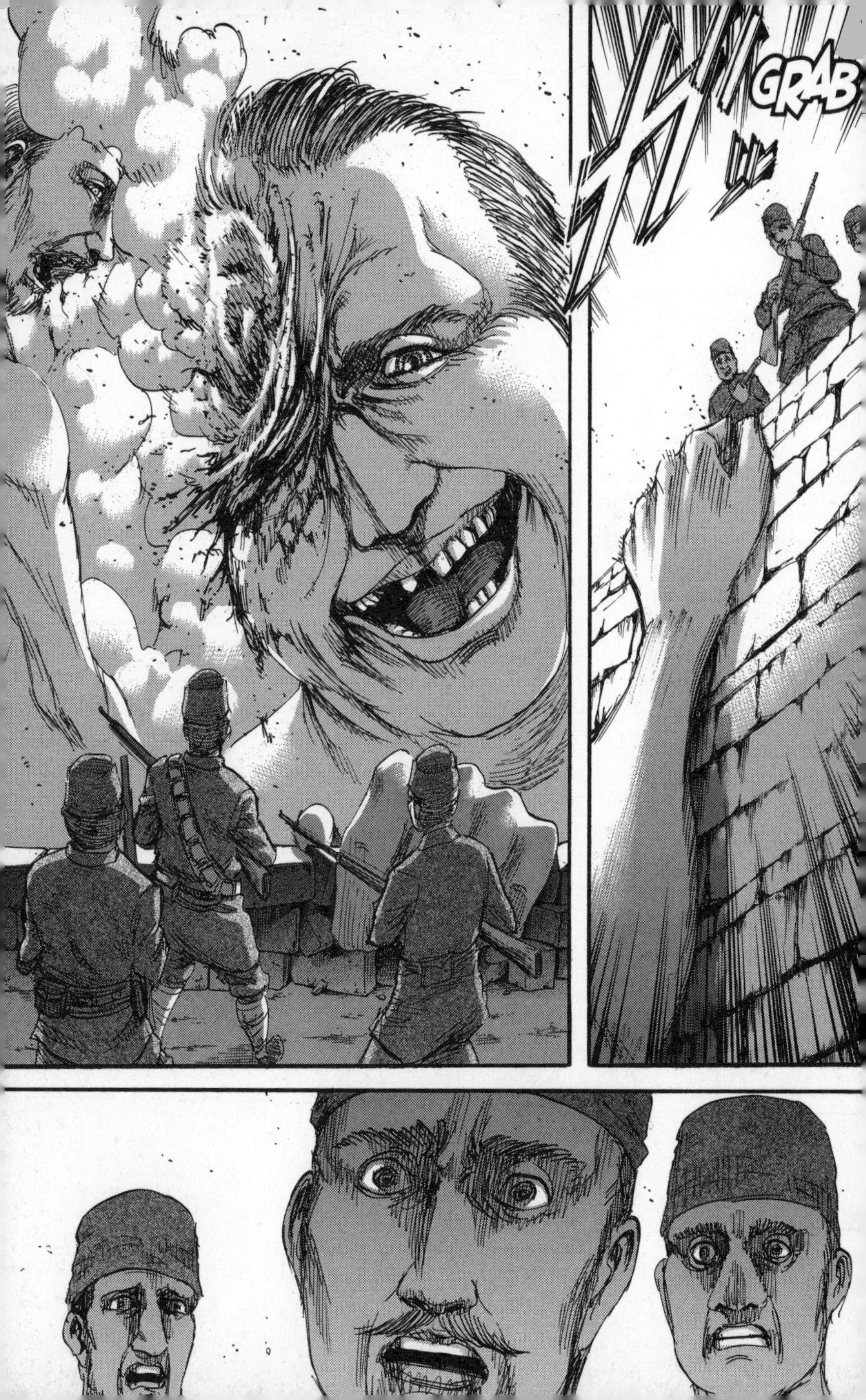
GRAB

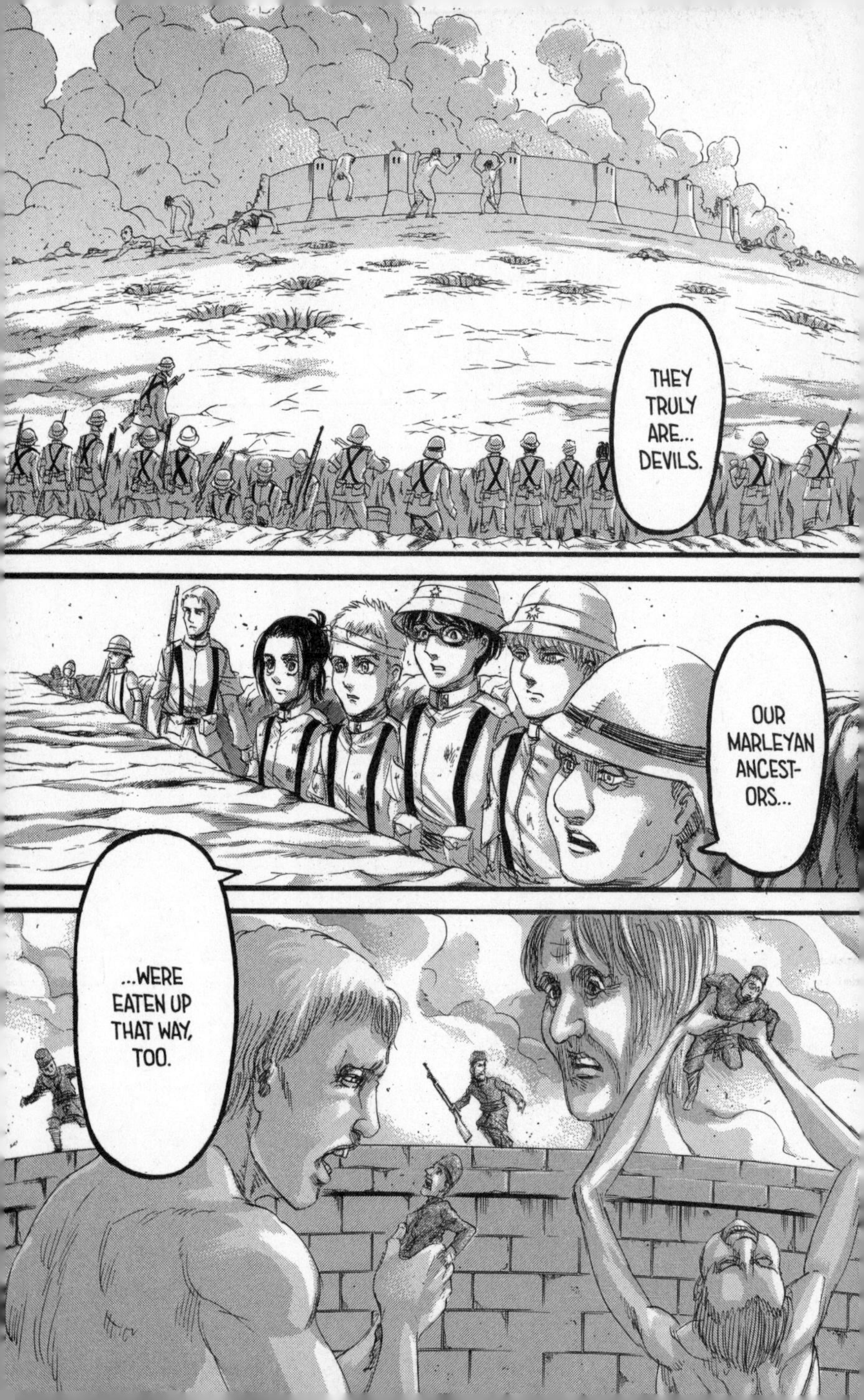
THEY TRULY ARE... DEVILS.
OUR MARLEYAN ANCEST-ORS...
...WERE EATEN UP THAT WAY, TOO.

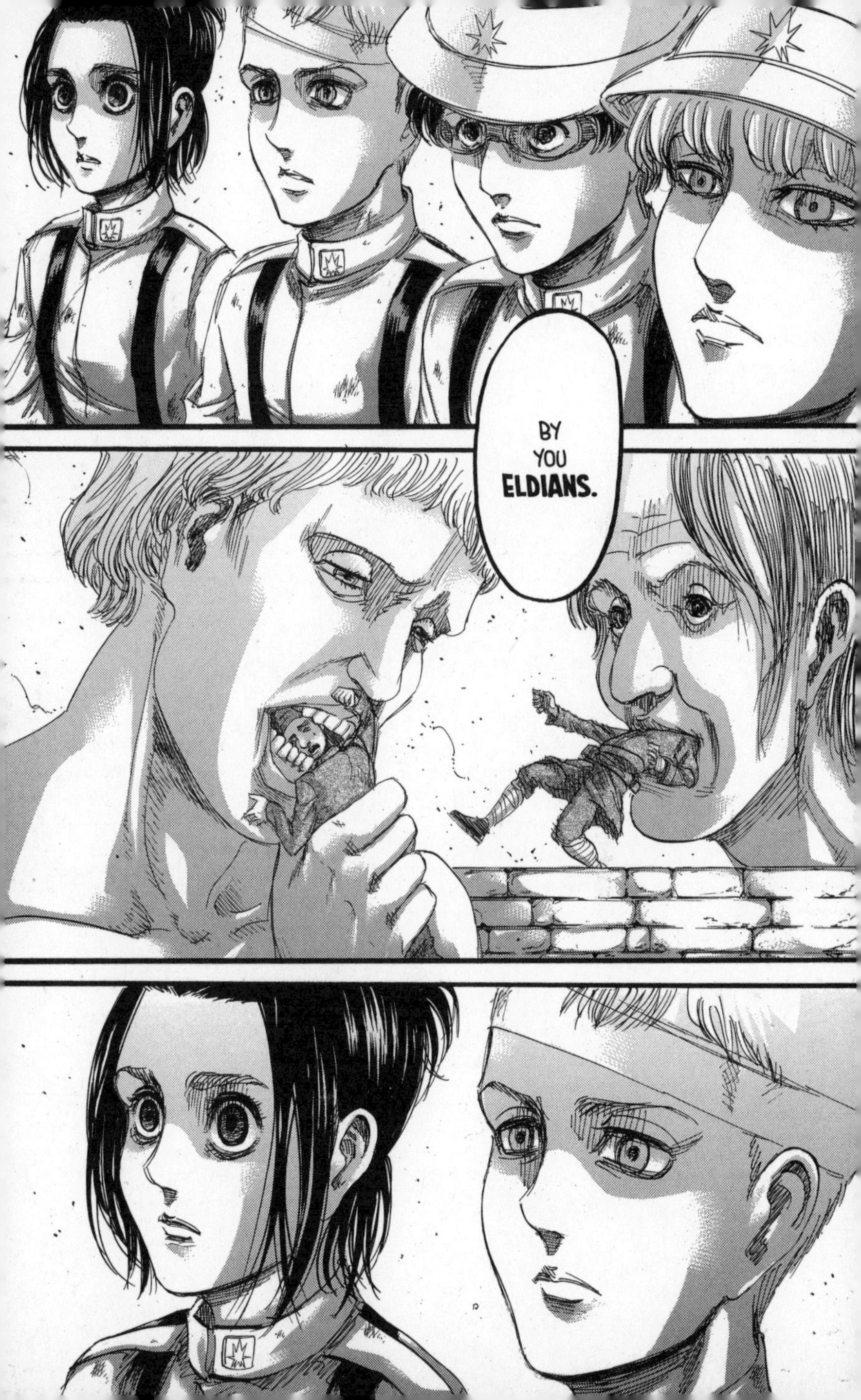
BY YOU **ELDIANS.**

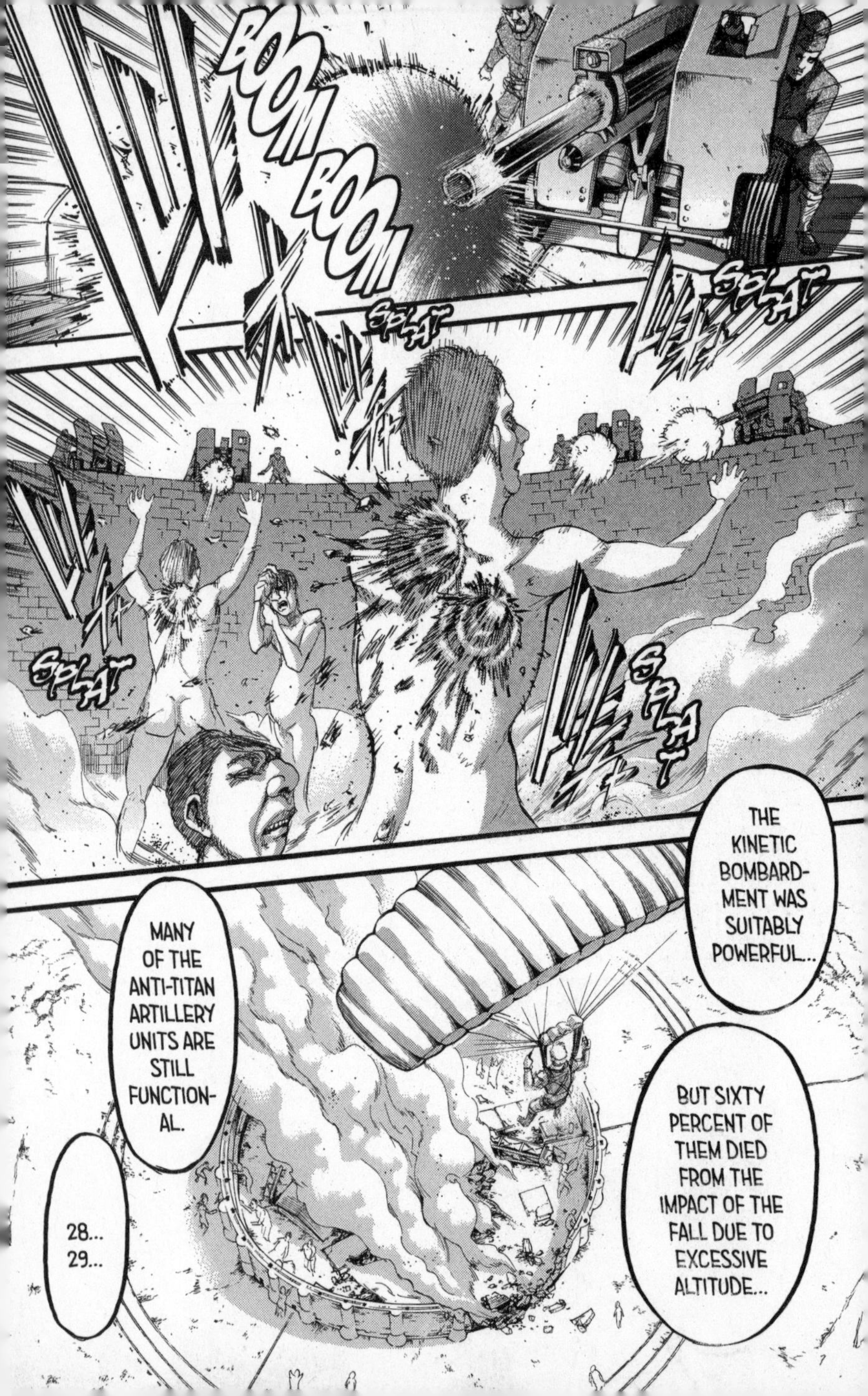
BOOM BOOM
SPLAT
SPLAT
SPLAT
SPLAT
THE KINETIC BOMBARDMENT WAS SUITABLY POWERFUL...
BUT SIXTY PERCENT OF THEM DIED FROM THE IMPACT OF THE FALL DUE TO EXCESSIVE ALTITUDE...
MANY OF THE ANTI-TITAN ARTILLERY UNITS ARE STILL FUNCTIONAL.
28... 29...

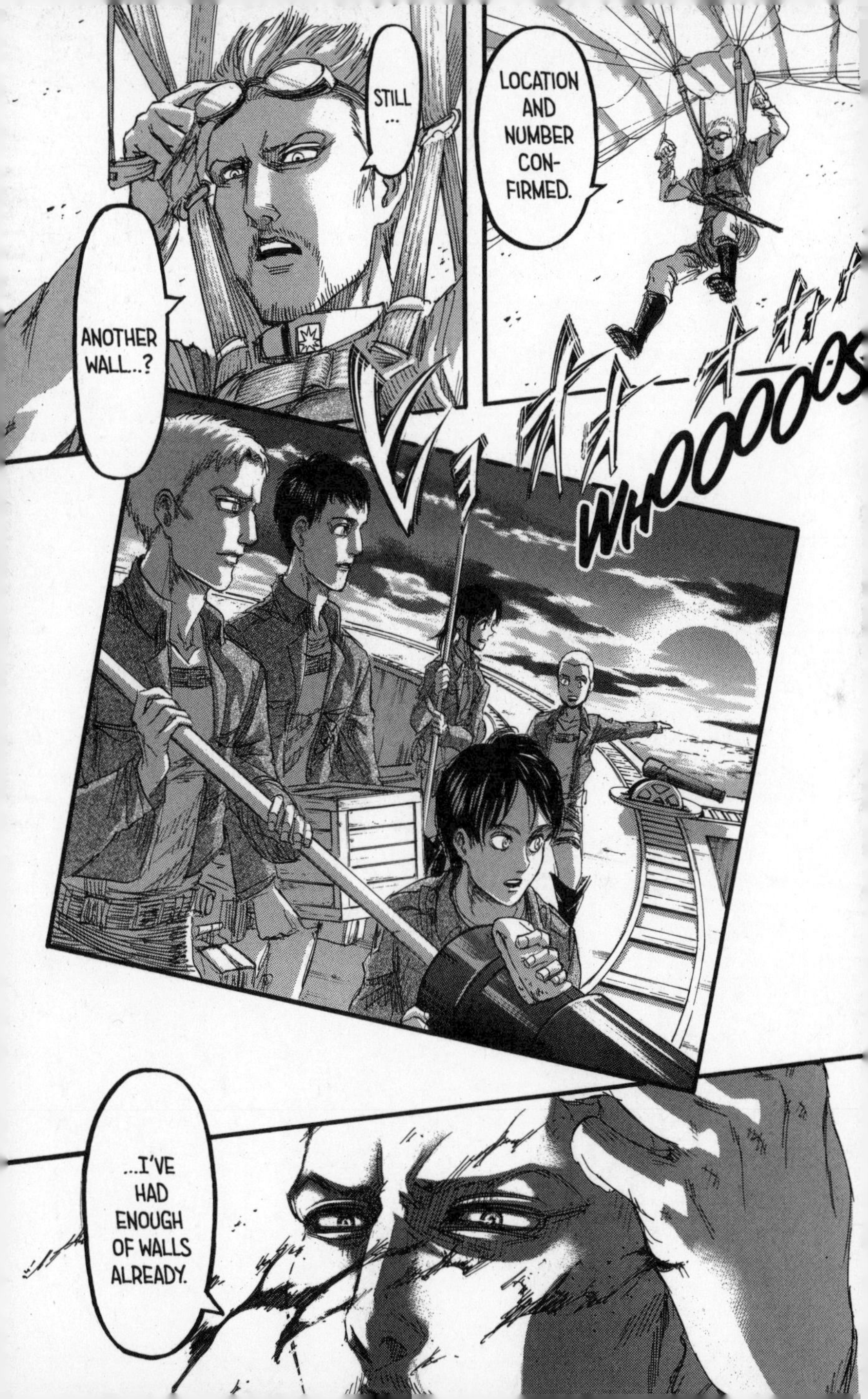
LOCATION AND NUMBER CON-FIRMED.
STILL ...
ANOTHER WALL...?
WHOOOOOOS
...I'VE HAD ENOUGH OF WALLS ALREADY.

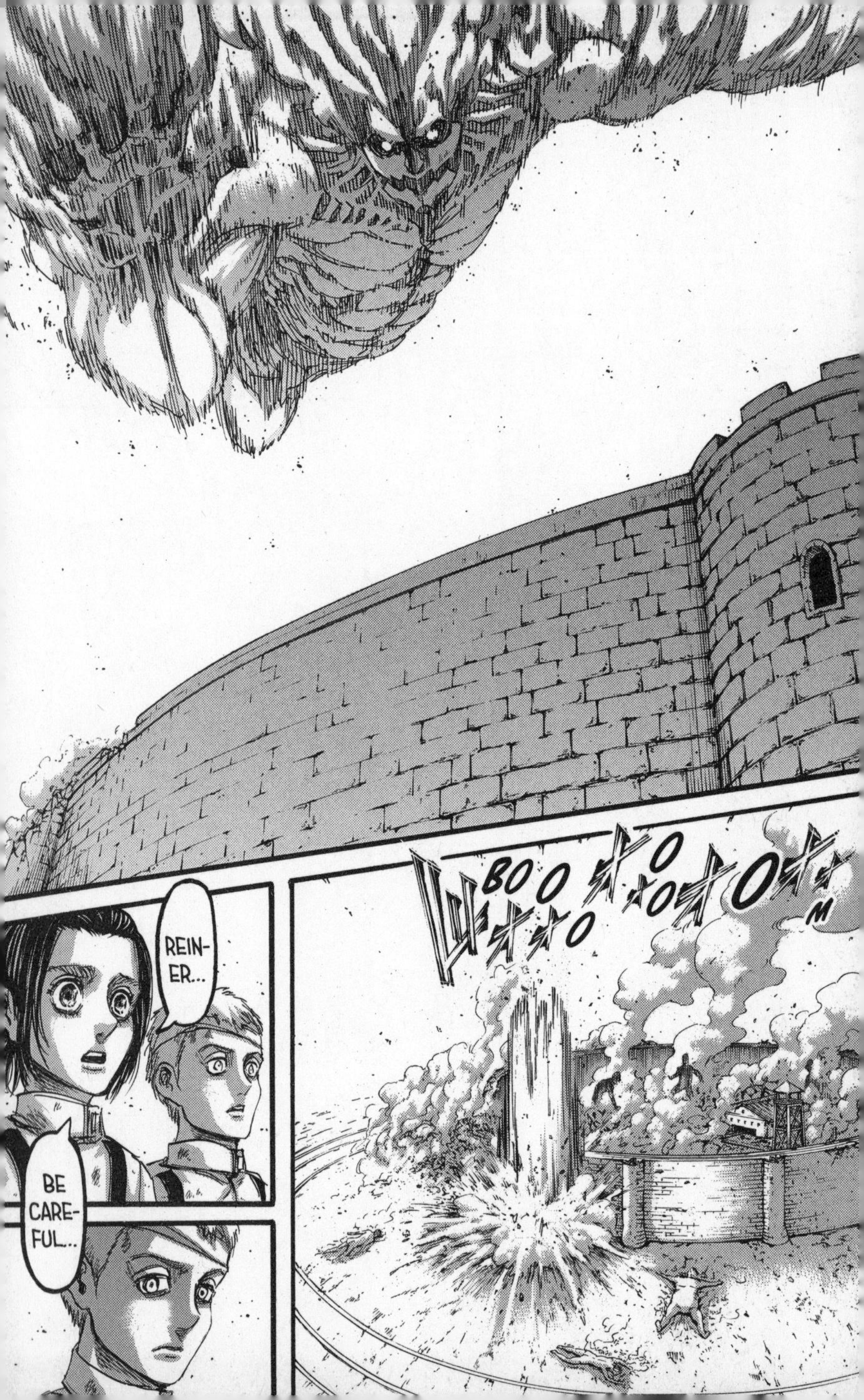
REIN-ER...
BE CARE-FUL...

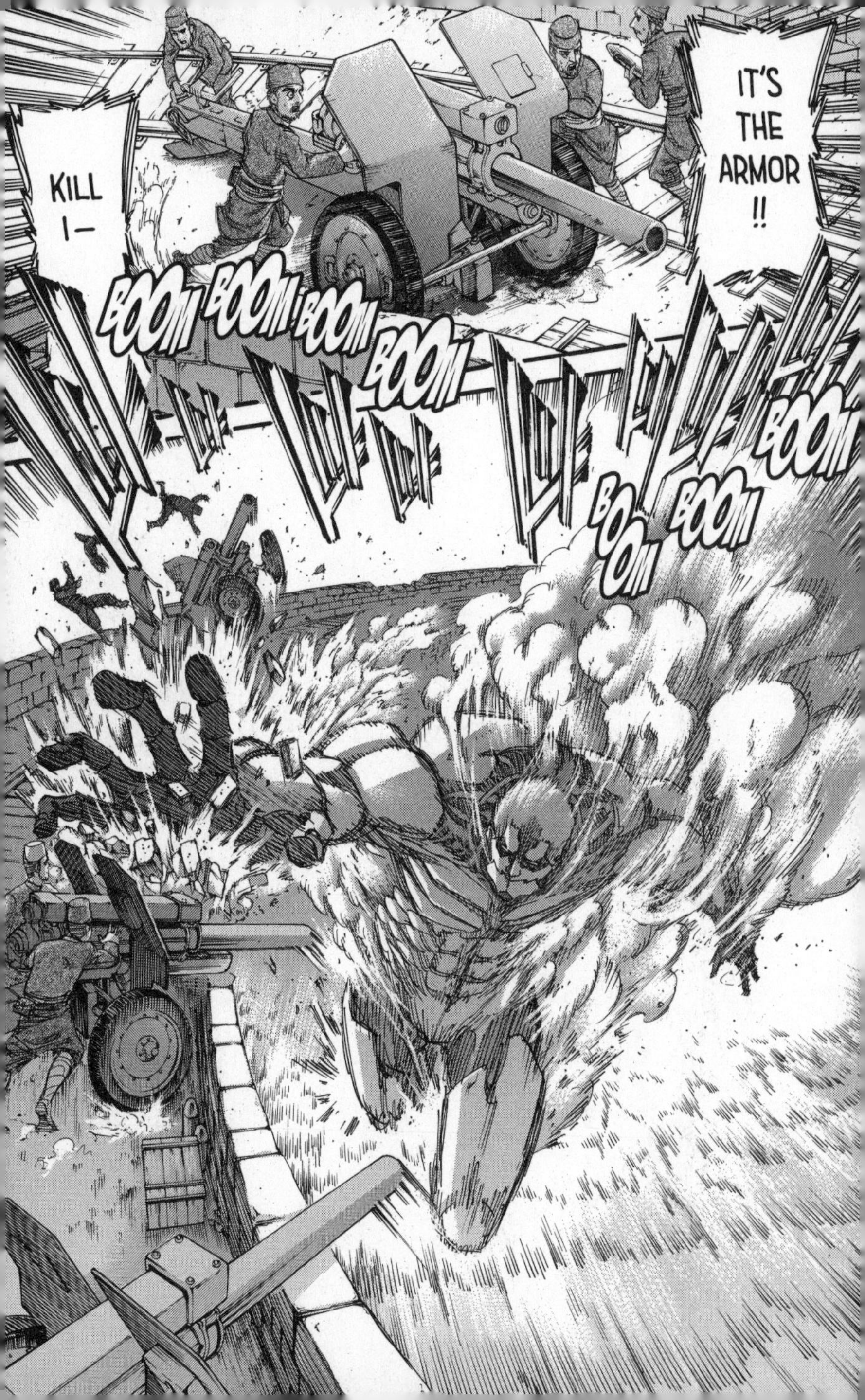
IT'S THE ARMOR !!
KILL I—
BOOM
BOOM
BOOM
BOOM
BOOM
BOOM
BOOM
BOOM

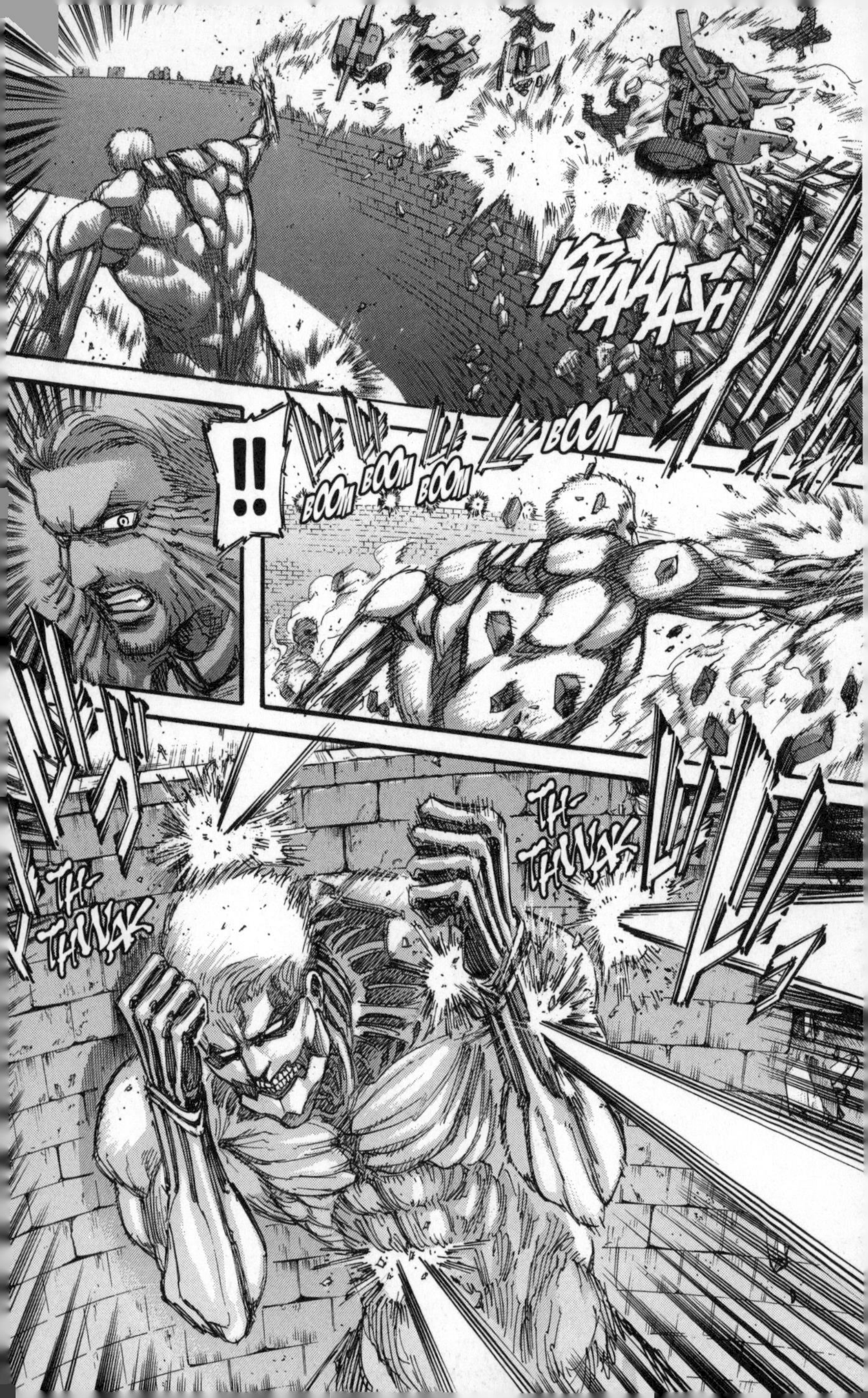
KRAAASH
BOOM
BOOM
BOOM
BOOM
!!
TH-THUNK
TH-THUNK

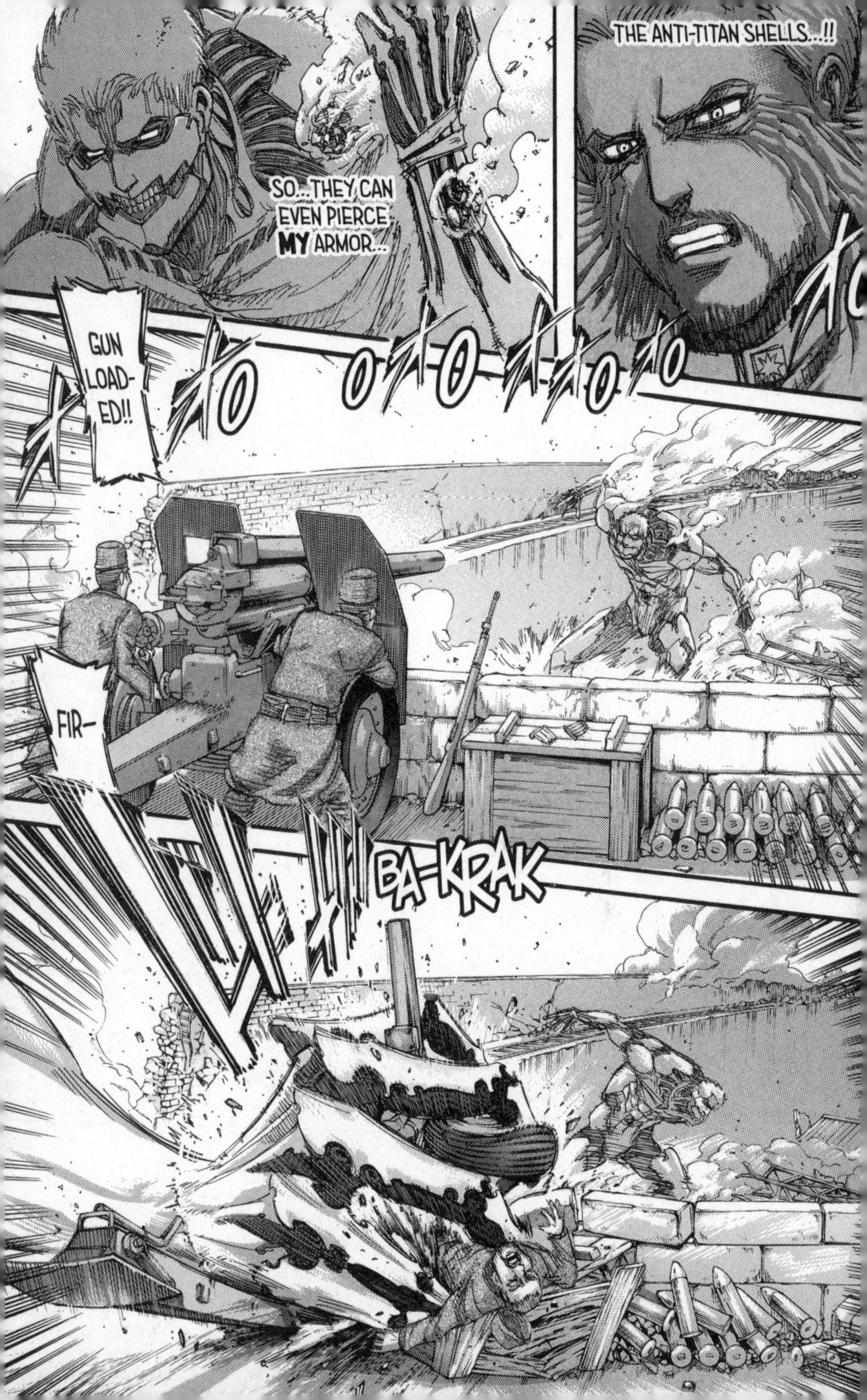
THE ANTI-TITAN SHELLS...!!
SO...THEY CAN EVEN PIERCE MY ARMOR...
GUN LOAD-ED!!
FIR-
BA-KRAK

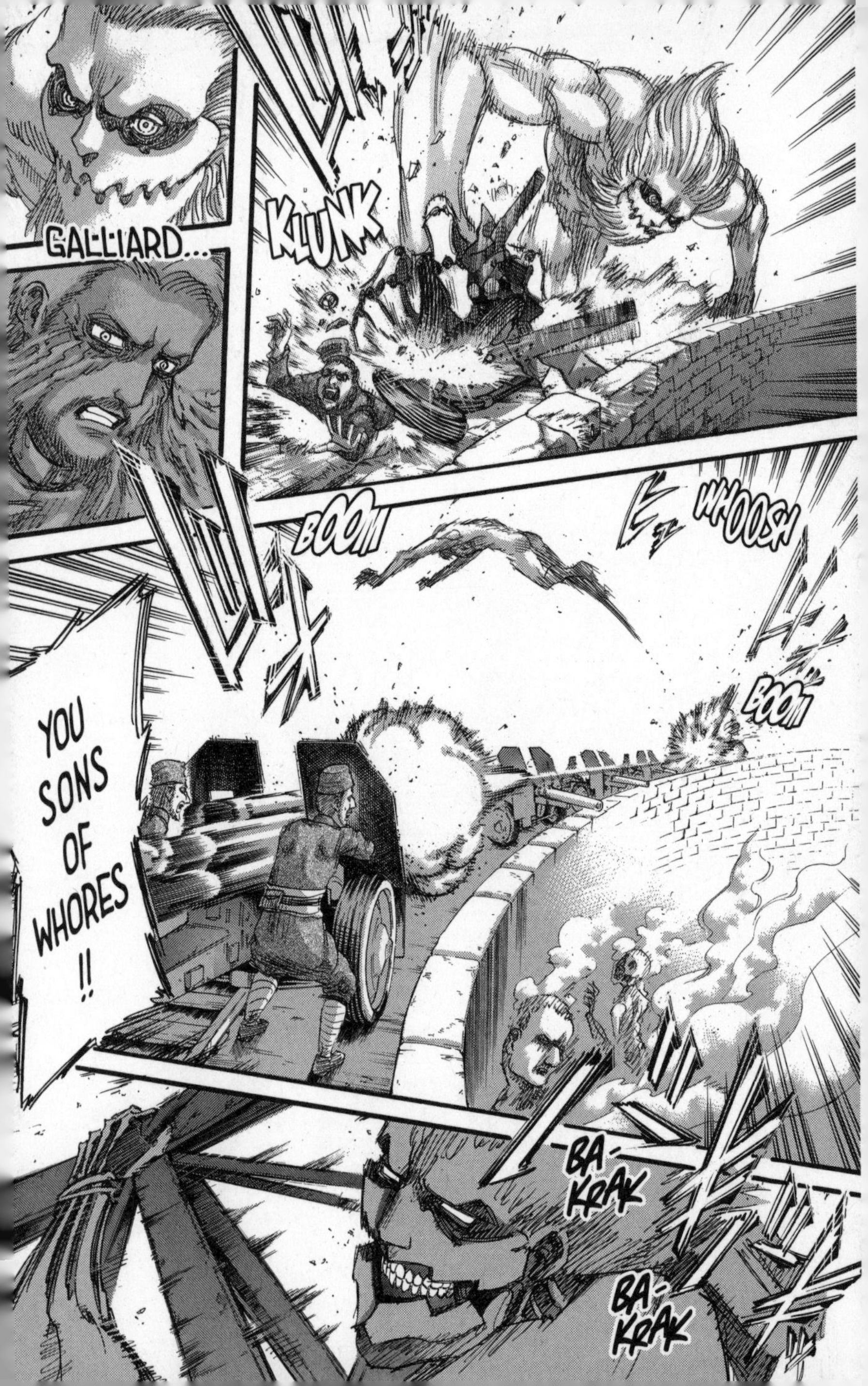
KLUNK
GALLIARD...
WHOOSH
BOOM
BOOM
YOU SONS OF WHORES!!
BA-KRAK
BA-KRAK

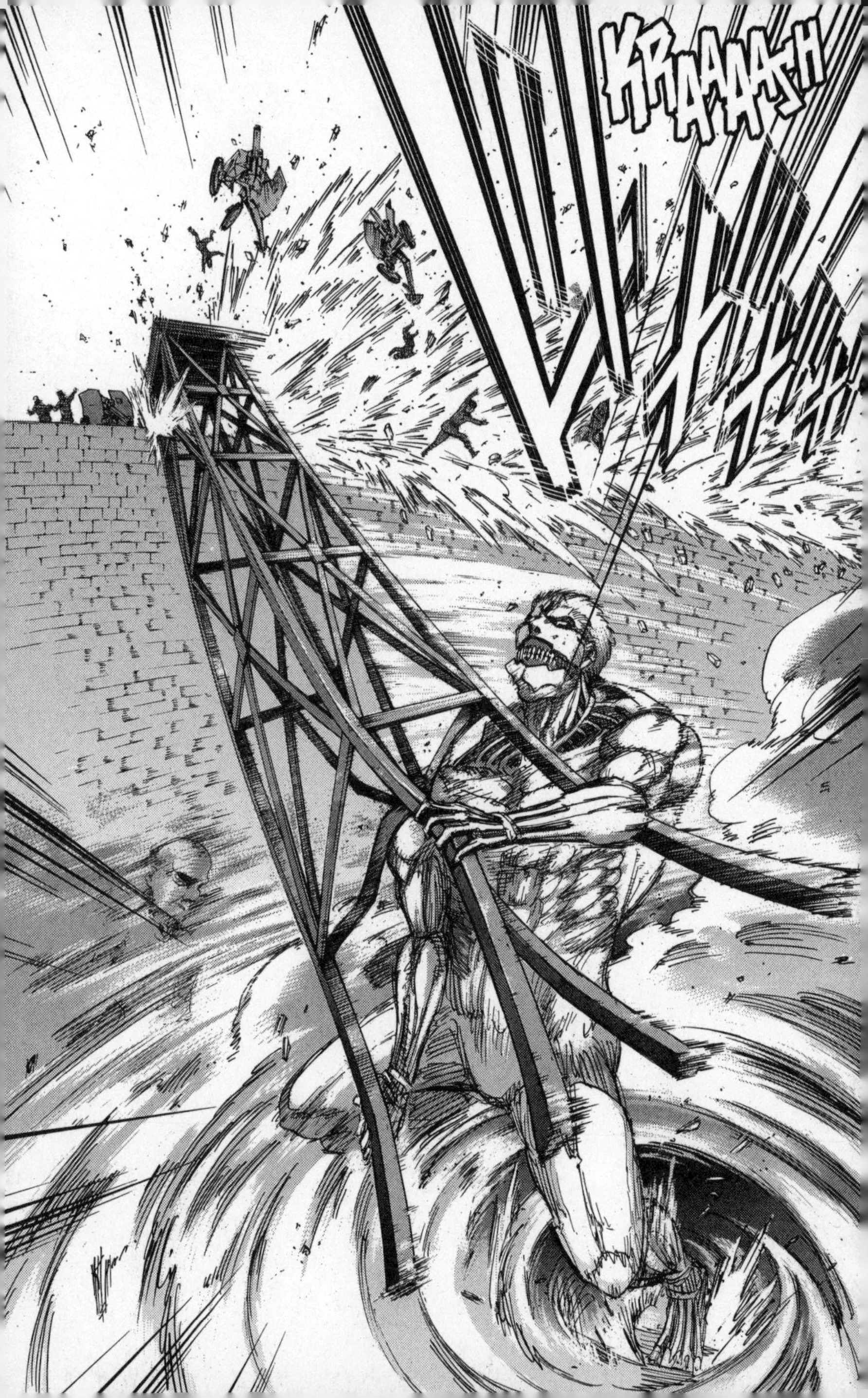
KRAAAASH

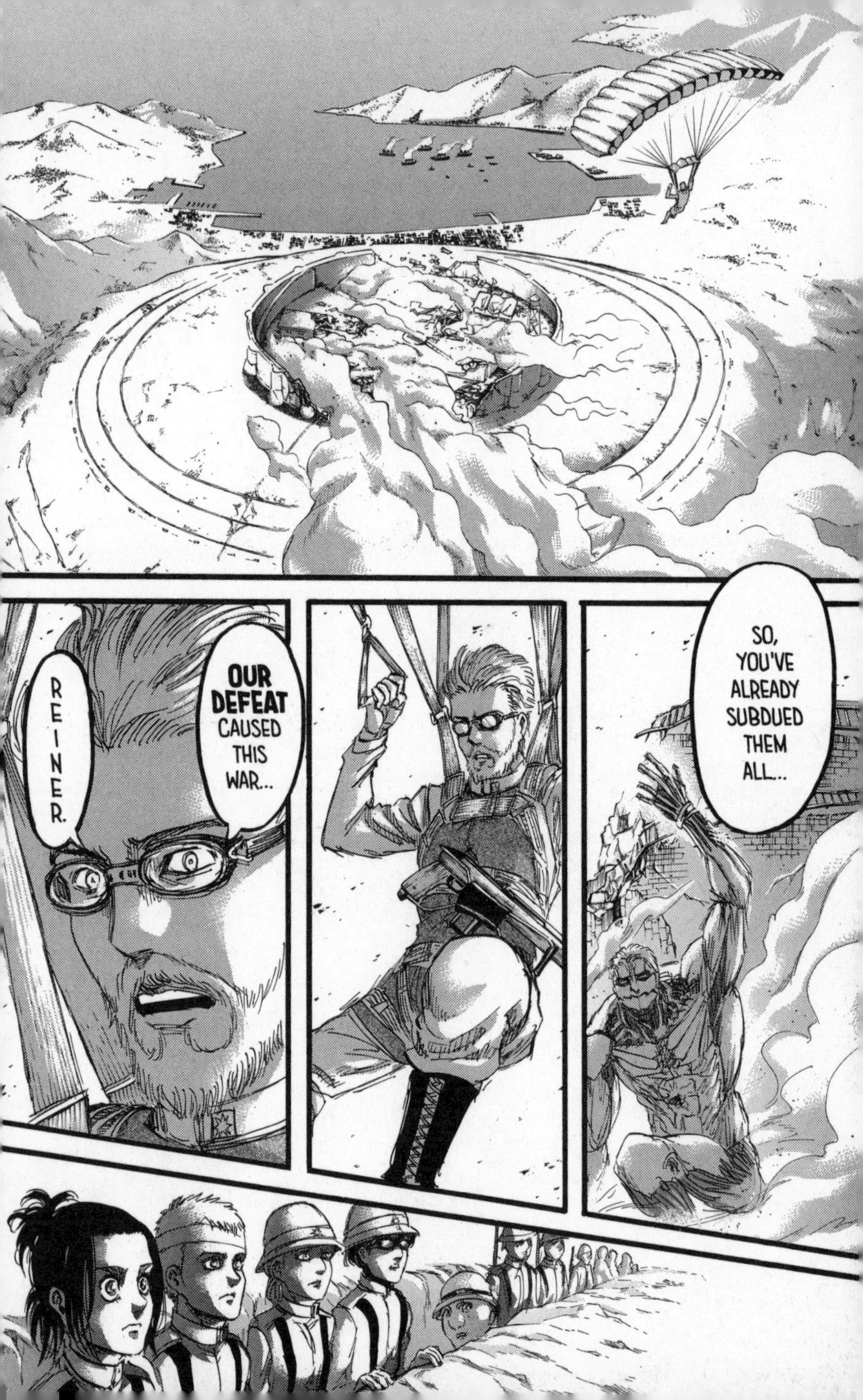

SO, YOU'VE ALREADY SUBDUED THEM ALL...
OUR DEFEAT CAUSED THIS WAR...
REINER.

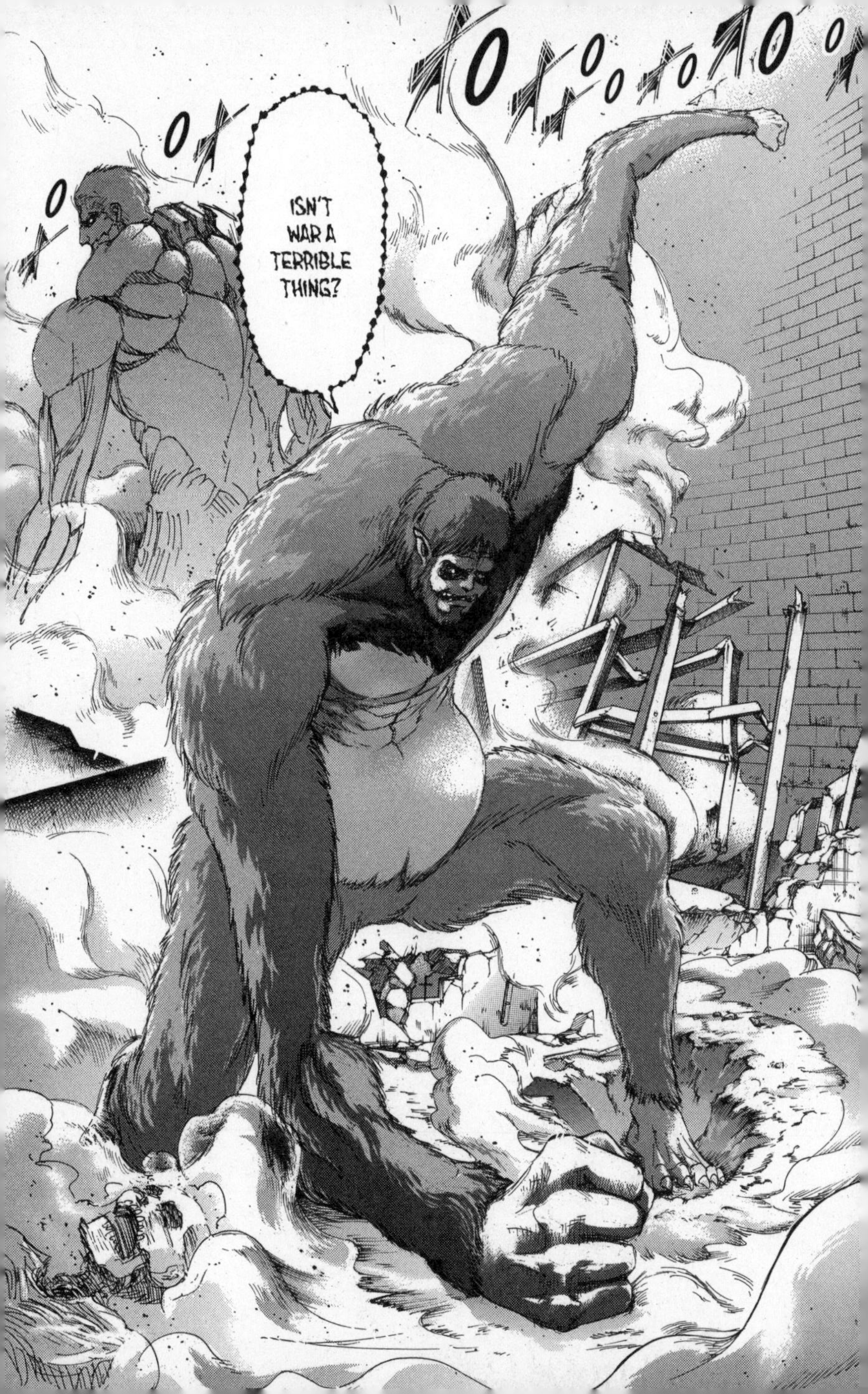
ISN'T WAR A TERRIBLE THING?

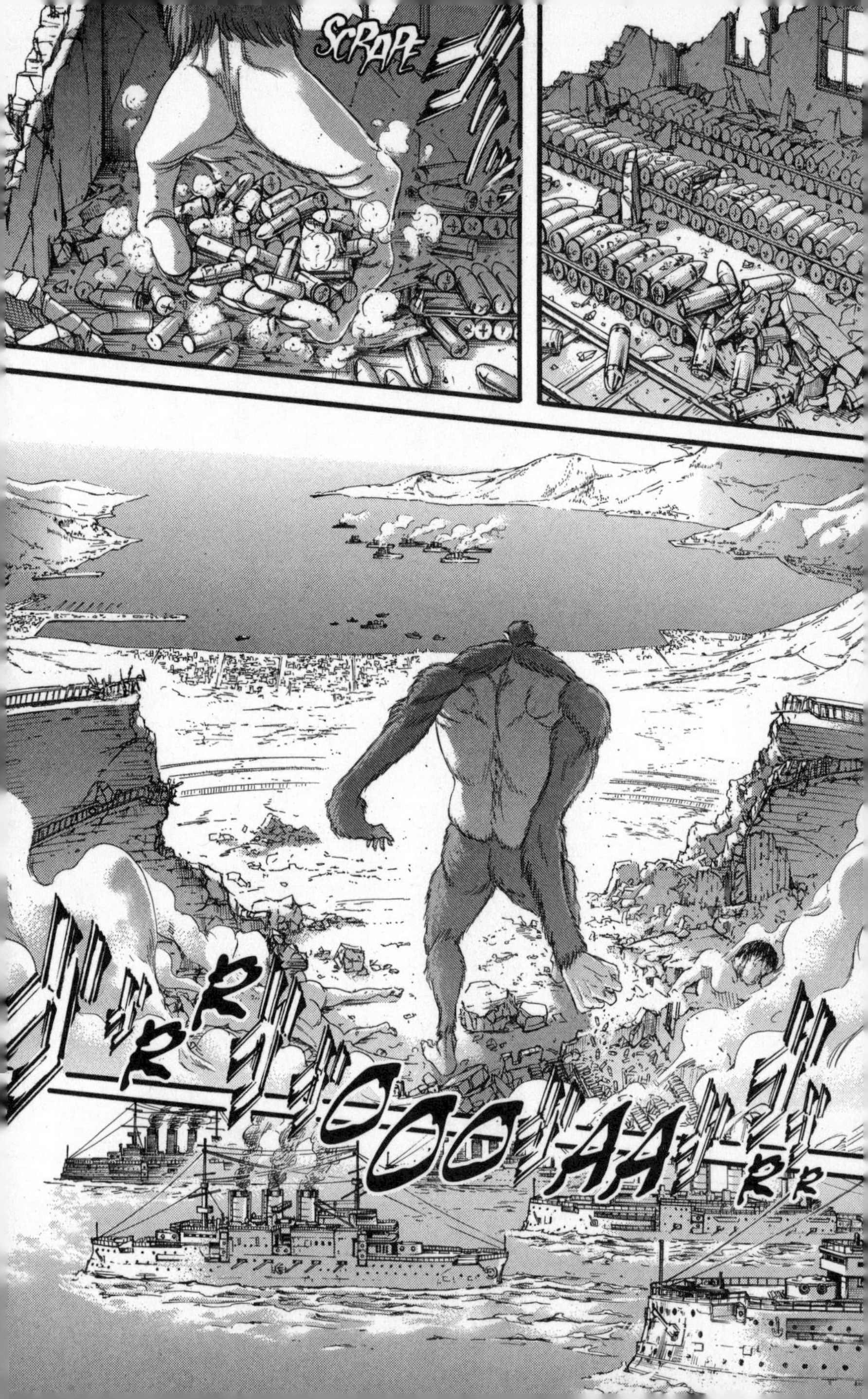
SCRAPE
RROOOAARR

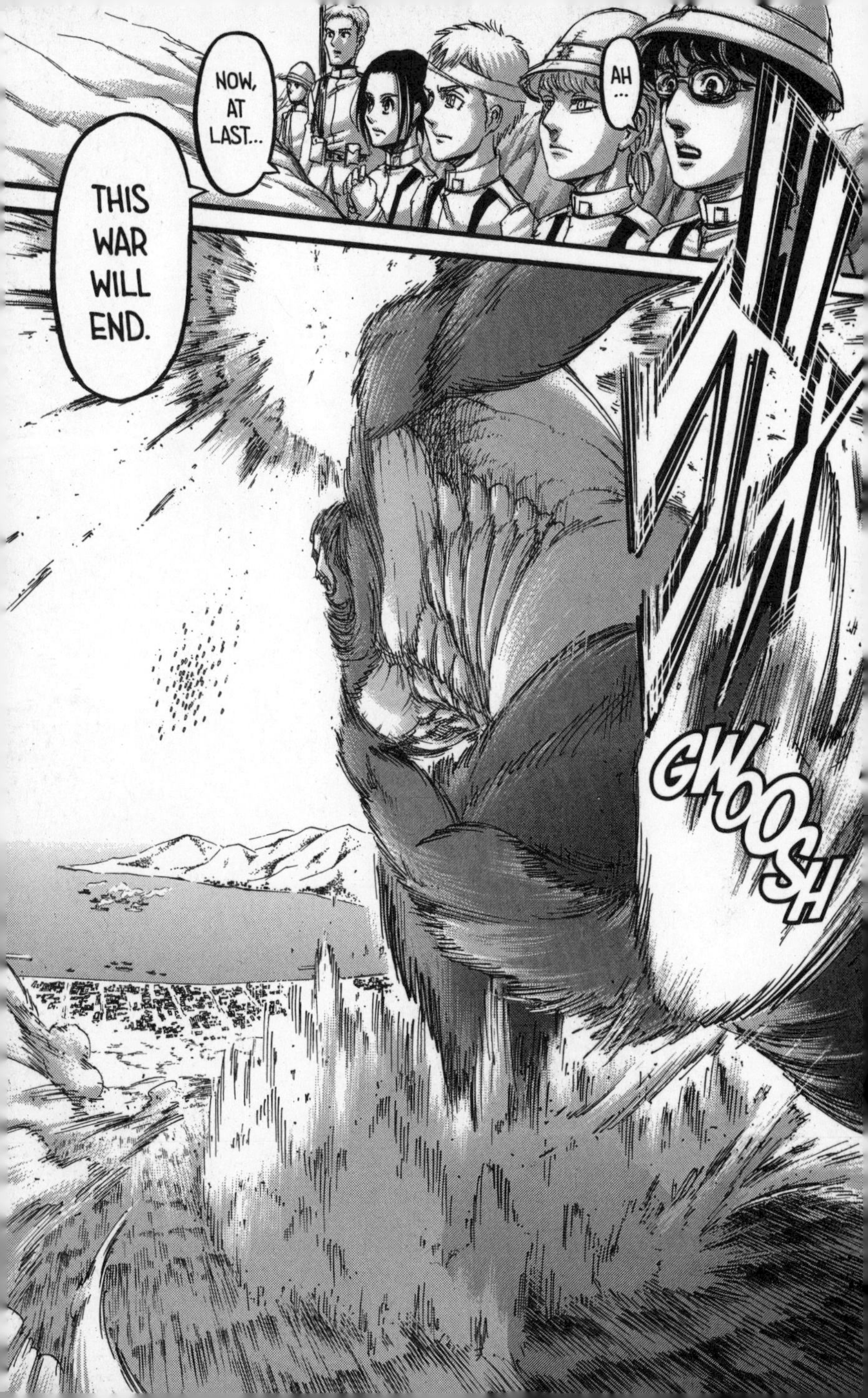
AH ...
NOW, AT LAST...
THIS WAR WILL END.
GWOOSH

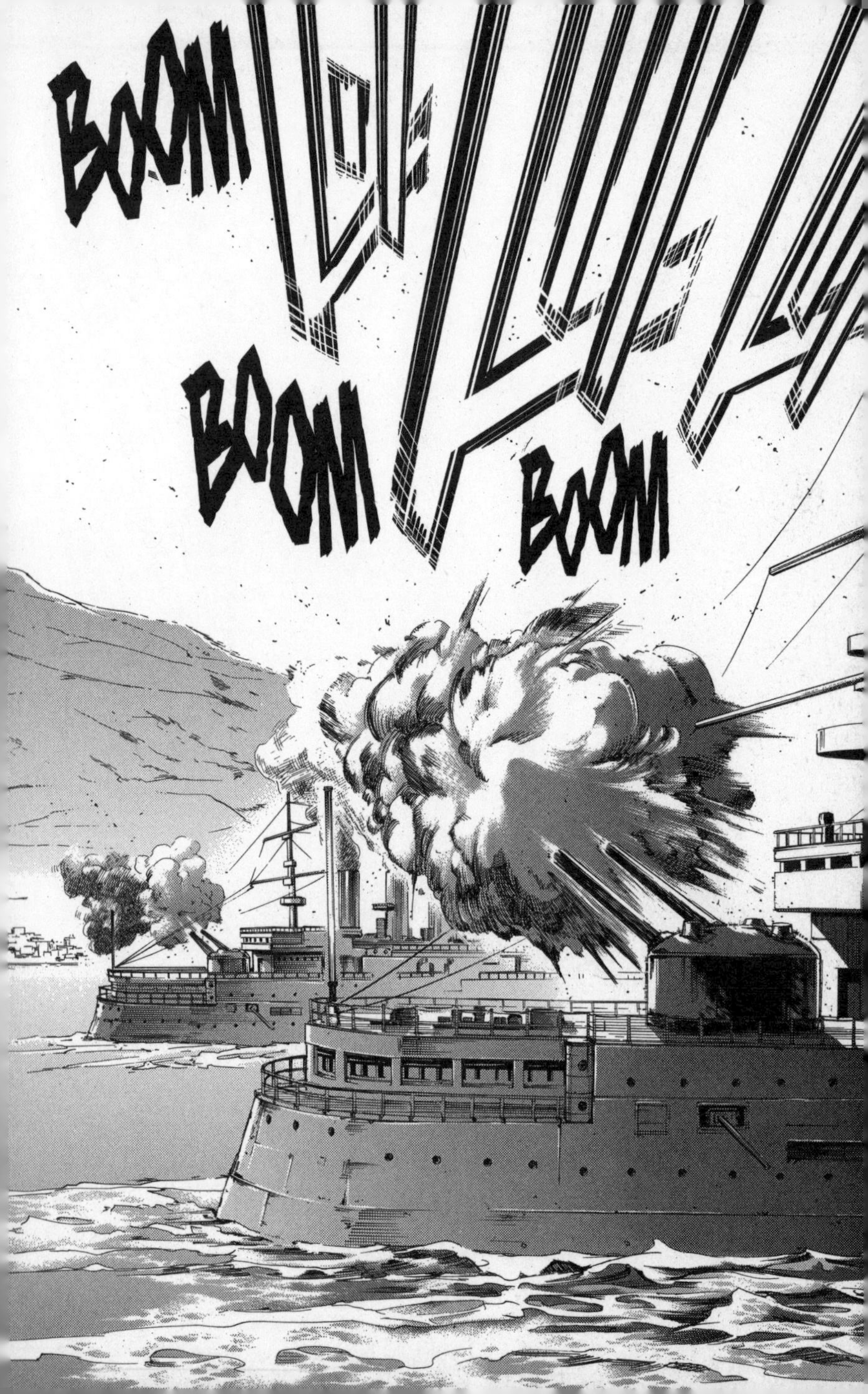
BOOM
BOOM
BOOM

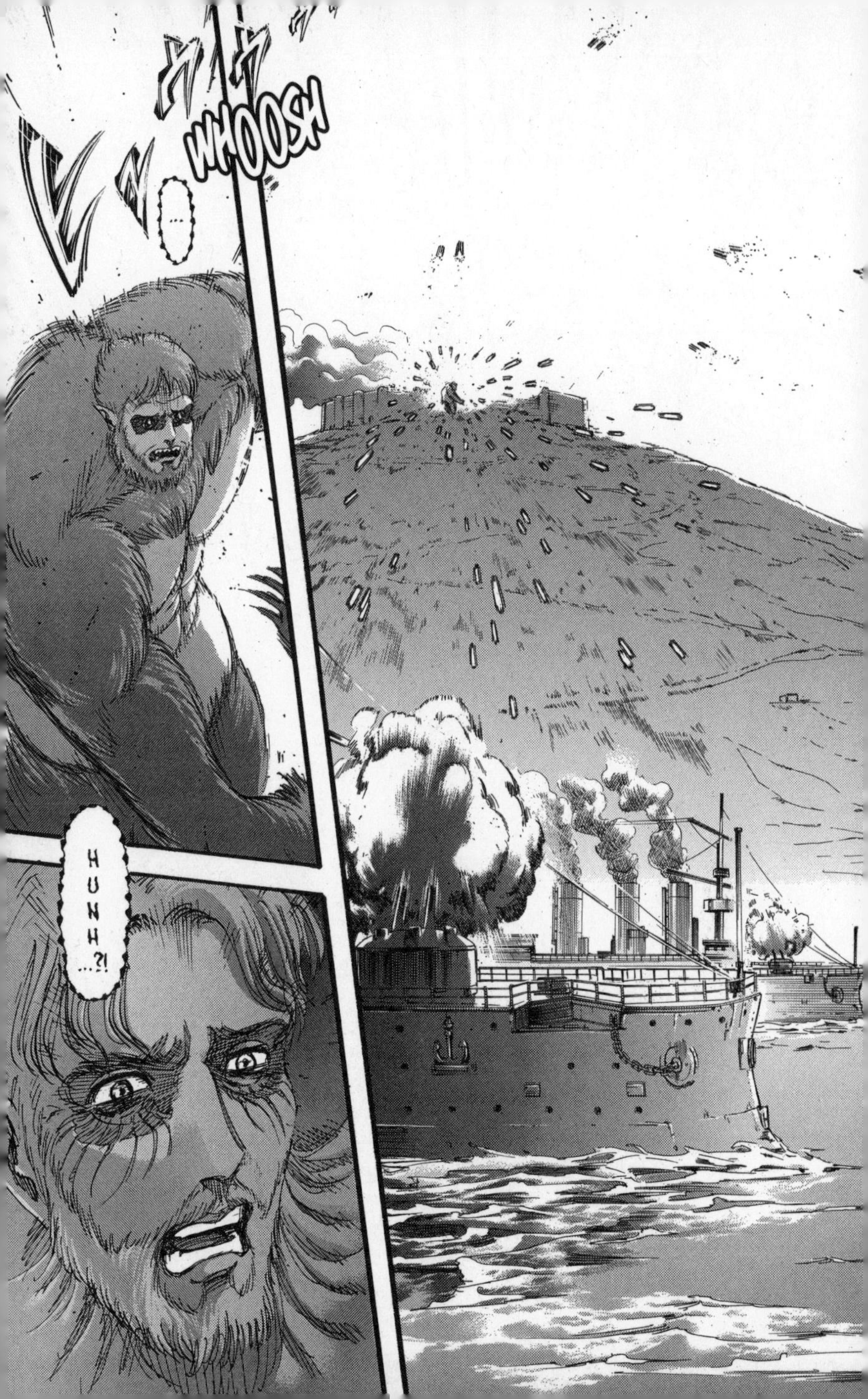
WHOOSH
...!
HUNH...?!

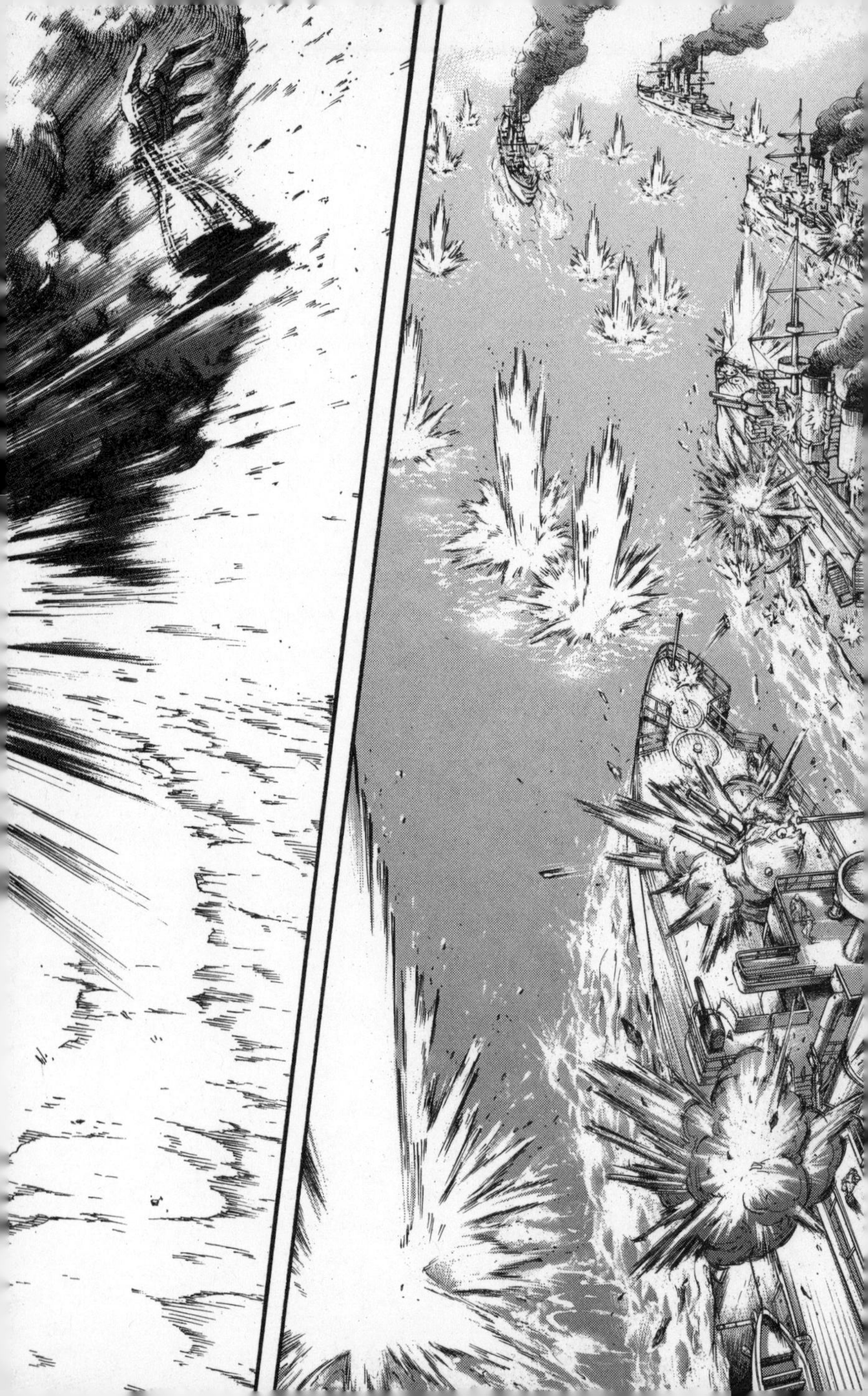

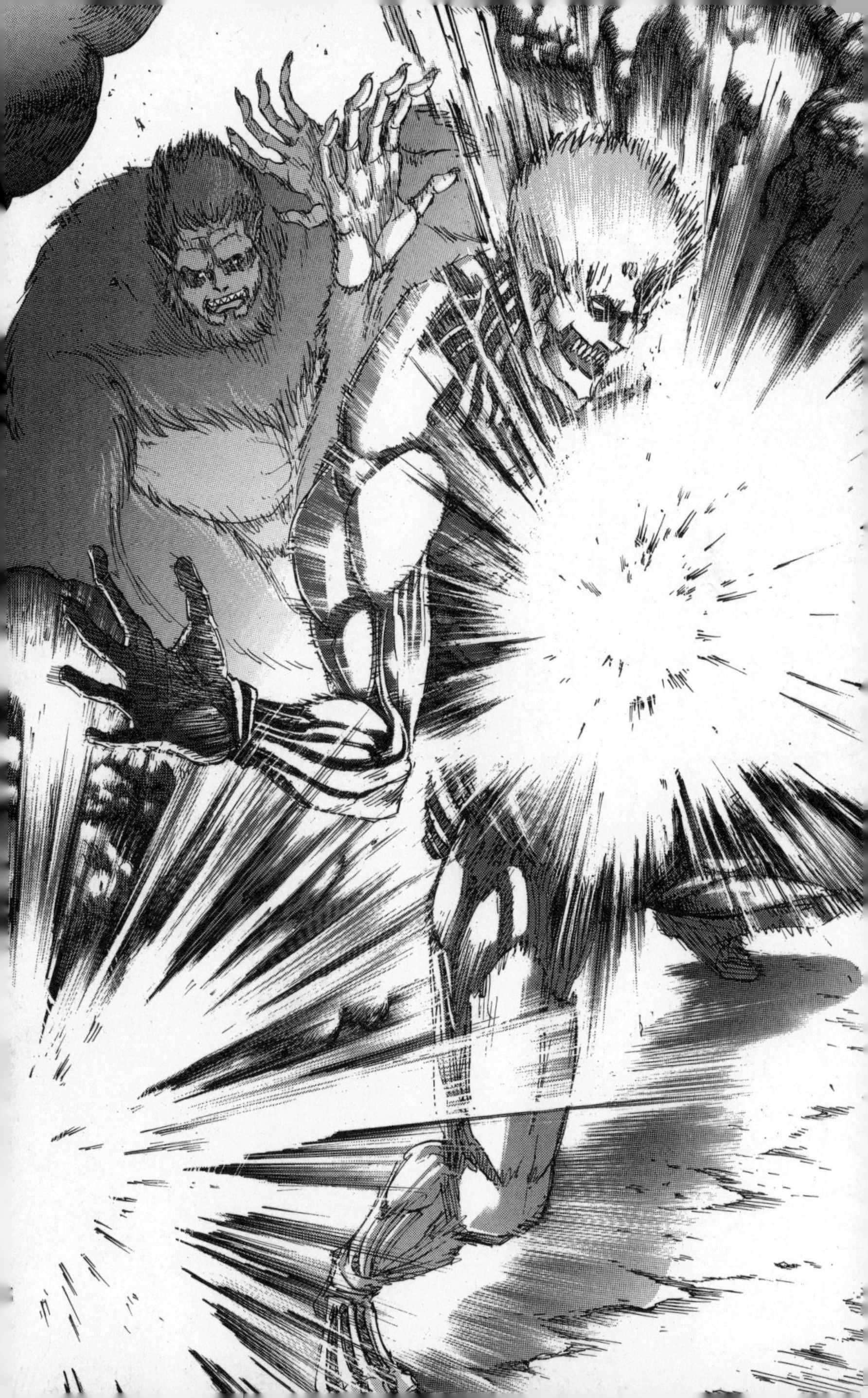

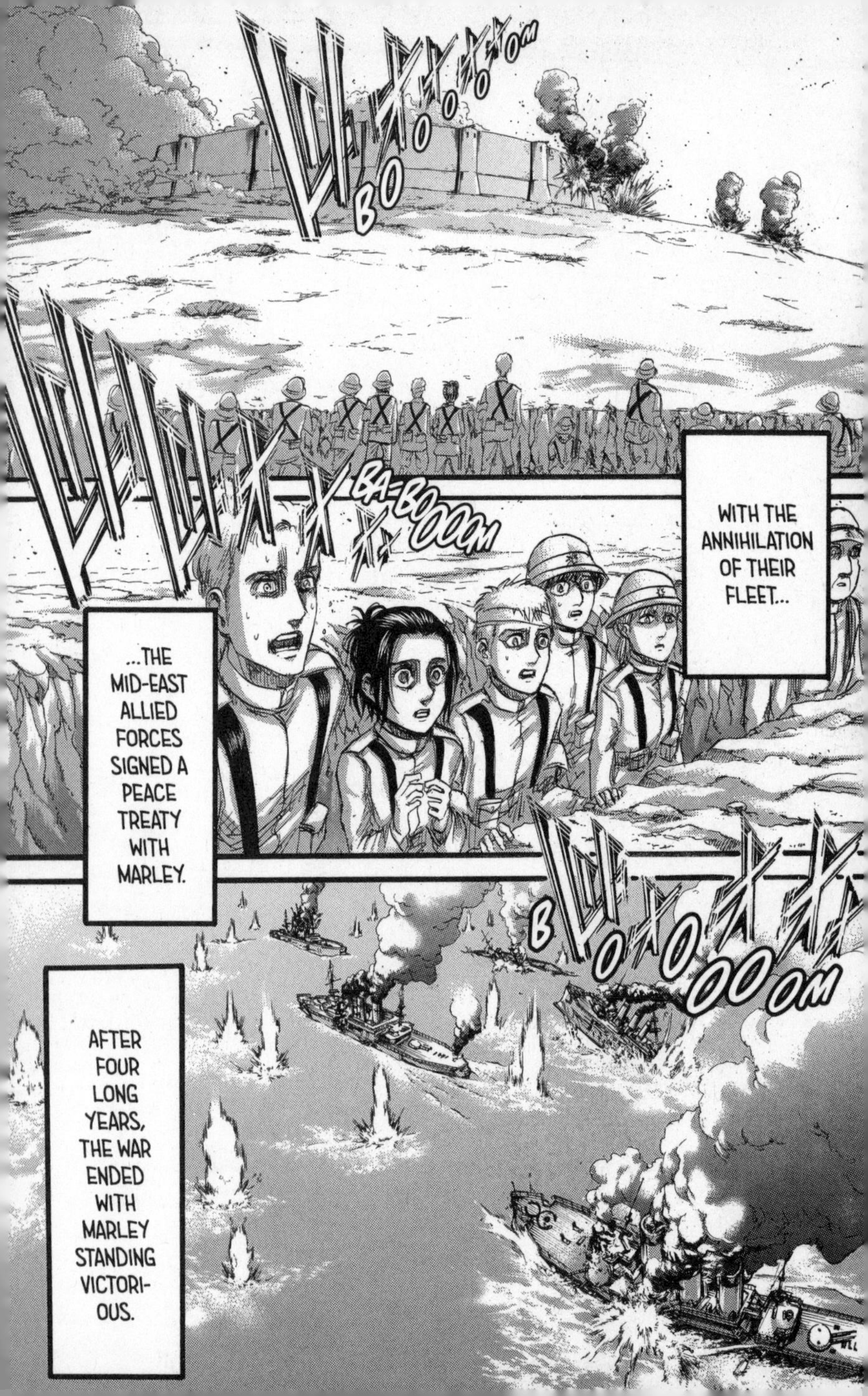
BOOOOOOM
WITH THE ANNIHILATION OF THEIR FLEET...
BA-BOOOOOM
...THE MID-EAST ALLIED FORCES SIGNED A PEACE TREATY WITH MARLEY.
BOOOOOOOM
AFTER FOUR LONG YEARS, THE WAR ENDED WITH MARLEY STANDING VICTORI-OUS.

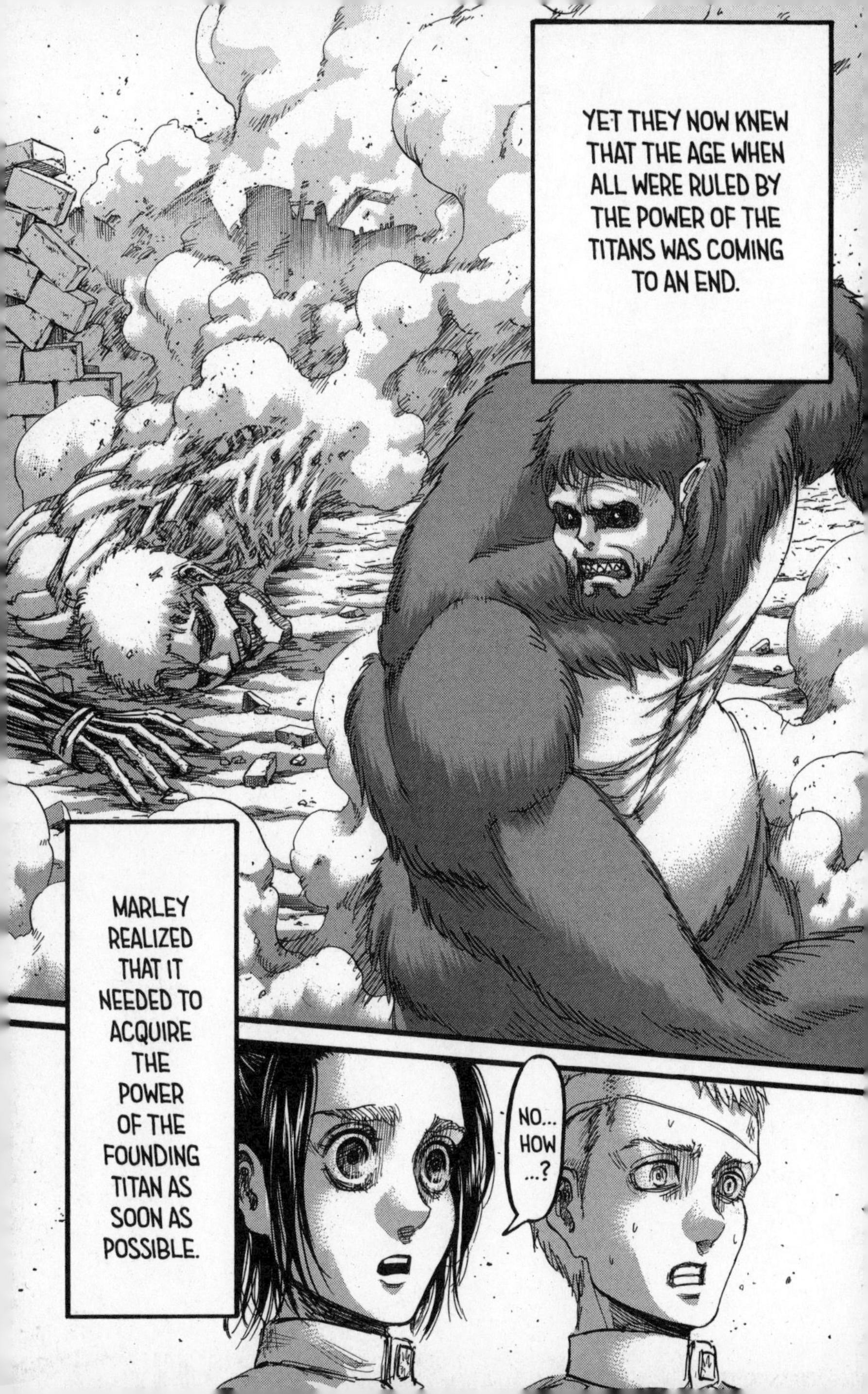
YET THEY NOW KNEW THAT THE AGE WHEN ALL WERE RULED BY THE POWER OF THE TITANS WAS COMING TO AN END.
MARLEY REALIZED THAT IT NEEDED TO ACQUIRE THE POWER OF THE FOUNDING TITAN AS SOON AS POSSIBLE.
NO... HOW ...?

ATTACK on TITAN

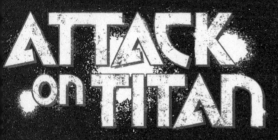

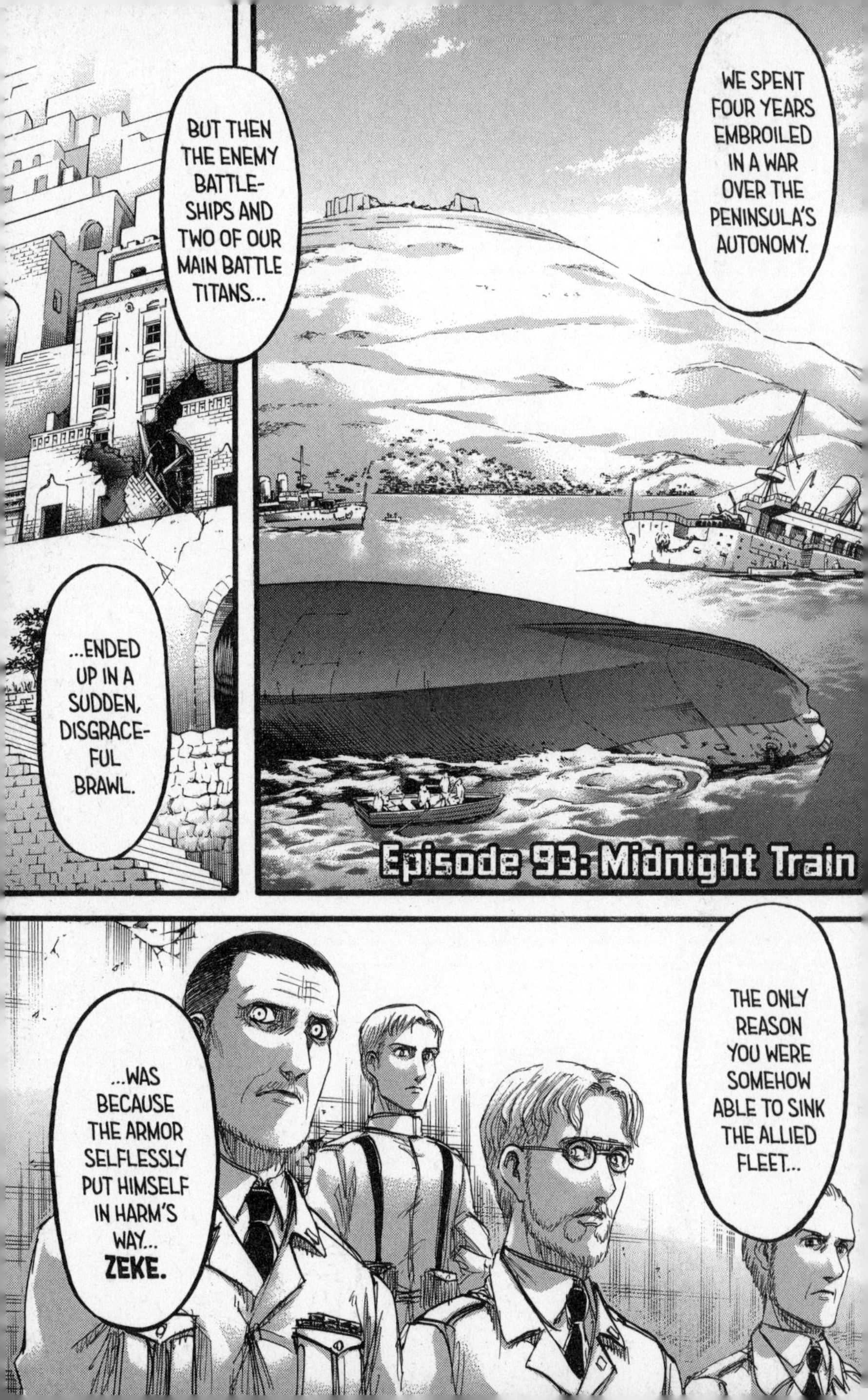
WE SPENT FOUR YEARS EMBROILED IN A WAR OVER THE PENINSULA'S AUTONOMY.
Episode 93: Midnight Train
BUT THEN THE ENEMY BATTLE-SHIPS AND TWO OF OUR MAIN BATTLE TITANS...
...ENDED UP IN A SUDDEN, DISGRACE-FUL BRAWL.
THE ONLY REASON YOU WERE SOMEHOW ABLE TO SINK THE ALLIED FLEET...
...WAS BECAUSE THE ARMOR SELFLESSLY PUT HIMSELF IN HARM'S WAY... **ZEKE.**

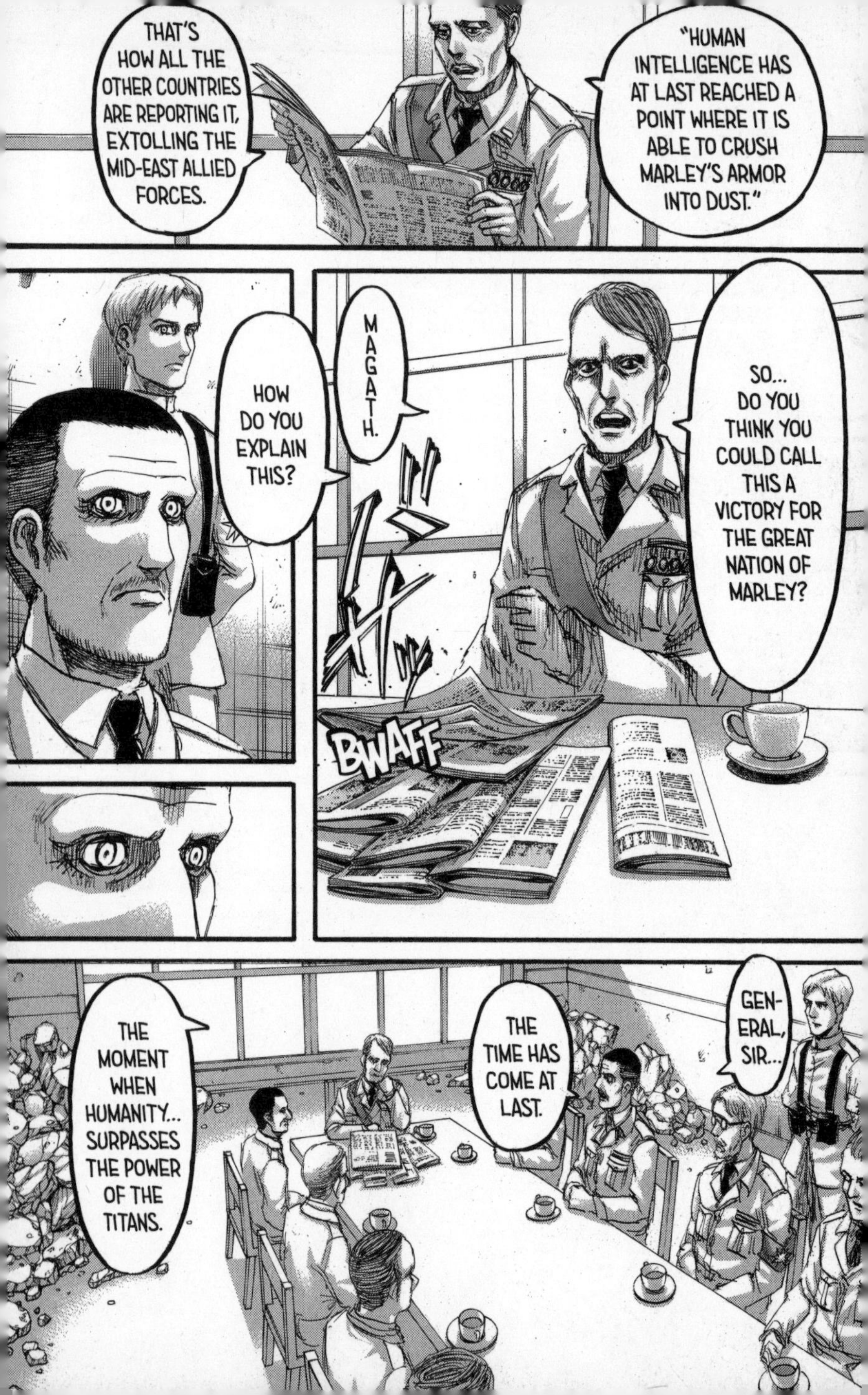
"HUMAN INTELLIGENCE HAS AT LAST REACHED A POINT WHERE IT IS ABLE TO CRUSH MARLEY'S ARMOR INTO DUST."
THAT'S HOW ALL THE OTHER COUNTRIES ARE REPORTING IT, EXTOLLING THE MID-EAST ALLIED FORCES.
SO... DO YOU THINK YOU COULD CALL THIS A VICTORY FOR THE GREAT NATION OF MARLEY?
MAGATH.
BWAFF
HOW DO YOU EXPLAIN THIS?
GEN-ERAL, SIR...
THE TIME HAS COME AT LAST.
THE MOMENT WHEN HUMANITY... SURPASSES THE POWER OF THE TITANS.

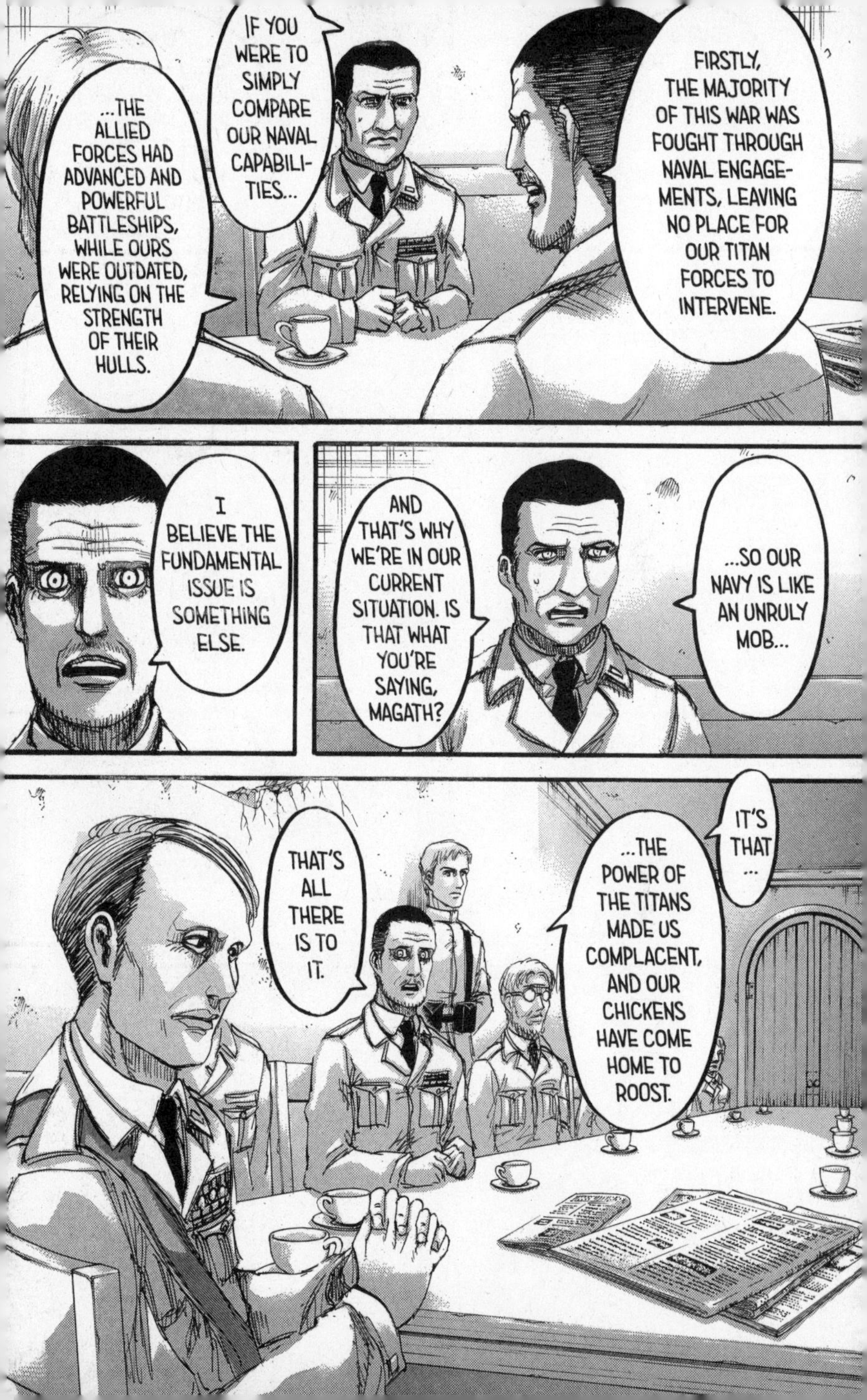
FIRSTLY, THE MAJORITY OF THIS WAR WAS FOUGHT THROUGH NAVAL ENGAGEMENTS, LEAVING NO PLACE FOR OUR TITAN FORCES TO INTERVENE.
IF YOU WERE TO SIMPLY COMPARE OUR NAVAL CAPABILITIES...
...THE ALLIED FORCES HAD ADVANCED AND POWERFUL BATTLESHIPS, WHILE OURS WERE OUTDATED, RELYING ON THE STRENGTH OF THEIR HULLS.
...SO OUR NAVY IS LIKE AN UNRULY MOB...
AND THAT'S WHY WE'RE IN OUR CURRENT SITUATION. IS THAT WHAT YOU'RE SAYING, MAGATH?
I BELIEVE THE FUNDAMENTAL ISSUE IS SOMETHING ELSE.
IT'S THAT ...
...THE POWER OF THE TITANS MADE US COMPLACENT, AND OUR CHICKENS HAVE COME HOME TO ROOST.
THAT'S ALL THERE IS TO IT.

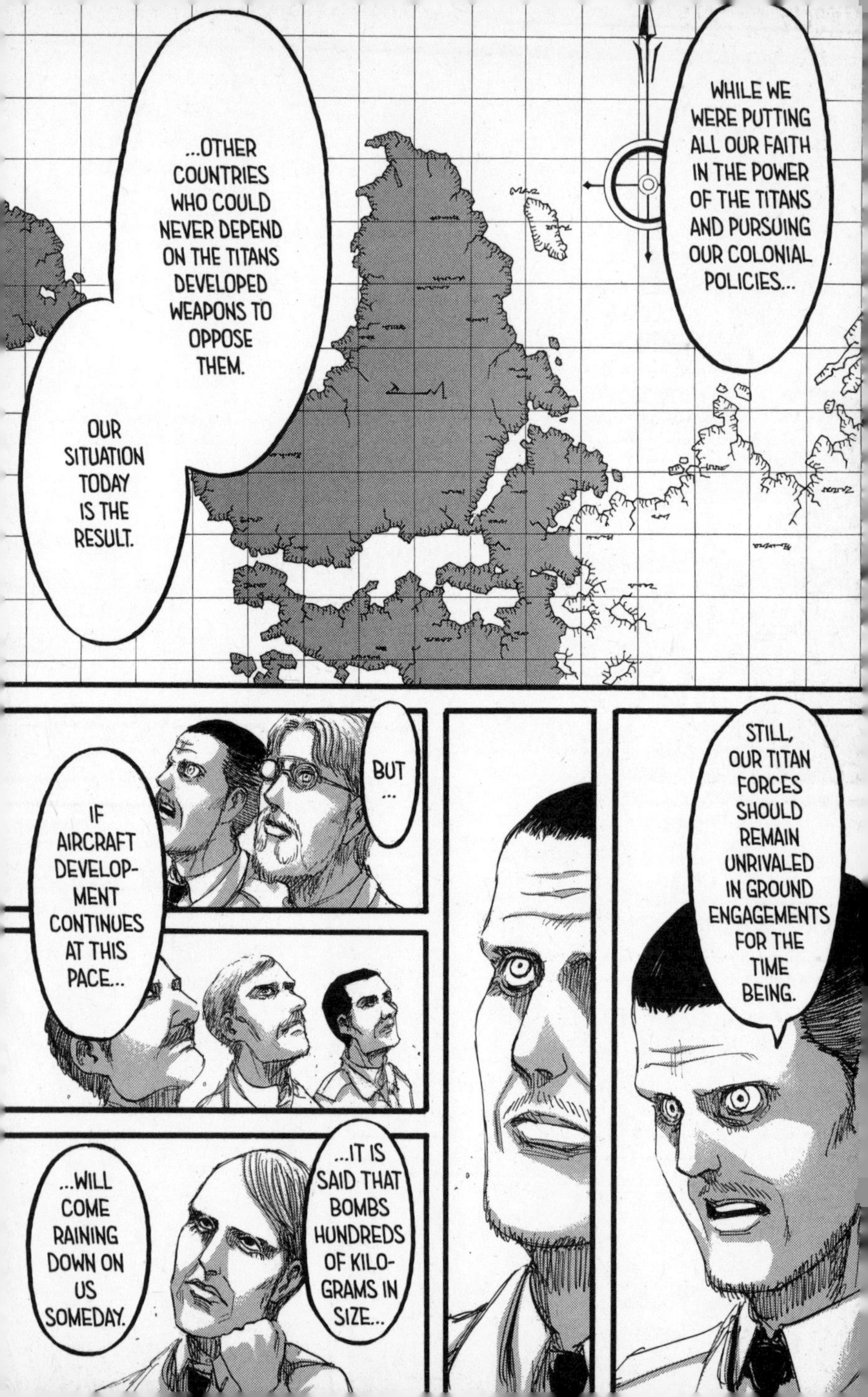
WHILE WE WERE PUTTING ALL OUR FAITH IN THE POWER OF THE TITANS AND PURSUING OUR COLONIAL POLICIES...
...OTHER COUNTRIES WHO COULD NEVER DEPEND ON THE TITANS DEVELOPED WEAPONS TO OPPOSE THEM.
OUR SITUATION TODAY IS THE RESULT.
STILL, OUR TITAN FORCES SHOULD REMAIN UNRIVALED IN GROUND ENGAGEMENTS FOR THE TIME BEING.
BUT ...
IF AIRCRAFT DEVELOP-MENT CONTINUES AT THIS PACE...
...IT IS SAID THAT BOMBS HUNDREDS OF KILO-GRAMS IN SIZE...
...WILL COME RAINING DOWN ON US SOMEDAY.

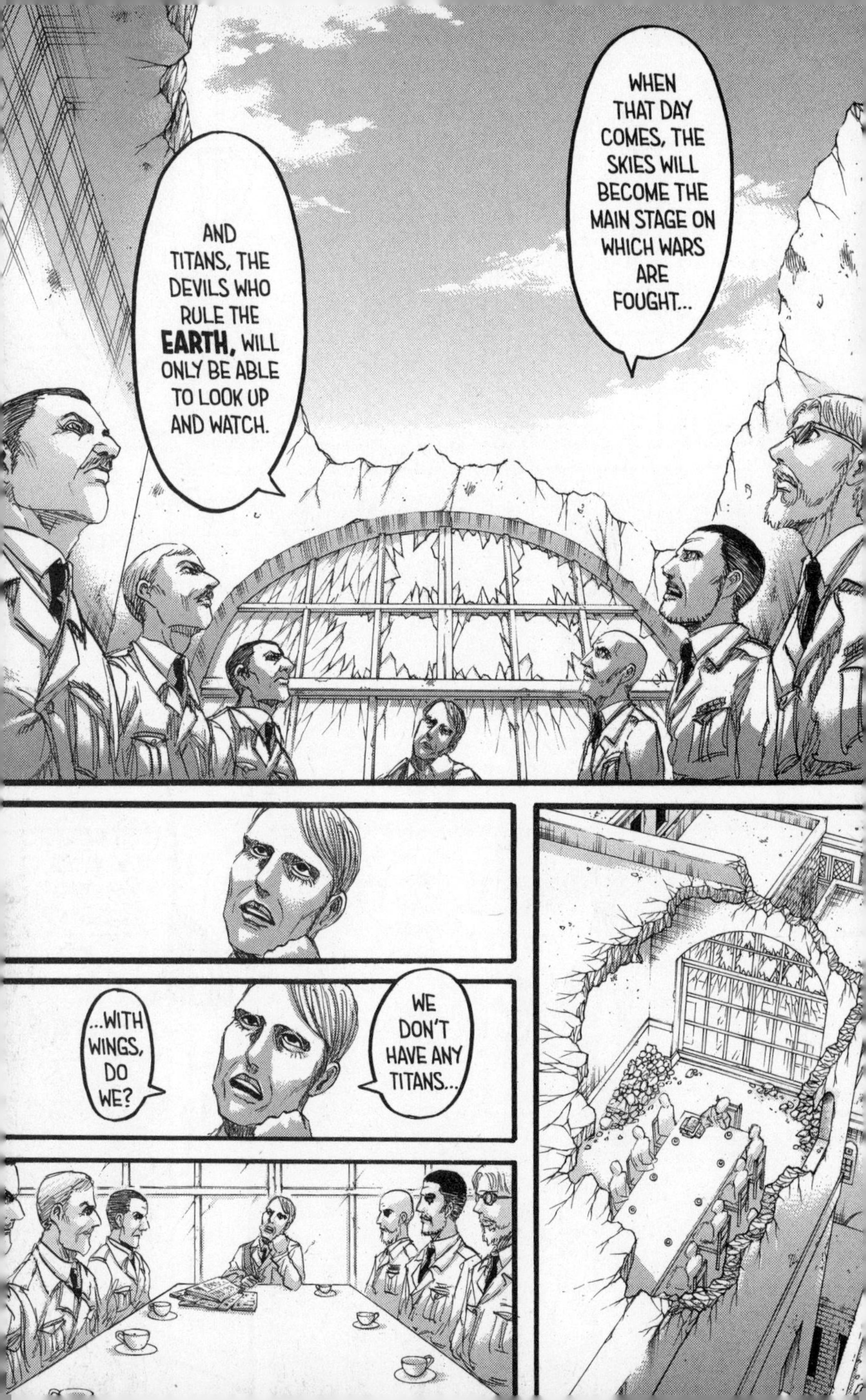
WHEN THAT DAY COMES, THE SKIES WILL BECOME THE MAIN STAGE ON WHICH WARS ARE FOUGHT...
AND TITANS, THE DEVILS WHO RULE THE **EARTH,** WILL ONLY BE ABLE TO LOOK UP AND WATCH.
WE DON'T HAVE ANY TITANS...
...WITH WINGS, DO WE?

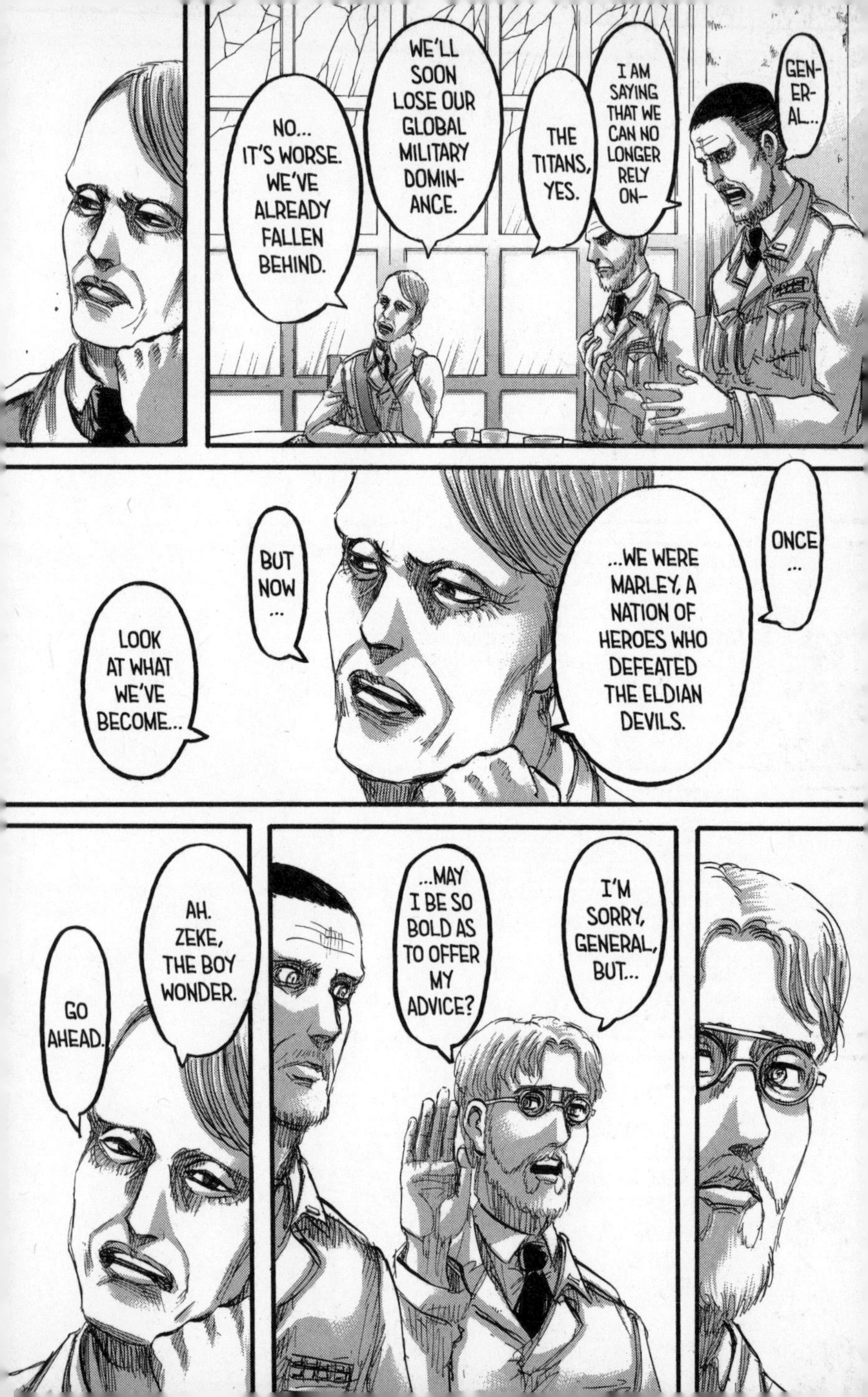
GEN-ER-AL...
I AM SAYING THAT WE CAN NO LONGER RELY ON–
THE TITANS, YES.
WE'LL SOON LOSE OUR GLOBAL MILITARY DOMIN-ANCE.
NO... IT'S WORSE. WE'VE ALREADY FALLEN BEHIND.
ONCE...
...WE WERE MARLEY, A NATION OF HEROES WHO DEFEATED THE ELDIAN DEVILS.
BUT NOW...
LOOK AT WHAT WE'VE BECOME...
I'M SORRY, GENERAL, BUT...
...MAY I BE SO BOLD AS TO OFFER MY ADVICE?
AH. ZEKE, THE BOY WONDER.
GO AHEAD.

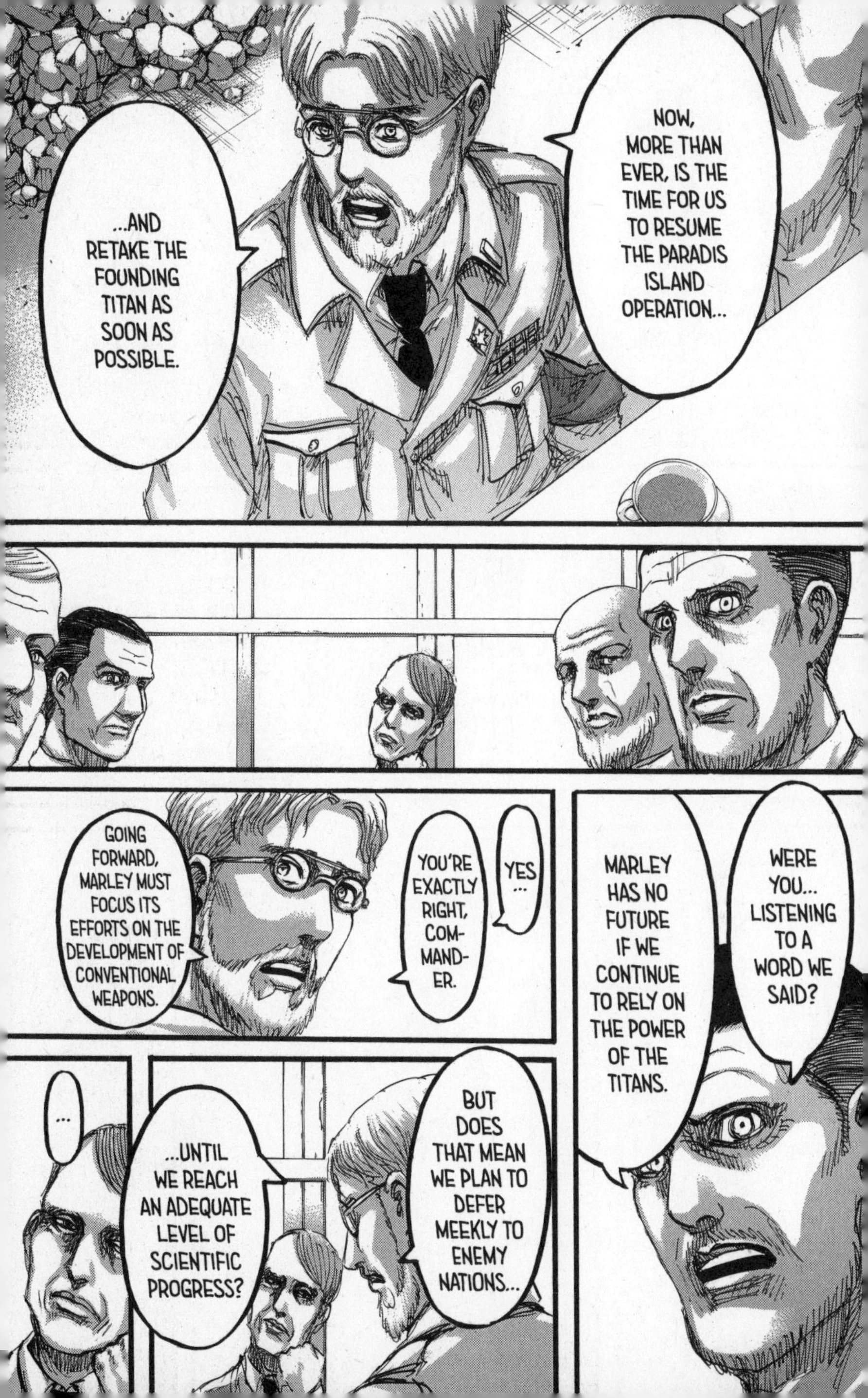
NOW, MORE THAN EVER, IS THE TIME FOR US TO RESUME THE PARADIS ISLAND OPERATION...
...AND RETAKE THE FOUNDING TITAN AS SOON AS POSSIBLE.
WERE YOU... LISTENING TO A WORD WE SAID?
MARLEY HAS NO FUTURE IF WE CONTINUE TO RELY ON THE POWER OF THE TITANS.
YES...
YOU'RE EXACTLY RIGHT, COMMANDER.
GOING FORWARD, MARLEY MUST FOCUS ITS EFFORTS ON THE DEVELOPMENT OF CONVENTIONAL WEAPONS.
BUT DOES THAT MEAN WE PLAN TO DEFER MEEKLY TO ENEMY NATIONS...
...UNTIL WE REACH AN ADEQUATE LEVEL OF SCIENTIFIC PROGRESS?
...

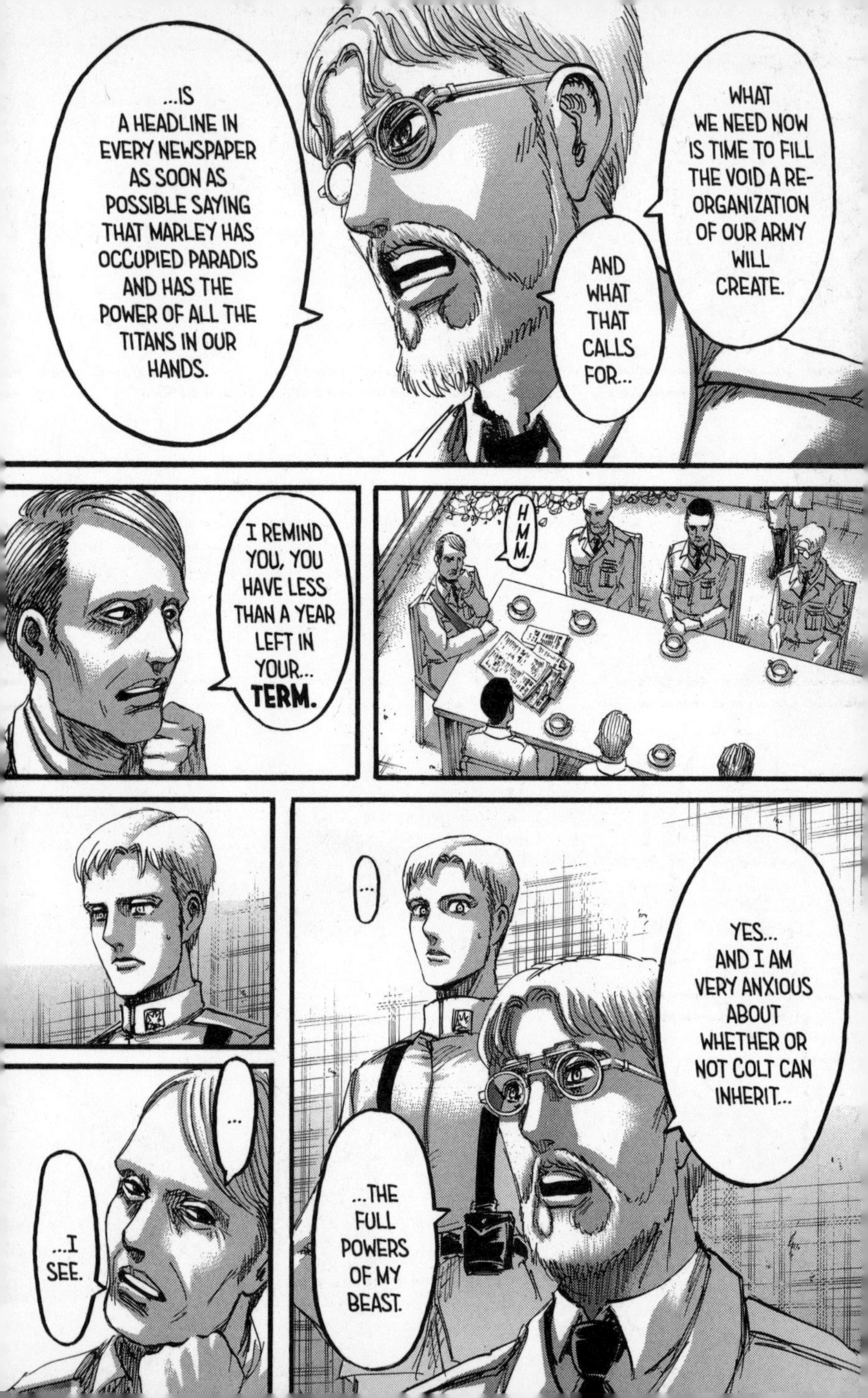
WHAT WE NEED NOW IS TIME TO FILL THE VOID A RE-ORGANIZATION OF OUR ARMY WILL CREATE.
AND WHAT THAT CALLS FOR...
...IS A HEADLINE IN EVERY NEWSPAPER AS SOON AS POSSIBLE SAYING THAT MARLEY HAS OCCUPIED PARADIS AND HAS THE POWER OF ALL THE TITANS IN OUR HANDS.
HMM.
I REMIND YOU, YOU HAVE LESS THAN A YEAR LEFT IN YOUR... **TERM.**
YES... AND I AM VERY ANXIOUS ABOUT WHETHER OR NOT COLT CAN INHERIT...
...
...THE FULL POWERS OF MY BEAST.
...
...I SEE.

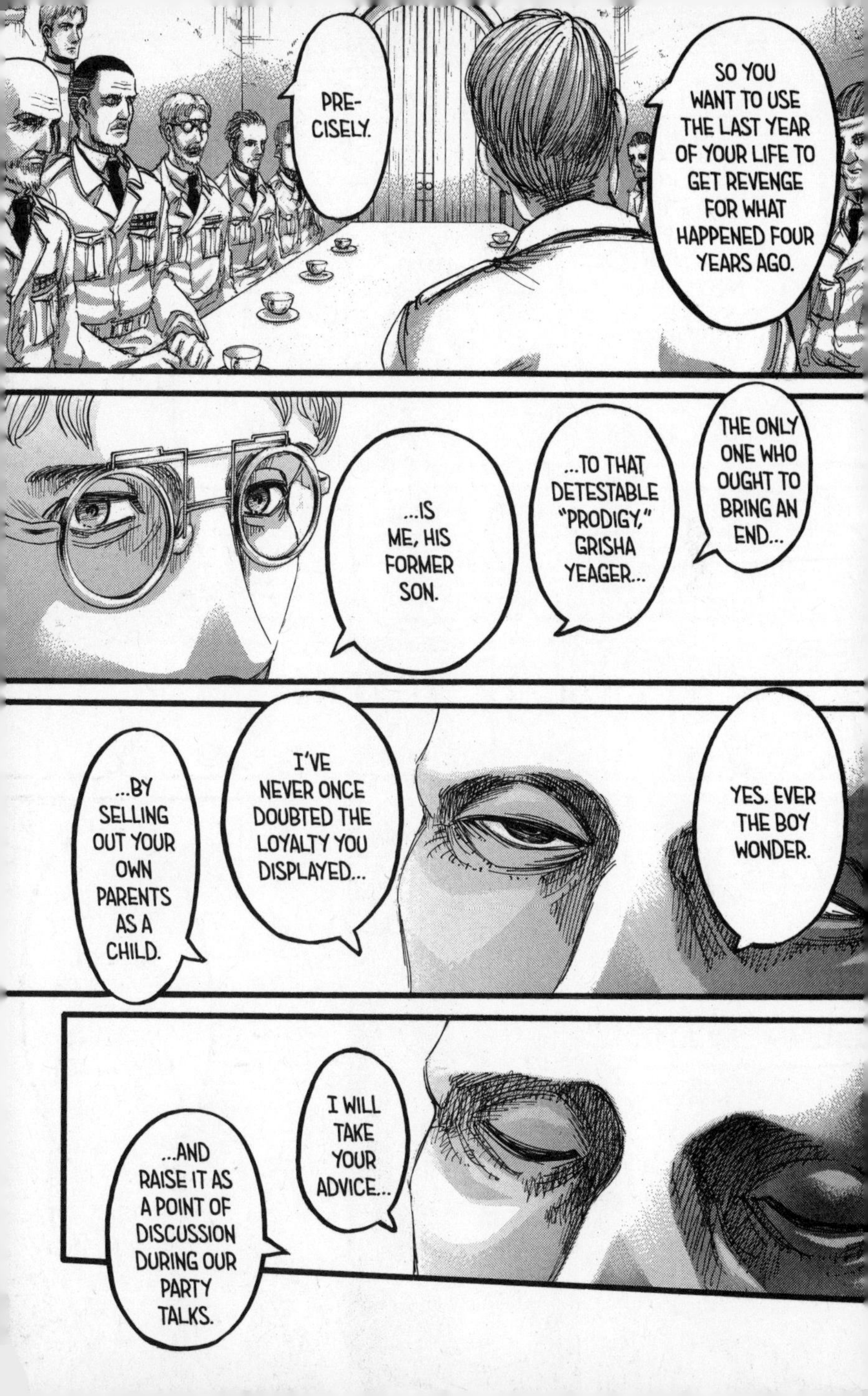
SO YOU WANT TO USE THE LAST YEAR OF YOUR LIFE TO GET REVENGE FOR WHAT HAPPENED FOUR YEARS AGO.
PRE-CISELY.
THE ONLY ONE WHO OUGHT TO BRING AN END...
...TO THAT DETESTABLE "PRODIGY," GRISHA YEAGER...
...IS ME, HIS FORMER SON.
YES. EVER THE BOY WONDER.
I'VE NEVER ONCE DOUBTED THE LOYALTY YOU DISPLAYED...
...BY SELLING OUT YOUR OWN PARENTS AS A CHILD.
I WILL TAKE YOUR ADVICE...
...AND RAISE IT AS A POINT OF DISCUSSION DURING OUR PARTY TALKS.

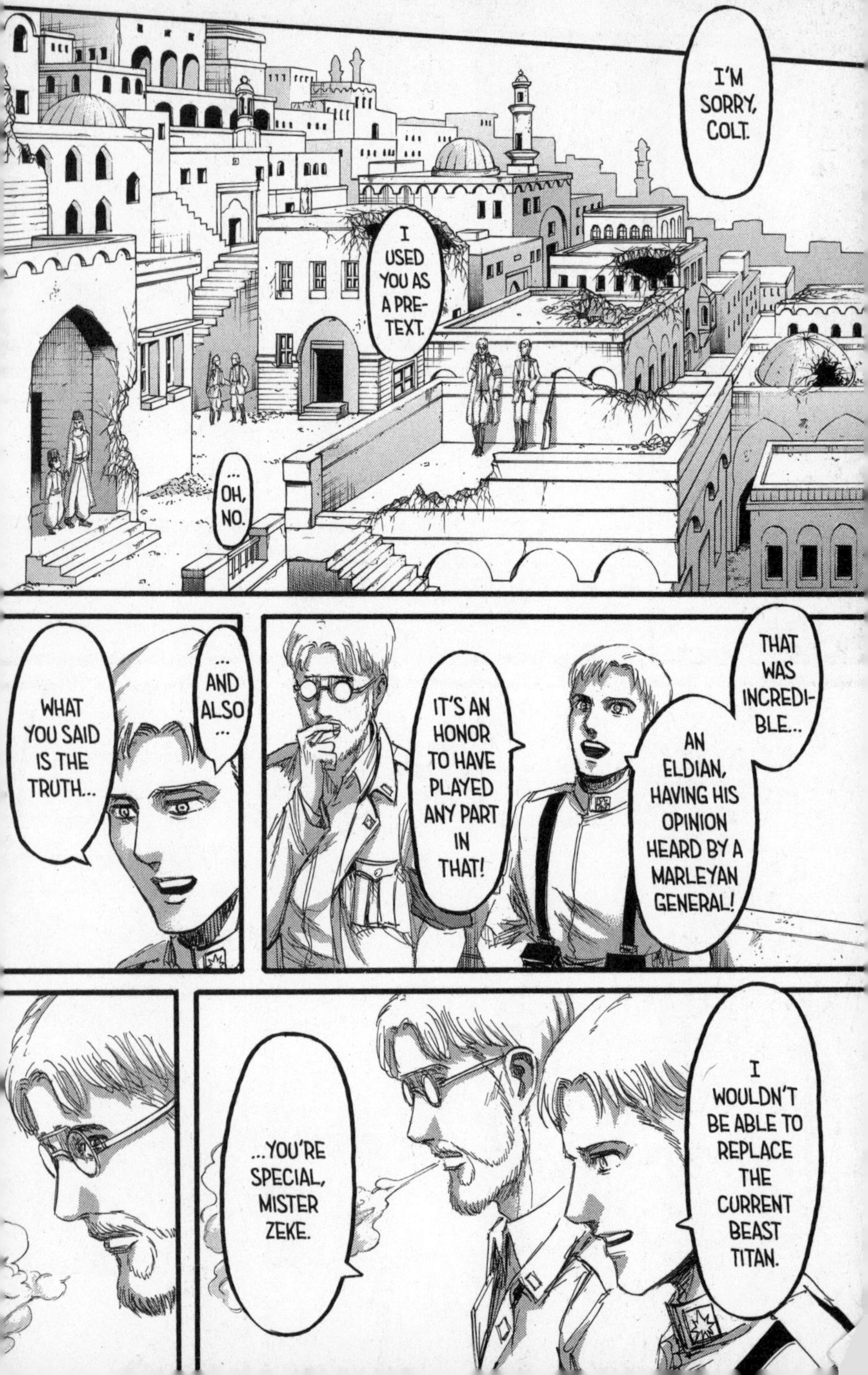
I'M SORRY, COLT.
I USED YOU AS A PRE-TEXT.
...OH, NO.
THAT WAS INCREDI-BLE...
AN ELDIAN, HAVING HIS OPINION HEARD BY A MARLEYAN GENERAL!
IT'S AN HONOR TO HAVE PLAYED ANY PART IN THAT!
...AND ALSO...
WHAT YOU SAID IS THE TRUTH...
I WOULDN'T BE ABLE TO REPLACE THE CURRENT BEAST TITAN.
...YOU'RE SPECIAL, MISTER ZEKE.

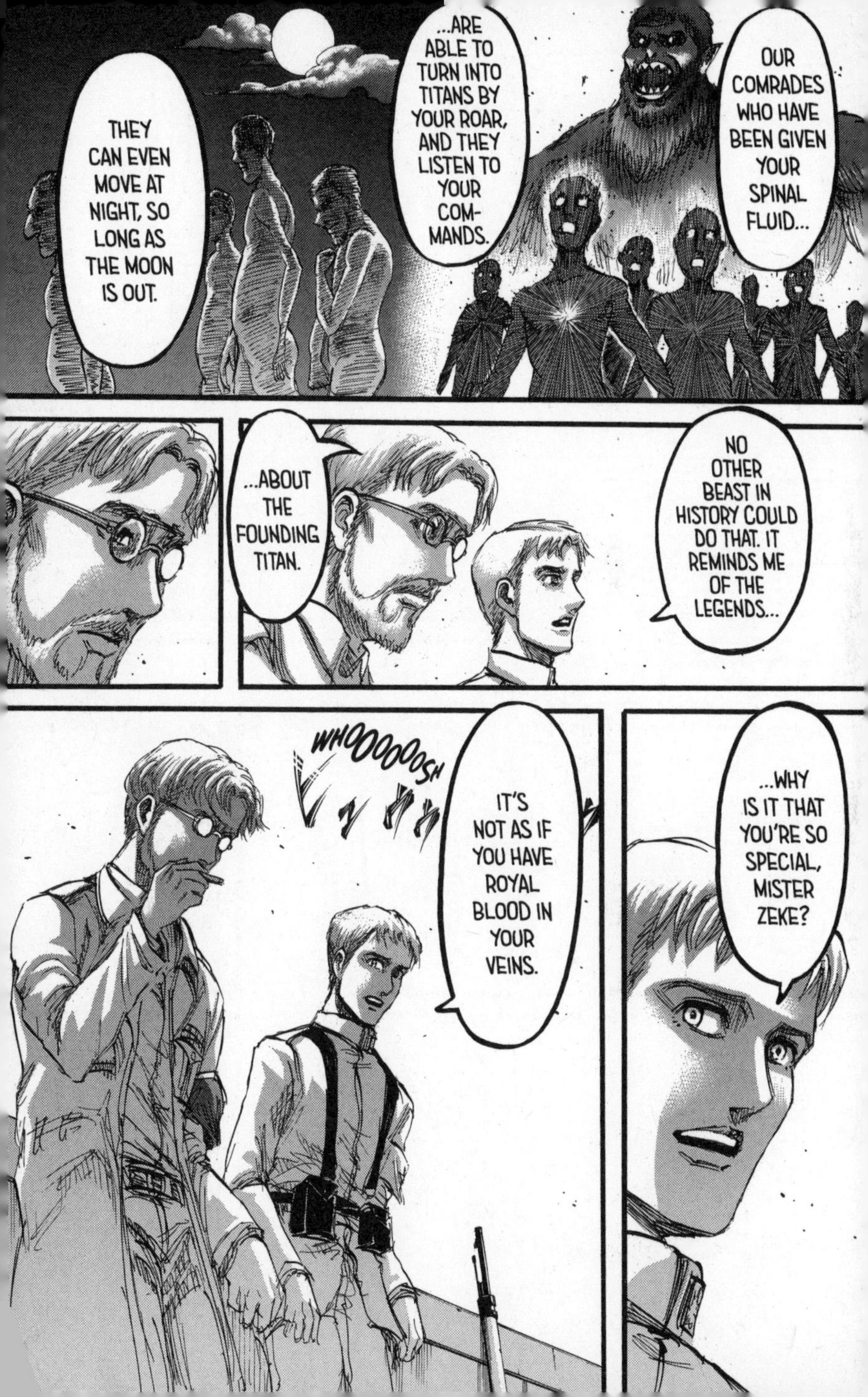
OUR COMRADES WHO HAVE BEEN GIVEN YOUR SPINAL FLUID...
...ARE ABLE TO TURN INTO TITANS BY YOUR ROAR, AND THEY LISTEN TO YOUR COM-MANDS.
THEY CAN EVEN MOVE AT NIGHT, SO LONG AS THE MOON IS OUT.
NO OTHER BEAST IN HISTORY COULD DO THAT. IT REMINDS ME OF THE LEGENDS...
...ABOUT THE FOUNDING TITAN.
...WHY IS IT THAT YOU'RE SO SPECIAL, MISTER ZEKE?
IT'S NOT AS IF YOU HAVE ROYAL BLOOD IN YOUR VEINS.
WHOOOOOOOSH

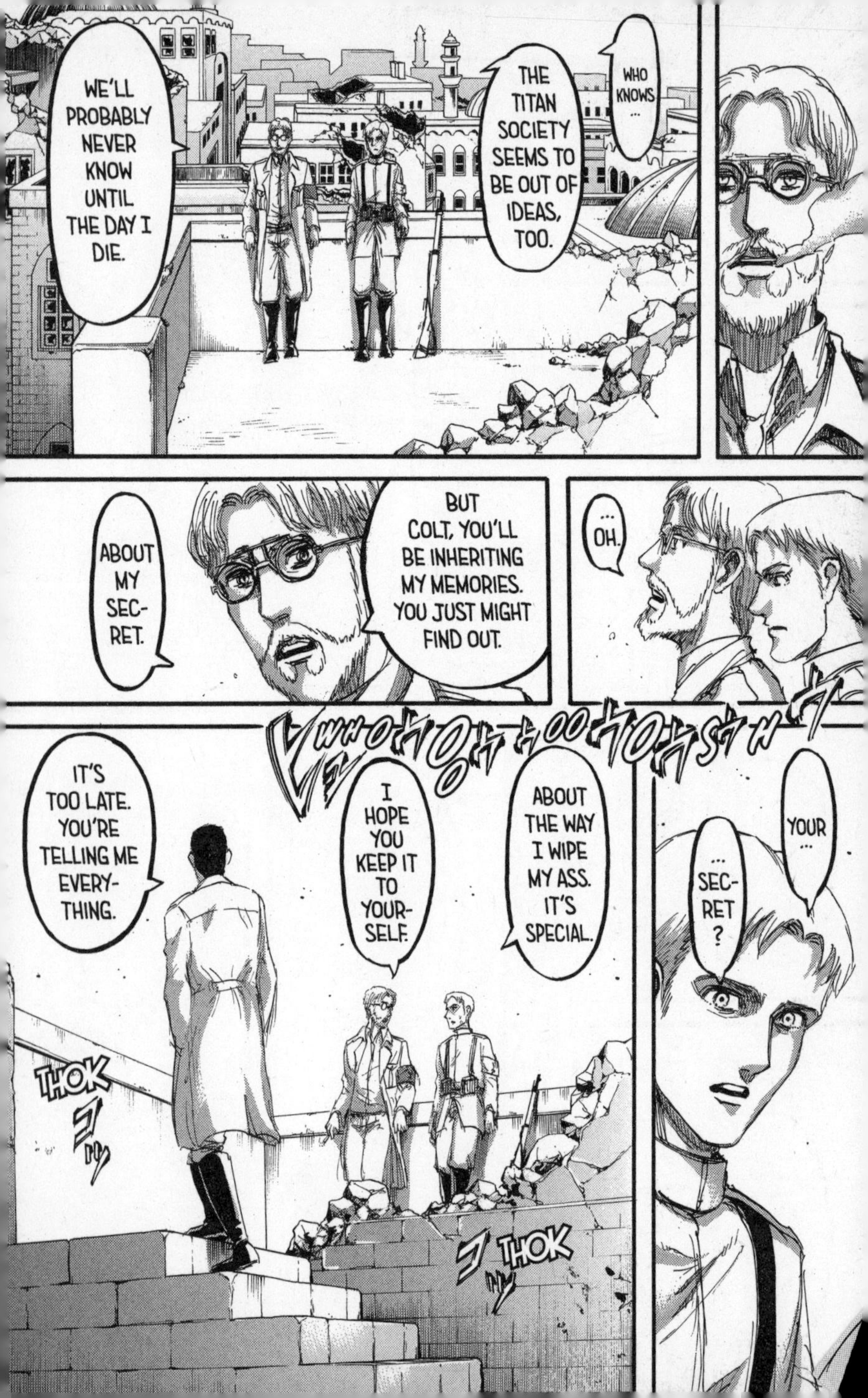
WHO KNOWS...
THE TITAN SOCIETY SEEMS TO BE OUT OF IDEAS, TOO.
WE'LL PROBABLY NEVER KNOW UNTIL THE DAY I DIE.
...OH.
BUT COLT, YOU'LL BE INHERITING MY MEMORIES. YOU JUST MIGHT FIND OUT.
ABOUT MY SECRET.
YOUR...
...SECRET?
ABOUT THE WAY I WIPE MY ASS. IT'S SPECIAL.
I HOPE YOU KEEP IT TO YOURSELF.
IT'S TOO LATE. YOU'RE TELLING ME EVERYTHING.
THOK
THOK

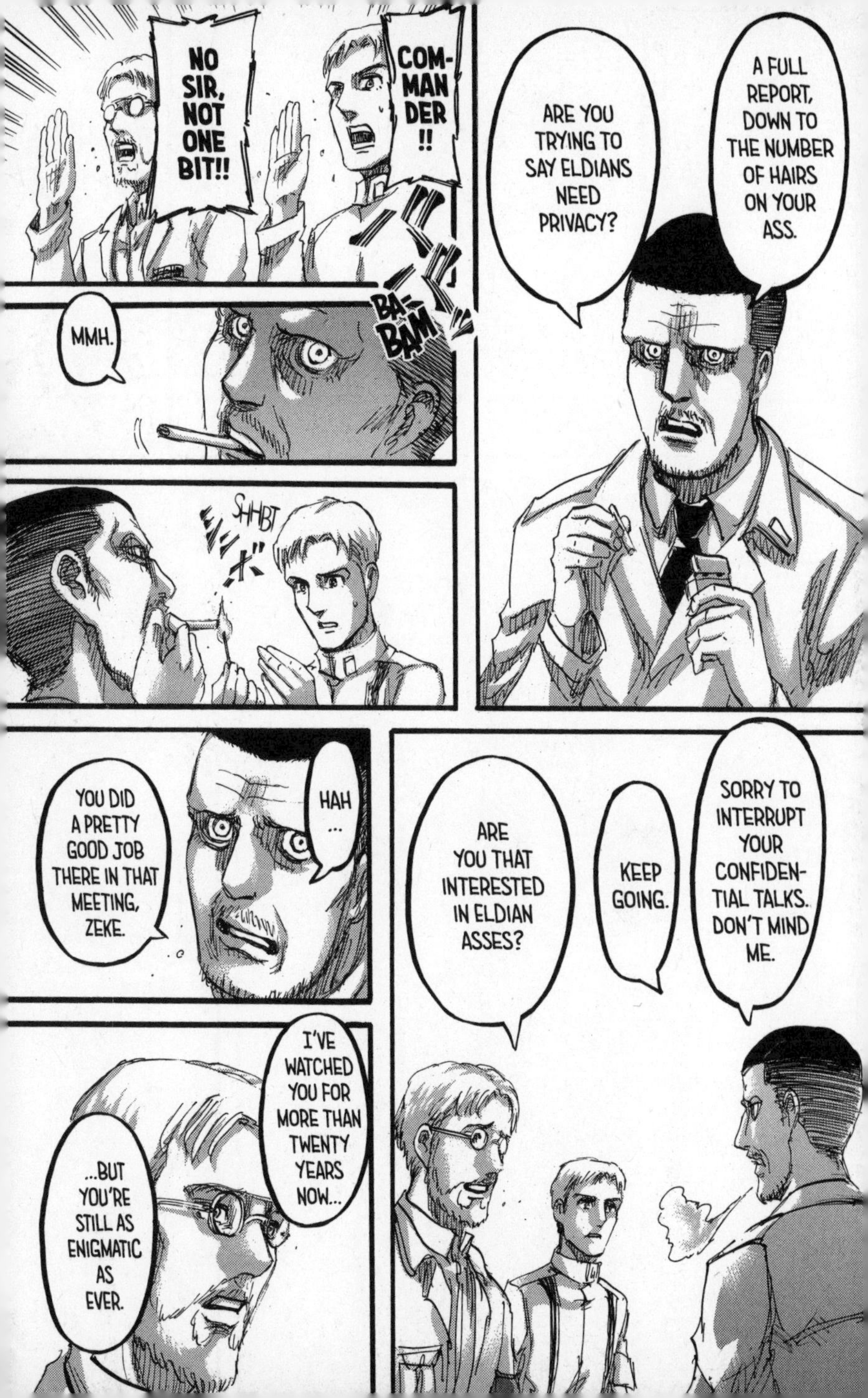
A FULL REPORT, DOWN TO THE NUMBER OF HAIRS ON YOUR ASS.
ARE YOU TRYING TO SAY ELDIANS NEED PRIVACY?
COM-MAN DER !!
NO SIR, NOT ONE BIT!!
BA-BAM
MMH.
SHHBT
SORRY TO INTERRUPT YOUR CONFIDEN-TIAL TALKS. DON'T MIND ME.
KEEP GOING.
ARE YOU THAT INTERESTED IN ELDIAN ASSES?
HAH ...
YOU DID A PRETTY GOOD JOB THERE IN THAT MEETING, ZEKE.
I'VE WATCHED YOU FOR MORE THAN TWENTY YEARS NOW...
...BUT YOU'RE STILL AS ENIGMATIC AS EVER.

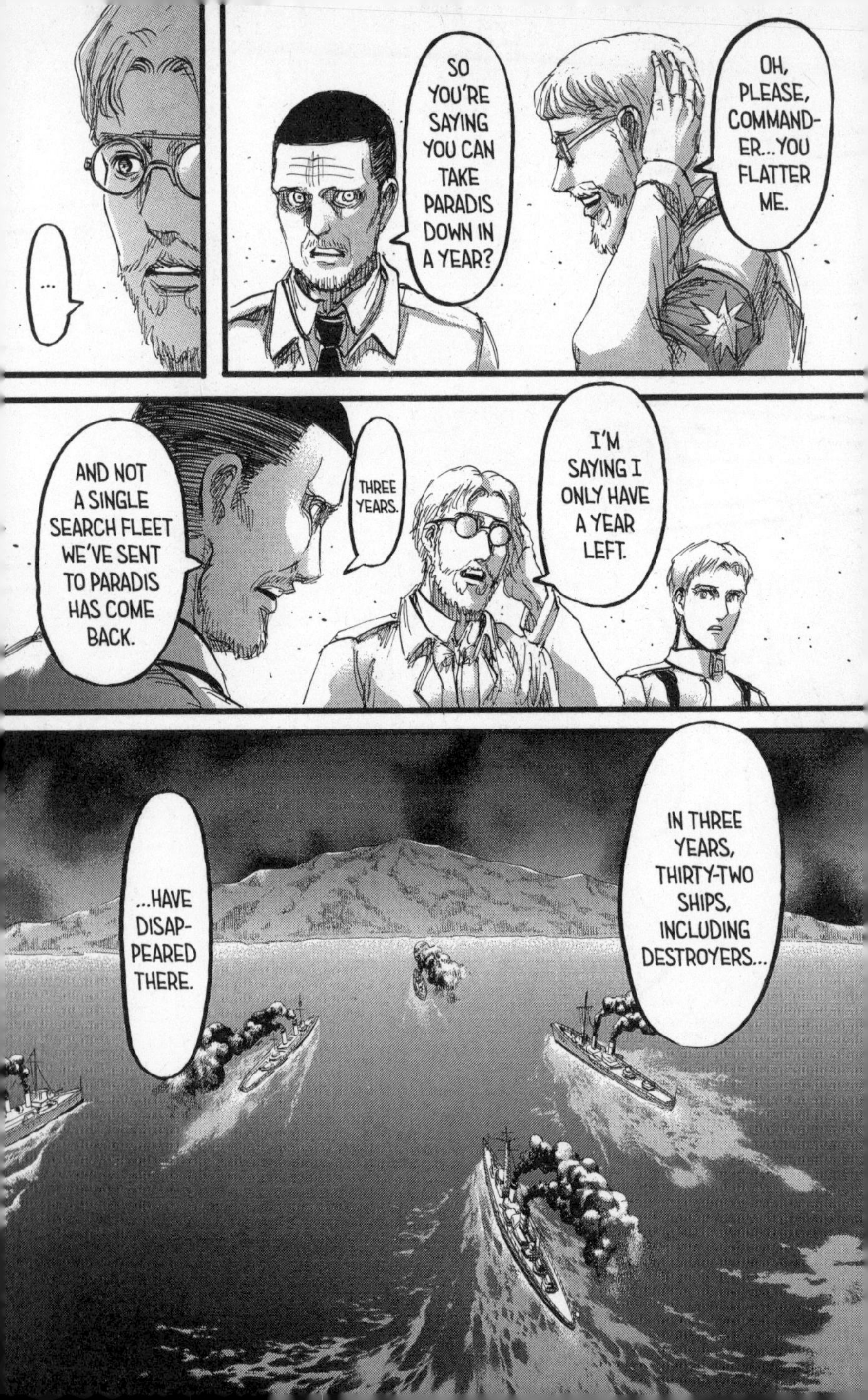
SO YOU'RE SAYING YOU CAN TAKE PARADIS DOWN IN A YEAR?
OH, PLEASE, COMMANDER...YOU FLATTER ME.
...
I'M SAYING I ONLY HAVE A YEAR LEFT.
THREE YEARS.
AND NOT A SINGLE SEARCH FLEET WE'VE SENT TO PARADIS HAS COME BACK.
IN THREE YEARS, THIRTY-TWO SHIPS, INCLUDING DESTROYERS...
...HAVE DISAPPEARED THERE.

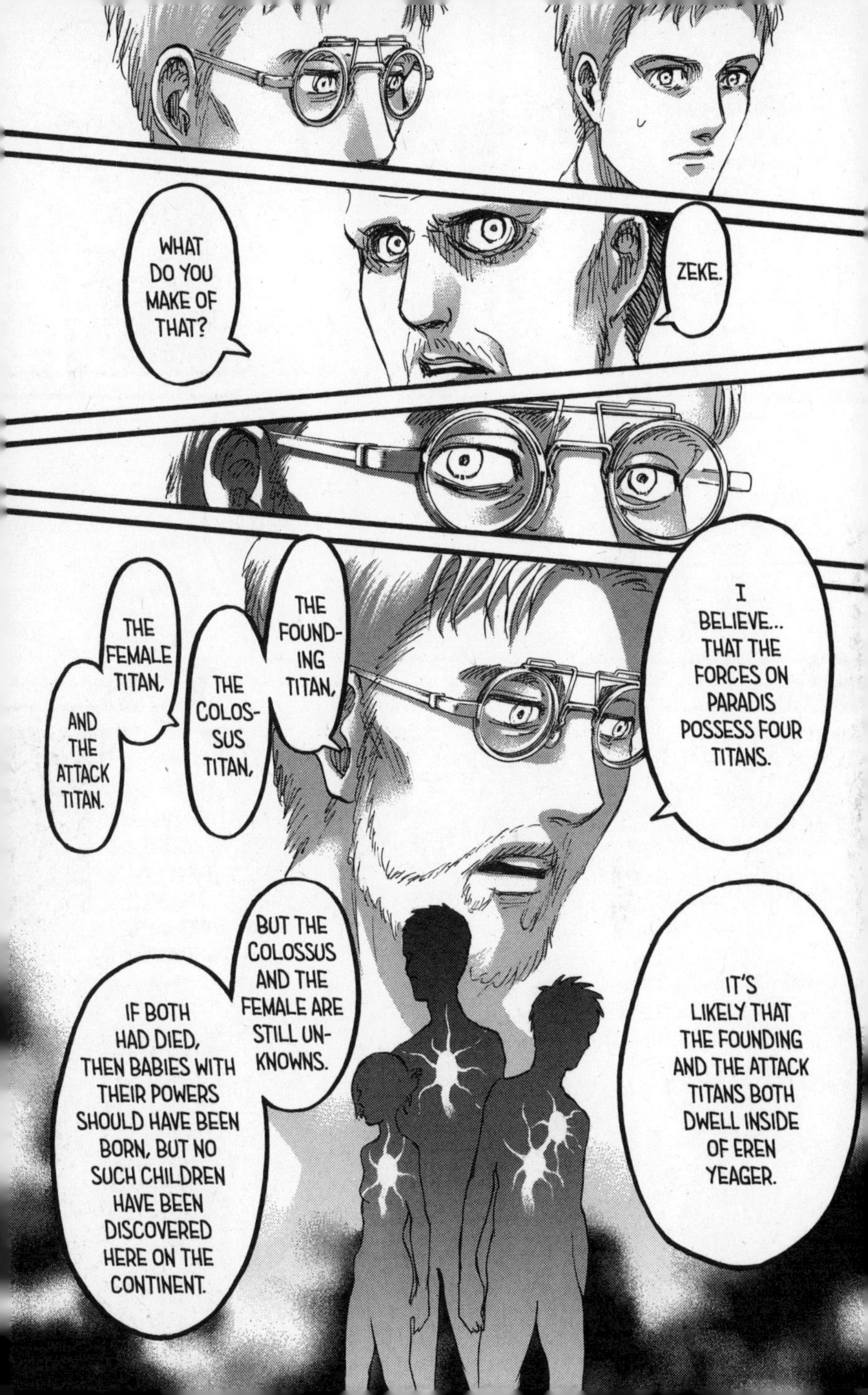
ZEKE.
WHAT DO YOU MAKE OF THAT?
I BELIEVE... THAT THE FORCES ON PARADIS POSSESS FOUR TITANS.
THE FOUNDING TITAN,
THE COLOSSUS TITAN,
THE FEMALE TITAN,
AND THE ATTACK TITAN.
IT'S LIKELY THAT THE FOUNDING AND THE ATTACK TITANS BOTH DWELL INSIDE OF EREN YEAGER.
BUT THE COLOSSUS AND THE FEMALE ARE STILL UNKNOWNS.
IF BOTH HAD DIED, THEN BABIES WITH THEIR POWERS SHOULD HAVE BEEN BORN, BUT NO SUCH CHILDREN HAVE BEEN DISCOVERED HERE ON THE CONTINENT.

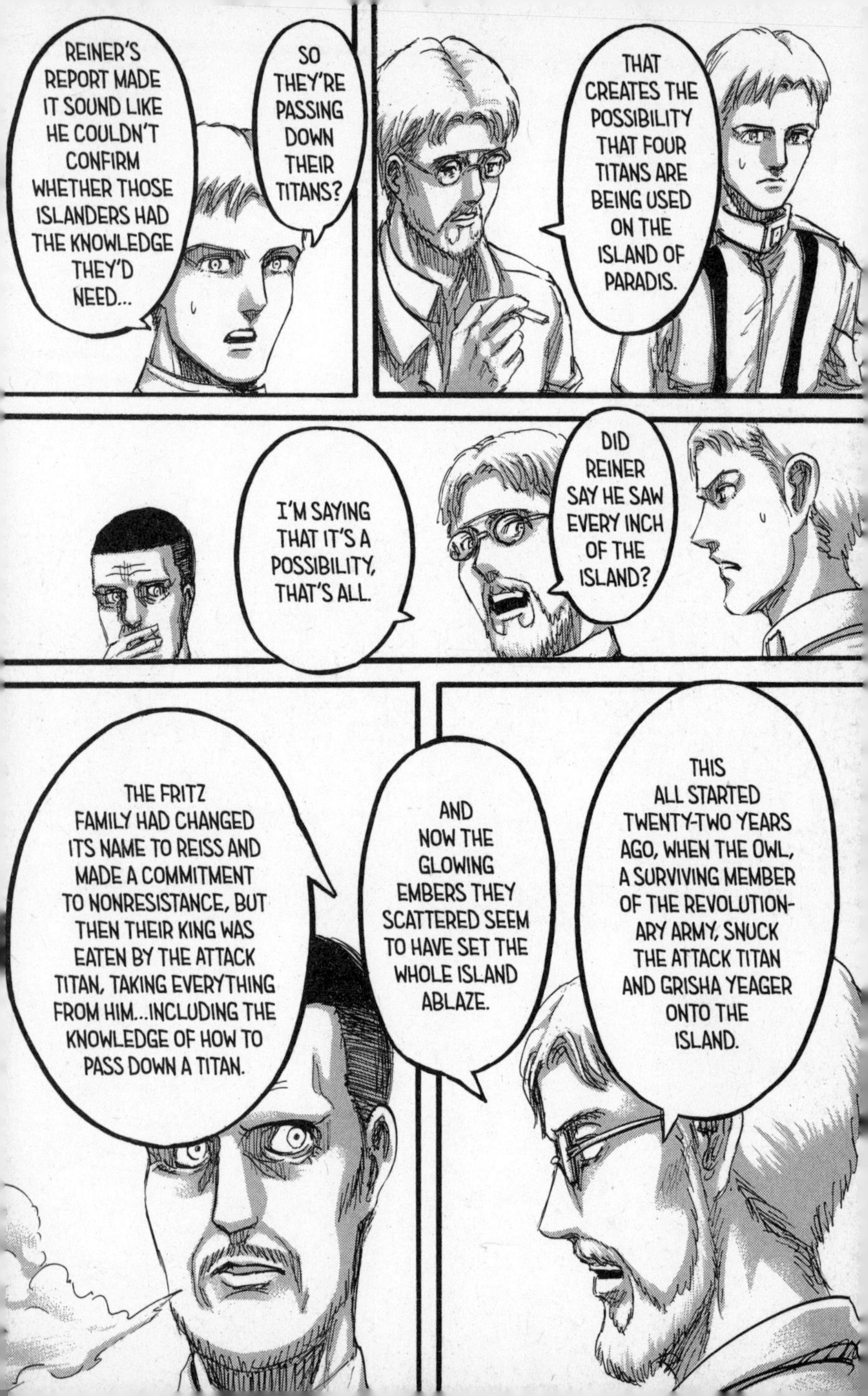
THAT CREATES THE POSSIBILITY THAT FOUR TITANS ARE BEING USED ON THE ISLAND OF PARADIS.
SO THEY'RE PASSING DOWN THEIR TITANS?
REINER'S REPORT MADE IT SOUND LIKE HE COULDN'T CONFIRM WHETHER THOSE ISLANDERS HAD THE KNOWLEDGE THEY'D NEED...
DID REINER SAY HE SAW EVERY INCH OF THE ISLAND?
I'M SAYING THAT IT'S A POSSIBILITY, THAT'S ALL.
THIS ALL STARTED TWENTY-TWO YEARS AGO, WHEN THE OWL, A SURVIVING MEMBER OF THE REVOLUTION-ARY ARMY, SNUCK THE ATTACK TITAN AND GRISHA YEAGER ONTO THE ISLAND.
AND NOW THE GLOWING EMBERS THEY SCATTERED SEEM TO HAVE SET THE WHOLE ISLAND ABLAZE.
THE FRITZ FAMILY HAD CHANGED ITS NAME TO REISS AND MADE A COMMITMENT TO NONRESISTANCE, BUT THEN THEIR KING WAS EATEN BY THE ATTACK TITAN, TAKING EVERYTHING FROM HIM...INCLUDING THE KNOWLEDGE OF HOW TO PASS DOWN A TITAN.

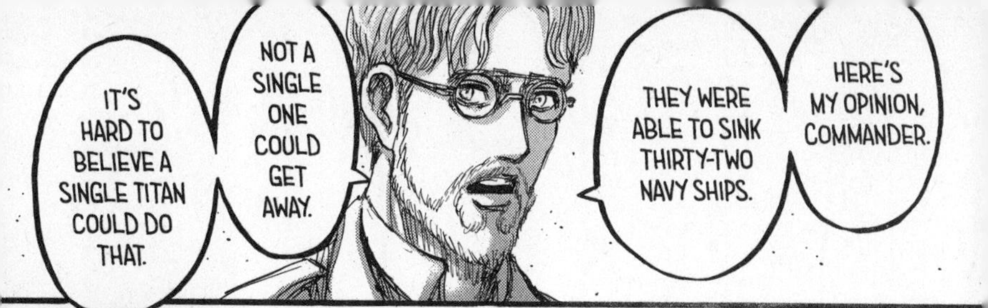
HERE'S MY OPINION, COMMANDER.
THEY WERE ABLE TO SINK THIRTY-TWO NAVY SHIPS.
NOT A SINGLE ONE COULD GET AWAY.
IT'S HARD TO BELIEVE A SINGLE TITAN COULD DO THAT.
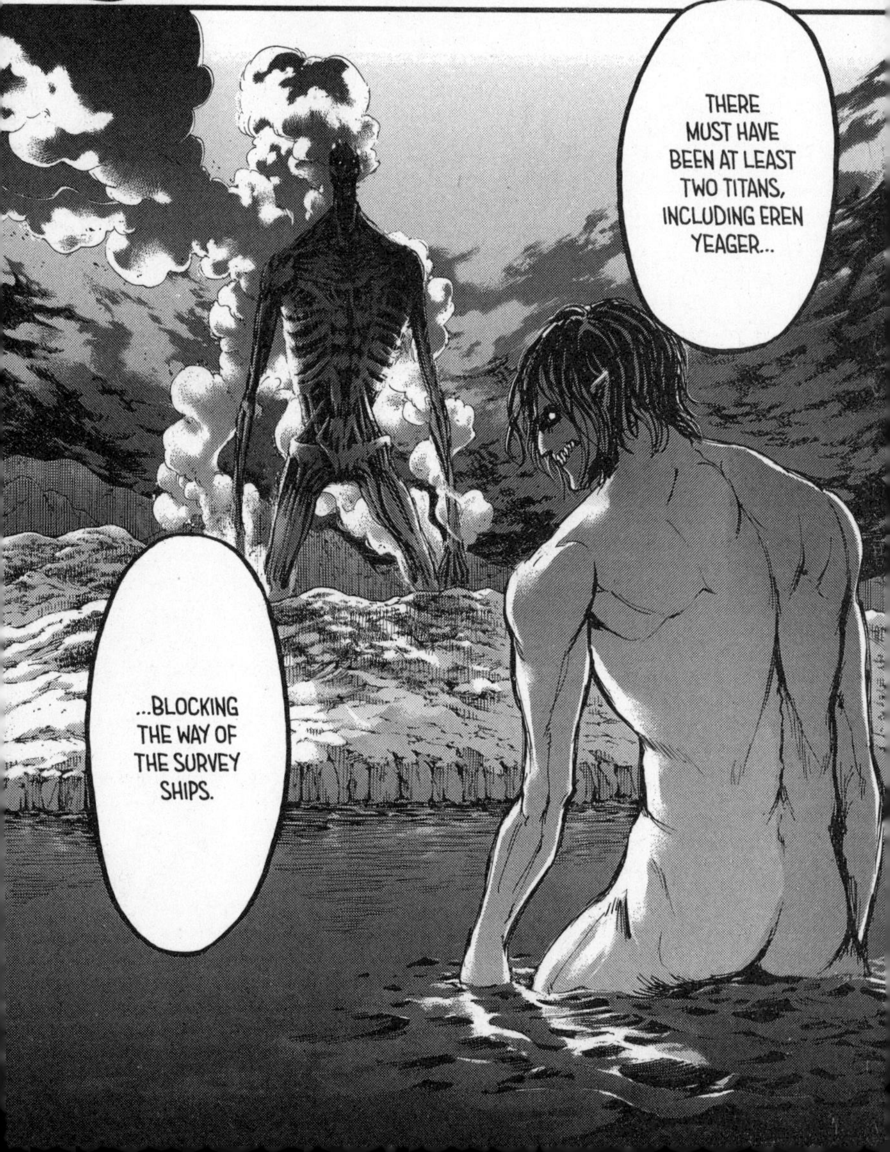
THERE MUST HAVE BEEN AT LEAST TWO TITANS, INCLUDING EREN YEAGER...
...BLOCKING THE WAY OF THE SURVEY SHIPS.

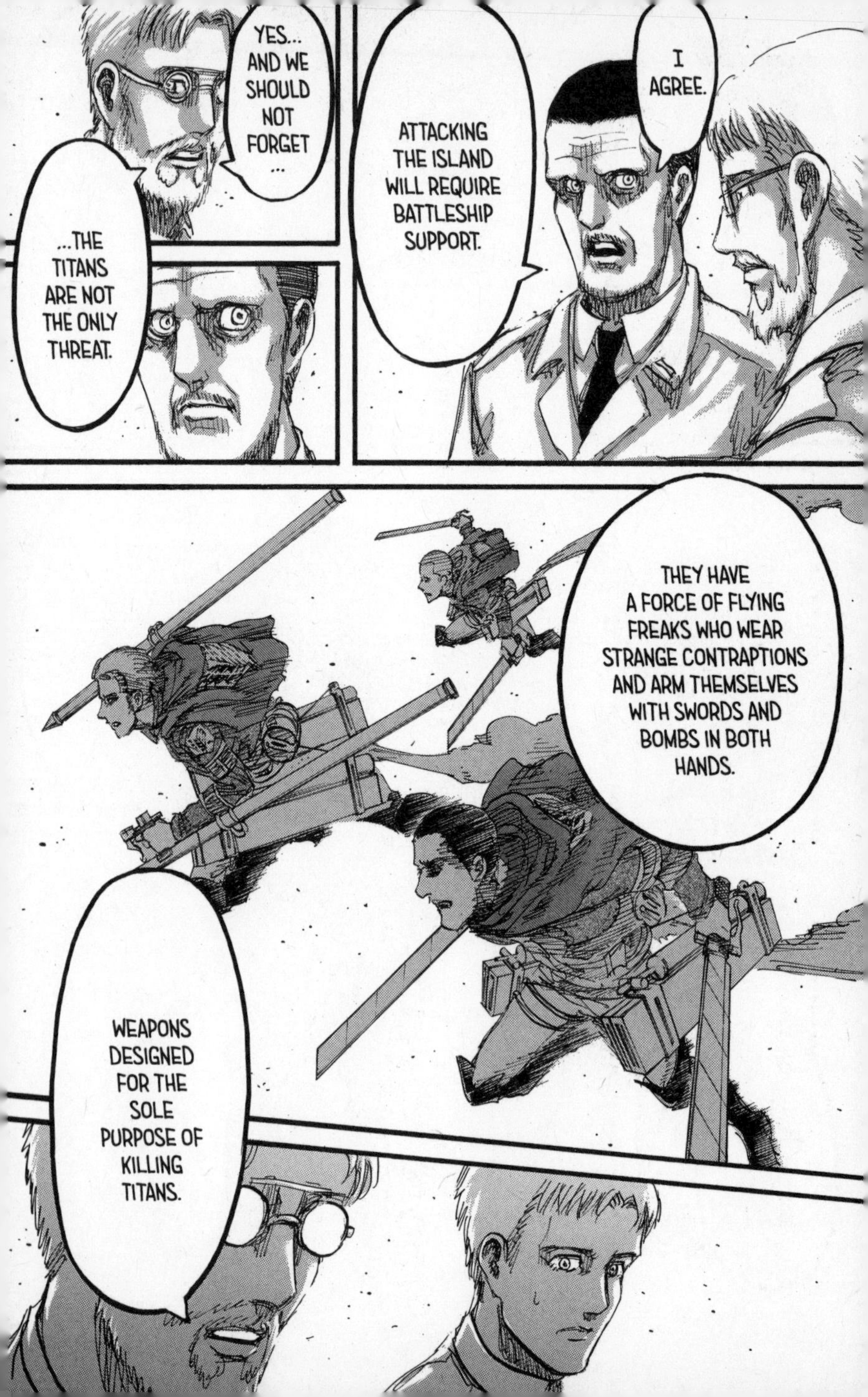
I AGREE.
ATTACKING THE ISLAND WILL REQUIRE BATTLESHIP SUPPORT.
YES... AND WE SHOULD NOT FORGET ...
...THE TITANS ARE NOT THE ONLY THREAT.
THEY HAVE A FORCE OF FLYING FREAKS WHO WEAR STRANGE CONTRAPTIONS AND ARM THEMSELVES WITH SWORDS AND BOMBS IN BOTH HANDS.
WEAPONS DESIGNED FOR THE SOLE PURPOSE OF KILLING TITANS.

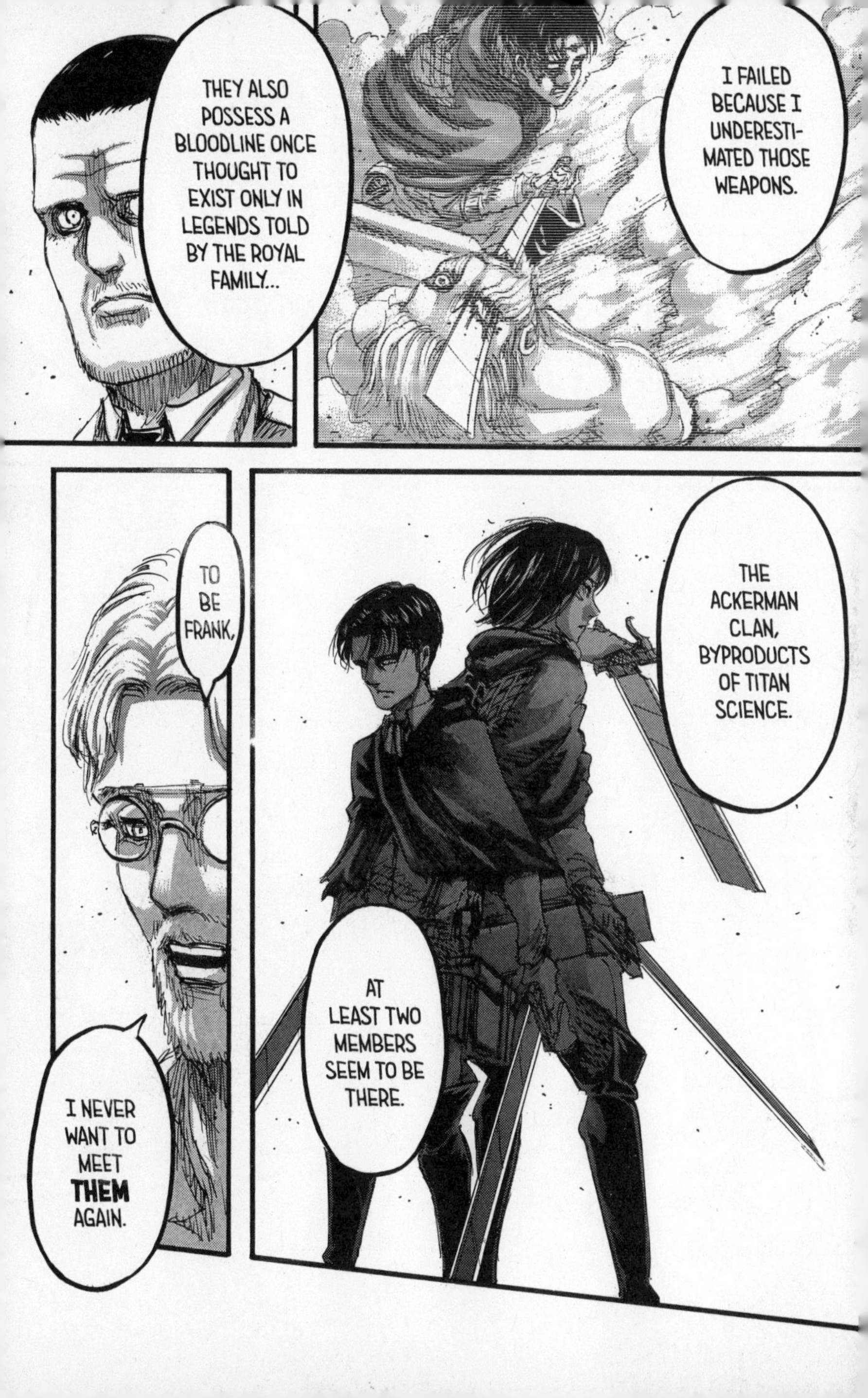
I FAILED BECAUSE I UNDERESTI-MATED THOSE WEAPONS.
THEY ALSO POSSESS A BLOODLINE ONCE THOUGHT TO EXIST ONLY IN LEGENDS TOLD BY THE ROYAL FAMILY...
THE ACKERMAN CLAN, BYPRODUCTS OF TITAN SCIENCE.
AT LEAST TWO MEMBERS SEEM TO BE THERE.
TO BE FRANK,
I NEVER WANT TO MEET **THEM** AGAIN.

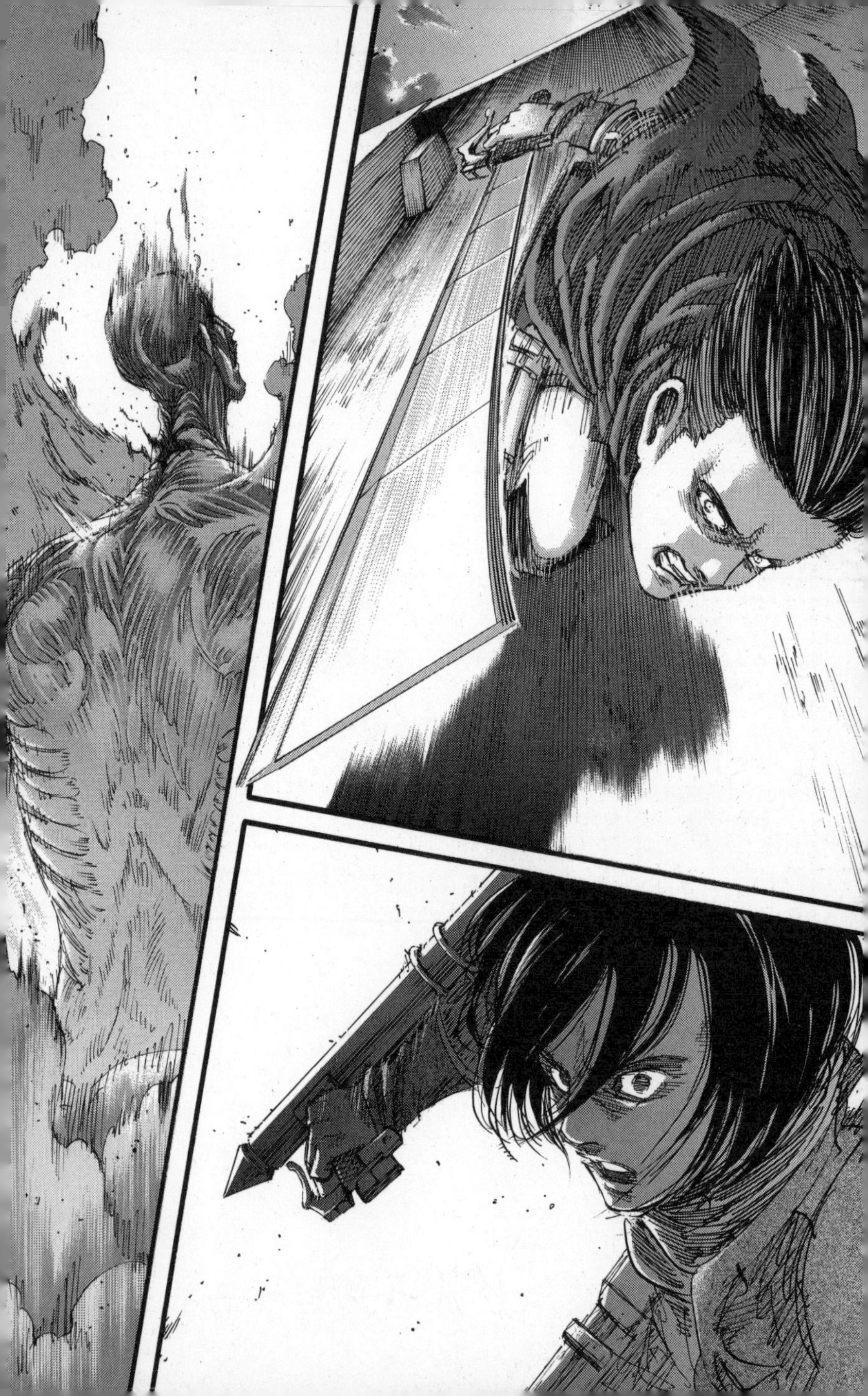

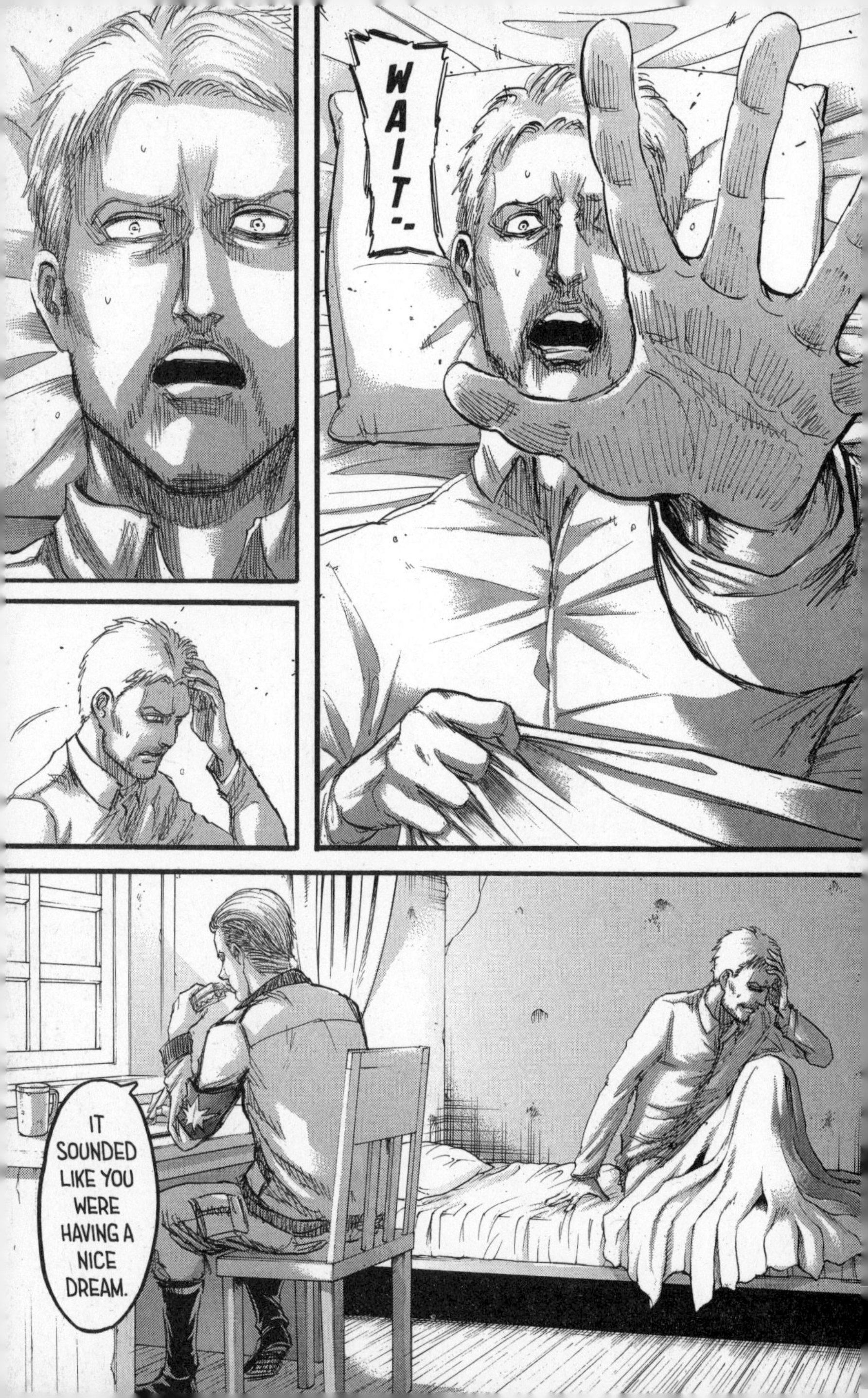
WAIT--
IT SOUNDED LIKE YOU WERE HAVING A NICE DREAM.

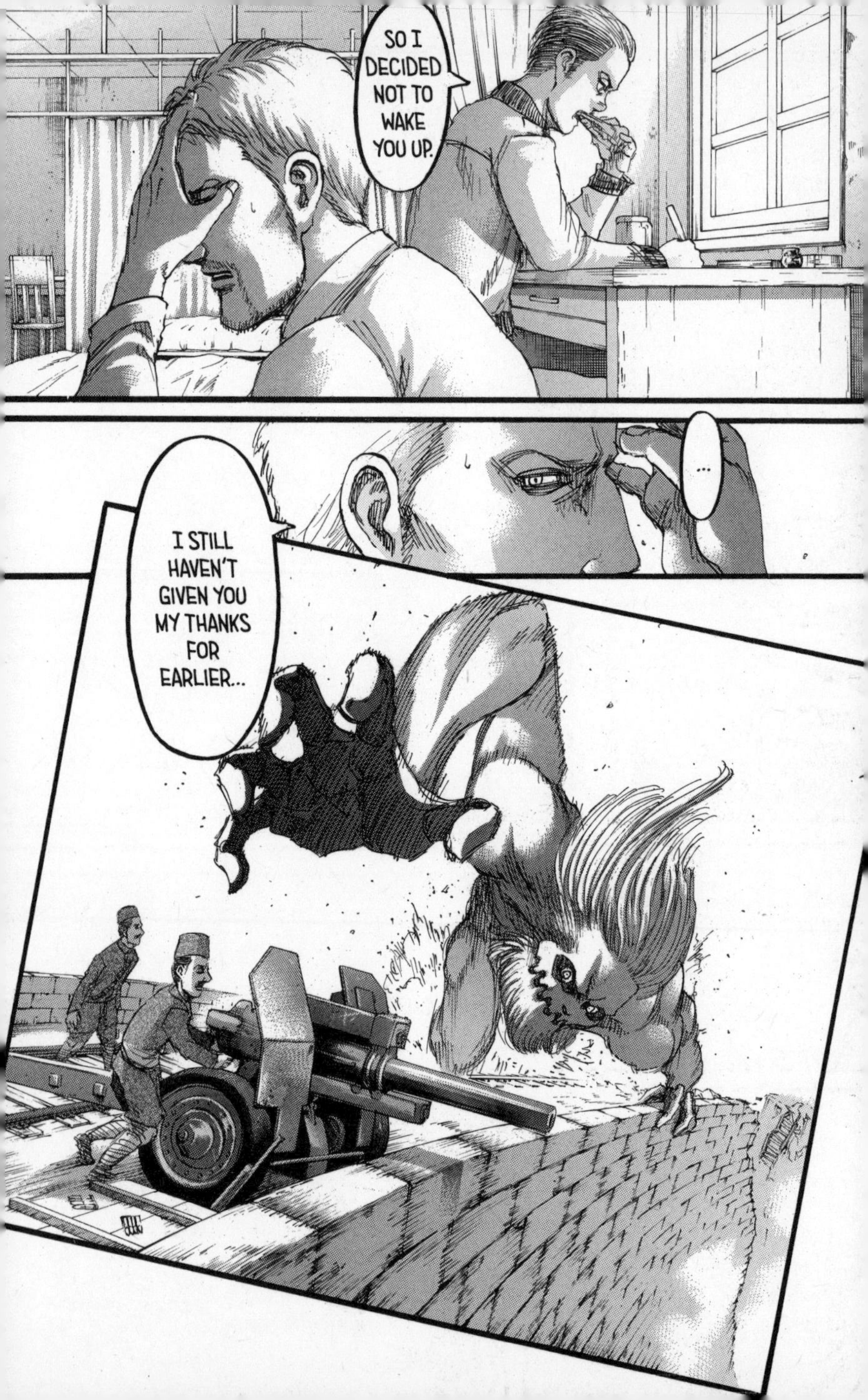
SO I DECIDED NOT TO WAKE YOU UP.
...
I STILL HAVEN'T GIVEN YOU MY THANKS FOR EARLIER...

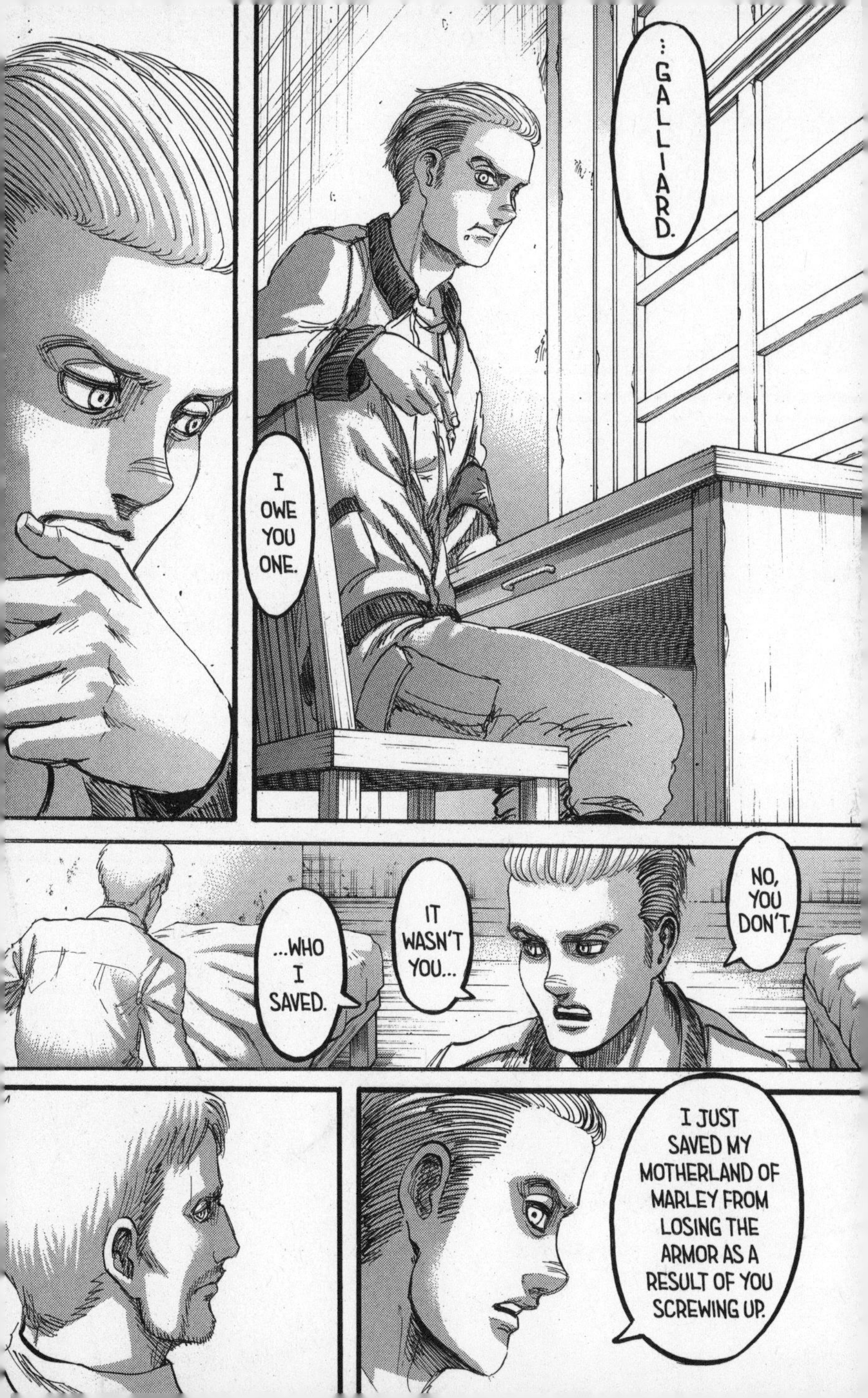
...GALLIARD.
I OWE YOU ONE.
NO, YOU DON'T.
IT WASN'T YOU...
...WHO I SAVED.
I JUST SAVED MY MOTHERLAND OF MARLEY FROM LOSING THE ARMOR AS A RESULT OF YOU SCREWING UP.

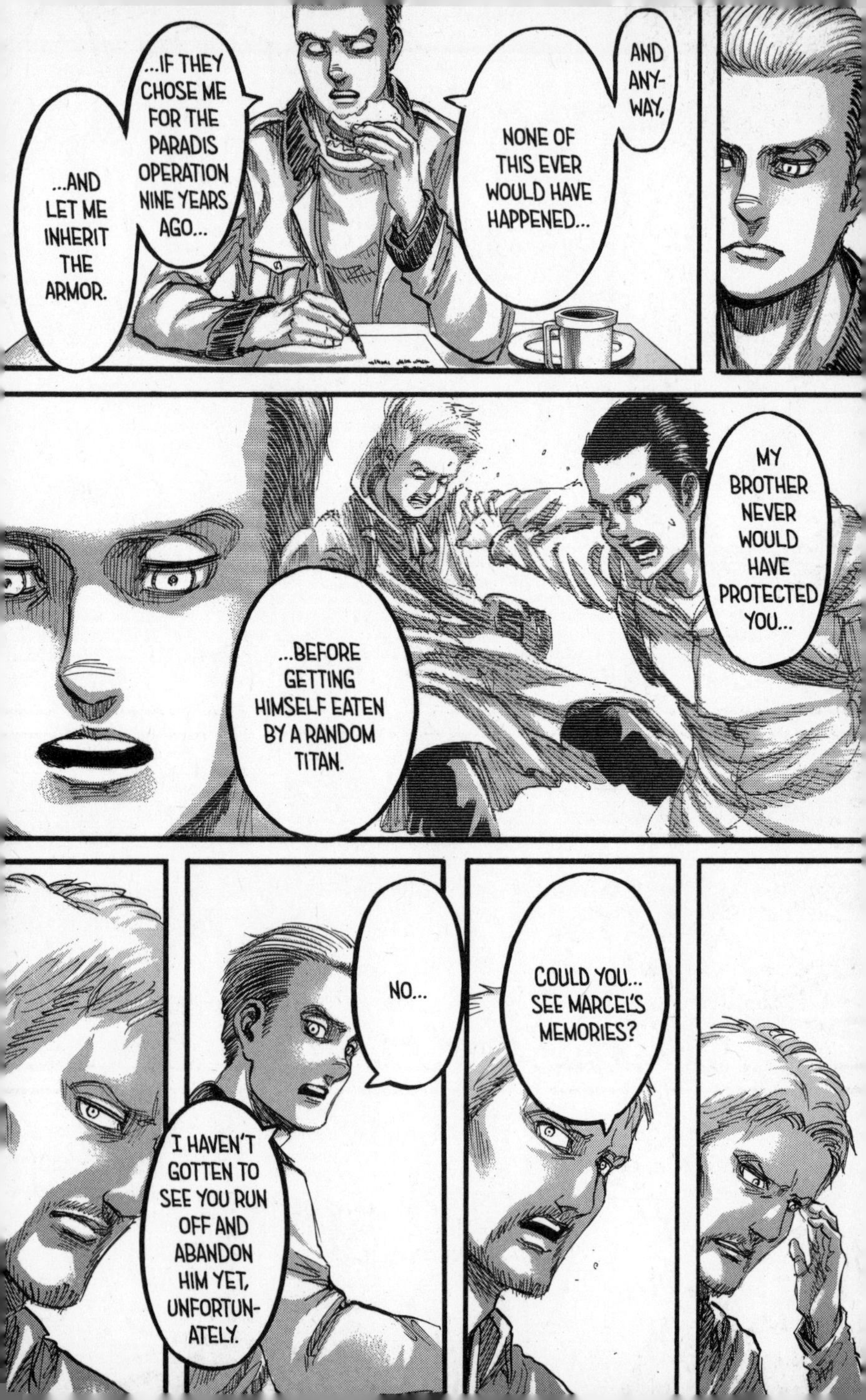
AND ANYWAY,
NONE OF THIS EVER WOULD HAVE HAPPENED...
...IF THEY CHOSE ME FOR THE PARADIS OPERATION NINE YEARS AGO...
...AND LET ME INHERIT THE ARMOR.
MY BROTHER NEVER WOULD HAVE PROTECTED YOU...
...BEFORE GETTING HIMSELF EATEN BY A RANDOM TITAN.
COULD YOU... SEE MARCEL'S MEMORIES?
NO...
I HAVEN'T GOTTEN TO SEE YOU RUN OFF AND ABANDON HIM YET, UNFORTUNATELY.

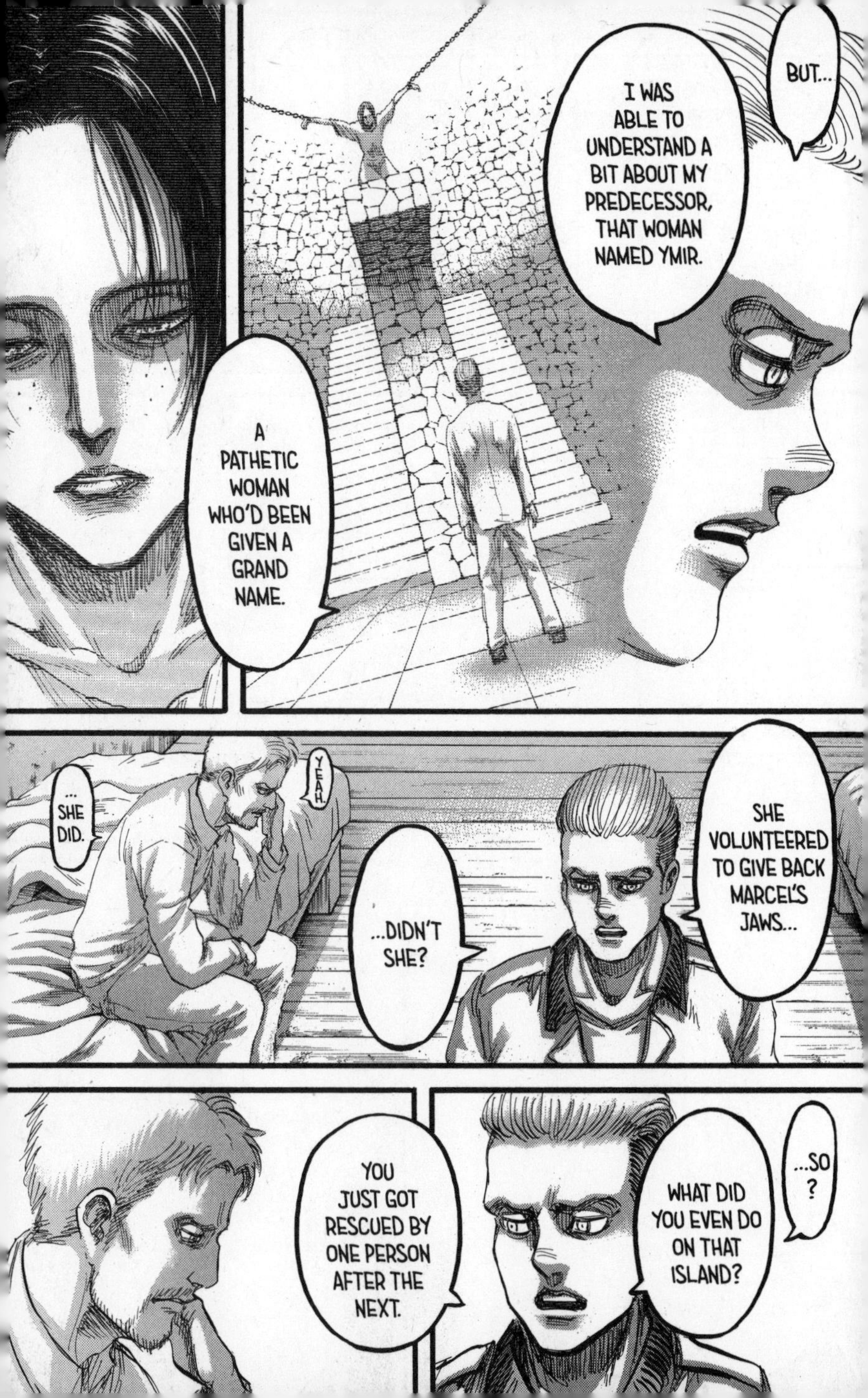
BUT...
I WAS ABLE TO UNDERSTAND A BIT ABOUT MY PREDECESSOR, THAT WOMAN NAMED YMIR.
A PATHETIC WOMAN WHO'D BEEN GIVEN A GRAND NAME.
SHE VOLUNTEERED TO GIVE BACK MARCEL'S JAWS...
...DIDN'T SHE?
YEAH.
... SHE DID.
...SO ?
WHAT DID YOU EVEN DO ON THAT ISLAND?
YOU JUST GOT RESCUED BY ONE PERSON AFTER THE NEXT.

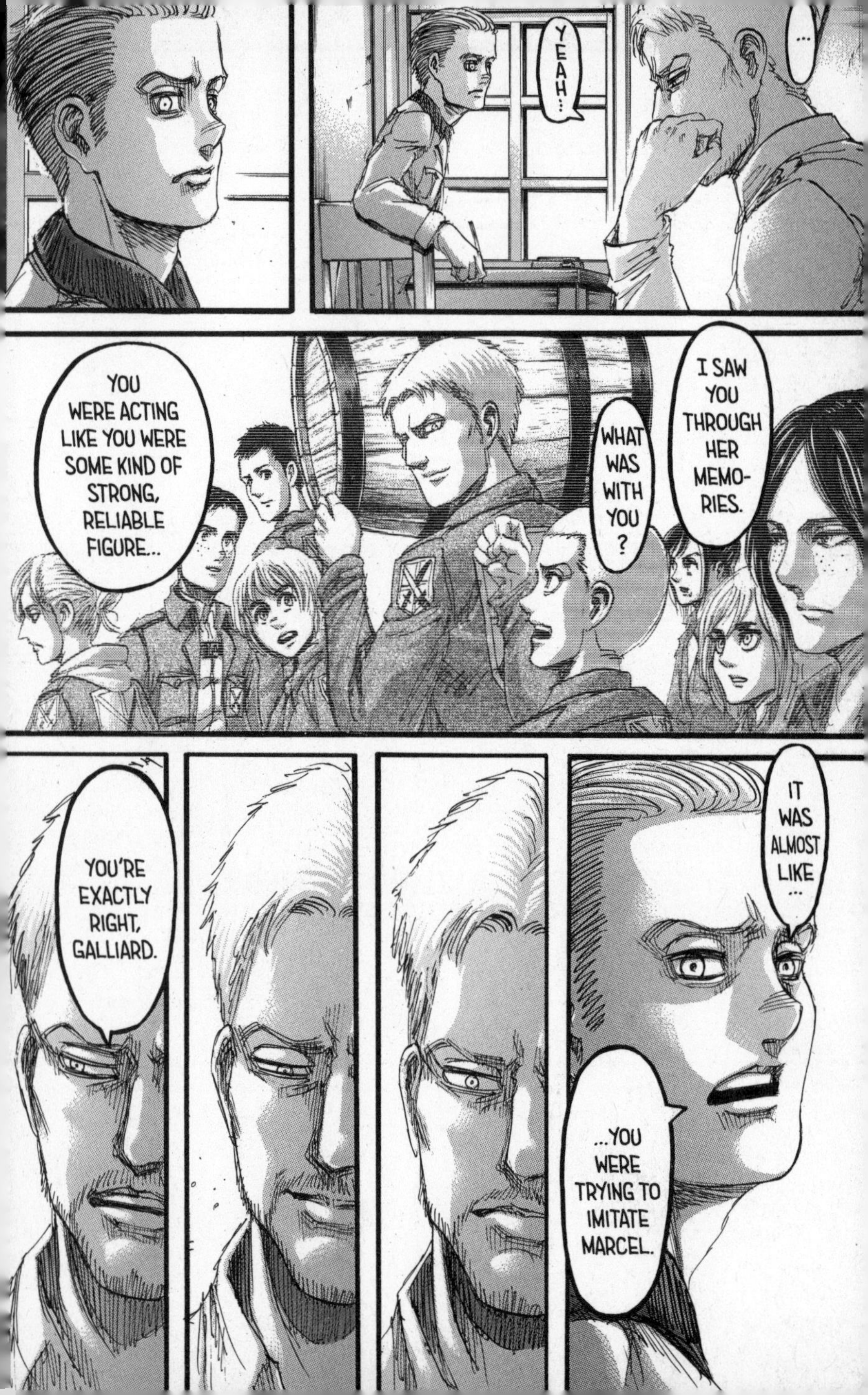
...
YEAH...
I SAW YOU THROUGH HER MEMORIES.
WHAT WAS WITH YOU?
YOU WERE ACTING LIKE YOU WERE SOME KIND OF STRONG, RELIABLE FIGURE...
IT WAS ALMOST LIKE...
...YOU WERE TRYING TO IMITATE MARCEL.
YOU'RE EXACTLY RIGHT, GALLIARD.

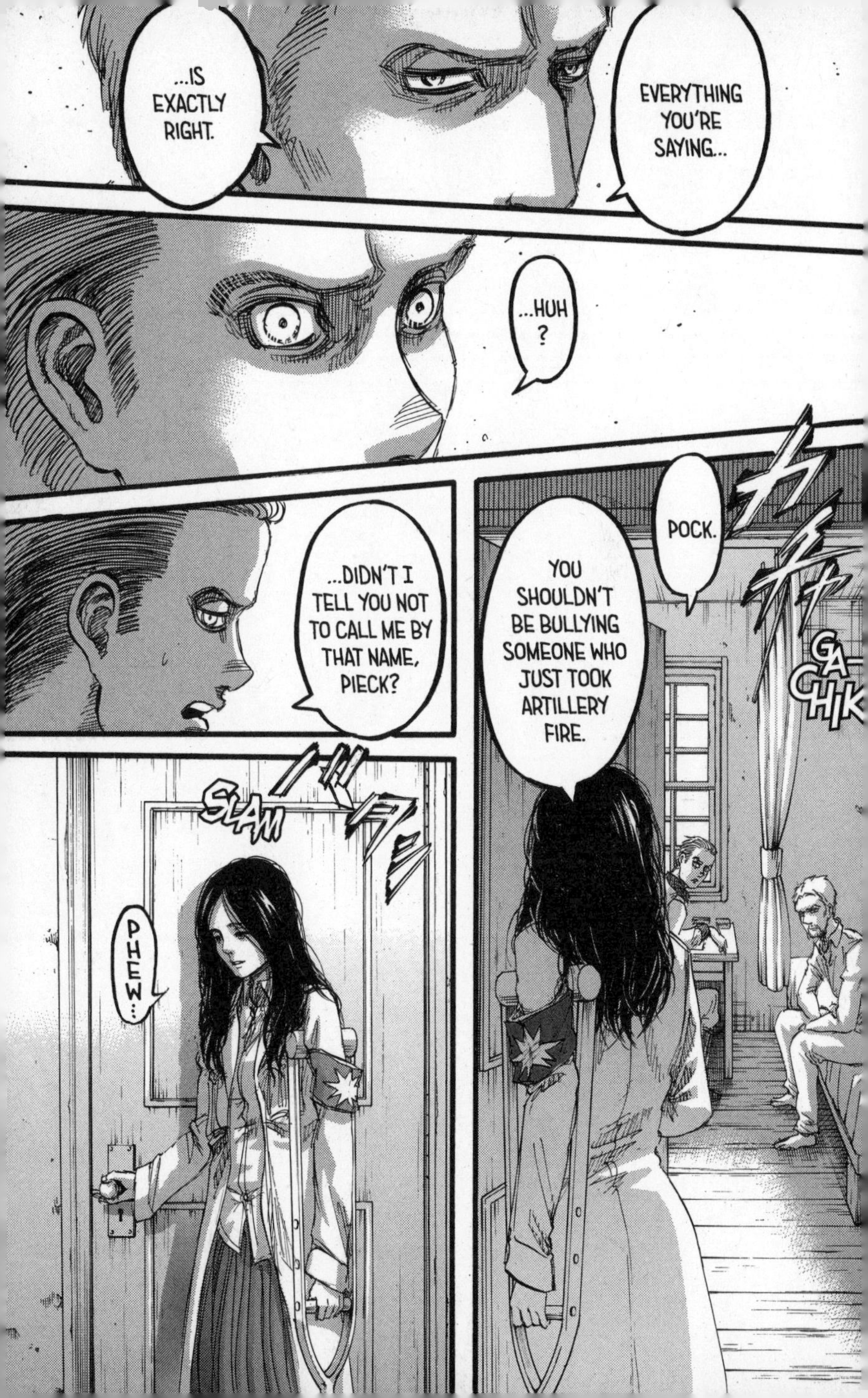
EVERYTHING YOU'RE SAYING...
...IS EXACTLY RIGHT.
...HUH ?
POCK.
GA-CHIK
YOU SHOULDN'T BE BULLYING SOMEONE WHO JUST TOOK ARTILLERY FIRE.
...DIDN'T I TELL YOU NOT TO CALL ME BY THAT NAME, PIECK?
SLAM
PHEW...

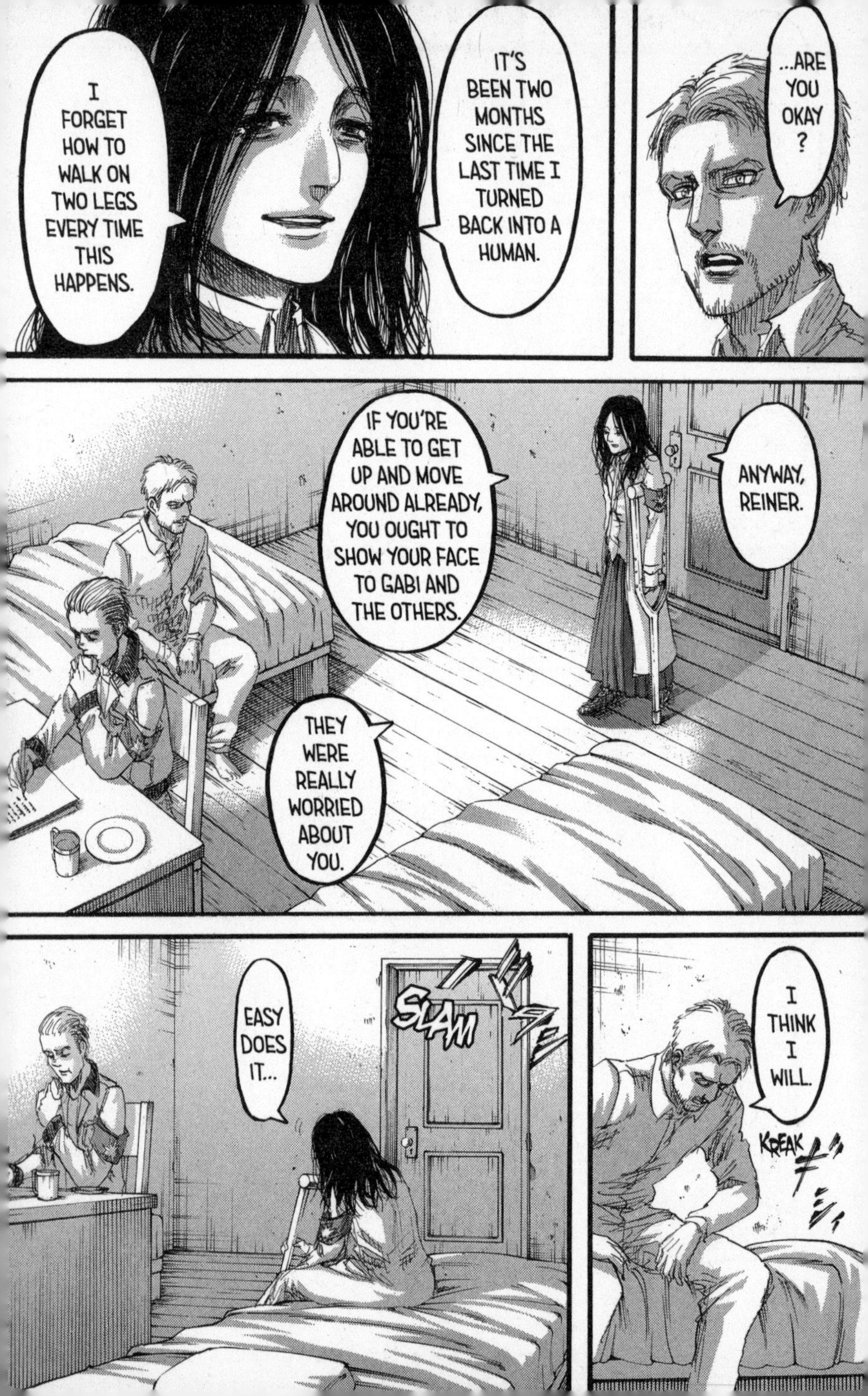
...ARE YOU OKAY?
IT'S BEEN TWO MONTHS SINCE THE LAST TIME I TURNED BACK INTO A HUMAN.
I FORGET HOW TO WALK ON TWO LEGS EVERY TIME THIS HAPPENS.
ANYWAY, REINER.
IF YOU'RE ABLE TO GET UP AND MOVE AROUND ALREADY, YOU OUGHT TO SHOW YOUR FACE TO GABI AND THE OTHERS.
THEY WERE REALLY WORRIED ABOUT YOU.
I THINK I WILL.
KREAK
SLAM
EASY DOES IT...

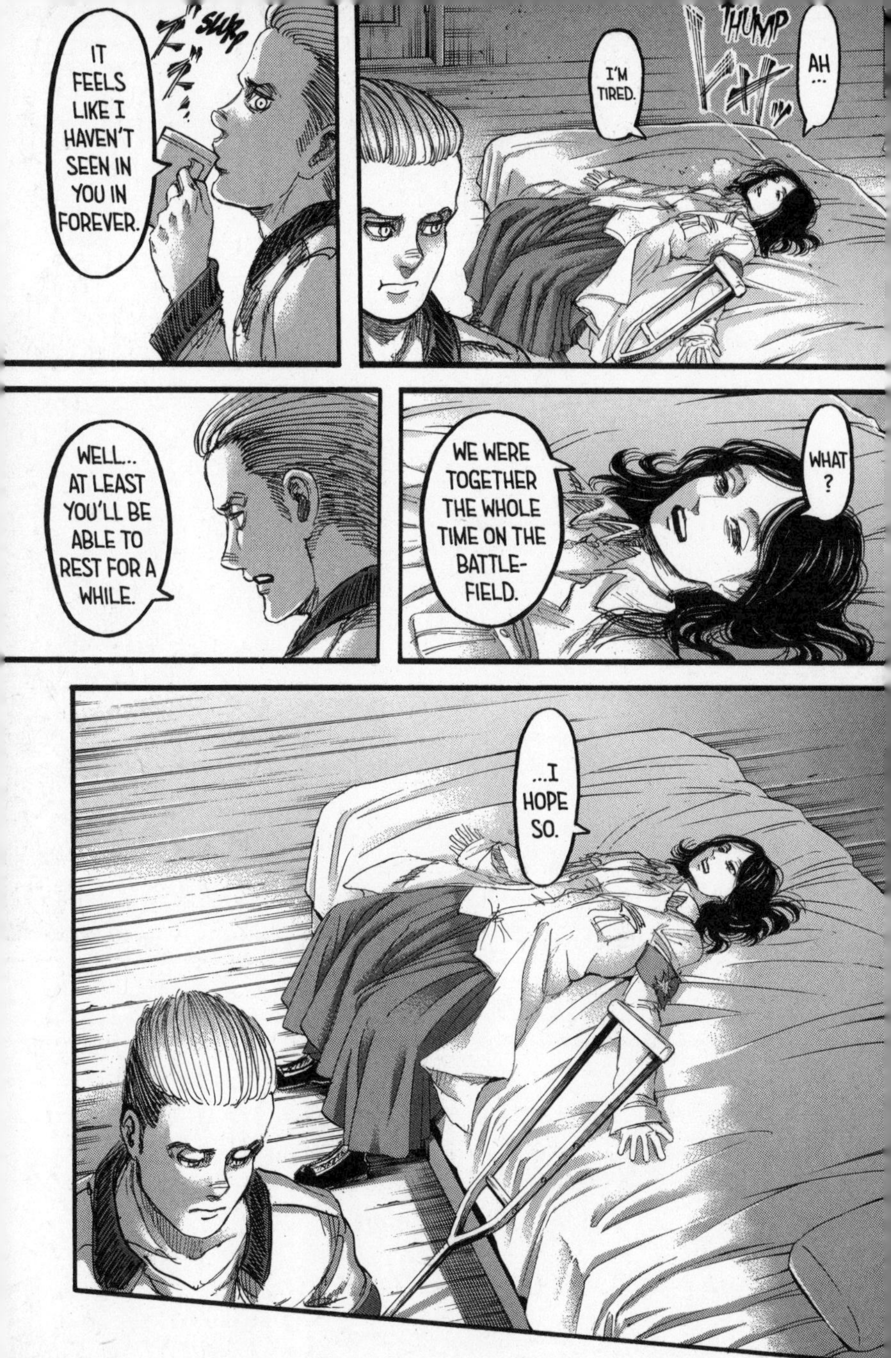
THUMP
AH...
I'M TIRED.
SLURP
IT FEELS LIKE I HAVEN'T SEEN IN YOU IN FOREVER.
WHAT?
WE WERE TOGETHER THE WHOLE TIME ON THE BATTLE-FIELD.
WELL... AT LEAST YOU'LL BE ABLE TO REST FOR A WHILE.
...I HOPE SO.

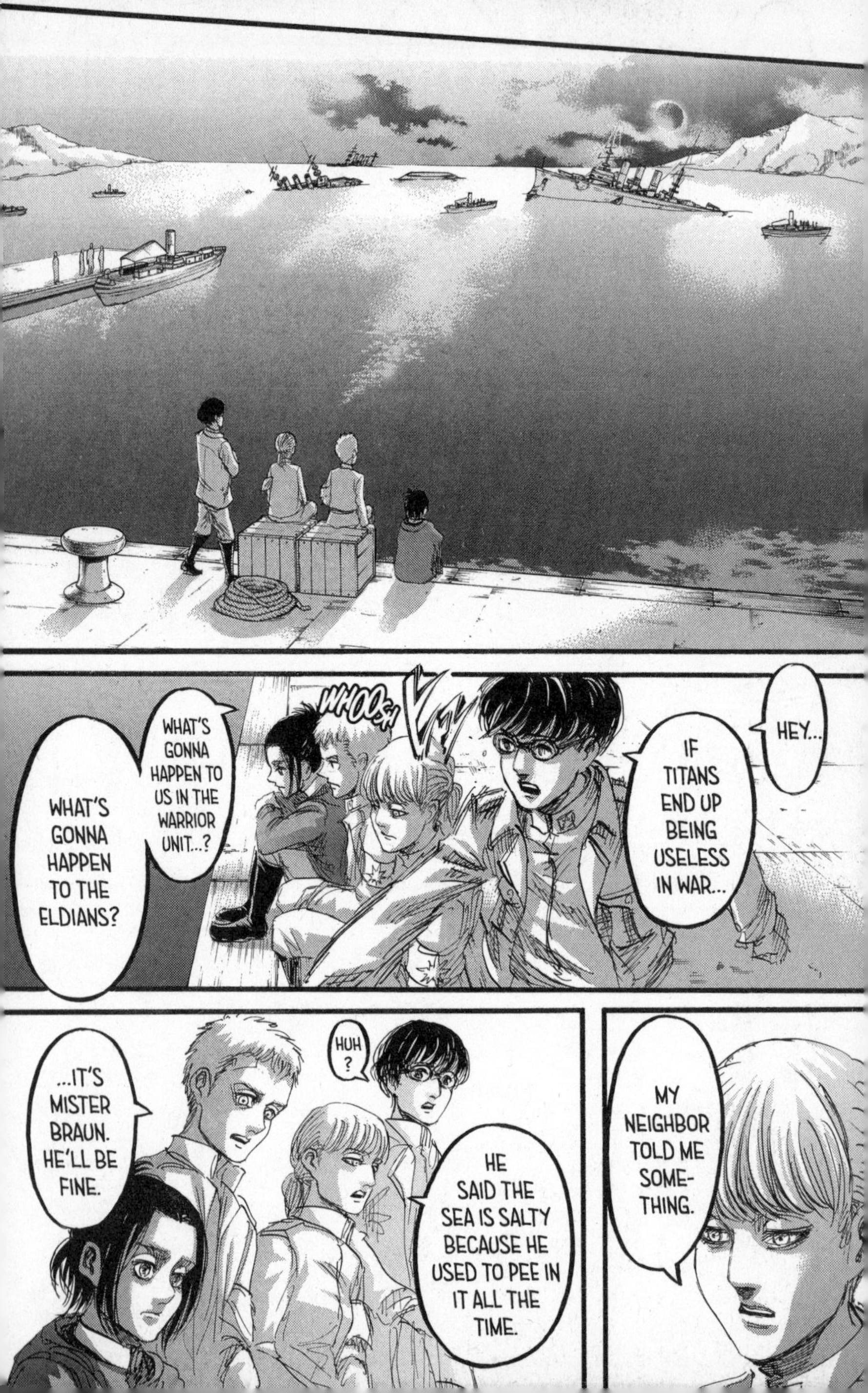
HEY...
IF TITANS END UP BEING USELESS IN WAR...
WHOOSH
WHAT'S GONNA HAPPEN TO US IN THE WARRIOR UNIT...?
WHAT'S GONNA HAPPEN TO THE ELDIANS?
MY NEIGHBOR TOLD ME SOME-THING.
HUH?
HE SAID THE SEA IS SALTY BECAUSE HE USED TO PEE IN IT ALL THE TIME.
...IT'S MISTER BRAUN. HE'LL BE FINE.

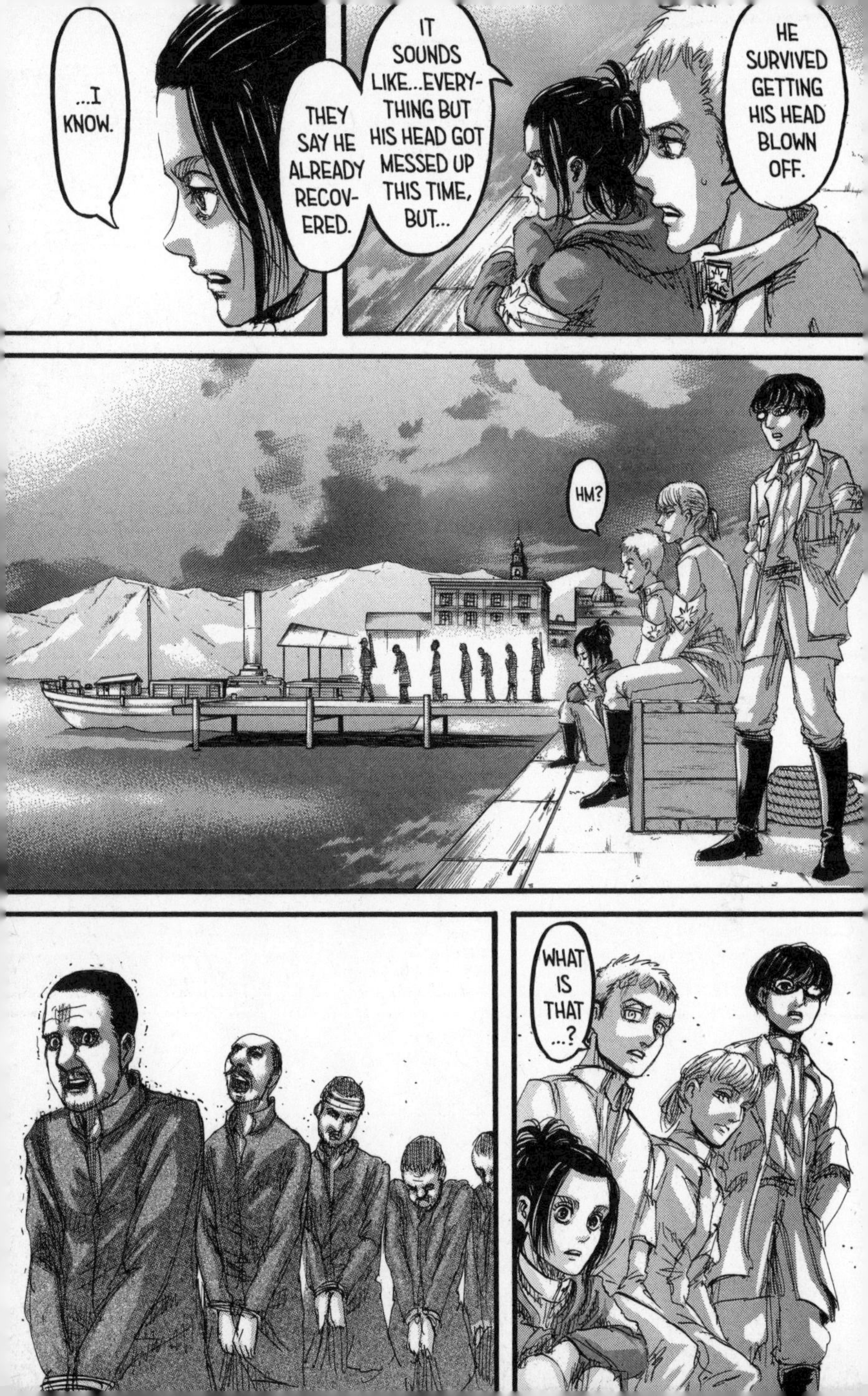
HE SURVIVED GETTING HIS HEAD BLOWN OFF.
IT SOUNDS LIKE...EVERYTHING BUT HIS HEAD GOT MESSED UP THIS TIME, BUT...
THEY SAY HE ALREADY RECOVERED.
...I KNOW.
HM?
WHAT IS THAT ...?

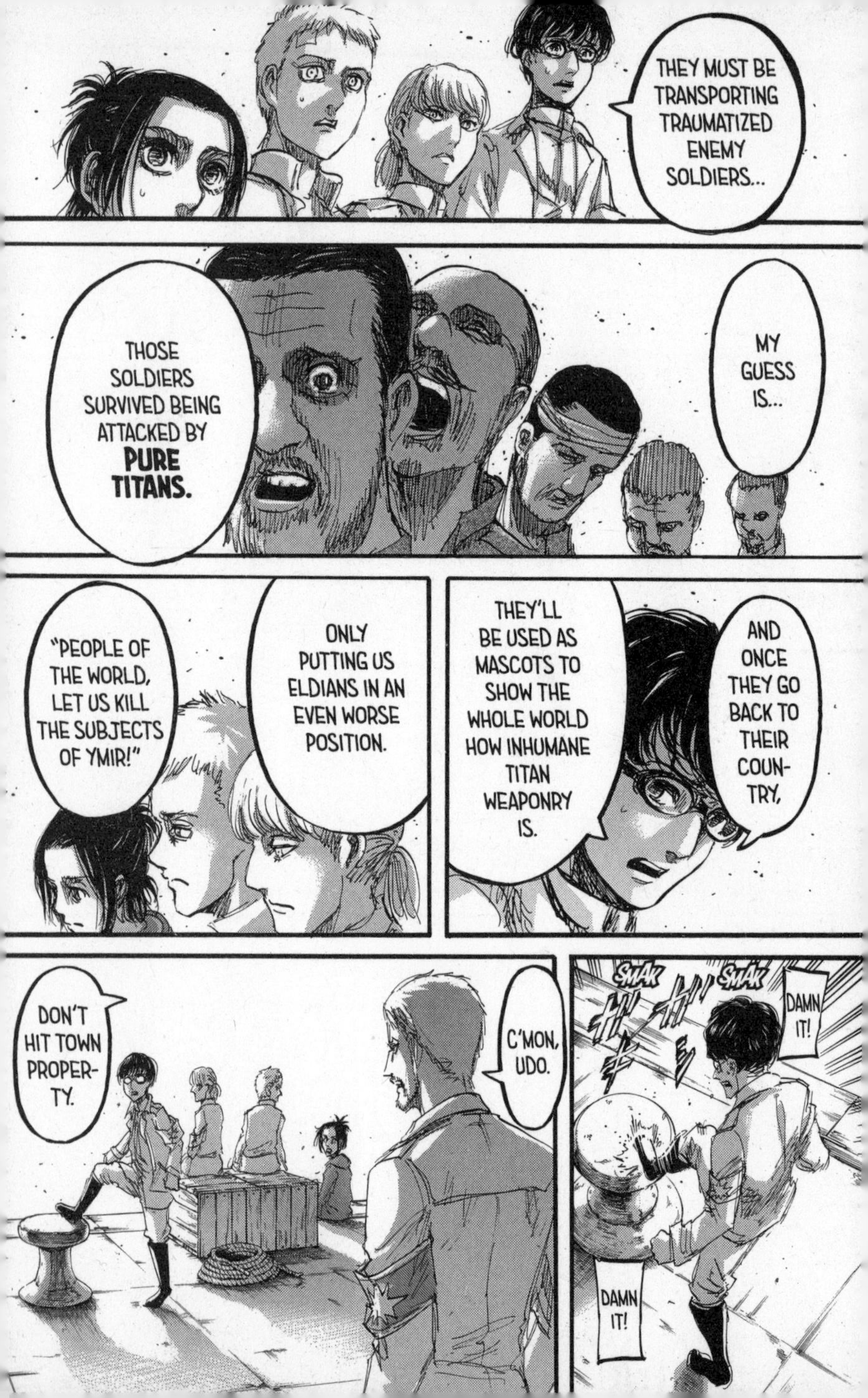
THEY MUST BE TRANSPORTING TRAUMATIZED ENEMY SOLDIERS...
MY GUESS IS...
THOSE SOLDIERS SURVIVED BEING ATTACKED BY **PURE TITANS.**
AND ONCE THEY GO BACK TO THEIR COUN-TRY,
THEY'LL BE USED AS MASCOTS TO SHOW THE WHOLE WORLD HOW INHUMANE TITAN WEAPONRY IS.
ONLY PUTTING US ELDIANS IN AN EVEN WORSE POSITION.
"PEOPLE OF THE WORLD, LET US KILL THE SUBJECTS OF YMIR!"
SMAK
SMAK
DAMN IT!
DAMN IT!
C'MON, UDO.
DON'T HIT TOWN PROPER-TY.

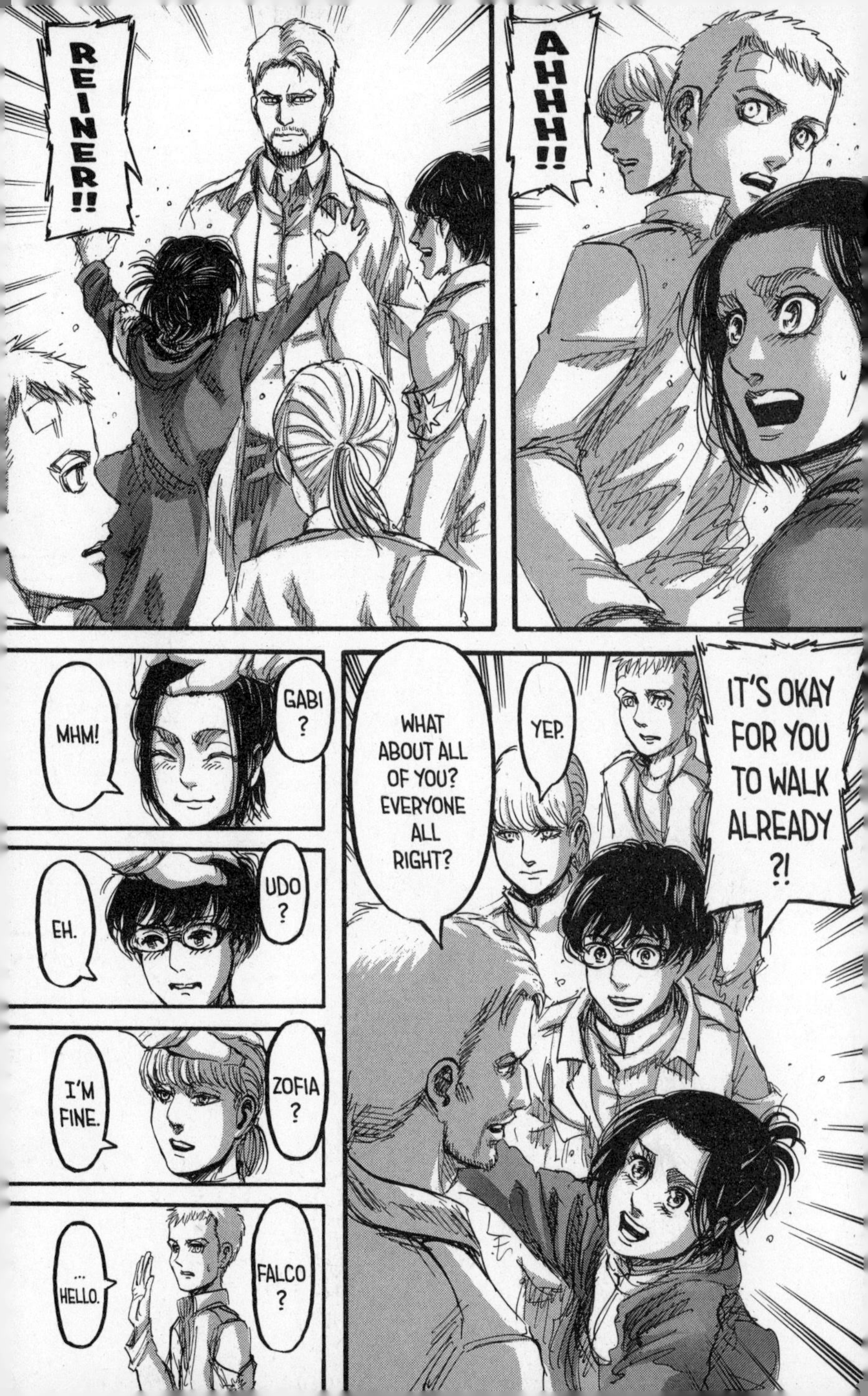
AHHHH!!
REINER!!
IT'S OKAY FOR YOU TO WALK ALREADY ?!
YEP.
WHAT ABOUT ALL OF YOU? EVERYONE ALL RIGHT?
GABI ?
MHM!
UDO ?
EH.
ZOFIA ?
I'M FINE.
FALCO ?
... HELLO.

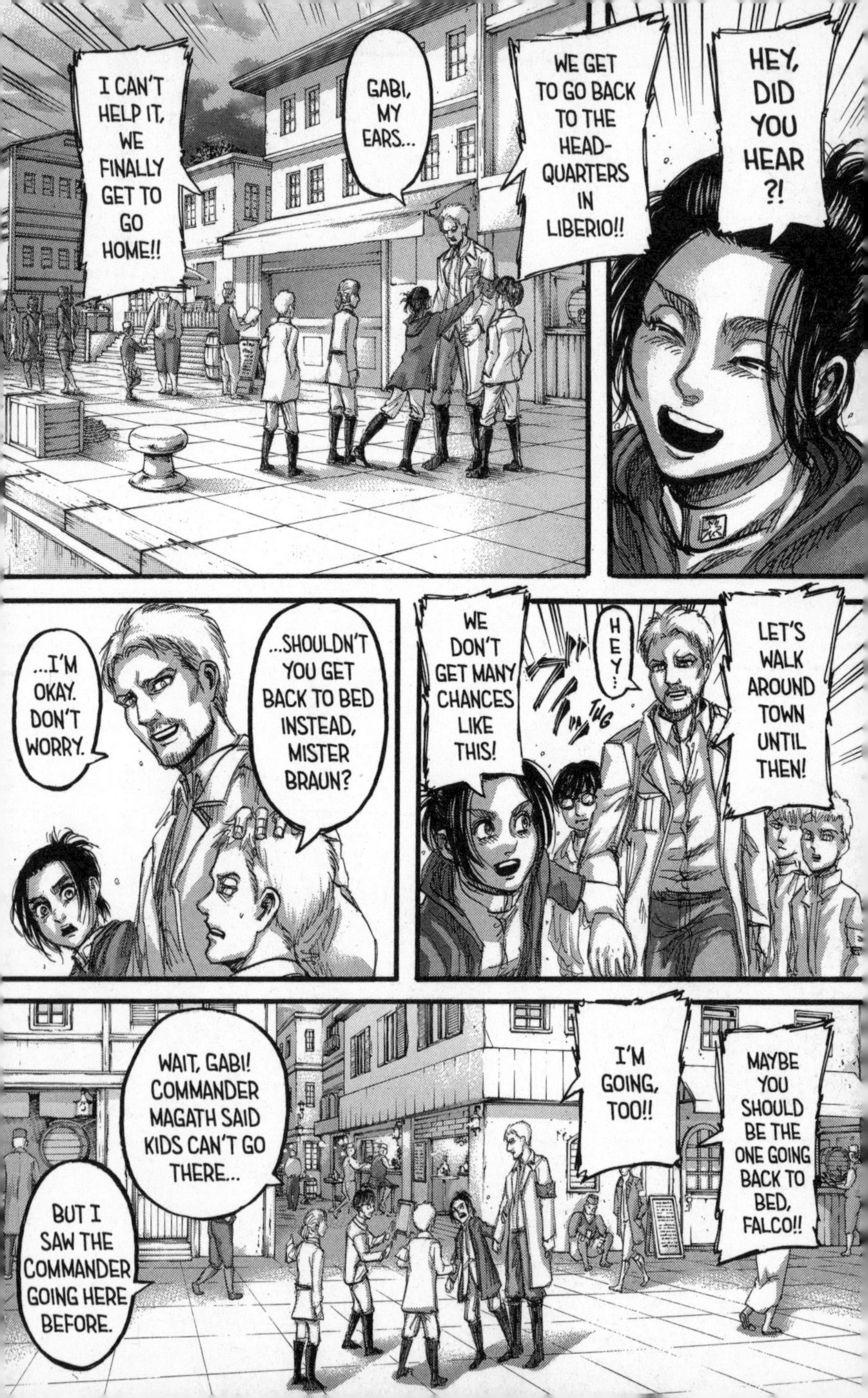
HEY, DID YOU HEAR?!
WE GET TO GO BACK TO THE HEAD-QUARTERS IN LIBERIO!!
GABI, MY EARS...
I CAN'T HELP IT, WE FINALLY GET TO GO HOME!!
LET'S WALK AROUND TOWN UNTIL THEN!
HEY...
WE DON'T GET MANY CHANCES LIKE THIS!
...SHOULDN'T YOU GET BACK TO BED INSTEAD, MISTER BRAUN?
...I'M OKAY. DON'T WORRY.
MAYBE YOU SHOULD BE THE ONE GOING BACK TO BED, FALCO!!
I'M GOING, TOO!!
WAIT, GABI! COMMANDER MAGATH SAID KIDS CAN'T GO THERE...
BUT I SAW THE COMMANDER GOING HERE BEFORE.

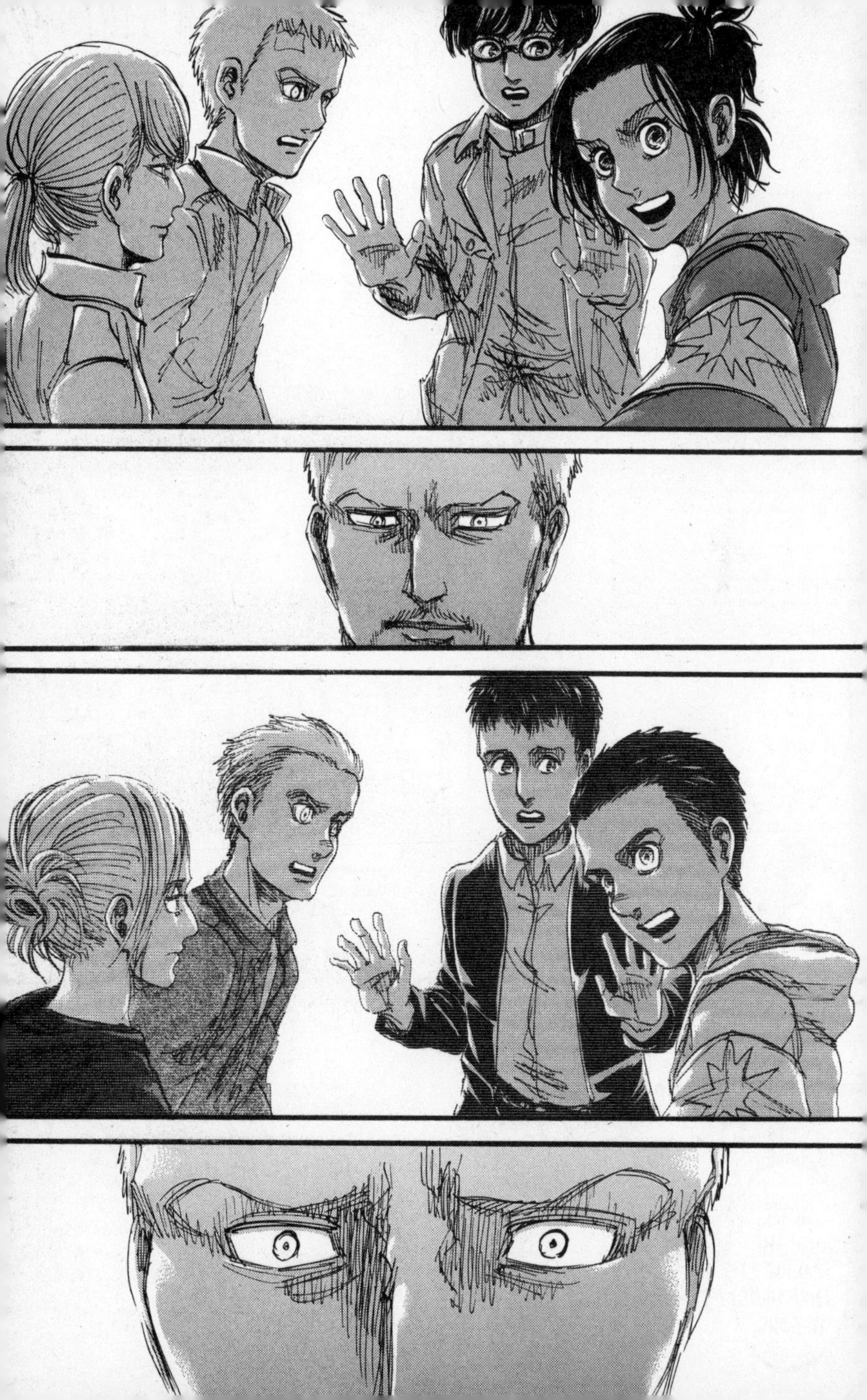

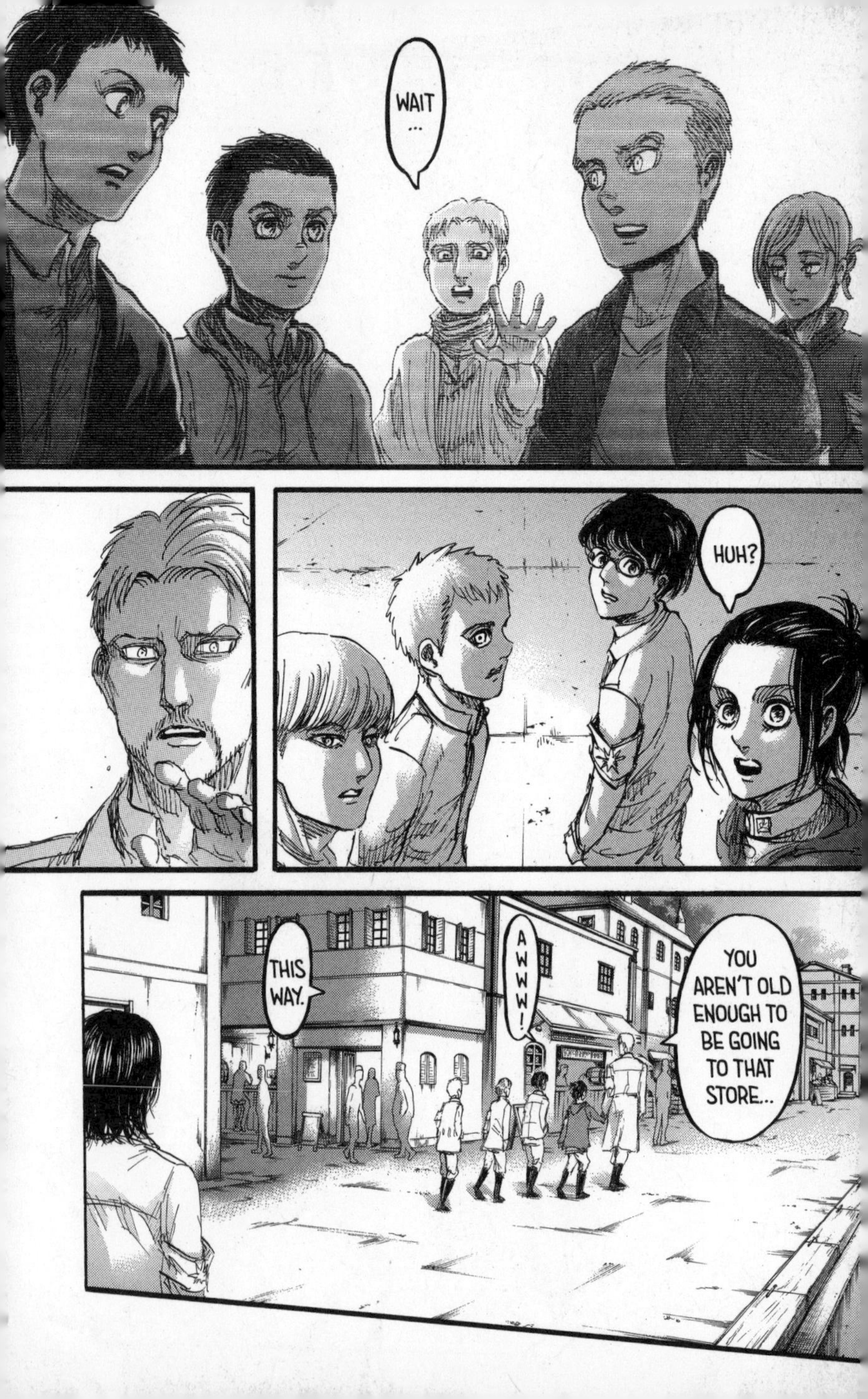
WAIT ...
HUH?
YOU AREN'T OLD ENOUGH TO BE GOING TO THAT STORE...
AWWW!
THIS WAY.

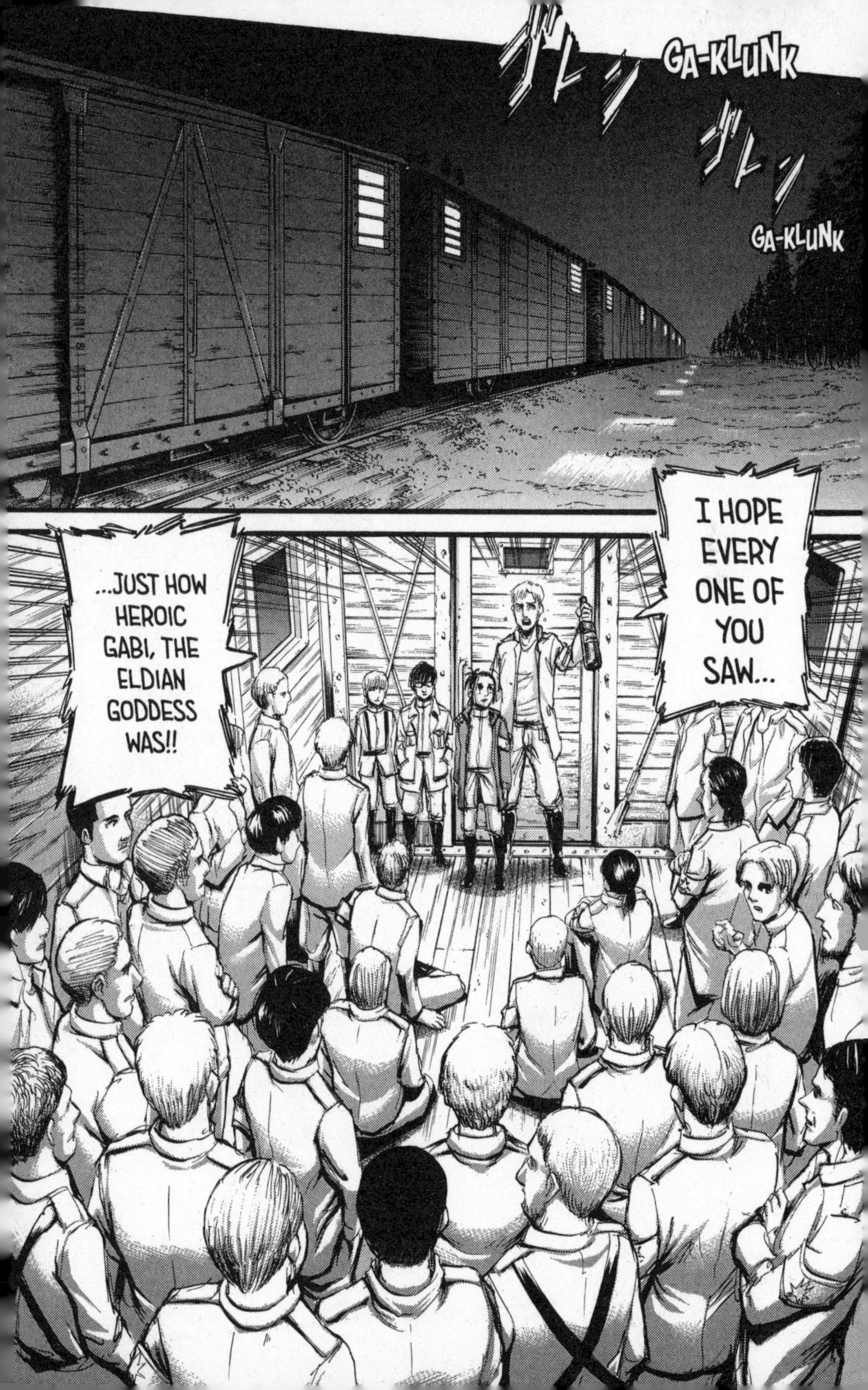
GA-KLUNK
GA-KLUNK
I HOPE EVERY ONE OF YOU SAW...
...JUST HOW HEROIC GABI, THE ELDIAN GODDESS WAS!!

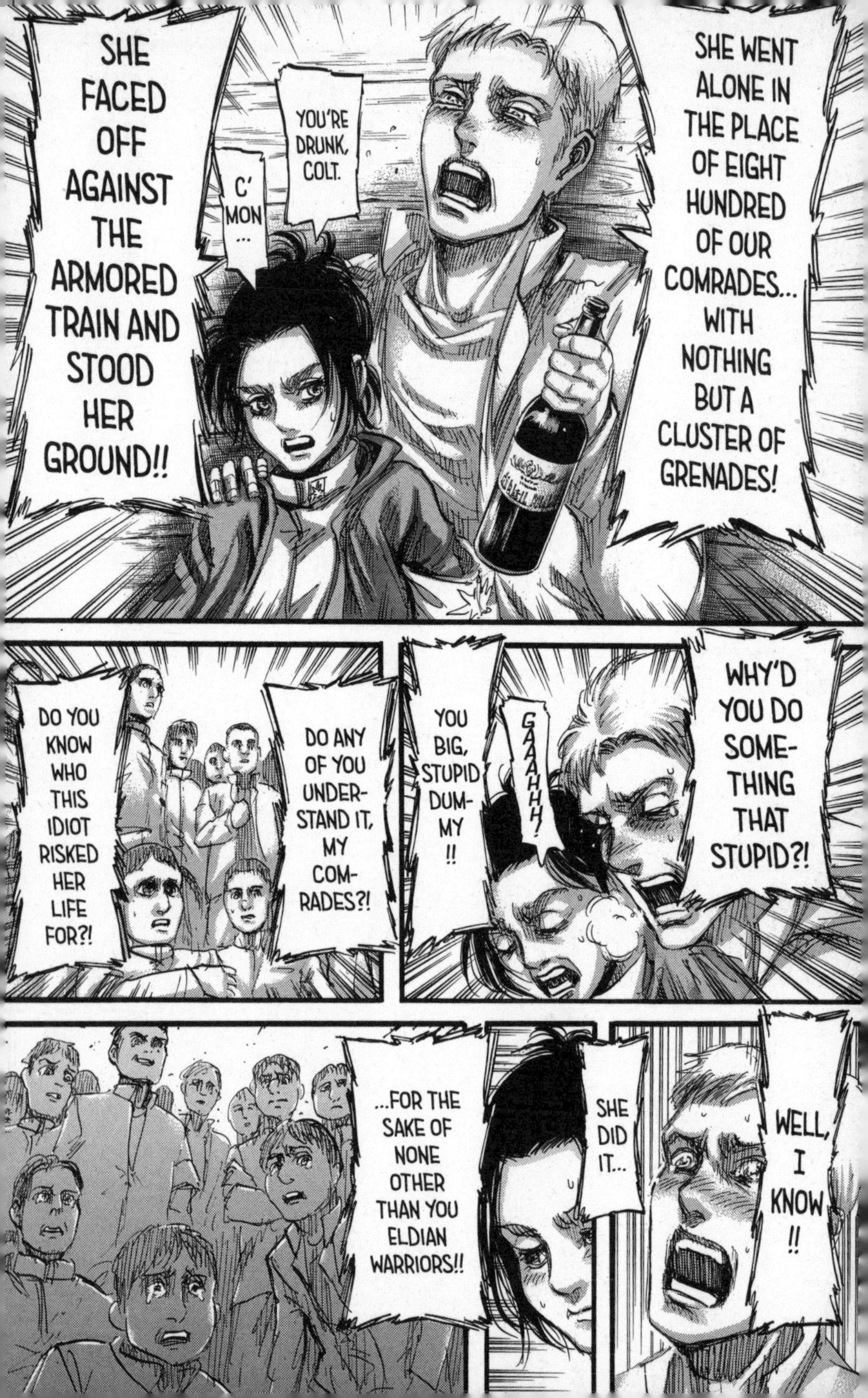
SHE WENT ALONE IN THE PLACE OF EIGHT HUNDRED OF OUR COMRADES... WITH NOTHING BUT A CLUSTER OF GRENADES!
YOU'RE DRUNK, COLT.
C'MON...
SHE FACED OFF AGAINST THE ARMORED TRAIN AND STOOD HER GROUND!!
WHY'D YOU DO SOME-THING THAT STUPID?!
GAAAHHH!
YOU BIG, STUPID DUM-MY!!
DO ANY OF YOU UNDER-STAND IT, MY COM-RADES?!
DO YOU KNOW WHO THIS IDIOT RISKED HER LIFE FOR?!
WELL, I KNOW!!
SHE DID IT...
...FOR THE SAKE OF NONE OTHER THAN YOU ELDIAN WARRIORS!!

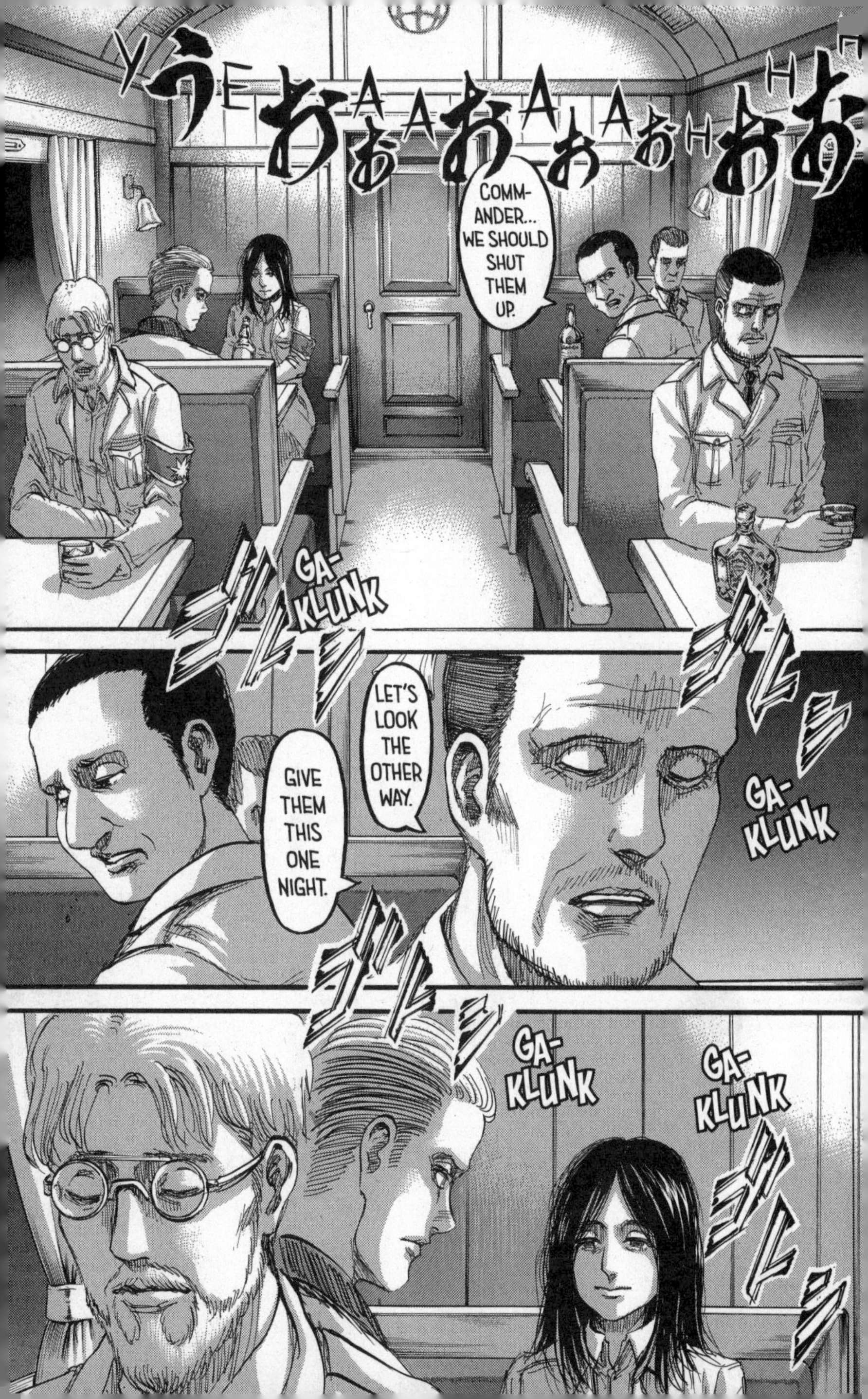
YEAAAAHH
COMMANDER... WE SHOULD SHUT THEM UP.
GA-KLUNK
GA-KLUNK
LET'S LOOK THE OTHER WAY.
GIVE THEM THIS ONE NIGHT.
GA-KLUNK
GA-KLUNK

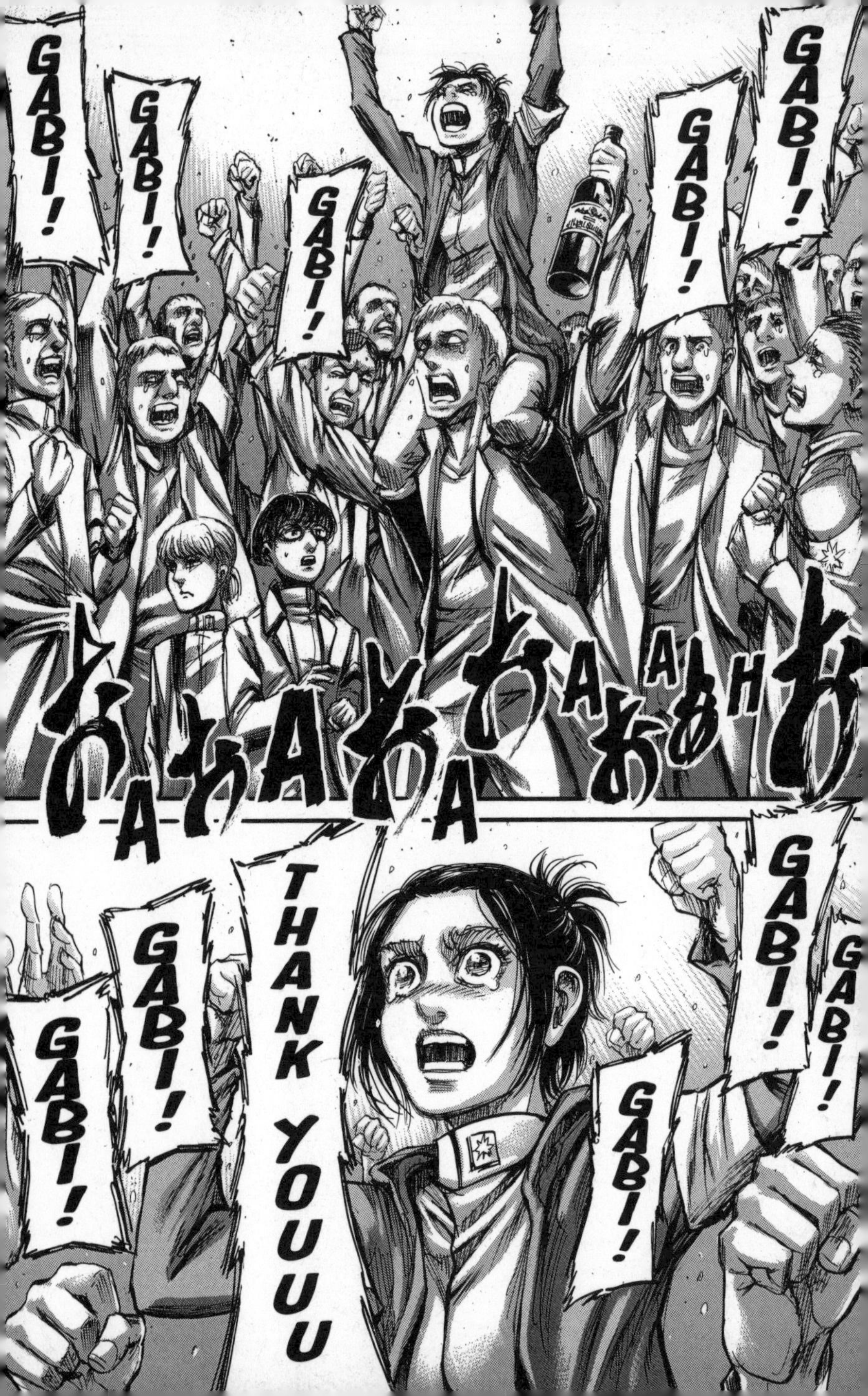
GABI!
GABI!
GABI!
GABI!
GABI!
AAAAAH
GABI!
GABI!
GABI!
THANK YOUUU
GABI!
GABI!

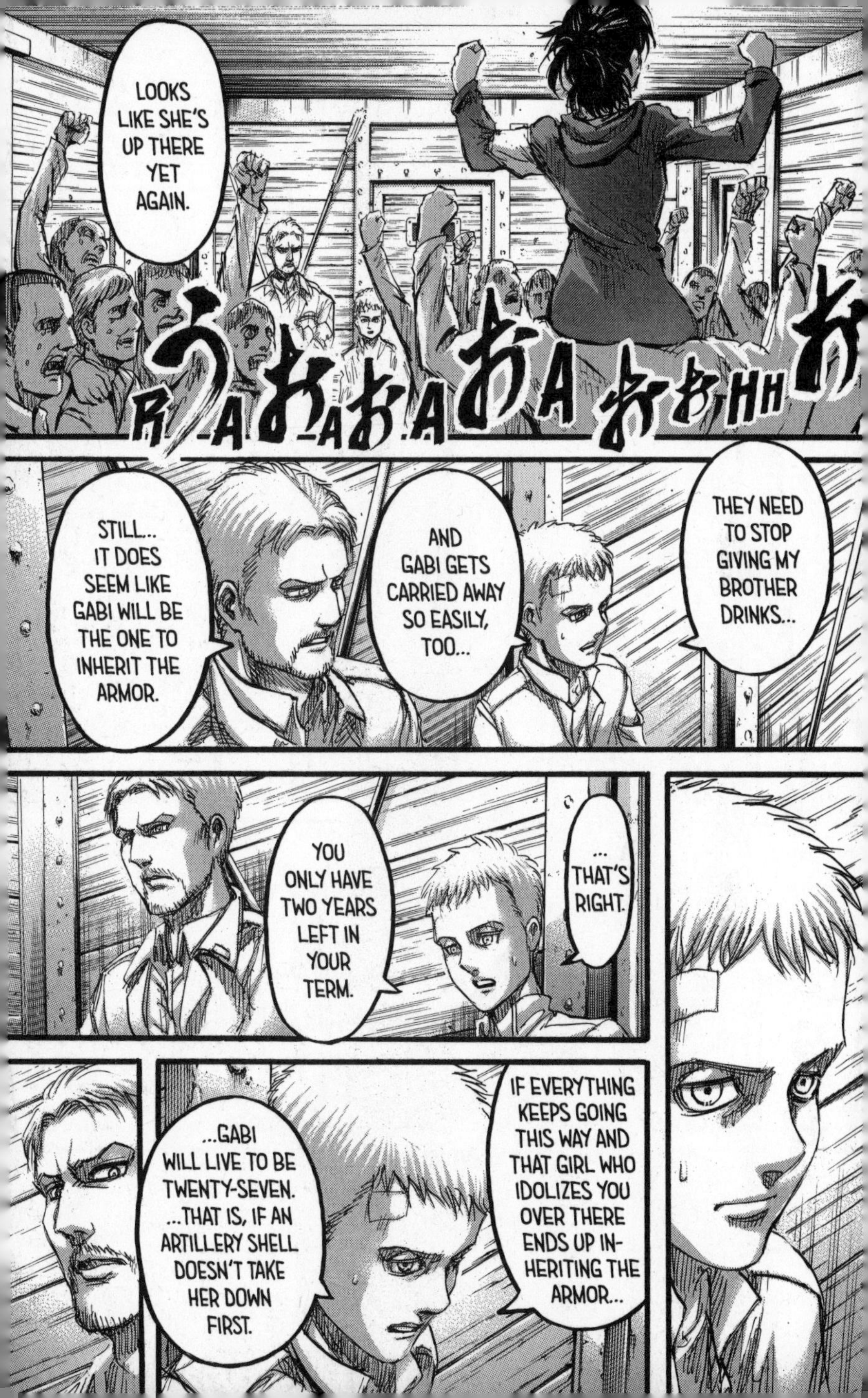
LOOKS LIKE SHE'S UP THERE YET AGAIN.
RAAAAHH
うおおおおおお
THEY NEED TO STOP GIVING MY BROTHER DRINKS...
AND GABI GETS CARRIED AWAY SO EASILY, TOO...
STILL... IT DOES SEEM LIKE GABI WILL BE THE ONE TO INHERIT THE ARMOR.
...THAT'S RIGHT.
YOU ONLY HAVE TWO YEARS LEFT IN YOUR TERM.
IF EVERYTHING KEEPS GOING THIS WAY AND THAT GIRL WHO IDOLIZES YOU OVER THERE ENDS UP INHERITING THE ARMOR...
...GABI WILL LIVE TO BE TWENTY-SEVEN. ...THAT IS, IF AN ARTILLERY SHELL DOESN'T TAKE HER DOWN FIRST.

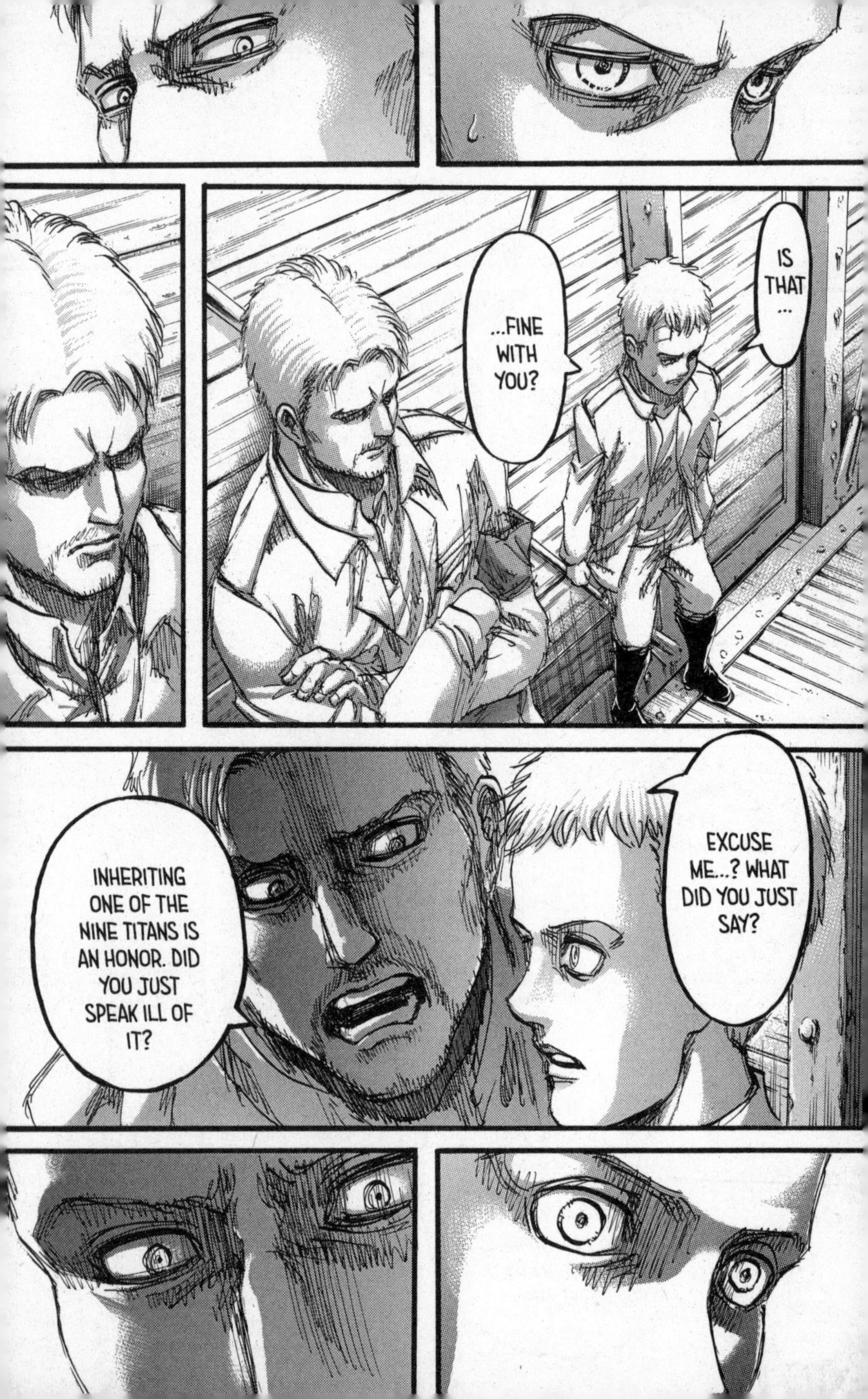
IS THAT ...
...FINE WITH YOU?
EXCUSE ME...? WHAT DID YOU JUST SAY?
INHERITING ONE OF THE NINE TITANS IS AN HONOR. DID YOU JUST SPEAK ILL OF IT?

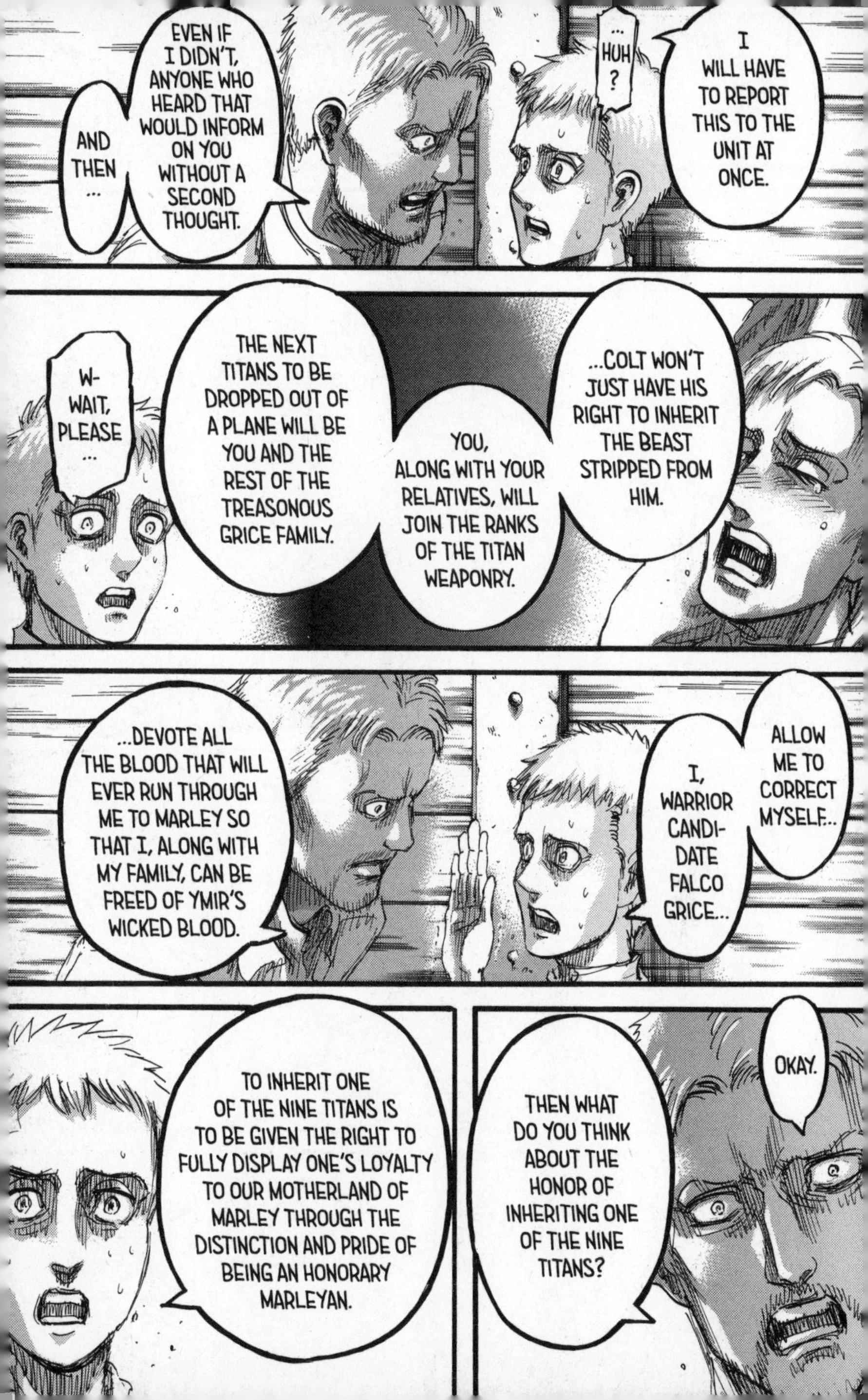
I WILL HAVE TO REPORT THIS TO THE UNIT AT ONCE.
...HUH?
EVEN IF I DIDN'T, ANYONE WHO HEARD THAT WOULD INFORM ON YOU WITHOUT A SECOND THOUGHT.
AND THEN ...
...COLT WON'T JUST HAVE HIS RIGHT TO INHERIT THE BEAST STRIPPED FROM HIM.
YOU, ALONG WITH YOUR RELATIVES, WILL JOIN THE RANKS OF THE TITAN WEAPONRY.
THE NEXT TITANS TO BE DROPPED OUT OF A PLANE WILL BE YOU AND THE REST OF THE TREASONOUS GRICE FAMILY.
W- WAIT, PLEASE ...
ALLOW ME TO CORRECT MYSELF...
I, WARRIOR CANDIDATE FALCO GRICE...
...DEVOTE ALL THE BLOOD THAT WILL EVER RUN THROUGH ME TO MARLEY SO THAT I, ALONG WITH MY FAMILY, CAN BE FREED OF YMIR'S WICKED BLOOD.
OKAY.
THEN WHAT DO YOU THINK ABOUT THE HONOR OF INHERITING ONE OF THE NINE TITANS?
TO INHERIT ONE OF THE NINE TITANS IS TO BE GIVEN THE RIGHT TO FULLY DISPLAY ONE'S LOYALTY TO OUR MOTHERLAND OF MARLEY THROUGH THE DISTINCTION AND PRIDE OF BEING AN HONORARY MARLEYAN.

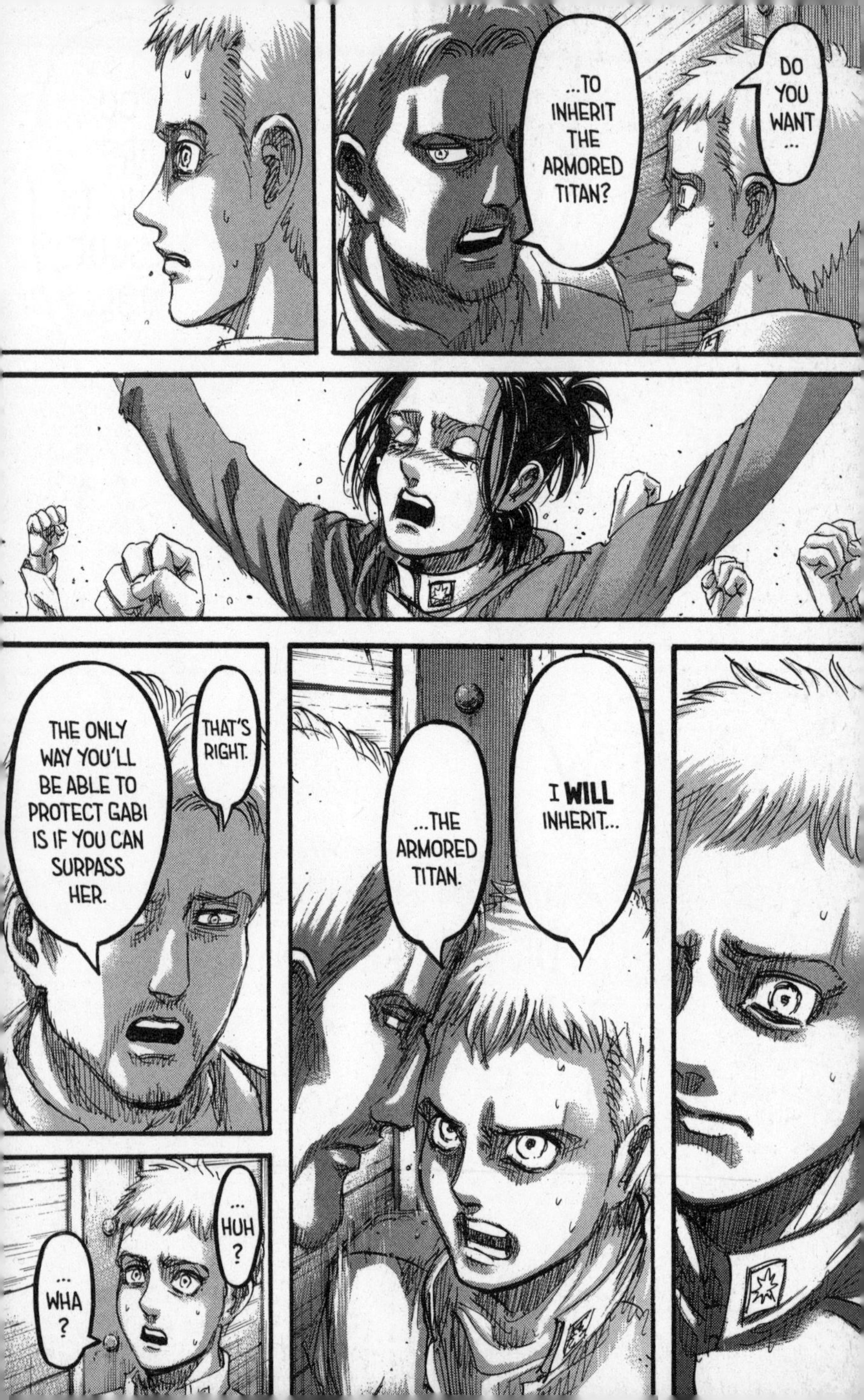
DO YOU WANT ...
...TO INHERIT THE ARMORED TITAN?
I **WILL** INHERIT...
...THE ARMORED TITAN.
THAT'S RIGHT.
THE ONLY WAY YOU'LL BE ABLE TO PROTECT GABI IS IF YOU CAN SURPASS HER.
... HUH ?
... WHA ?

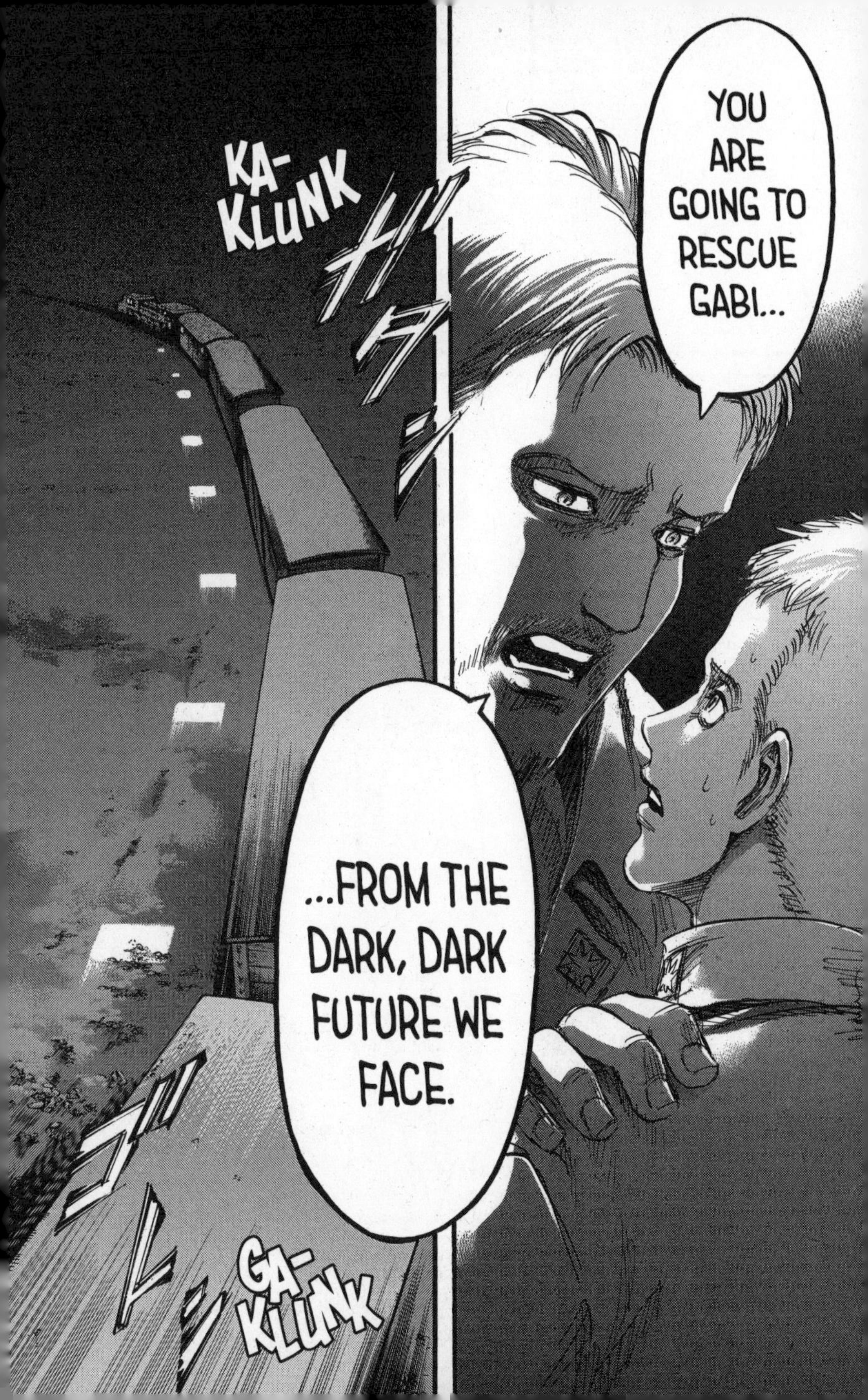
YOU ARE GOING TO RESCUE GABI...
...FROM THE DARK, DARK FUTURE WE FACE.
KA-KLUNK
GA-KLUNK

ATTACK on TITAN

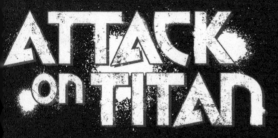

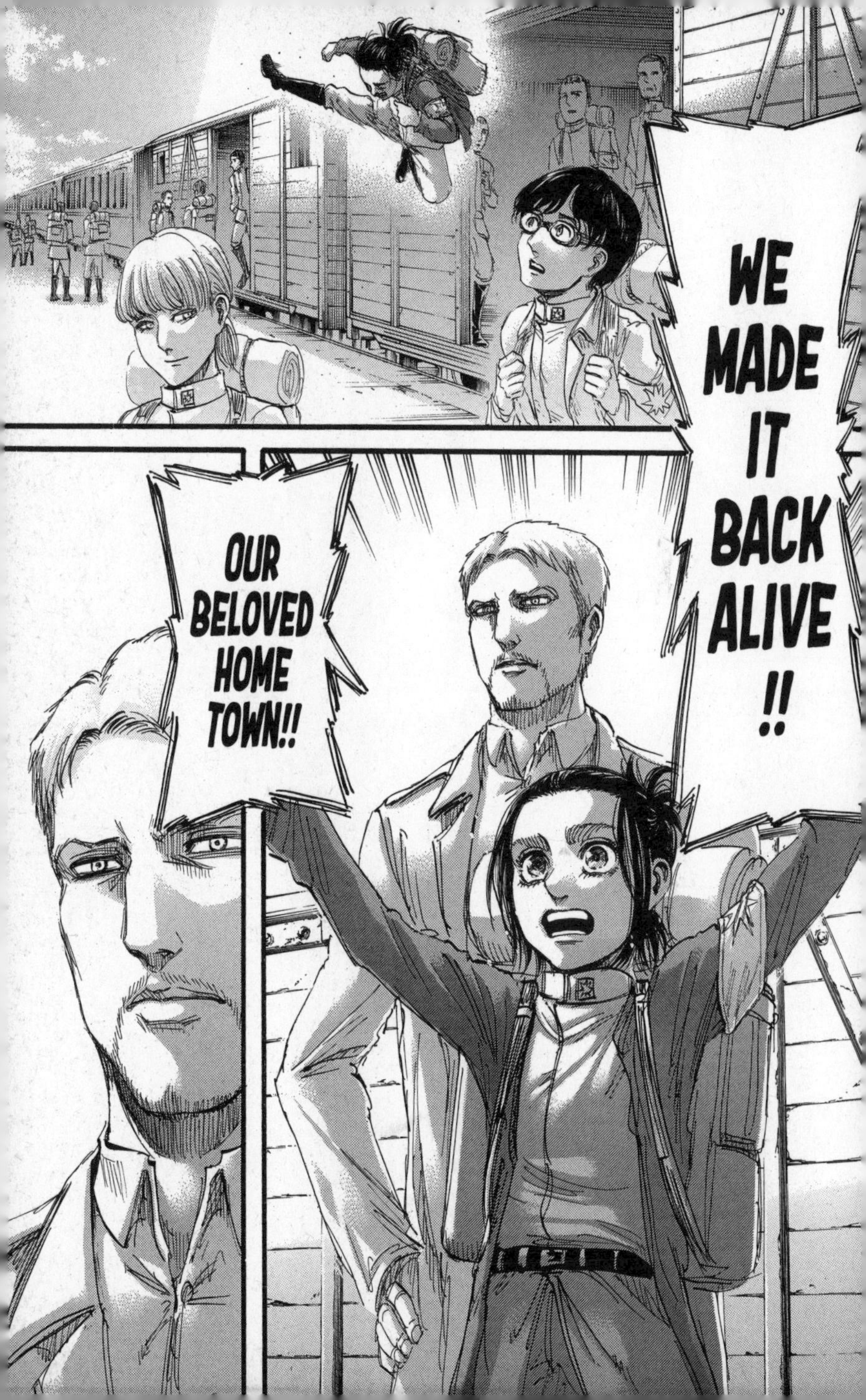
WE MADE IT BACK ALIVE!!
OUR BELOVED HOME TOWN!!

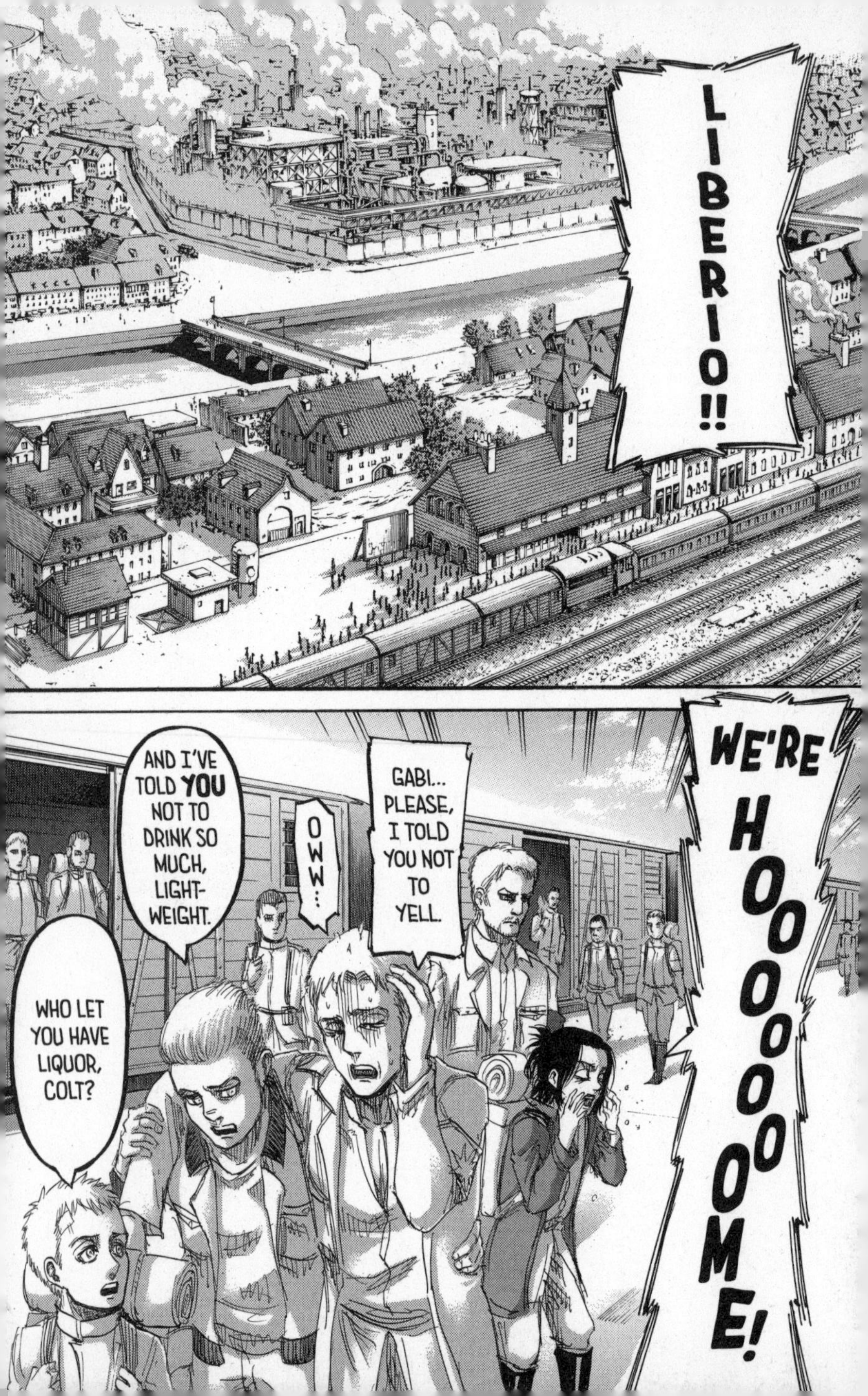
LIBERIO!!
WE'RE HOOOOOOOOOME!
GABI... PLEASE, I TOLD YOU NOT TO YELL.
OWW...
AND I'VE TOLD **YOU** NOT TO DRINK SO MUCH, LIGHTWEIGHT.
WHO LET YOU HAVE LIQUOR, COLT?

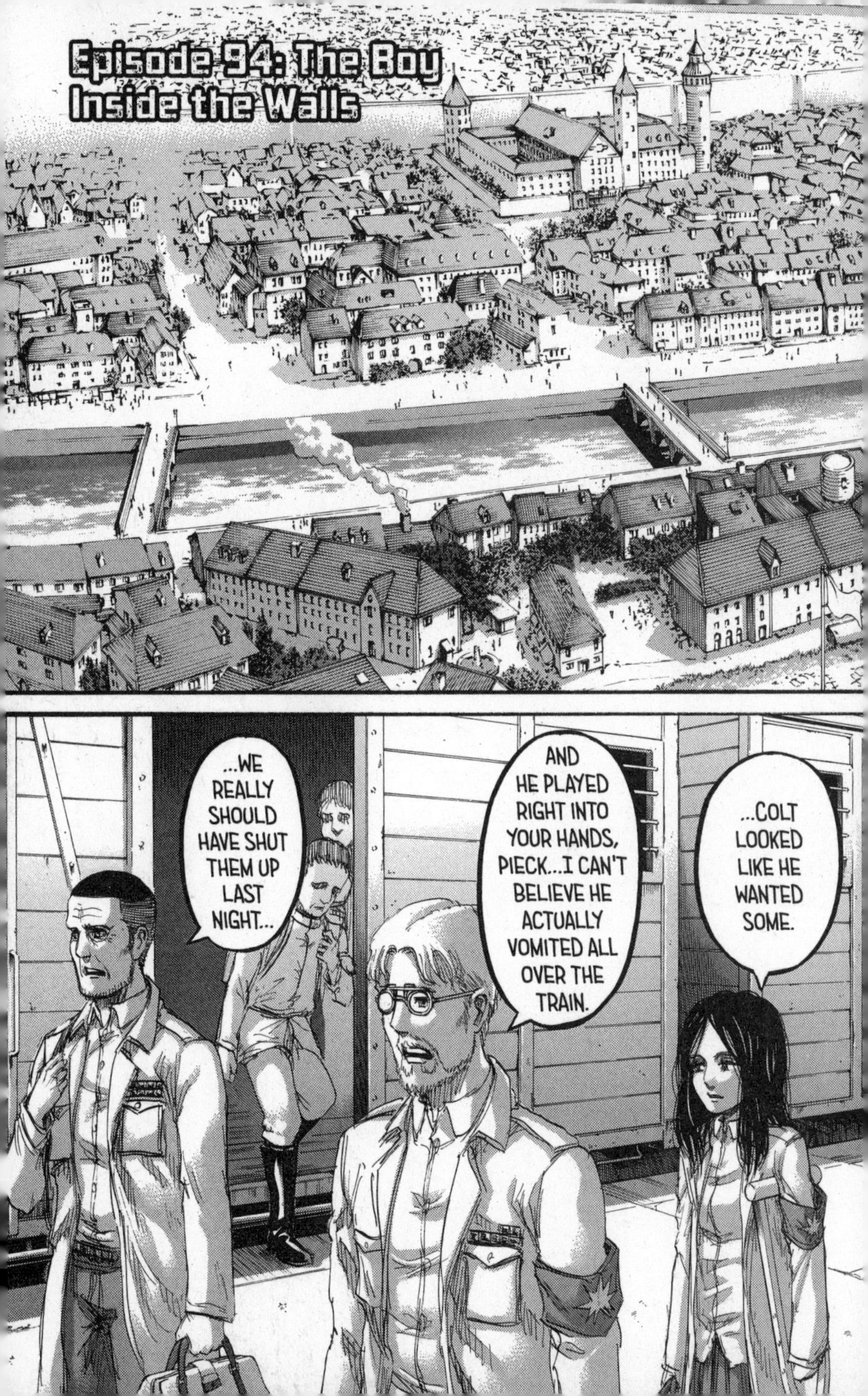
Episode 94: The Boy Inside the Walls
...COLT LOOKED LIKE HE WANTED SOME.
AND HE PLAYED RIGHT INTO YOUR HANDS, PIECK...I CAN'T BELIEVE HE ACTUALLY VOMITED ALL OVER THE TRAIN.
...WE REALLY SHOULD HAVE SHUT THEM UP LAST NIGHT...

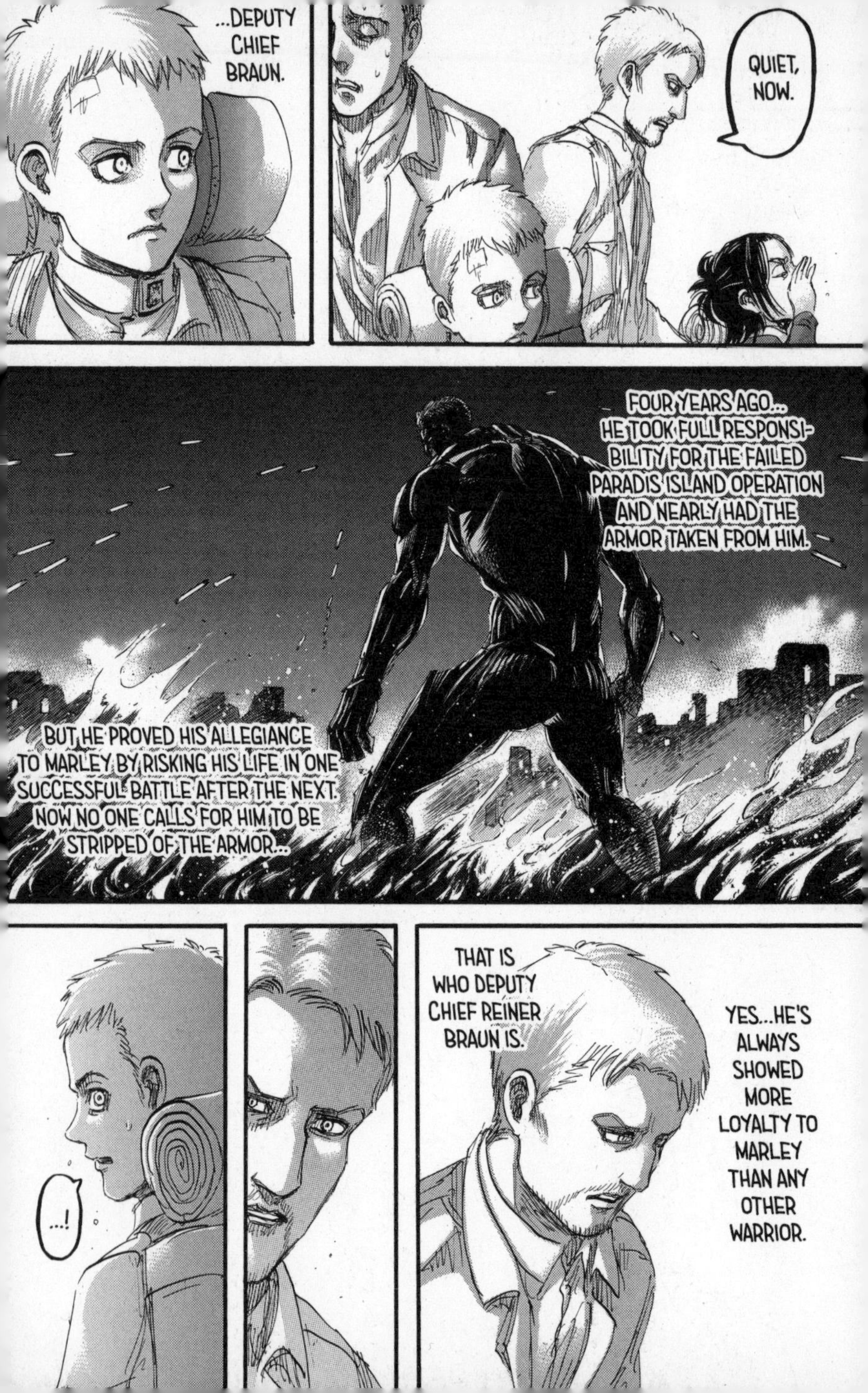
QUIET, NOW.
...DEPUTY CHIEF BRAUN.
FOUR YEARS AGO... HE TOOK FULL RESPONSI-BILITY FOR THE FAILED PARADIS ISLAND OPERATION AND NEARLY HAD THE ARMOR TAKEN FROM HIM.
BUT HE PROVED HIS ALLEGIANCE TO MARLEY BY RISKING HIS LIFE IN ONE SUCCESSFUL BATTLE AFTER THE NEXT. NOW NO ONE CALLS FOR HIM TO BE STRIPPED OF THE ARMOR...
THAT IS WHO DEPUTY CHIEF REINER BRAUN IS.
YES...HE'S ALWAYS SHOWED MORE LOYALTY TO MARLEY THAN ANY OTHER WARRIOR.
...!

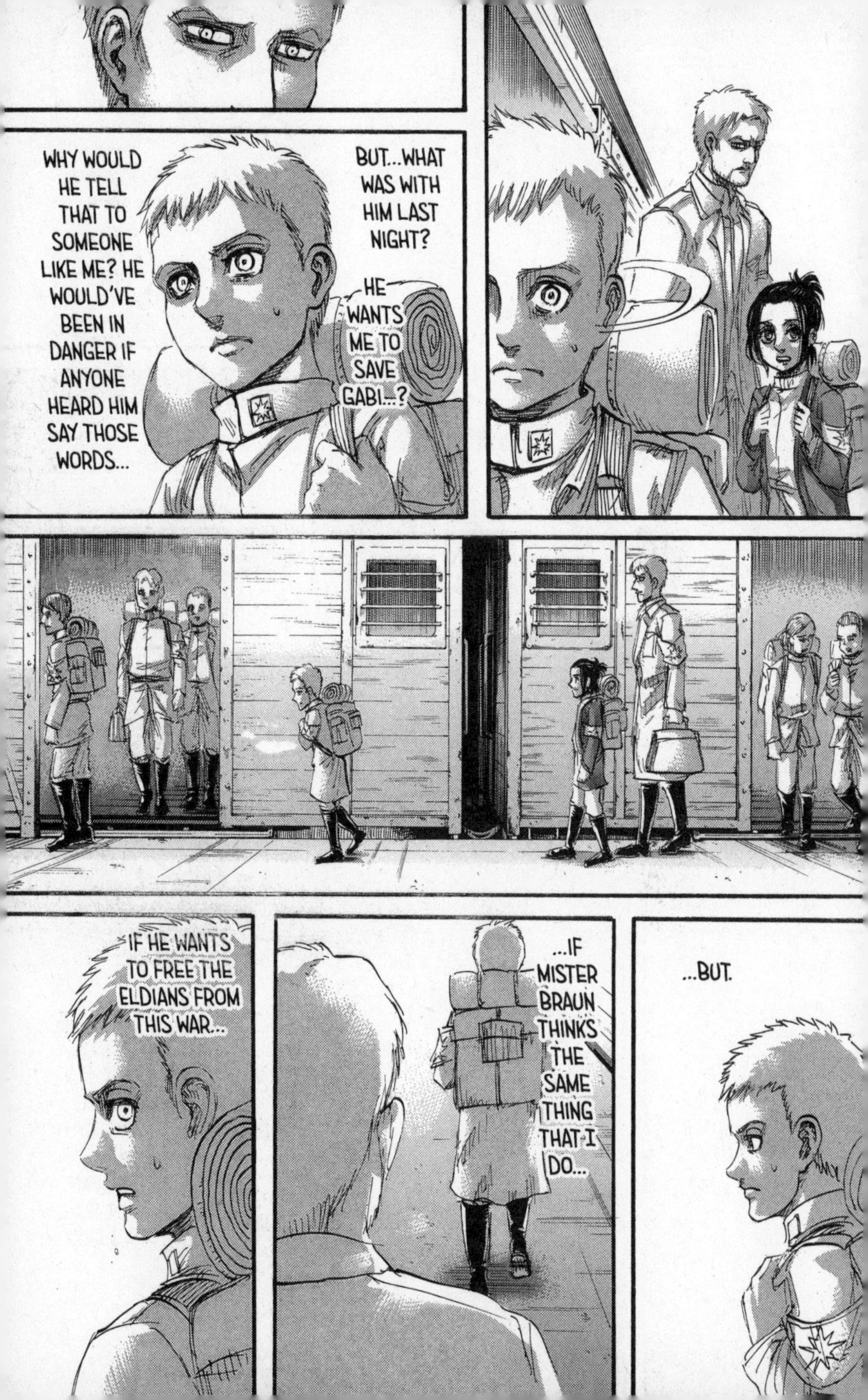
BUT...WHAT WAS WITH HIM LAST NIGHT?
WHY WOULD HE TELL THAT TO SOMEONE LIKE ME? HE WOULD'VE BEEN IN DANGER IF ANYONE HEARD HIM SAY THOSE WORDS...
HE WANTS ME TO SAVE GABI...?
...BUT.
...IF MISTER BRAUN THINKS THE SAME THING THAT I DO...
IF HE WANTS TO FREE THE ELDIANS FROM THIS WAR...

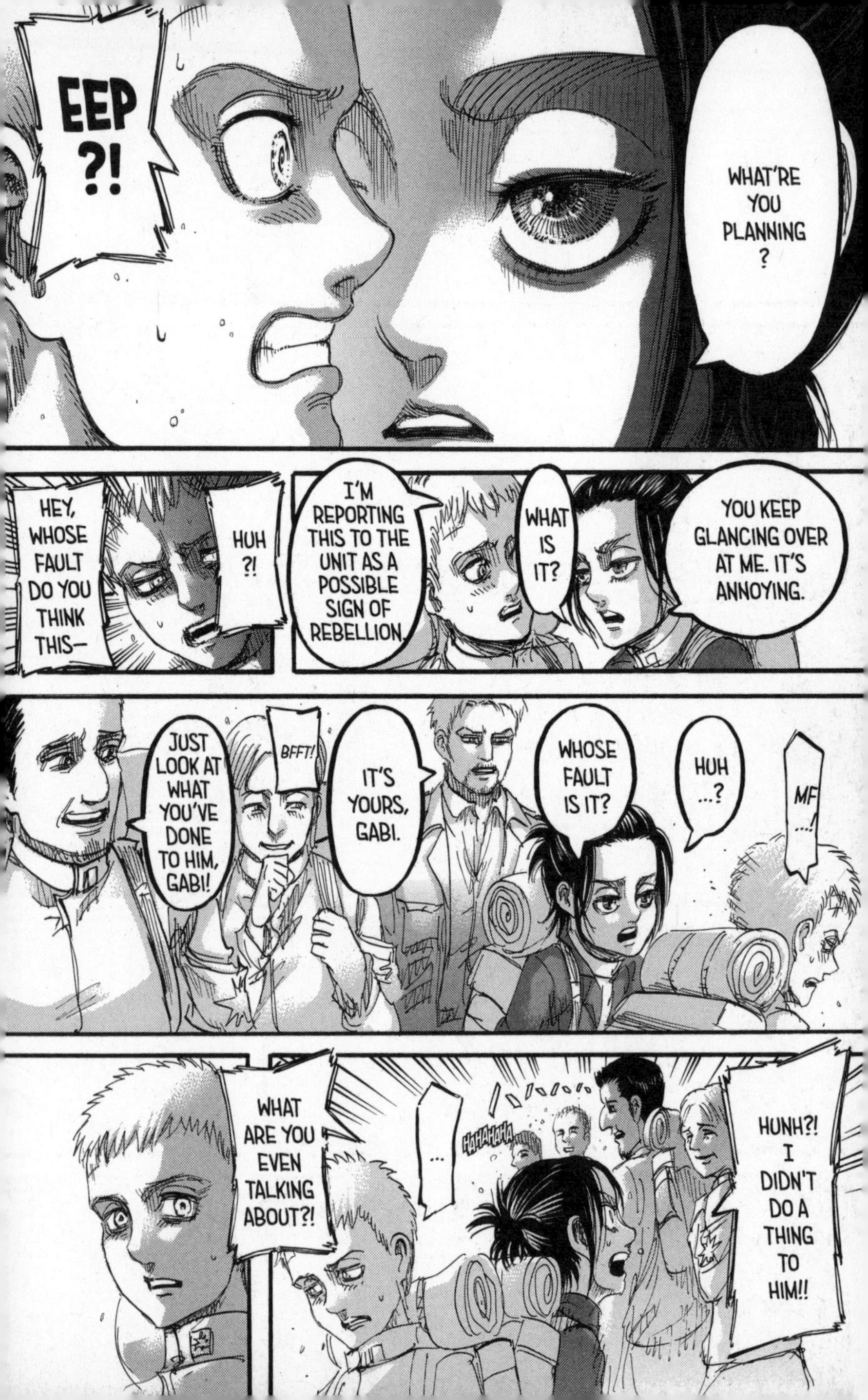
WHAT'RE YOU PLANNING?
EEP?!
YOU KEEP GLANCING OVER AT ME. IT'S ANNOYING.
WHAT IS IT?
I'M REPORTING THIS TO THE UNIT AS A POSSIBLE SIGN OF REBELLION.
HUH?!
HEY, WHOSE FAULT DO YOU THINK THIS—
MF...!
HUH...?
WHOSE FAULT IS IT?
IT'S YOURS, GABI.
BFFT!
JUST LOOK AT WHAT YOU'VE DONE TO HIM, GABI!
HUNH?! I DIDN'T DO A THING TO HIM!!
HAHAHAHA
...
WHAT ARE YOU EVEN TALKING ABOUT?!

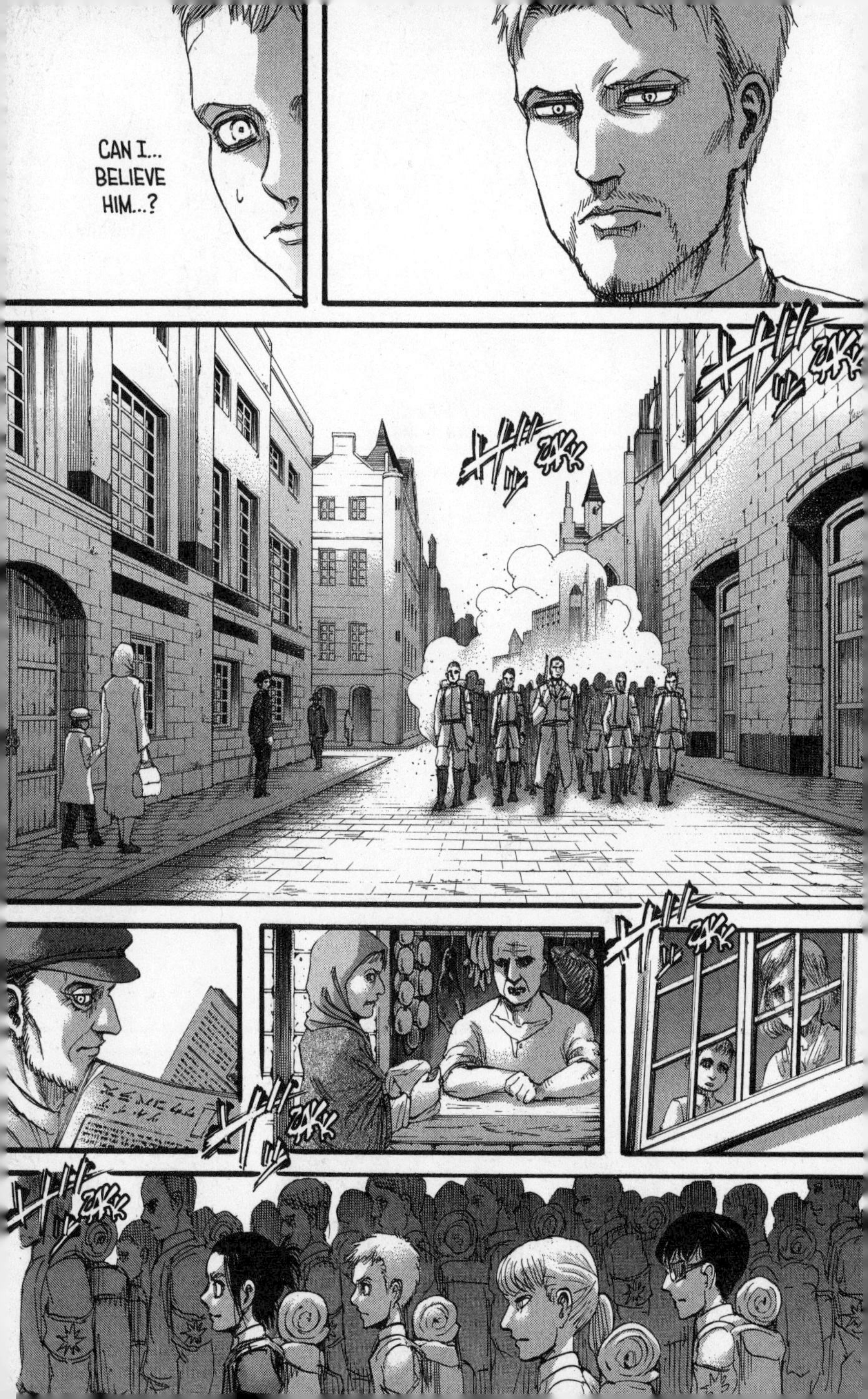
CAN I... BELIEVE HIM...?
ZAK
ZAK
ZAK
ZAK
ZAK

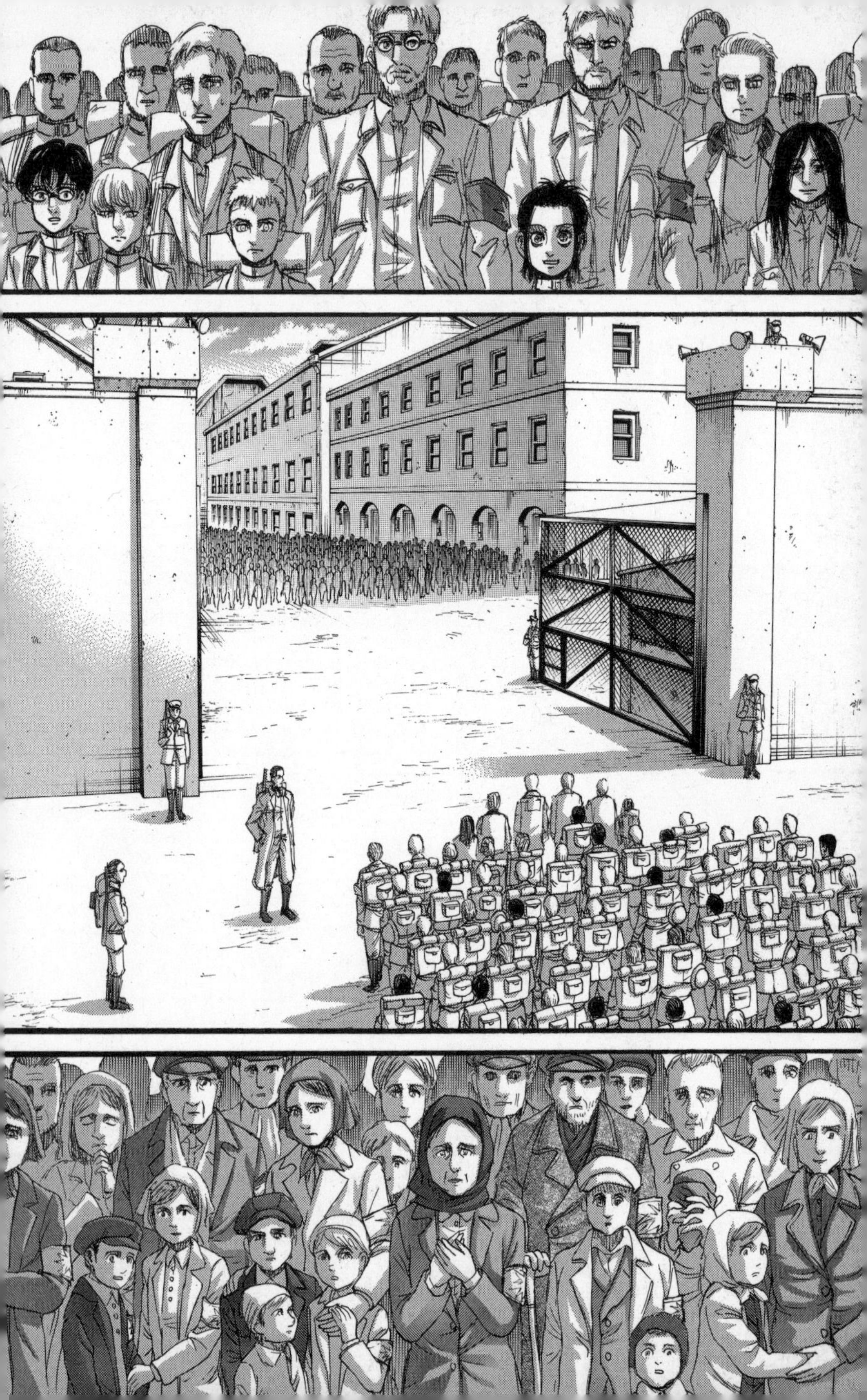

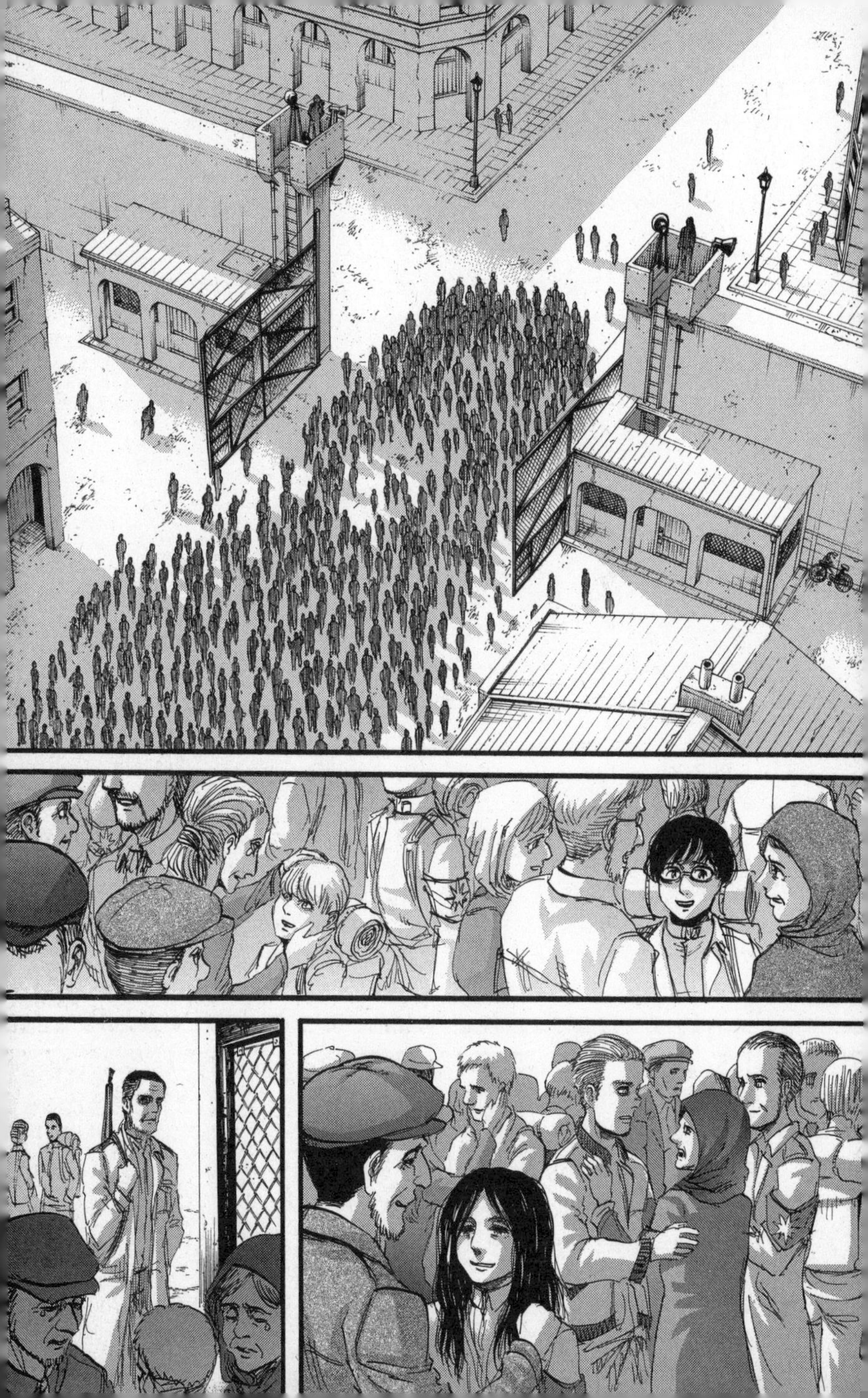

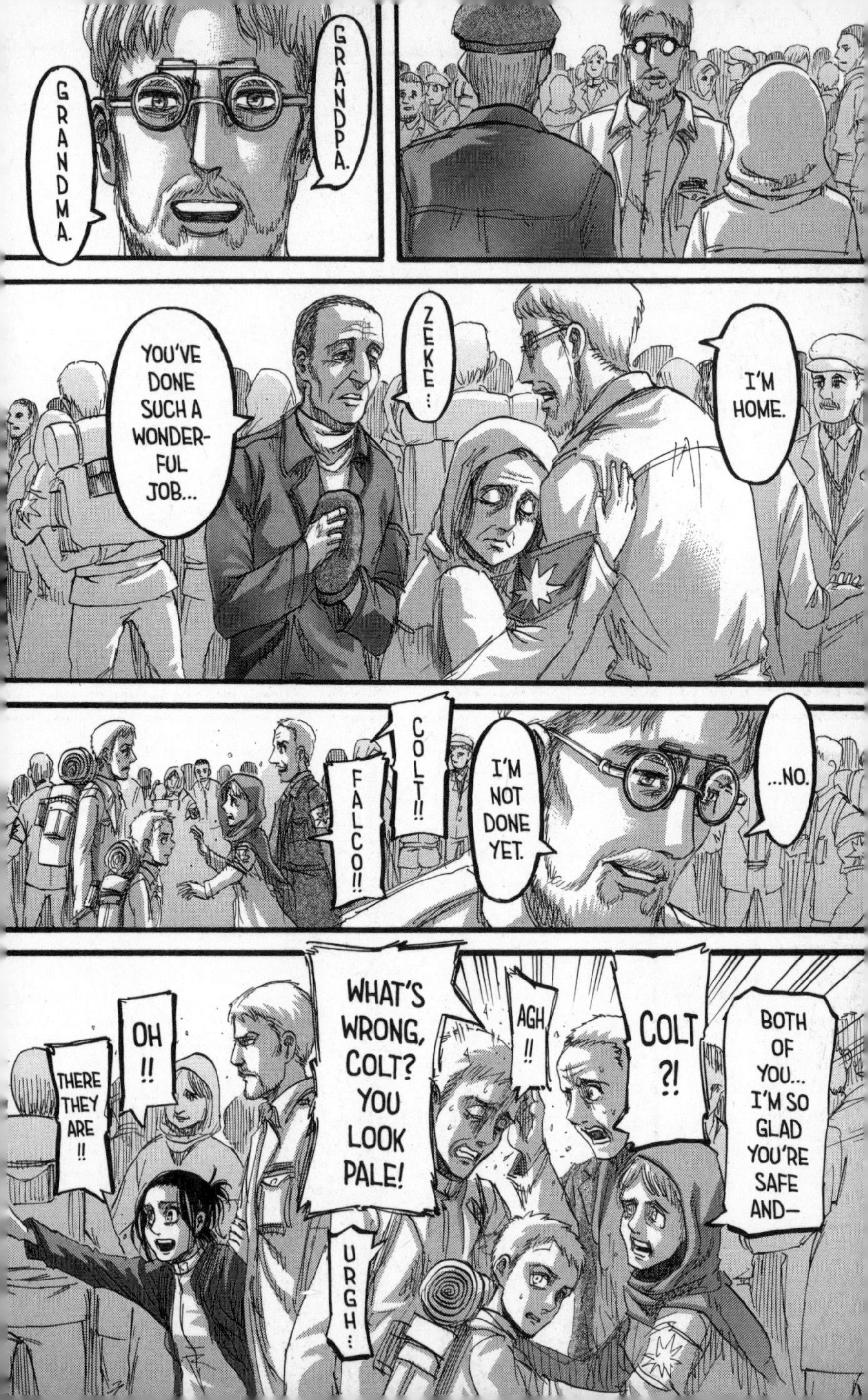
GRANDPA.
GRANDMA.
I'M HOME.
ZEKE...
YOU'VE DONE SUCH A WONDERFUL JOB...
...NO.
I'M NOT DONE YET.
COLT!!
FALCO!!
BOTH OF YOU... I'M SO GLAD YOU'RE SAFE AND—
COLT?!
AGH!!
WHAT'S WRONG, COLT? YOU LOOK PALE!
URGH...
OH!!
THERE THEY ARE!!

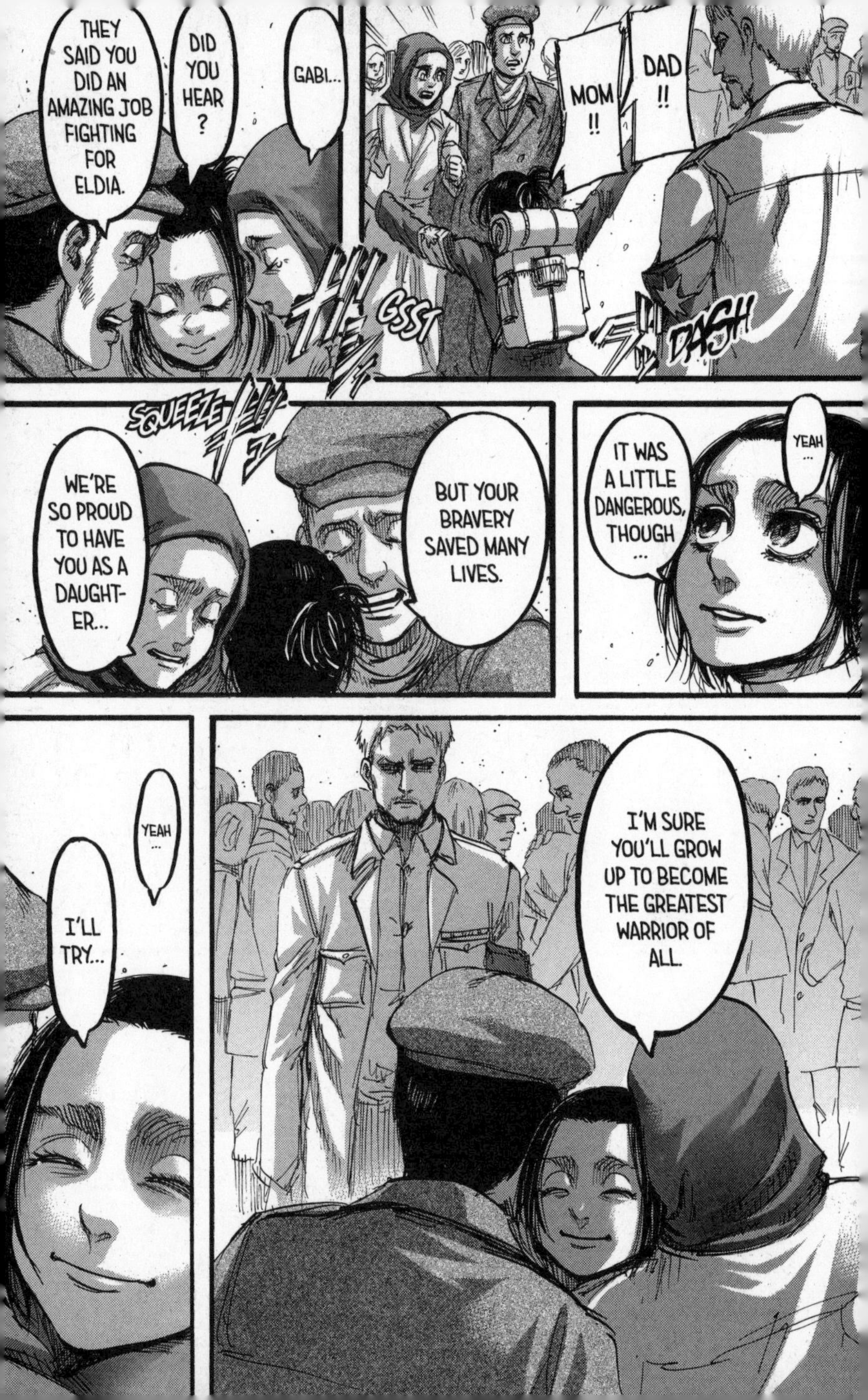
DAD !!
MOM !!
DASH
GABI...
DID YOU HEAR ?
THEY SAID YOU DID AN AMAZING JOB FIGHTING FOR ELDIA.
GSST
YEAH ...
IT WAS A LITTLE DANGEROUS, THOUGH ...
BUT YOUR BRAVERY SAVED MANY LIVES.
WE'RE SO PROUD TO HAVE YOU AS A DAUGHTER...
SQUEEZE
I'M SURE YOU'LL GROW UP TO BECOME THE GREATEST WARRIOR OF ALL.
YEAH ...
I'LL TRY...

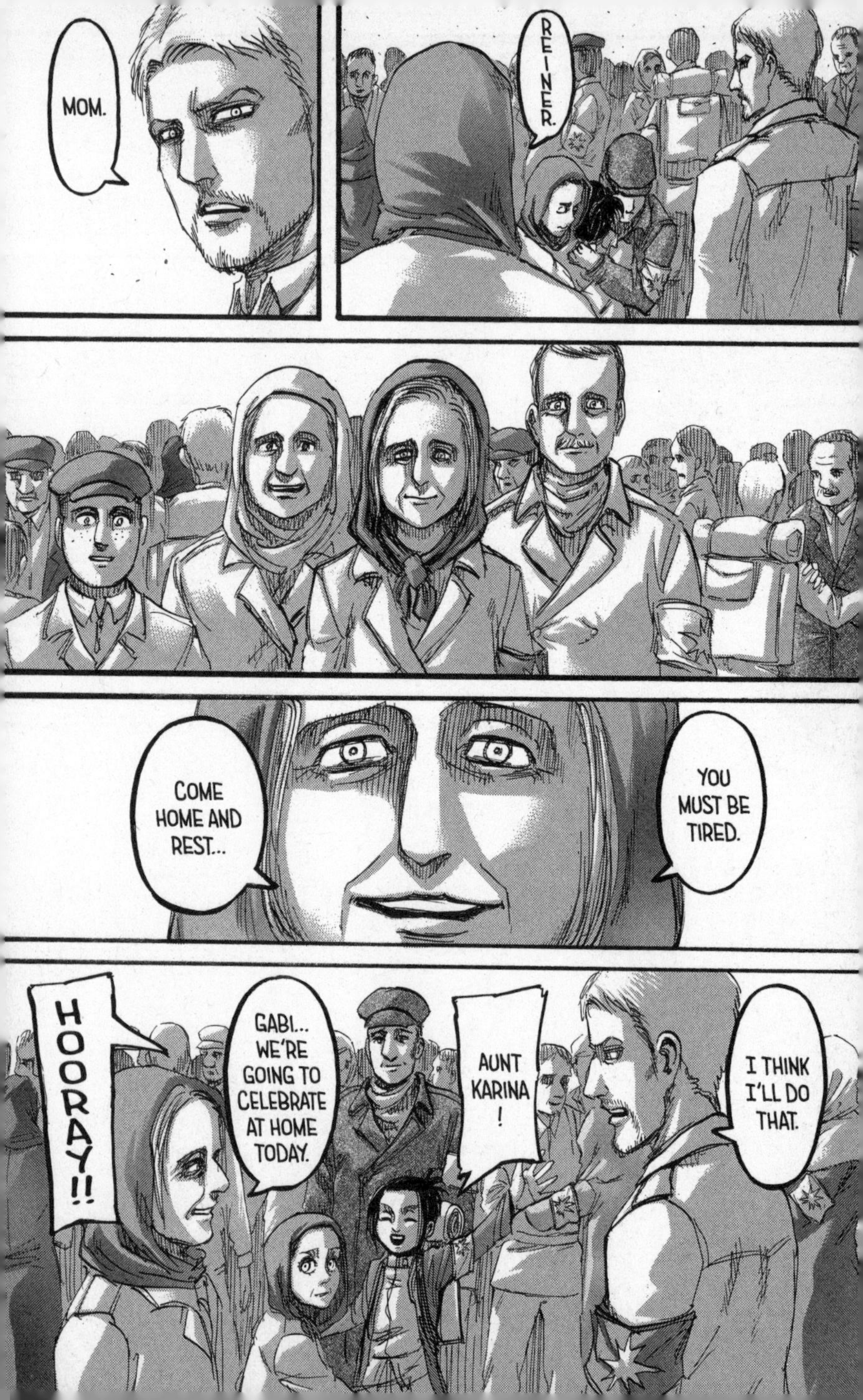
REINER.
MOM.
YOU MUST BE TIRED.
COME HOME AND REST...
I THINK I'LL DO THAT.
AUNT KARINA!
GABI... WE'RE GOING TO CELEBRATE AT HOME TODAY.
HOORAY!!

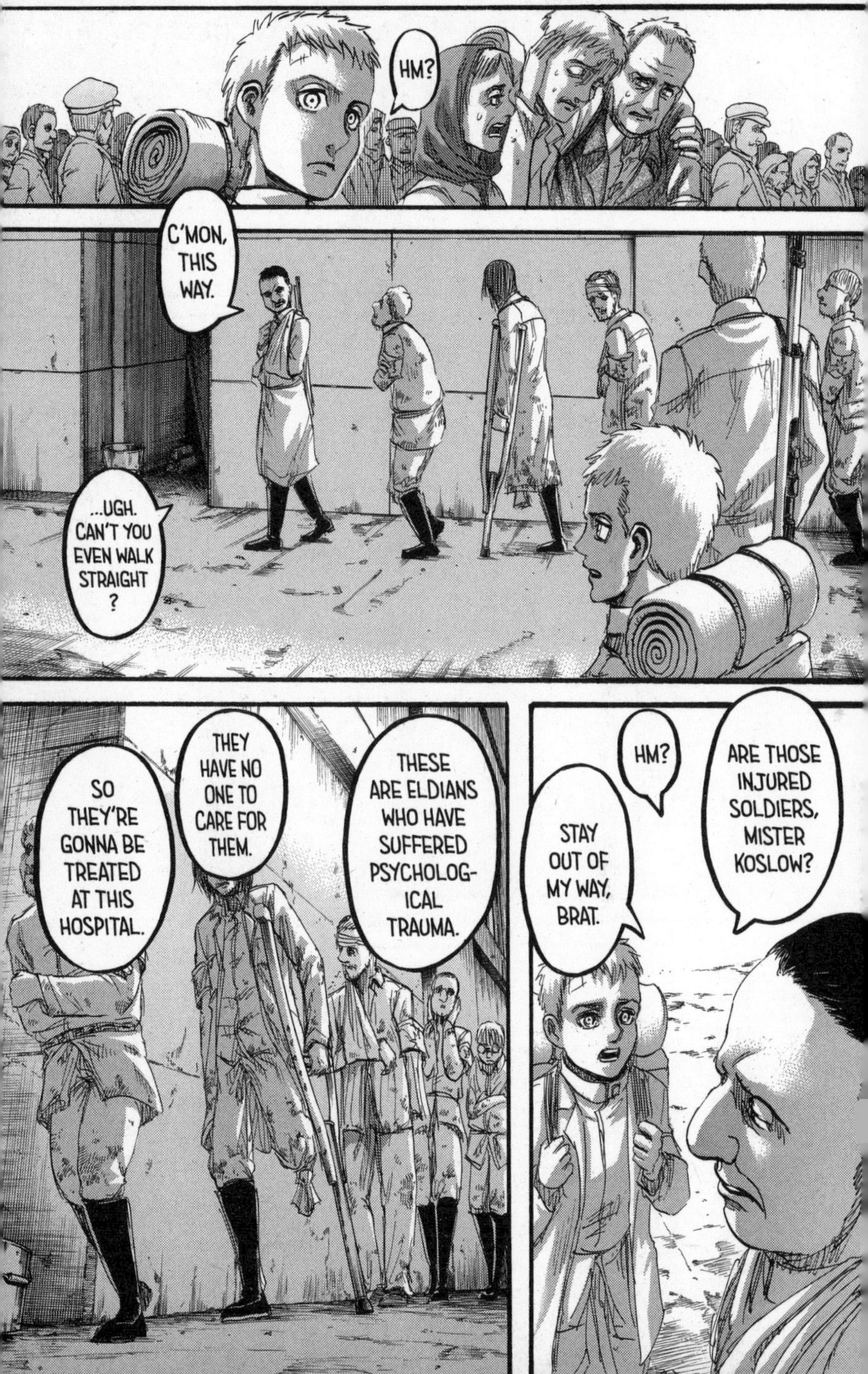
HM?
C'MON, THIS WAY.
...UGH. CAN'T YOU EVEN WALK STRAIGHT?
ARE THOSE INJURED SOLDIERS, MISTER KOSLOW?
HM?
STAY OUT OF MY WAY, BRAT.
THESE ARE ELDIANS WHO HAVE SUFFERED PSYCHOLOG-ICAL TRAUMA.
THEY HAVE NO ONE TO CARE FOR THEM.
SO THEY'RE GONNA BE TREATED AT THIS HOSPITAL.

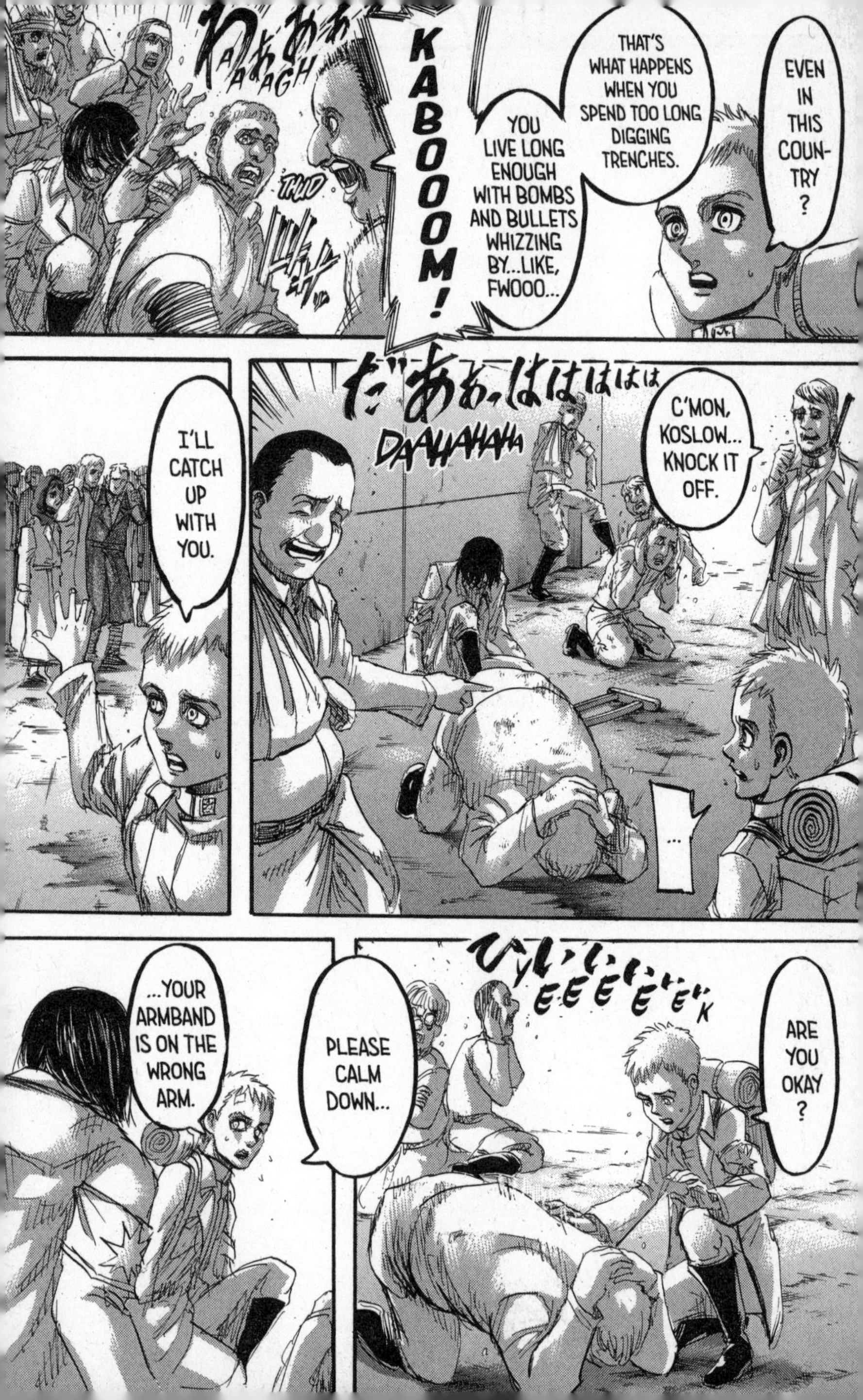
EVEN IN THIS COUNTRY?
THAT'S WHAT HAPPENS WHEN YOU SPEND TOO LONG DIGGING TRENCHES.
YOU LIVE LONG ENOUGH WITH BOMBS AND BULLETS WHIZZING BY...LIKE, FWOOO...
KABOOOOM!
THUD
AAAAGH
DAAHAHAHA
C'MON, KOSLOW... KNOCK IT OFF.
...
I'LL CATCH UP WITH YOU.
EEEEEEK
ARE YOU OKAY?
PLEASE CALM DOWN...
...YOUR ARMBAND IS ON THE WRONG ARM.

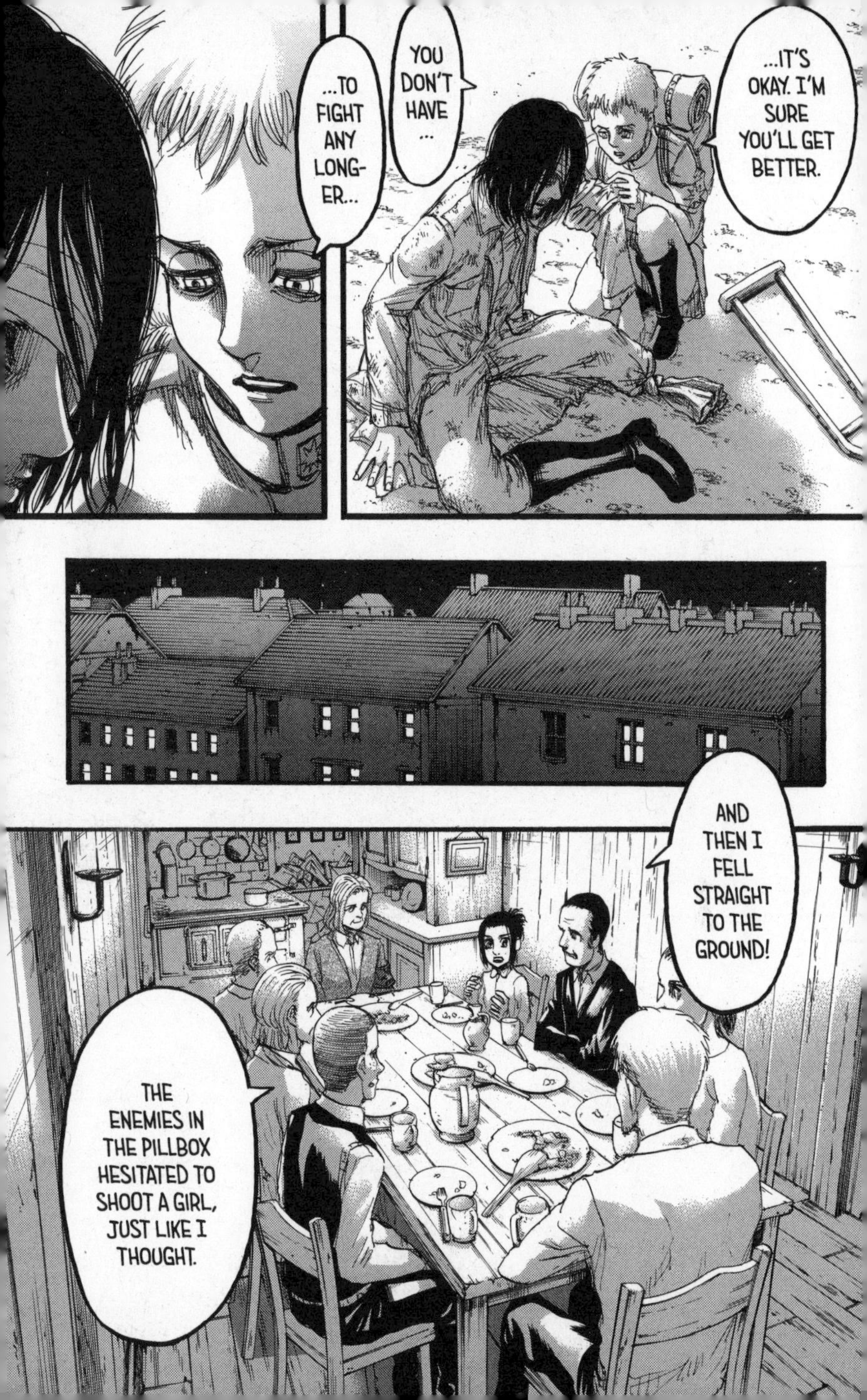
...IT'S OKAY. I'M SURE YOU'LL GET BETTER.
YOU DON'T HAVE...
...TO FIGHT ANY LONGER...
AND THEN I FELL STRAIGHT TO THE GROUND!
THE ENEMIES IN THE PILLBOX HESITATED TO SHOOT A GIRL, JUST LIKE I THOUGHT.

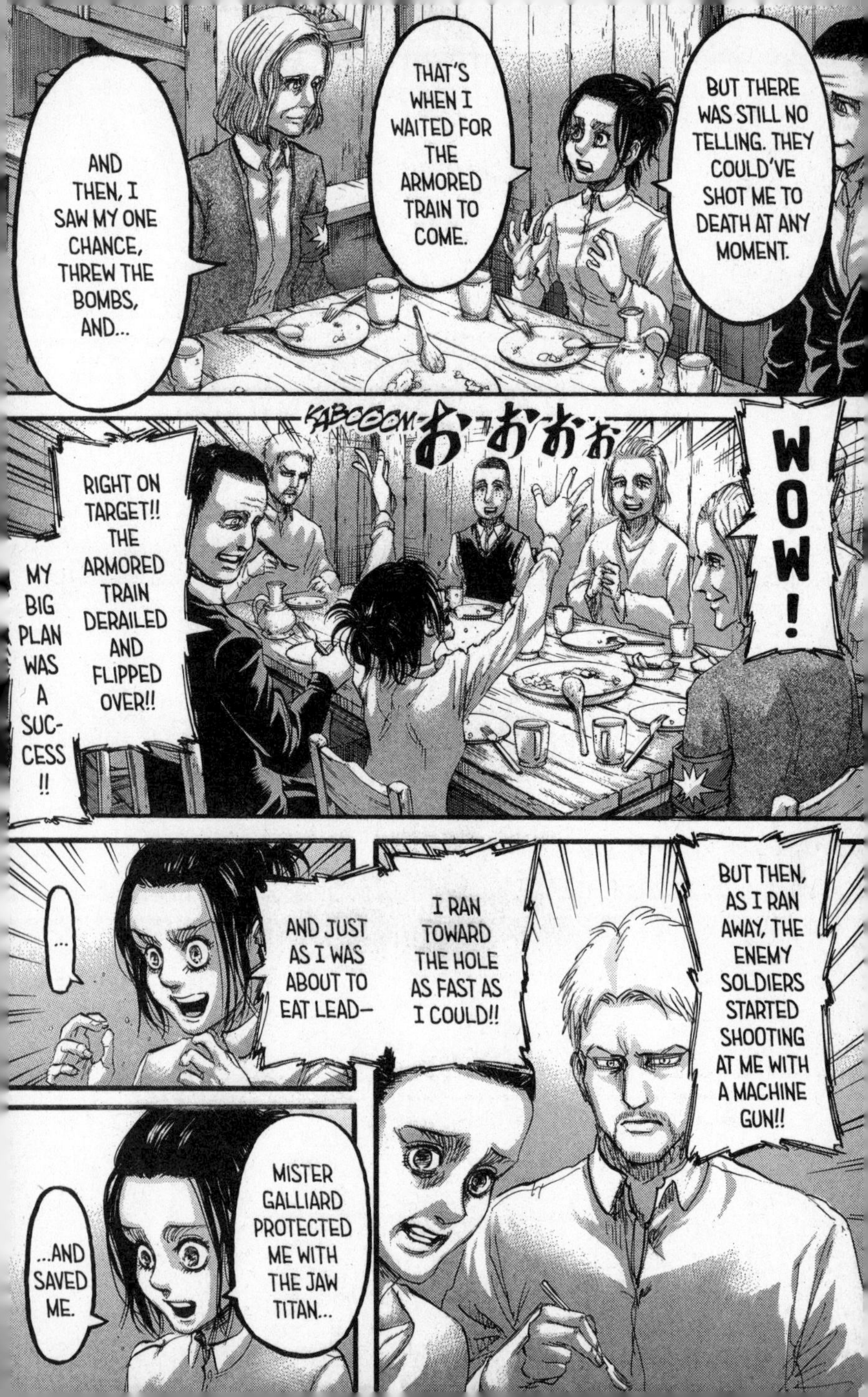
BUT THERE WAS STILL NO TELLING. THEY COULD'VE SHOT ME TO DEATH AT ANY MOMENT.
THAT'S WHEN I WAITED FOR THE ARMORED TRAIN TO COME.
AND THEN, I SAW MY ONE CHANCE, THREW THE BOMBS, AND...
WOW!
KABOOOOM- おおおぉ
RIGHT ON TARGET!! THE ARMORED TRAIN DERAILED AND FLIPPED OVER!!
MY BIG PLAN WAS A SUC-CESS!!
BUT THEN, AS I RAN AWAY, THE ENEMY SOLDIERS STARTED SHOOTING AT ME WITH A MACHINE GUN!!
I RAN TOWARD THE HOLE AS FAST AS I COULD!!
AND JUST AS I WAS ABOUT TO EAT LEAD—
...
MISTER GALLIARD PROTECTED ME WITH THE JAW TITAN...
...AND SAVED ME.

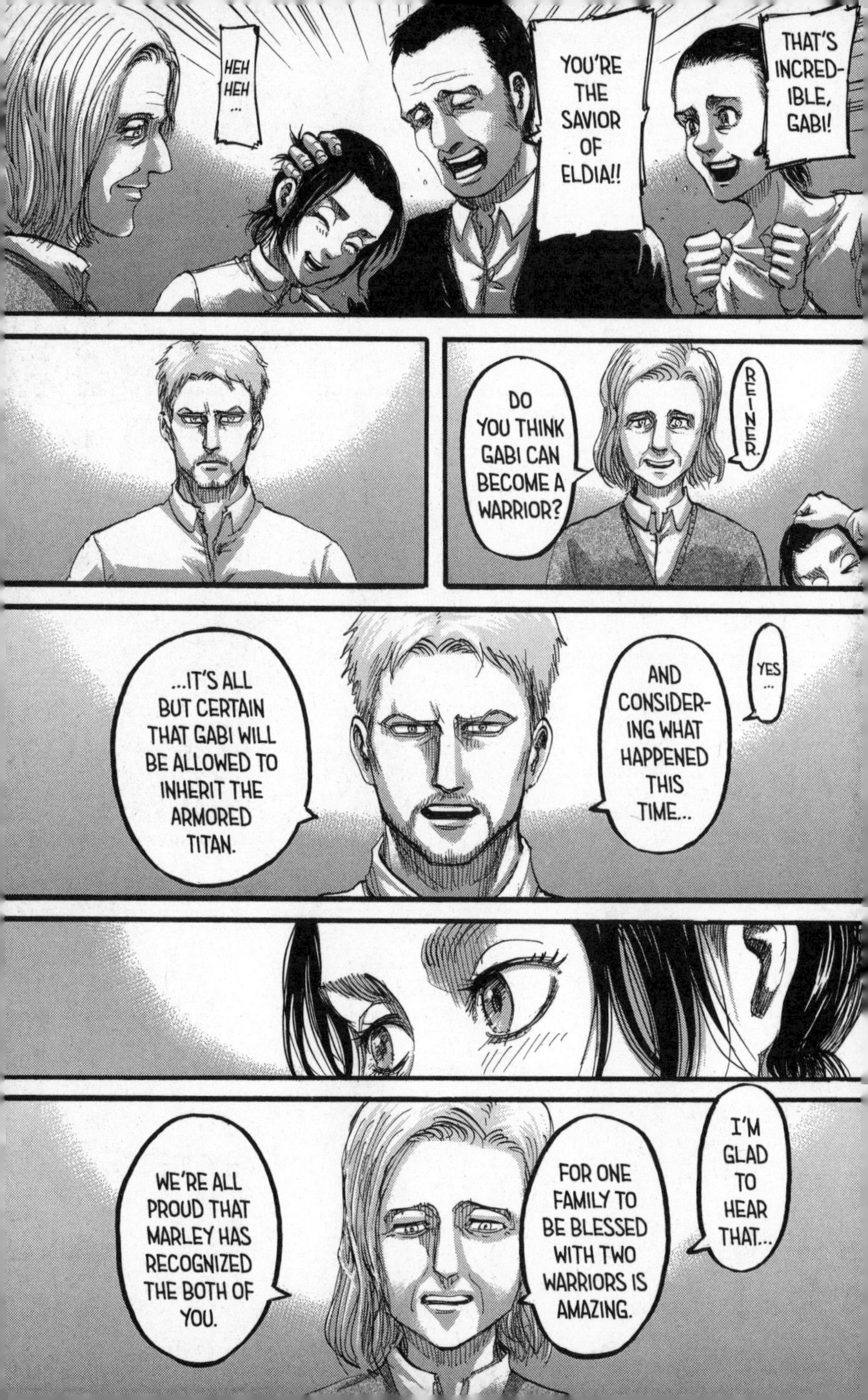
THAT'S INCREDIBLE, GABI!
YOU'RE THE SAVIOR OF ELDIA!!
HEH HEH ...
REINER.
DO YOU THINK GABI CAN BECOME A WARRIOR?
YES...
AND CONSIDERING WHAT HAPPENED THIS TIME...
...IT'S ALL BUT CERTAIN THAT GABI WILL BE ALLOWED TO INHERIT THE ARMORED TITAN.
I'M GLAD TO HEAR THAT...
FOR ONE FAMILY TO BE BLESSED WITH TWO WARRIORS IS AMAZING.
WE'RE ALL PROUD THAT MARLEY HAS RECOGNIZED THE BOTH OF YOU.

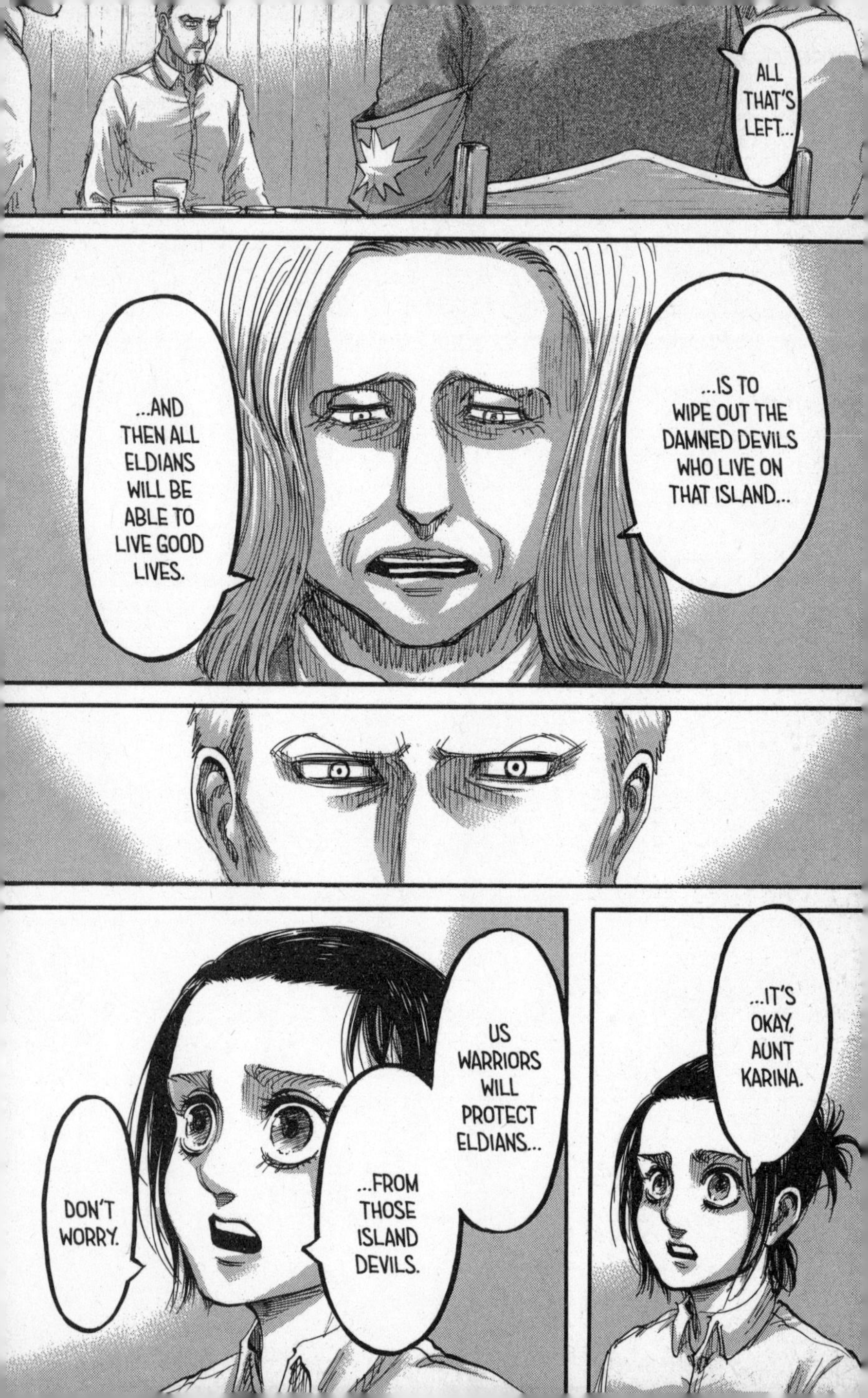
ALL THAT'S LEFT...
...IS TO WIPE OUT THE DAMNED DEVILS WHO LIVE ON THAT ISLAND...
...AND THEN ALL ELDIANS WILL BE ABLE TO LIVE GOOD LIVES.
...IT'S OKAY, AUNT KARINA.
US WARRIORS WILL PROTECT ELDIANS...
...FROM THOSE ISLAND DEVILS.
DON'T WORRY.

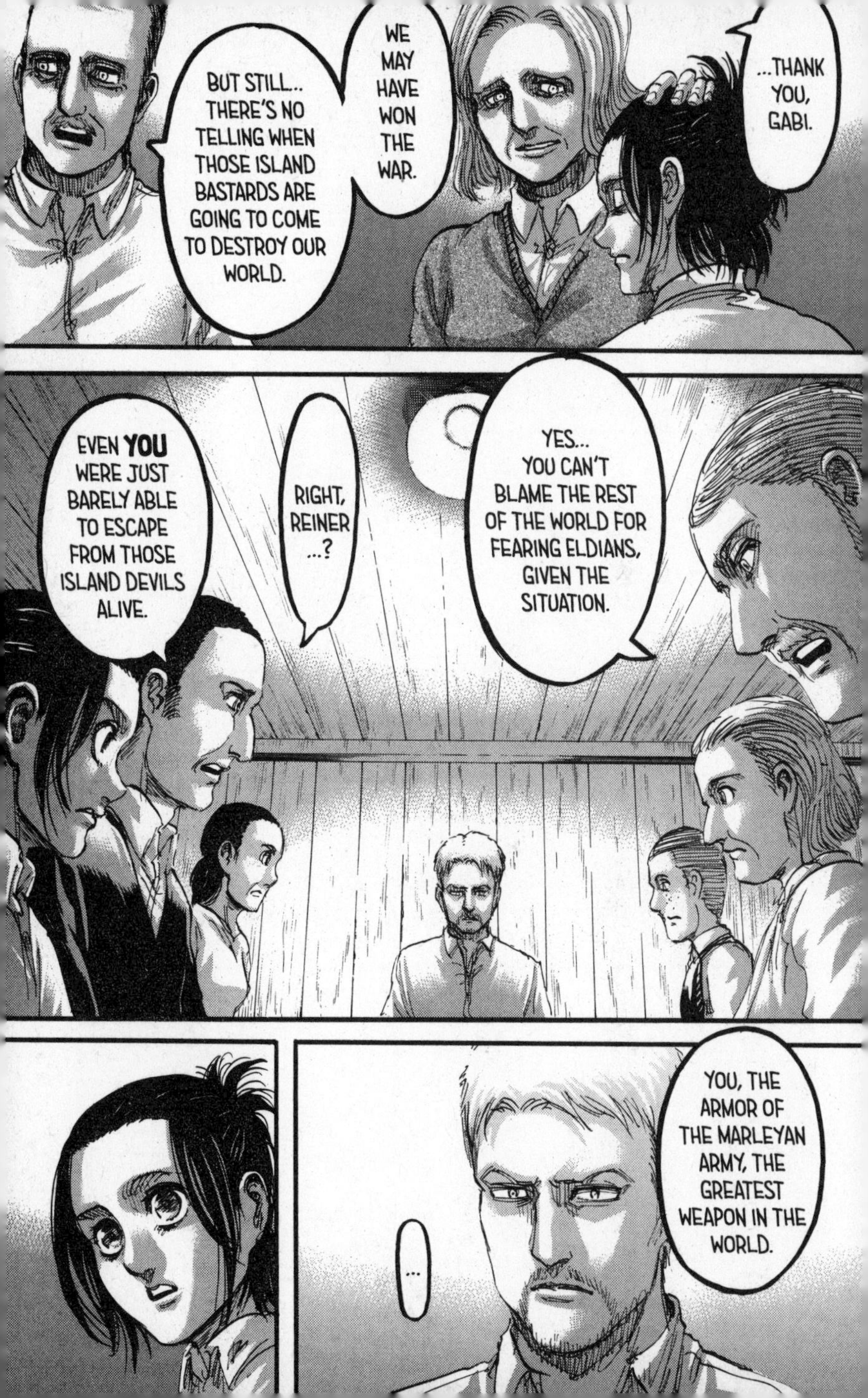
...THANK YOU, GABI.
WE MAY HAVE WON THE WAR.
BUT STILL.. THERE'S NO TELLING WHEN THOSE ISLAND BASTARDS ARE GOING TO COME TO DESTROY OUR WORLD.
YES... YOU CAN'T BLAME THE REST OF THE WORLD FOR FEARING ELDIANS, GIVEN THE SITUATION.
RIGHT, REINER ...?
EVEN **YOU** WERE JUST BARELY ABLE TO ESCAPE FROM THOSE ISLAND DEVILS ALIVE.
YOU, THE ARMOR OF THE MARLEYAN ARMY, THE GREATEST WEAPON IN THE WORLD.
...

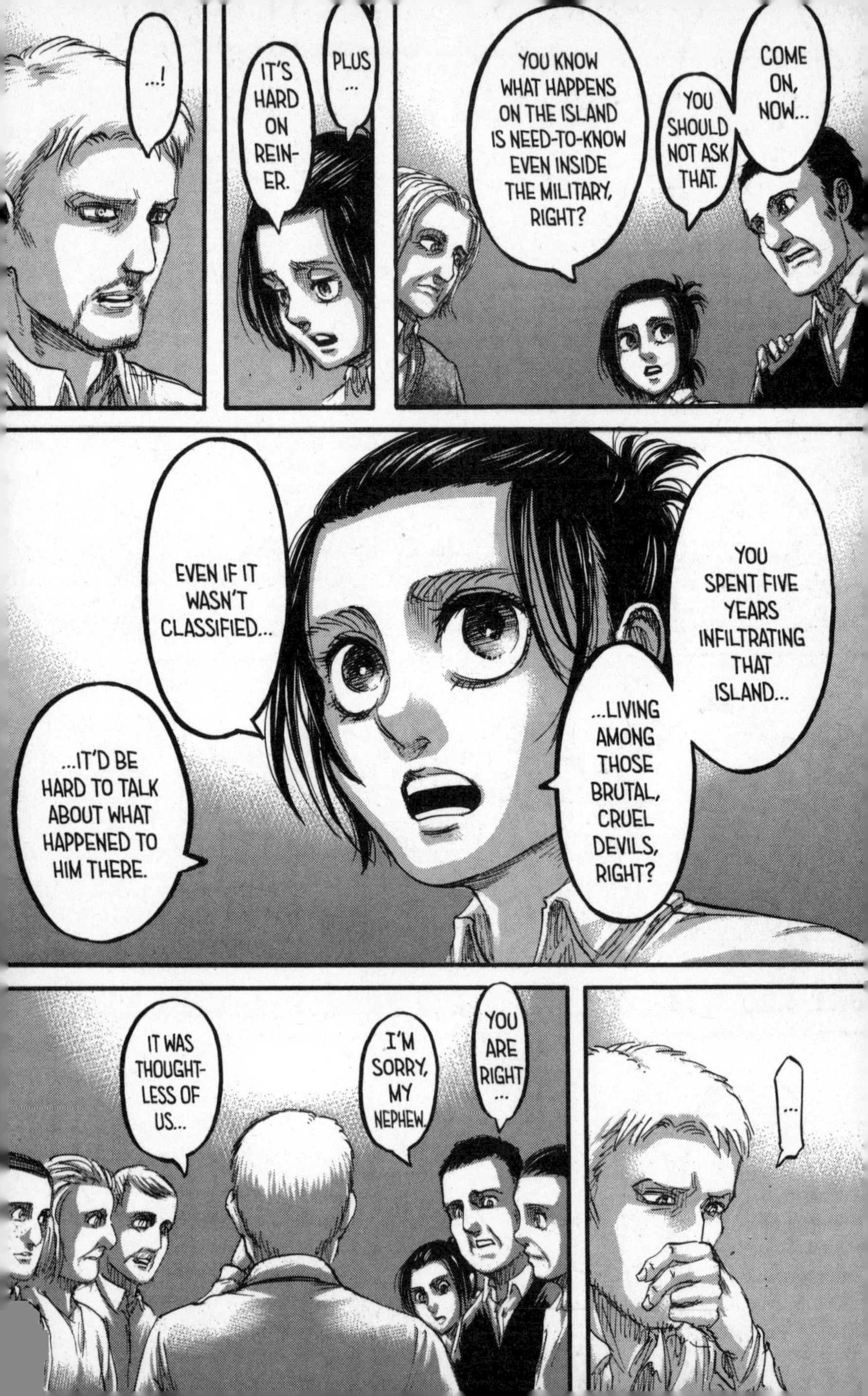
COME ON, NOW...
YOU SHOULD NOT ASK THAT.
YOU KNOW WHAT HAPPENS ON THE ISLAND IS NEED-TO-KNOW EVEN INSIDE THE MILITARY, RIGHT?
PLUS...
IT'S HARD ON REINER.
...!
YOU SPENT FIVE YEARS INFILTRATING THAT ISLAND...
...LIVING AMONG THOSE BRUTAL, CRUEL DEVILS, RIGHT?
EVEN IF IT WASN'T CLASSIFIED...
...IT'D BE HARD TO TALK ABOUT WHAT HAPPENED TO HIM THERE.
...
YOU ARE RIGHT...
I'M SORRY, MY NEPHEW.
IT WAS THOUGHTLESS OF US...

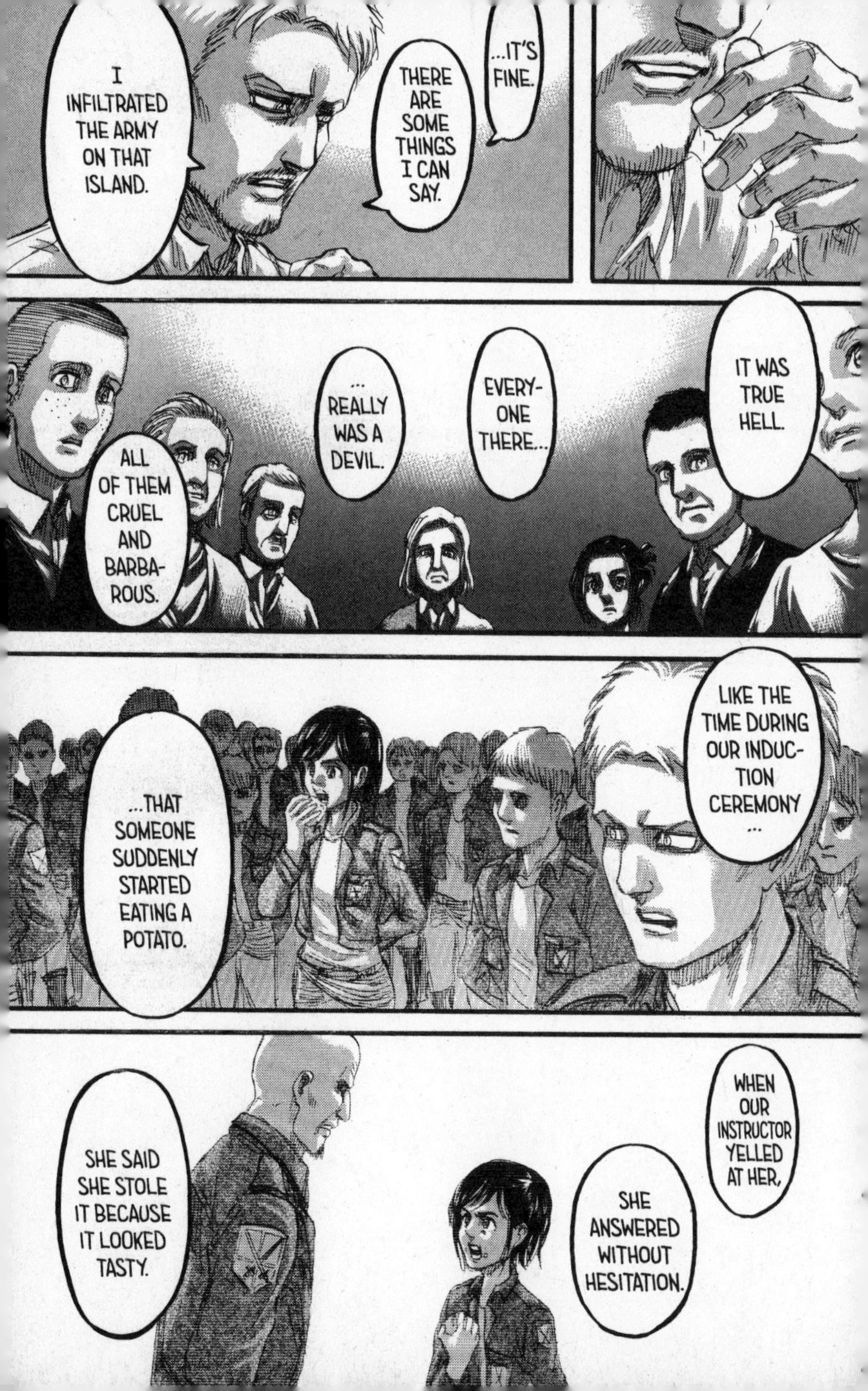
...IT'S FINE.
THERE ARE SOME THINGS I CAN SAY.
I INFILTRATED THE ARMY ON THAT ISLAND.
IT WAS TRUE HELL.
EVERY-ONE THERE...
... REALLY WAS A DEVIL.
ALL OF THEM CRUEL AND BARBA-ROUS.
LIKE THE TIME DURING OUR INDUC-TION CEREMONY ...
...THAT SOMEONE SUDDENLY STARTED EATING A POTATO.
WHEN OUR INSTRUCTOR YELLED AT HER,
SHE ANSWERED WITHOUT HESITATION.
SHE SAID SHE STOLE IT BECAUSE IT LOOKED TASTY.

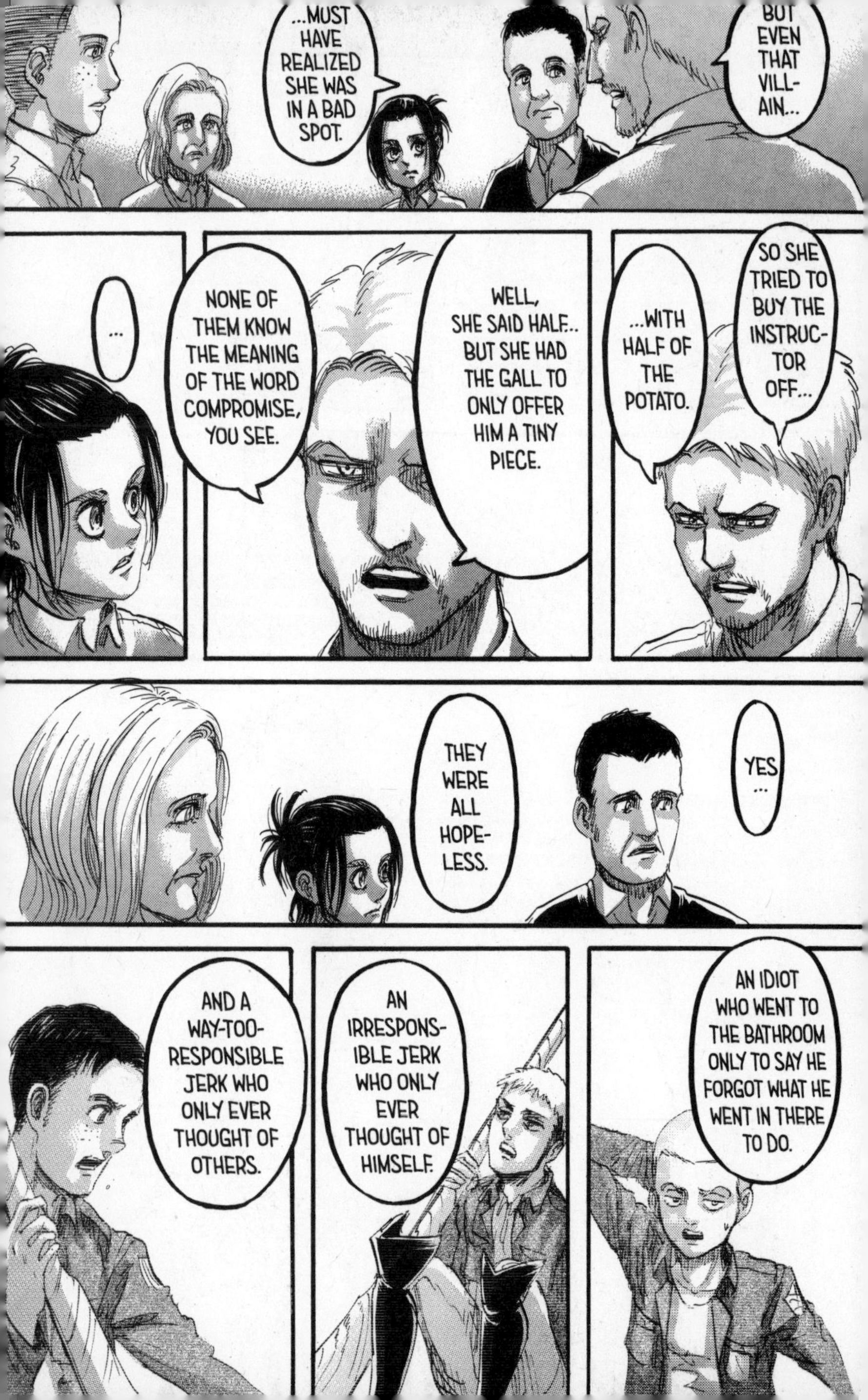
BUT EVEN THAT VILLAIN...
...MUST HAVE REALIZED SHE WAS IN A BAD SPOT.
SO SHE TRIED TO BUY THE INSTRUCTOR OFF...
...WITH HALF OF THE POTATO.
WELL, SHE SAID HALF... BUT SHE HAD THE GALL TO ONLY OFFER HIM A TINY PIECE.
NONE OF THEM KNOW THE MEANING OF THE WORD COMPROMISE, YOU SEE.
...
YES...
THEY WERE ALL HOPELESS.
AN IDIOT WHO WENT TO THE BATHROOM ONLY TO SAY HE FORGOT WHAT HE WENT IN THERE TO DO.
AN IRRESPONSIBLE JERK WHO ONLY EVER THOUGHT OF HIMSELF.
AND A WAY-TOO-RESPONSIBLE JERK WHO ONLY EVER THOUGHT OF OTHERS.

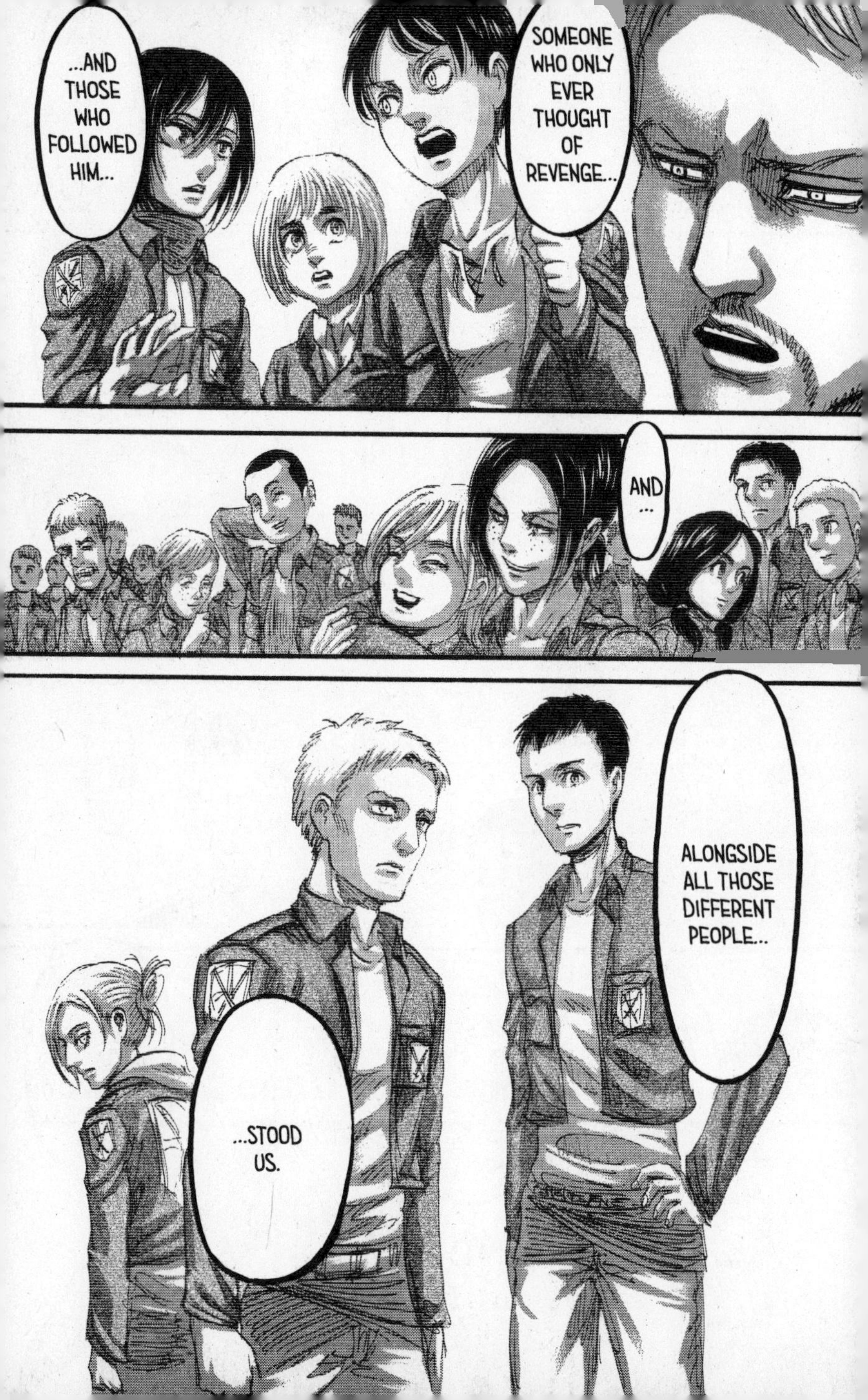
SOMEONE WHO ONLY EVER THOUGHT OF REVENGE...
...AND THOSE WHO FOLLOWED HIM...
AND ...
ALONGSIDE ALL THOSE DIFFERENT PEOPLE...
...STOOD US.

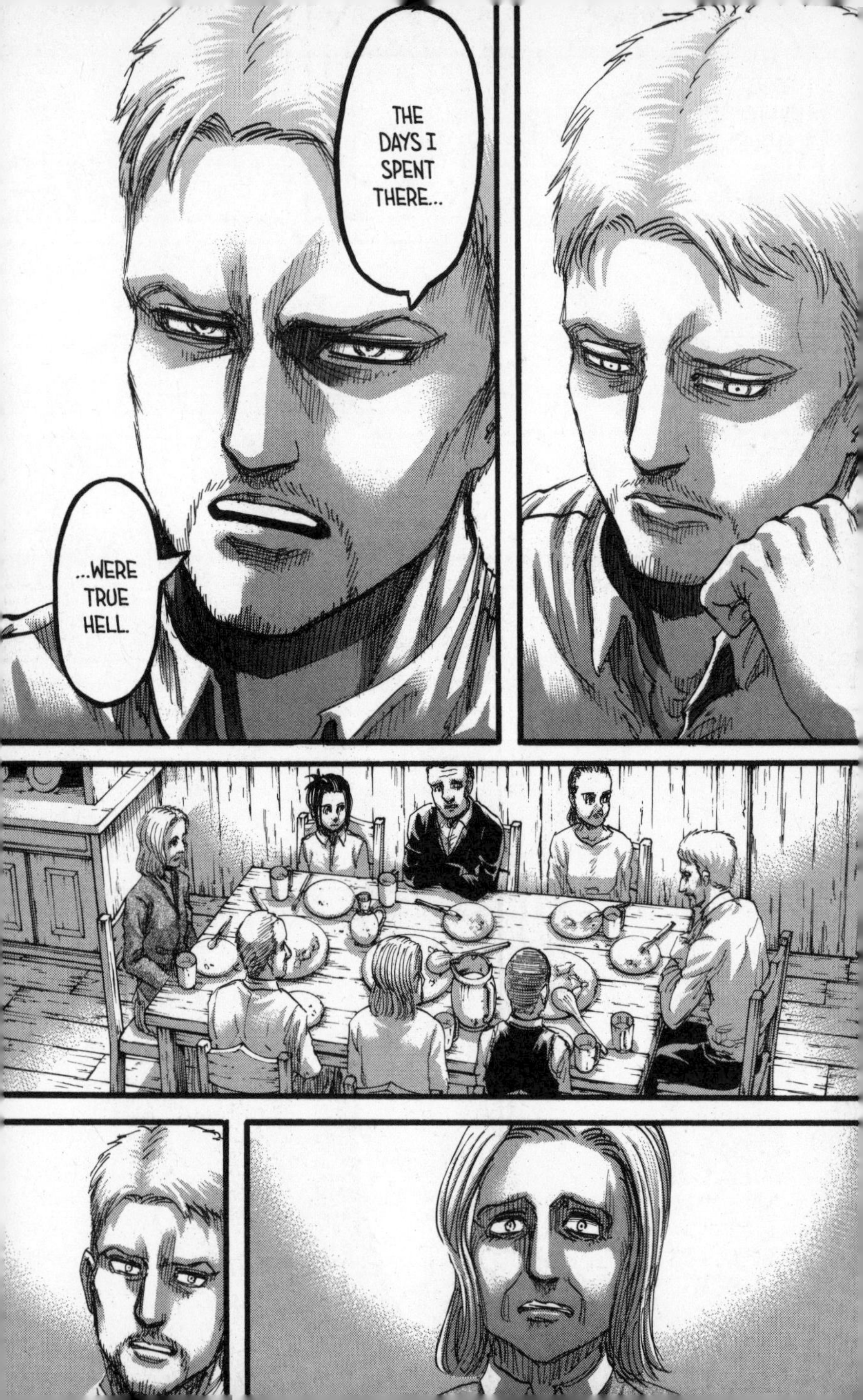
THE DAYS I SPENT THERE...
...WERE TRUE HELL.

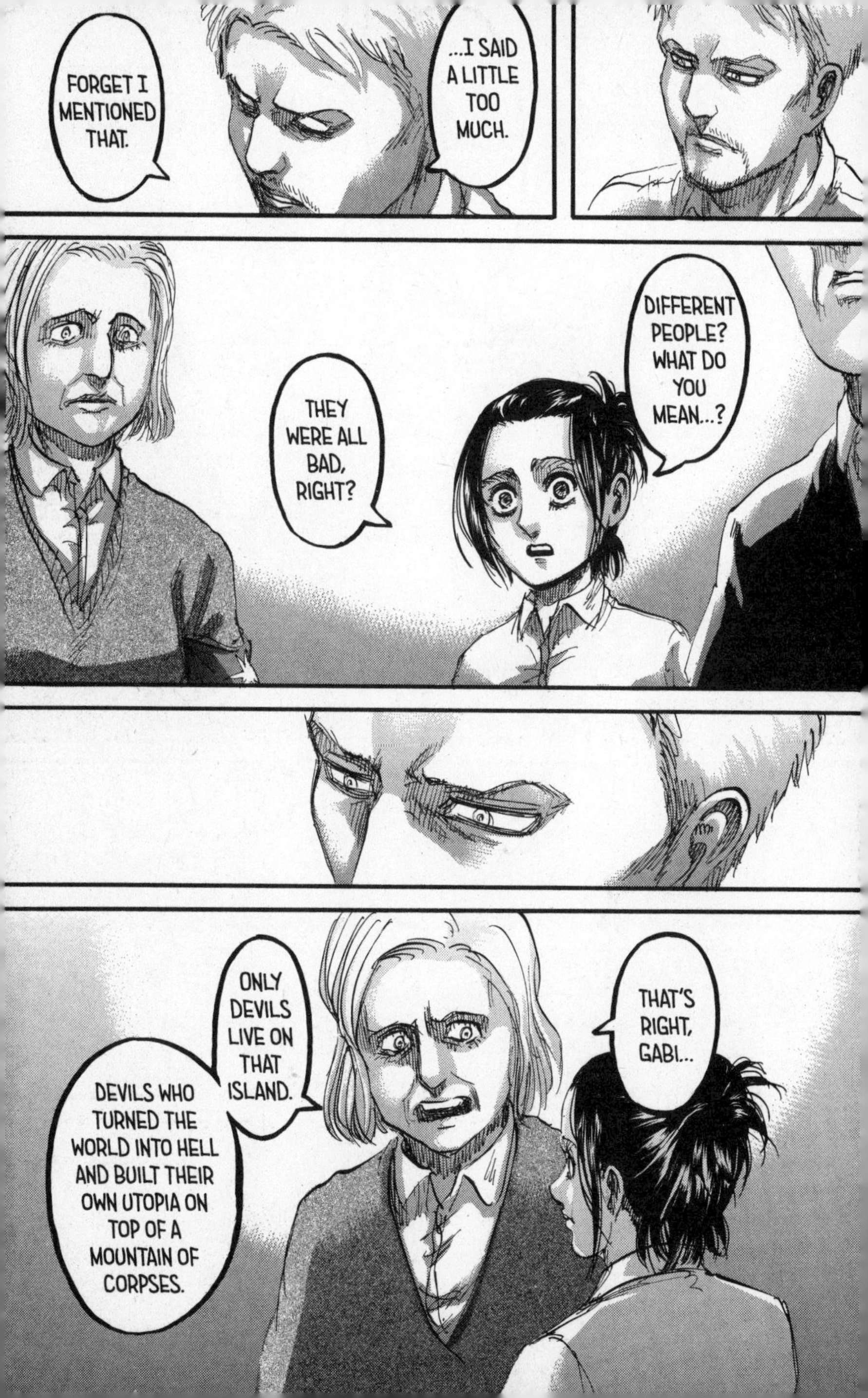
...I SAID A LITTLE TOO MUCH.
FORGET I MENTIONED THAT.
DIFFERENT PEOPLE? WHAT DO YOU MEAN...?
THEY WERE ALL BAD, RIGHT?
THAT'S RIGHT, GABI...
ONLY DEVILS LIVE ON THAT ISLAND.
DEVILS WHO TURNED THE WORLD INTO HELL AND BUILT THEIR OWN UTOPIA ON TOP OF A MOUNTAIN OF CORPSES.

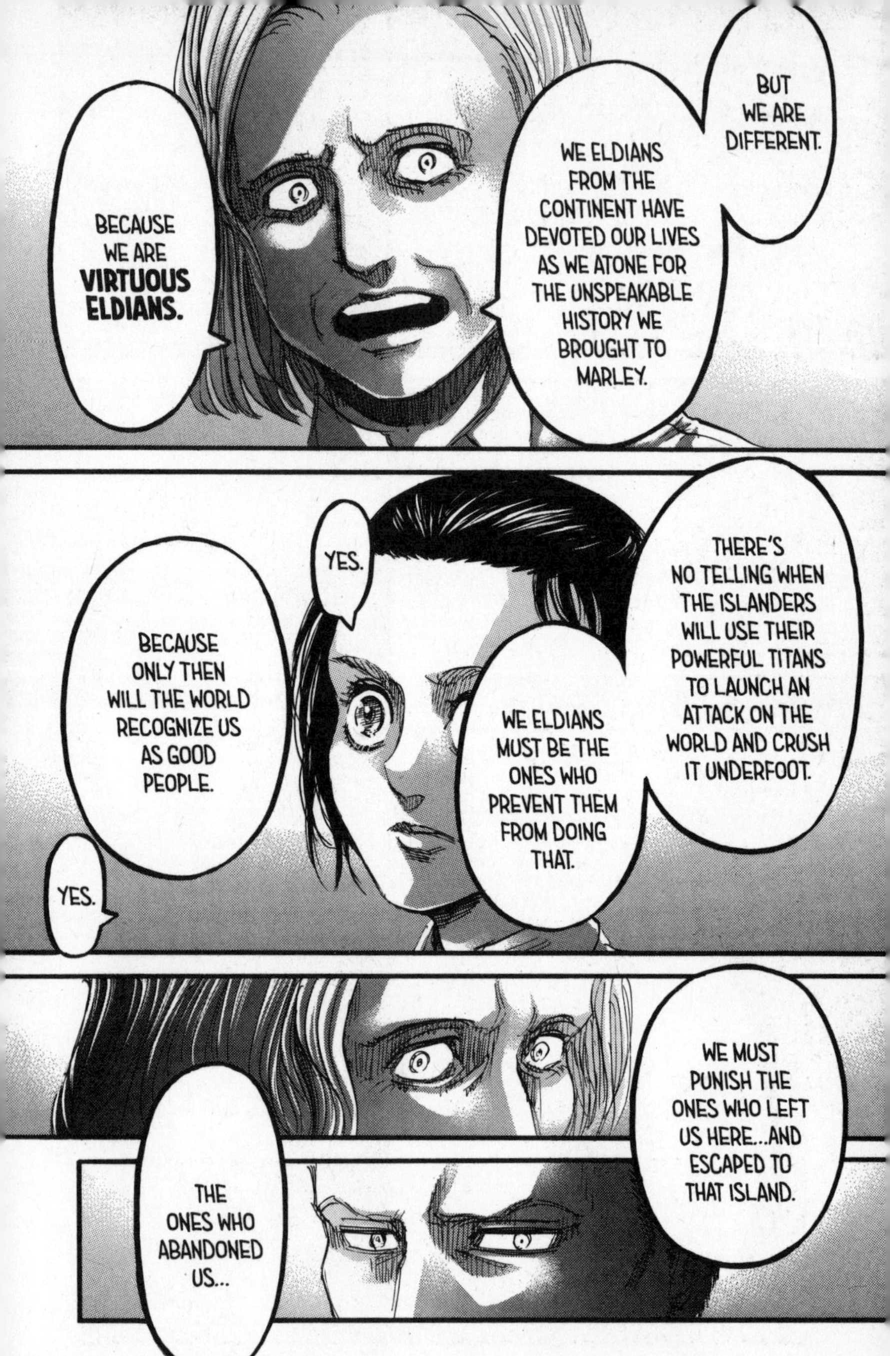
BUT WE ARE DIFFERENT.
WE ELDIANS FROM THE CONTINENT HAVE DEVOTED OUR LIVES AS WE ATONE FOR THE UNSPEAKABLE HISTORY WE BROUGHT TO MARLEY.
BECAUSE WE ARE **VIRTUOUS ELDIANS.**
THERE'S NO TELLING WHEN THE ISLANDERS WILL USE THEIR POWERFUL TITANS TO LAUNCH AN ATTACK ON THE WORLD AND CRUSH IT UNDERFOOT.
WE ELDIANS MUST BE THE ONES WHO PREVENT THEM FROM DOING THAT.
YES.
BECAUSE ONLY THEN WILL THE WORLD RECOGNIZE US AS GOOD PEOPLE.
YES.
WE MUST PUNISH THE ONES WHO LEFT US HERE...AND ESCAPED TO THAT ISLAND.
THE ONES WHO ABANDONED US...

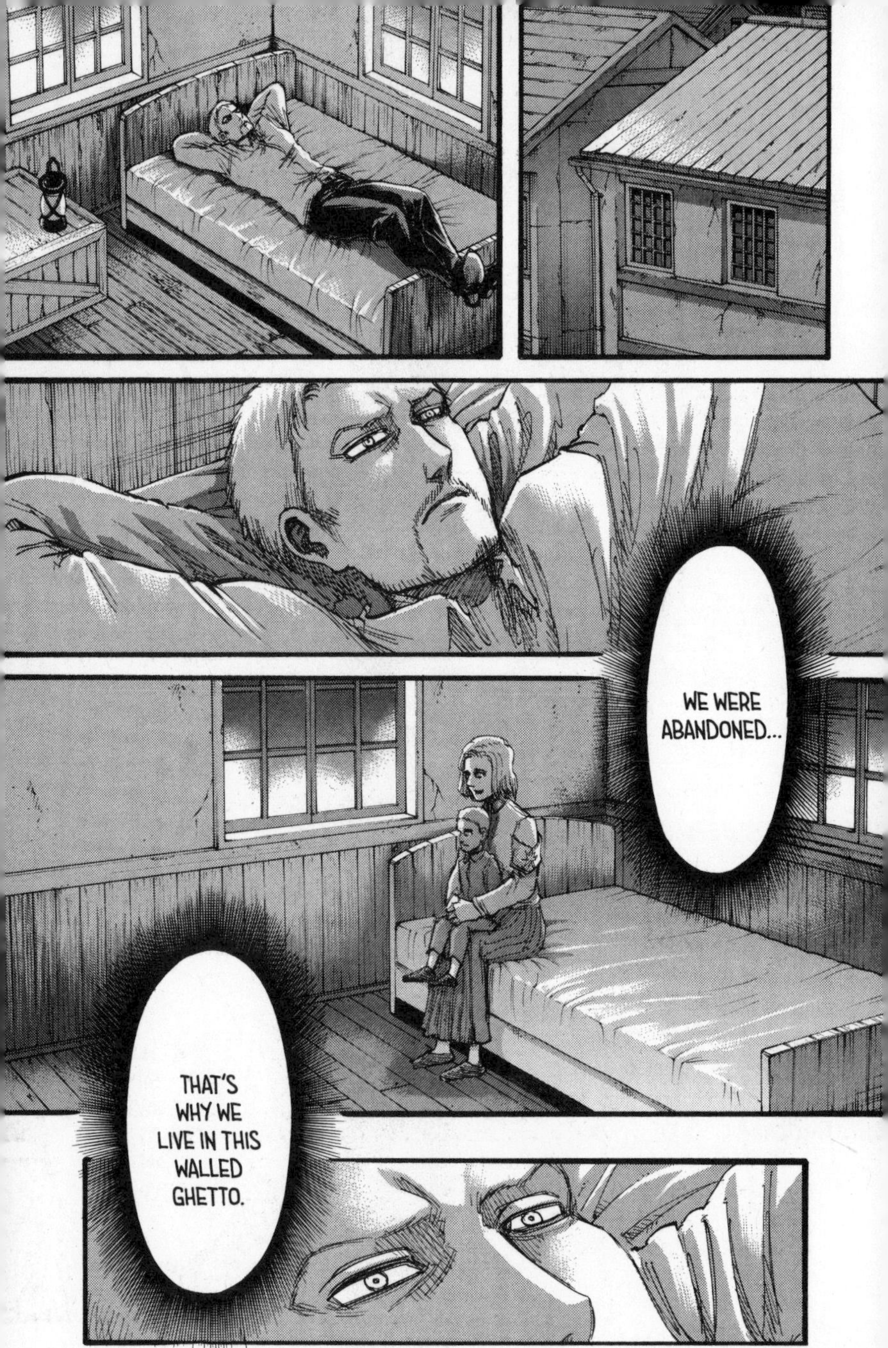
WE WERE ABANDONED...
THAT'S WHY WE LIVE IN THIS WALLED GHETTO.

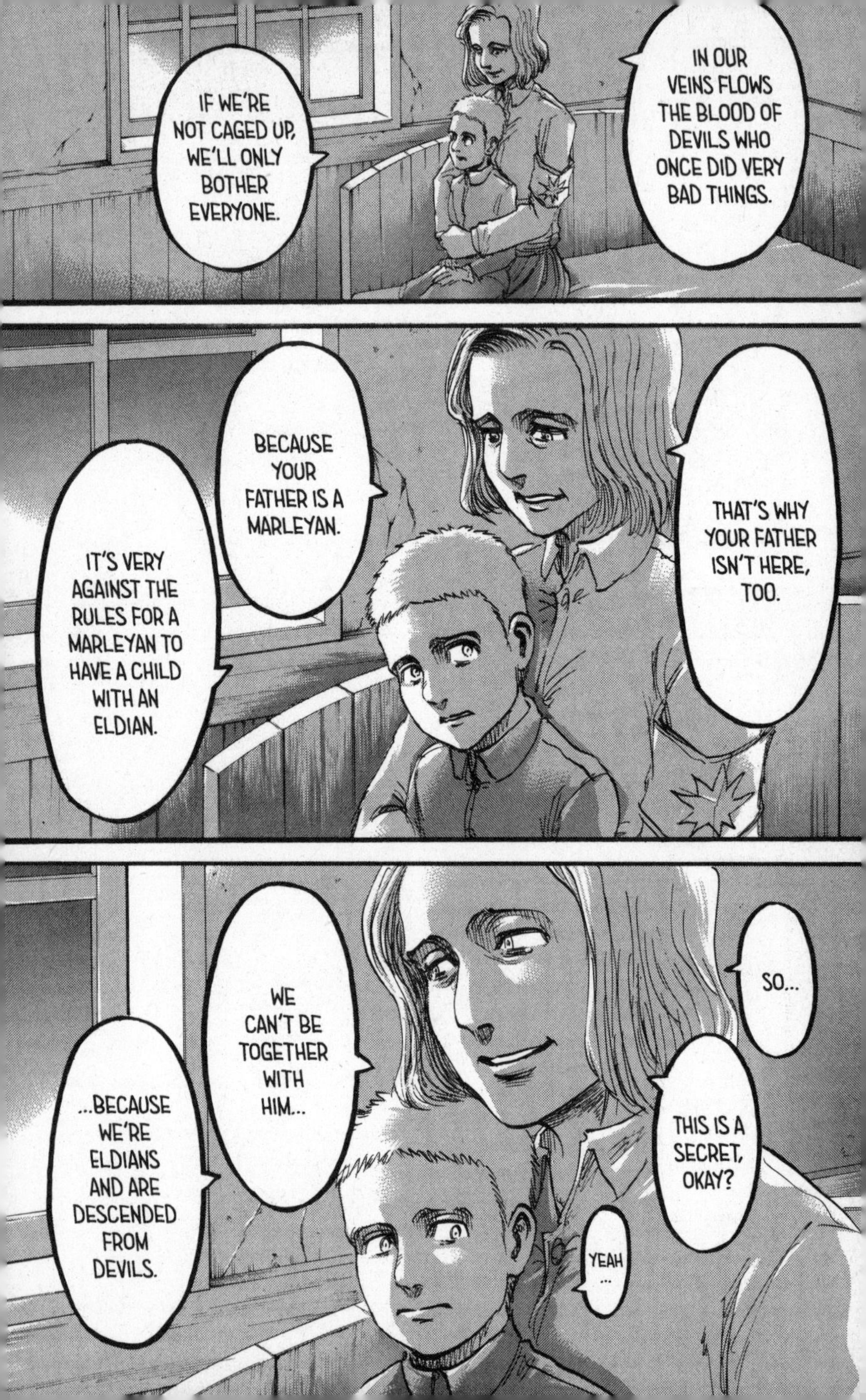
IN OUR VEINS FLOWS THE BLOOD OF DEVILS WHO ONCE DID VERY BAD THINGS.
IF WE'RE NOT CAGED UP, WE'LL ONLY BOTHER EVERYONE.
THAT'S WHY YOUR FATHER ISN'T HERE, TOO.
BECAUSE YOUR FATHER IS A MARLEYAN.
IT'S VERY AGAINST THE RULES FOR A MARLEYAN TO HAVE A CHILD WITH AN ELDIAN.
SO...
THIS IS A SECRET, OKAY?
YEAH ...
WE CAN'T BE TOGETHER WITH HIM...
...BECAUSE WE'RE ELDIANS AND ARE DESCENDED FROM DEVILS.

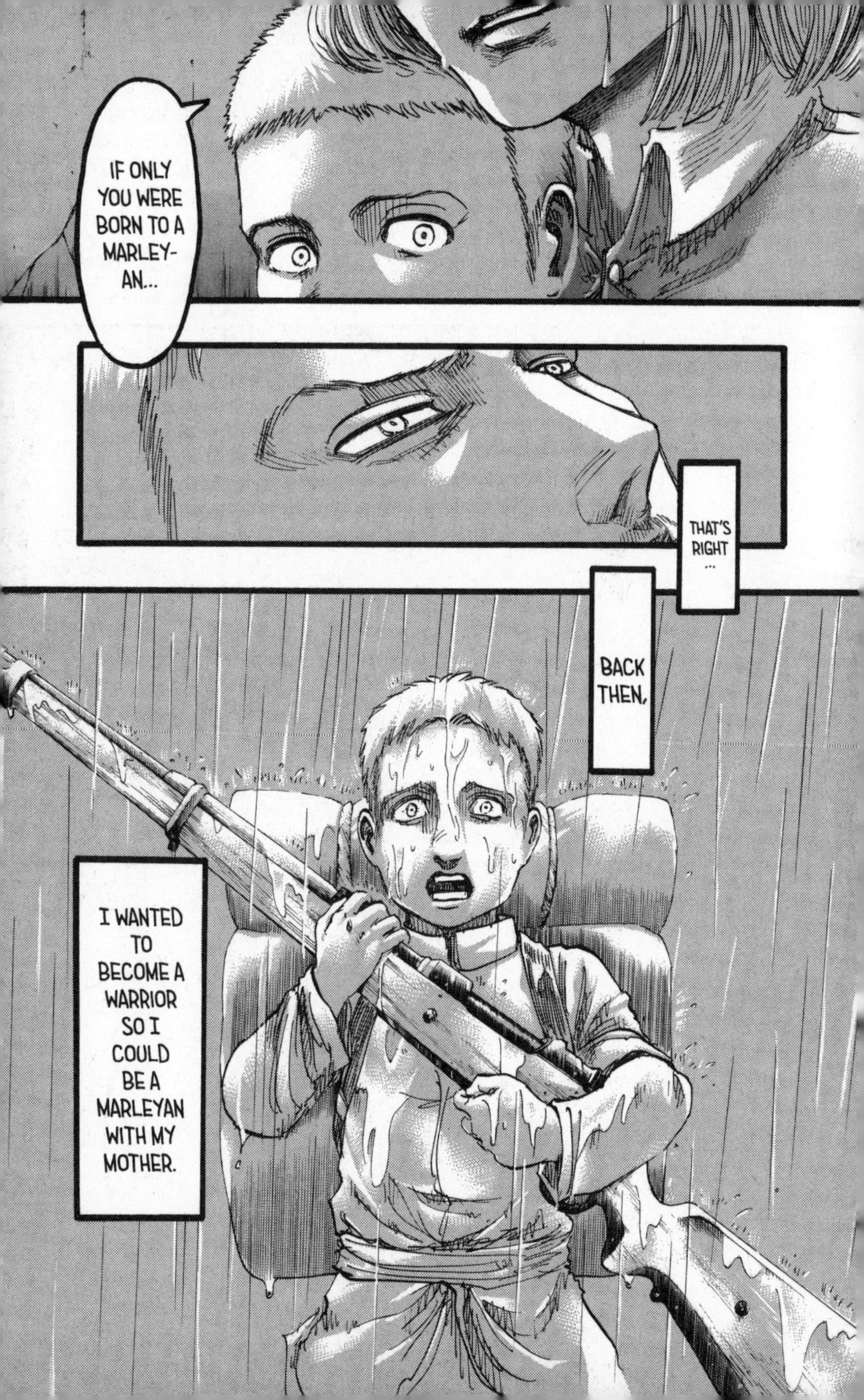
IF ONLY YOU WERE BORN TO A MARLEY-AN...
THAT'S RIGHT...
BACK THEN,
I WANTED TO BECOME A WARRIOR SO I COULD BE A MARLEYAN WITH MY MOTHER.

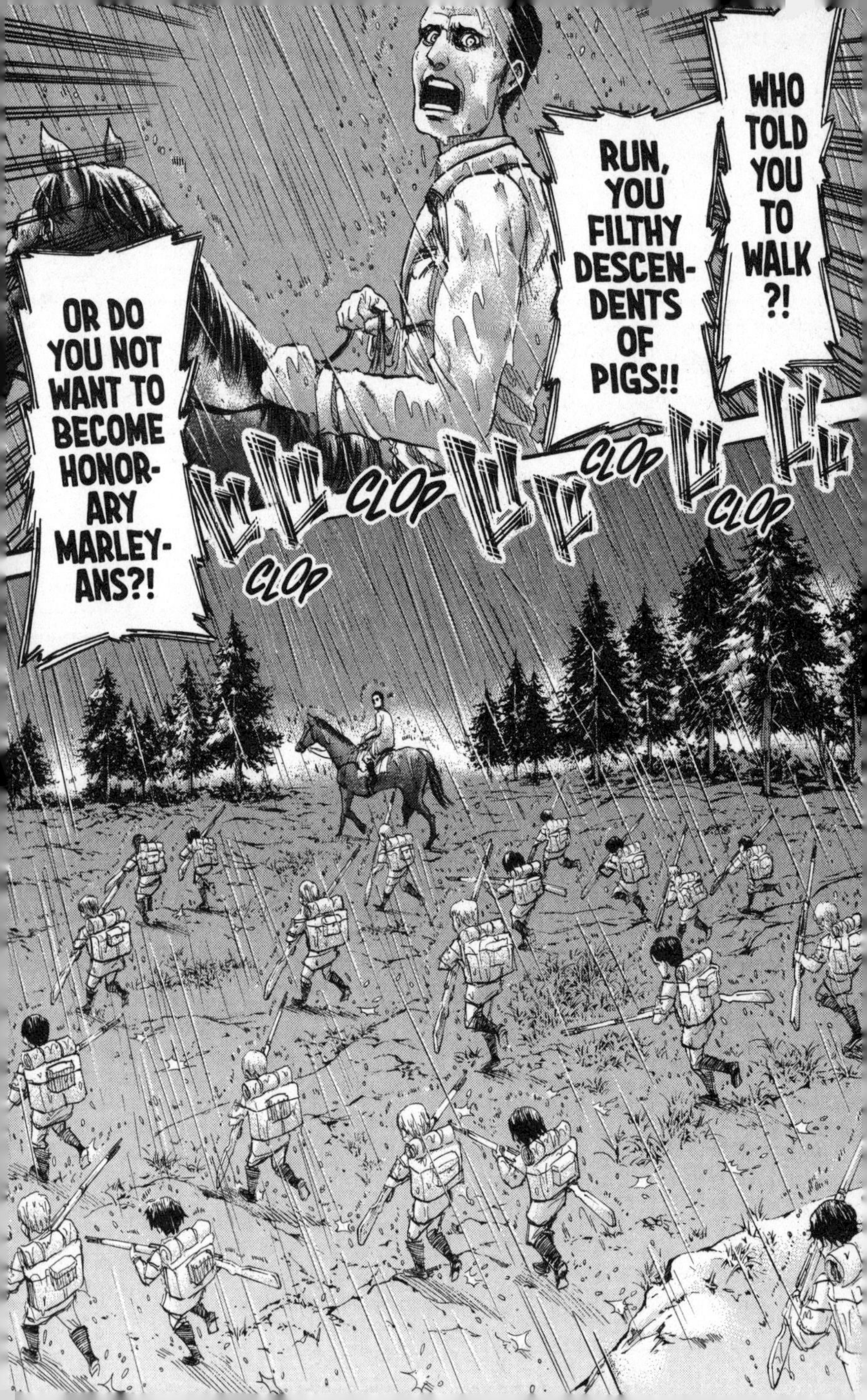
WHO TOLD YOU TO WALK?!
RUN, YOU FILTHY DESCEN-DENTS OF PIGS!!
OR DO YOU NOT WANT TO BECOME HONOR-ARY MARLEY-ANS?!
CLOP
CLOP
CLOP
CLOP

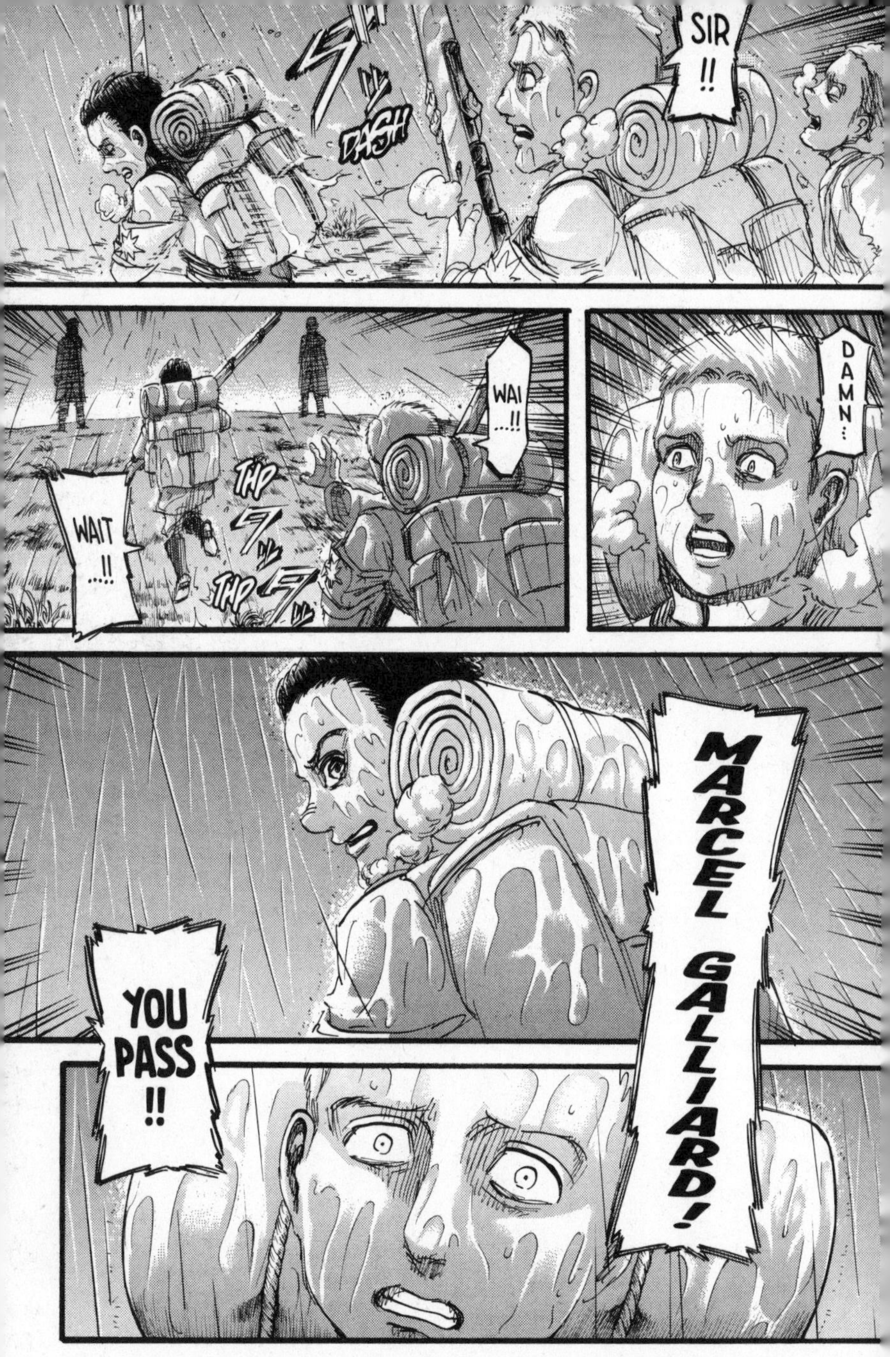
SIR !!
DASH
DAMN...
WAI ...!!
THP
THP
WAIT ...!!
MARCEL GALLIARD!
YOU PASS !!

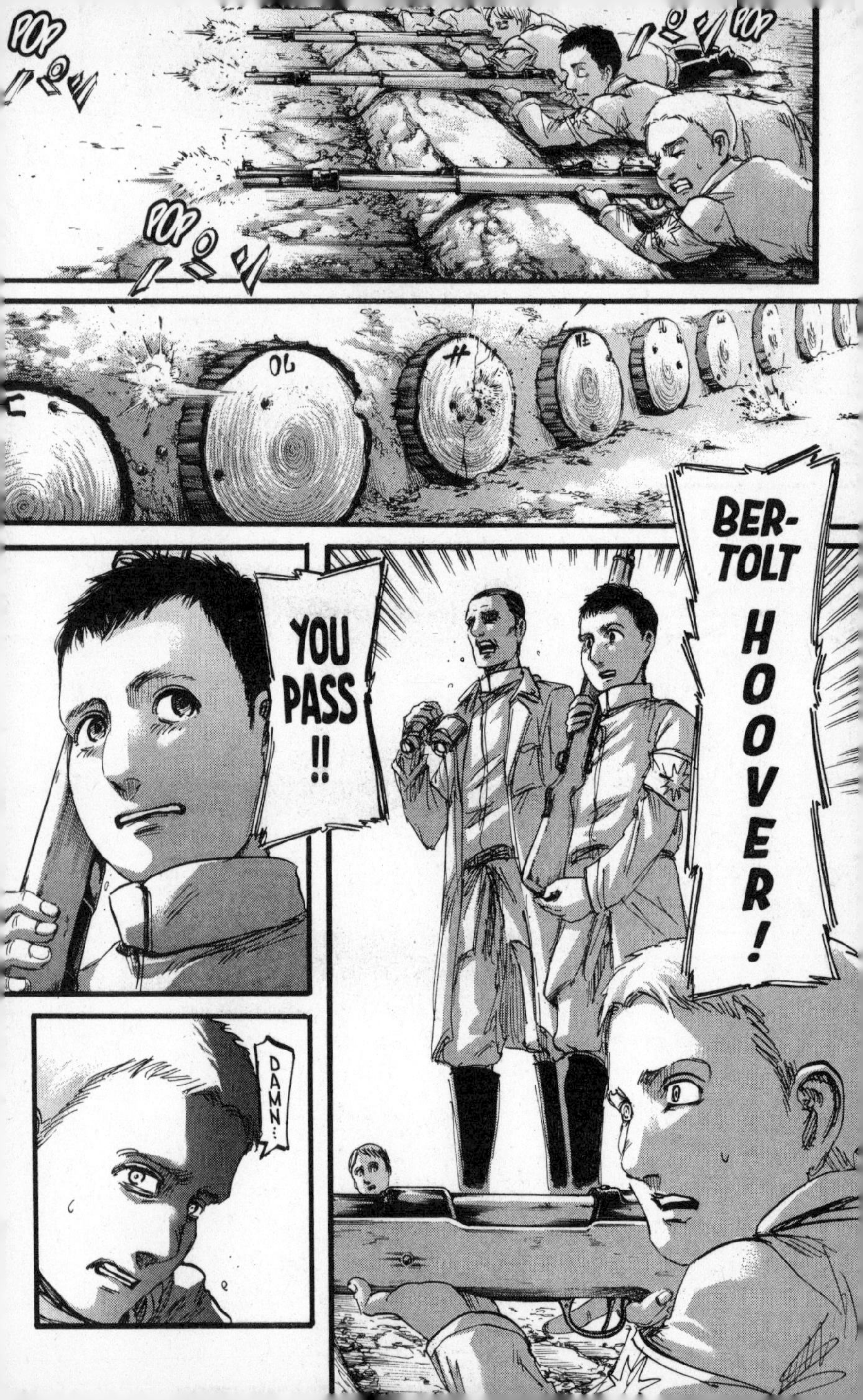
POP
POP
POP
BER-TOLT HOOVER!
YOU PASS!!
DAMN...

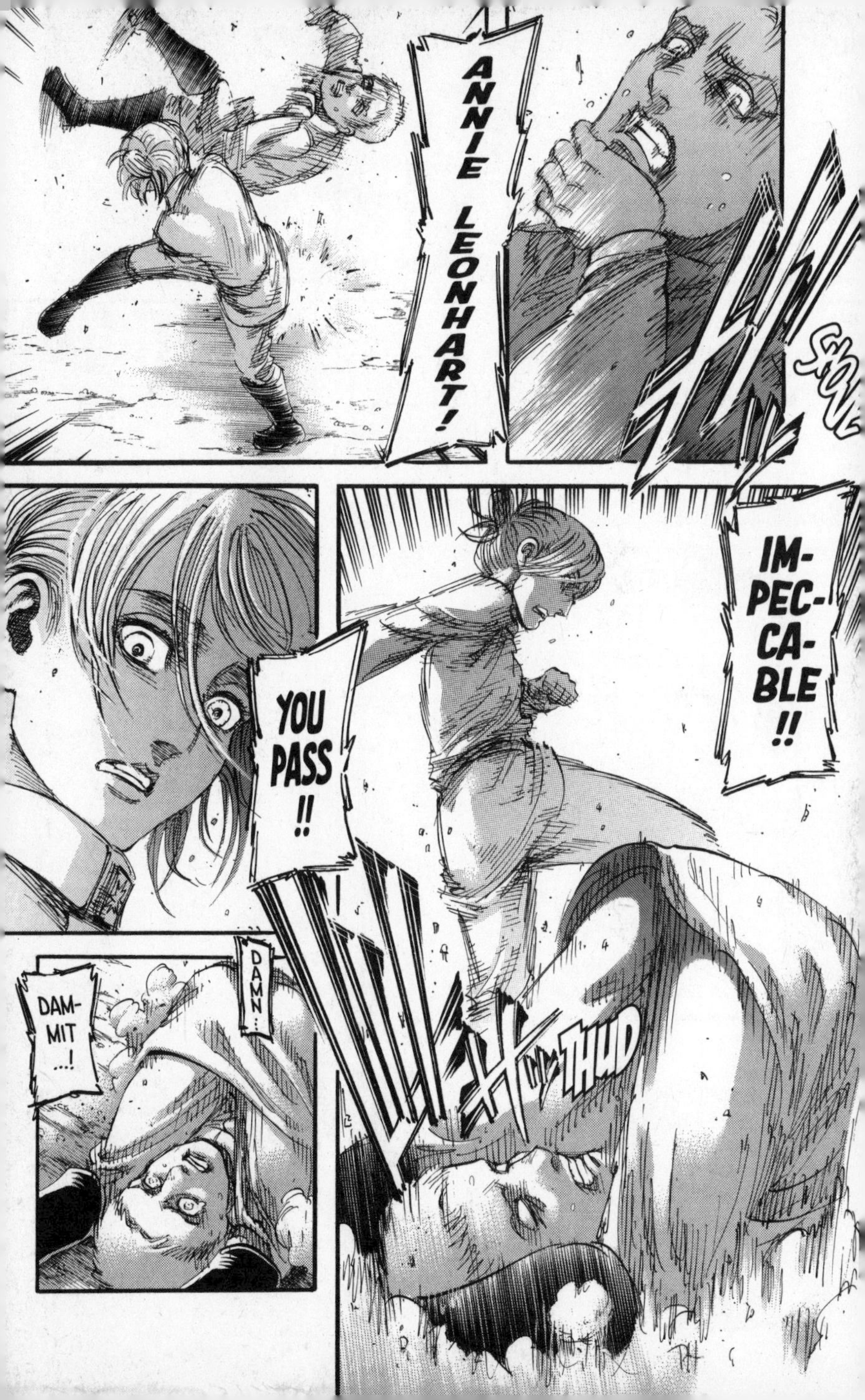
ANNIE LEONHART!
IMPECCABLE!!
YOU PASS!!
THUD
DAMN...
DAMMIT ...!

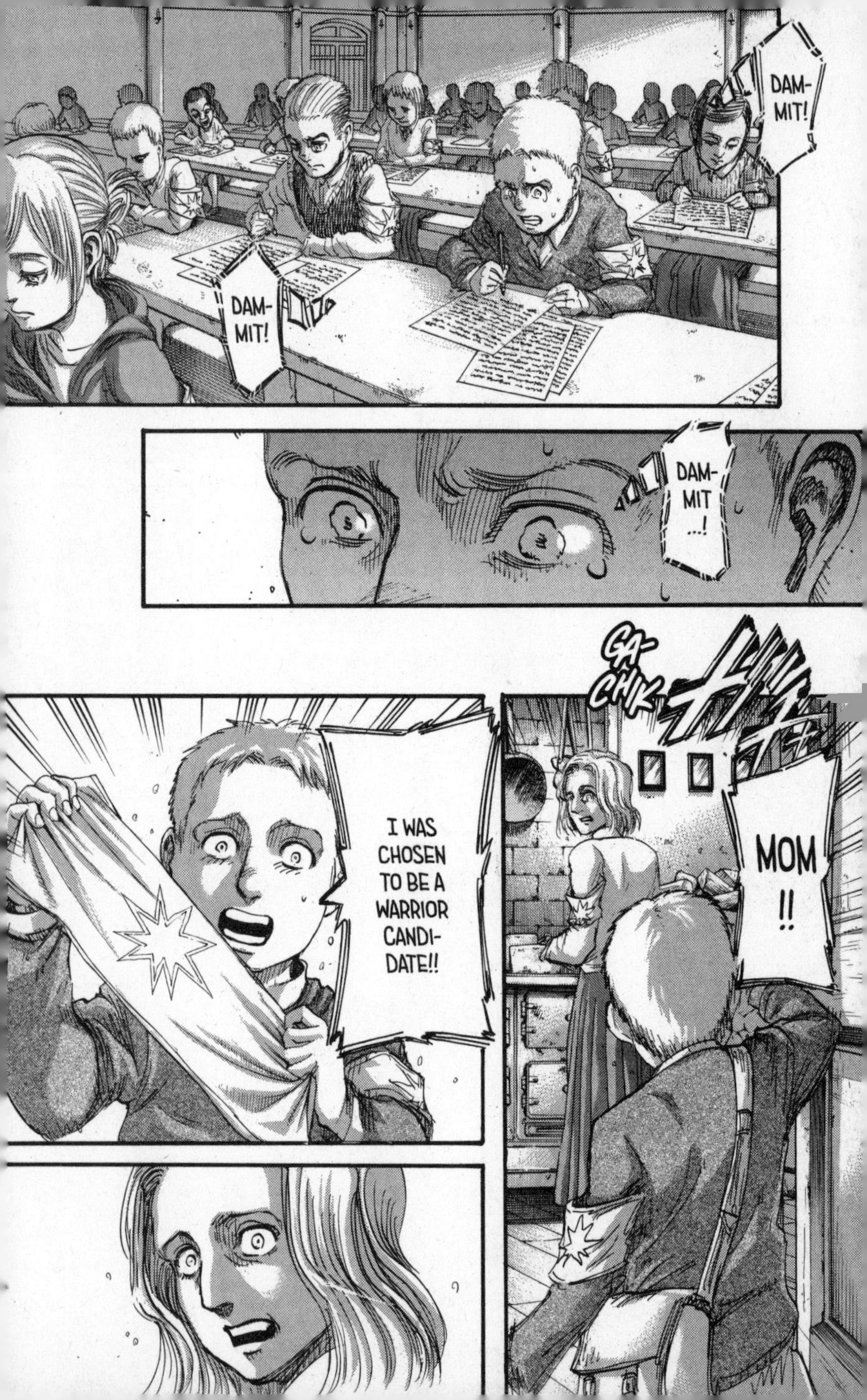
DAM-MIT!
DAM-MIT!
DAM-MIT ...!
GA-CHIK
MOM !!
I WAS CHOSEN TO BE A WARRIOR CANDI-DATE!!

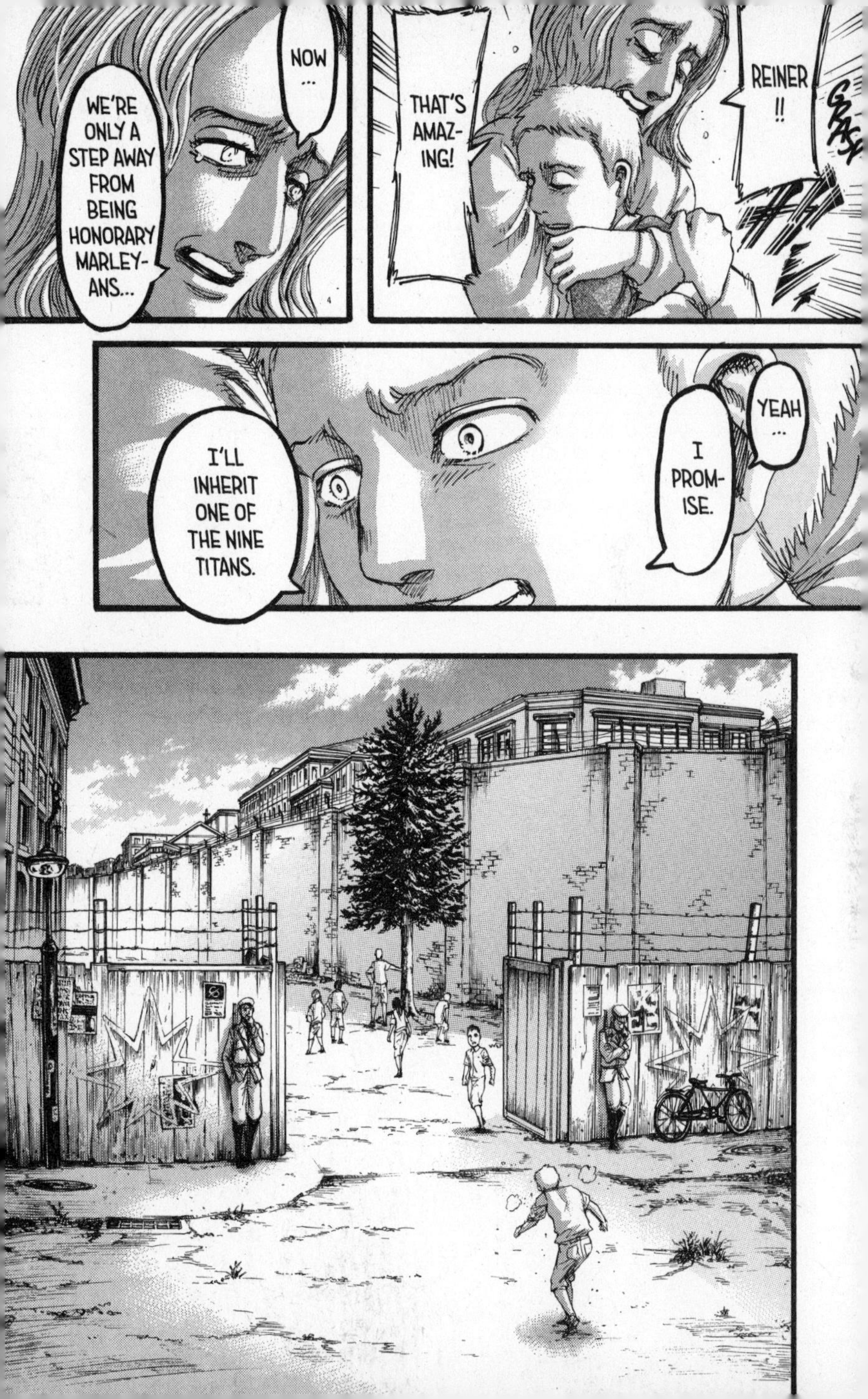
REINER !!
THAT'S AMAZING!
NOW ...
WE'RE ONLY A STEP AWAY FROM BEING HONORARY MARLEYANS...
YEAH ...
I PROMISE.
I'LL INHERIT ONE OF THE NINE TITANS.

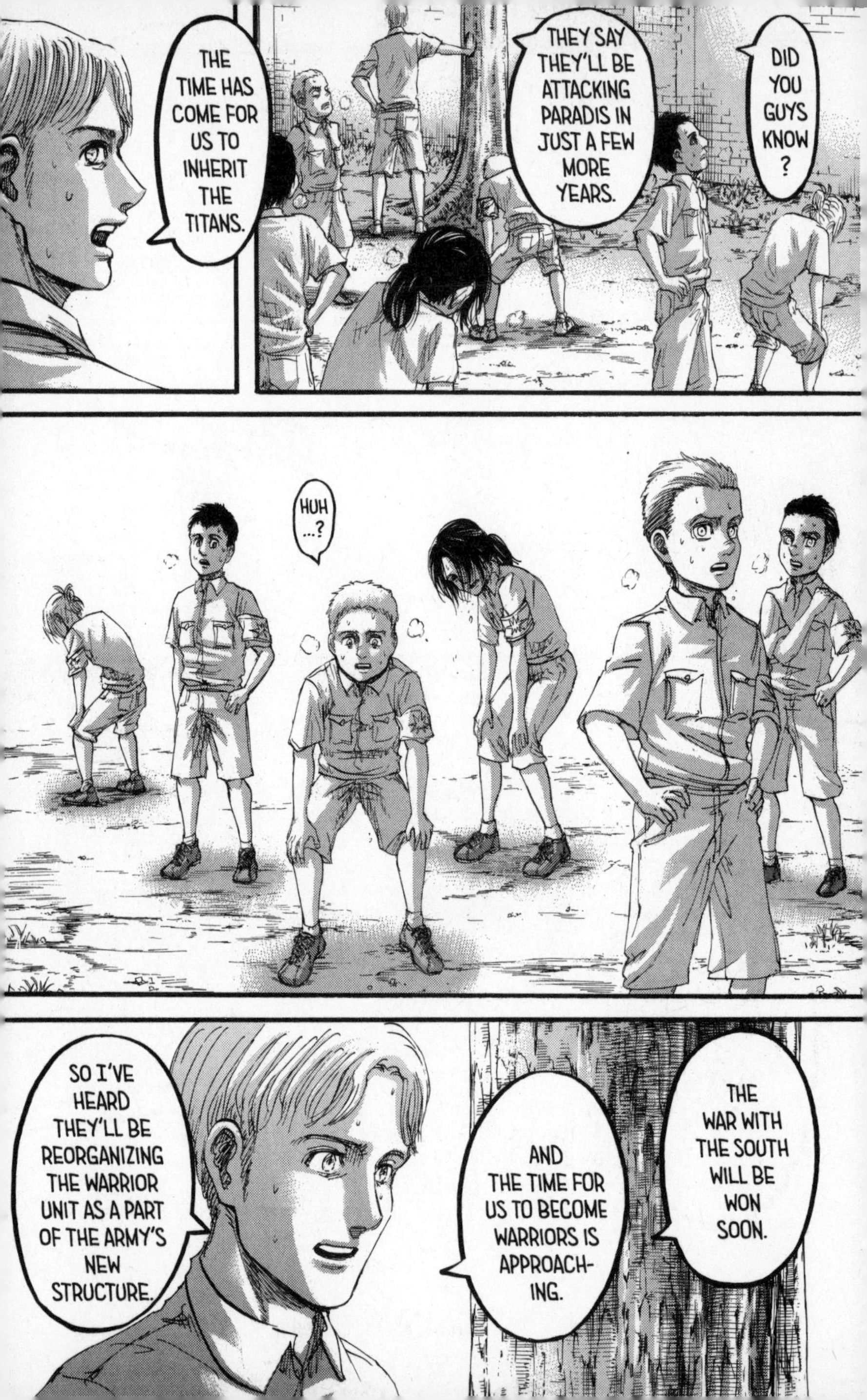
DID YOU GUYS KNOW?
THEY SAY THEY'LL BE ATTACKING PARADIS IN JUST A FEW MORE YEARS.
THE TIME HAS COME FOR US TO INHERIT THE TITANS.
HUH ...?
THE WAR WITH THE SOUTH WILL BE WON SOON.
AND THE TIME FOR US TO BECOME WARRIORS IS APPROACH-ING.
SO I'VE HEARD THEY'LL BE REORGANIZING THE WARRIOR UNIT AS A PART OF THE ARMY'S NEW STRUCTURE.

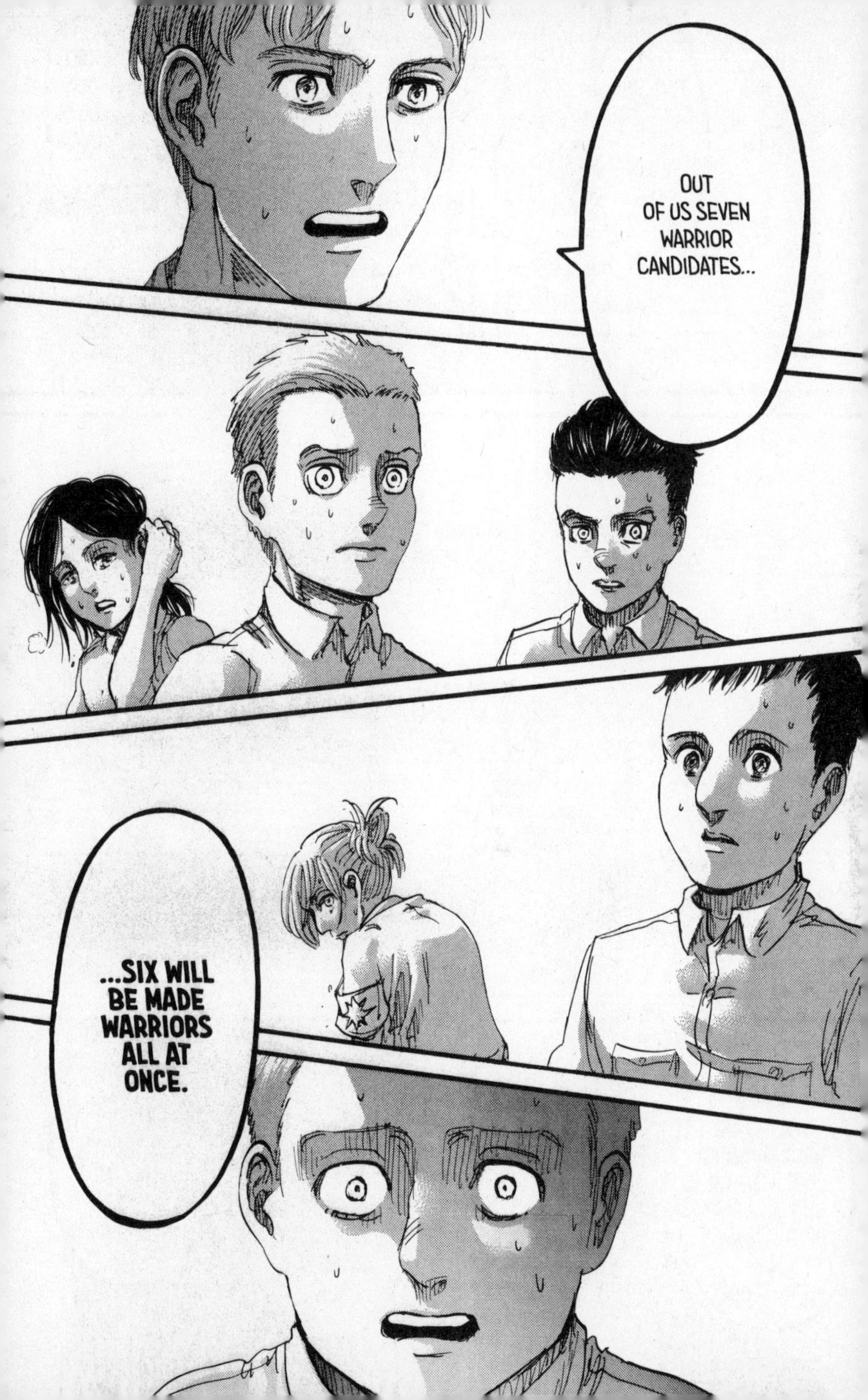
OUT OF US SEVEN WARRIOR CANDIDATES...
...SIX WILL BE MADE WARRIORS ALL AT ONCE.

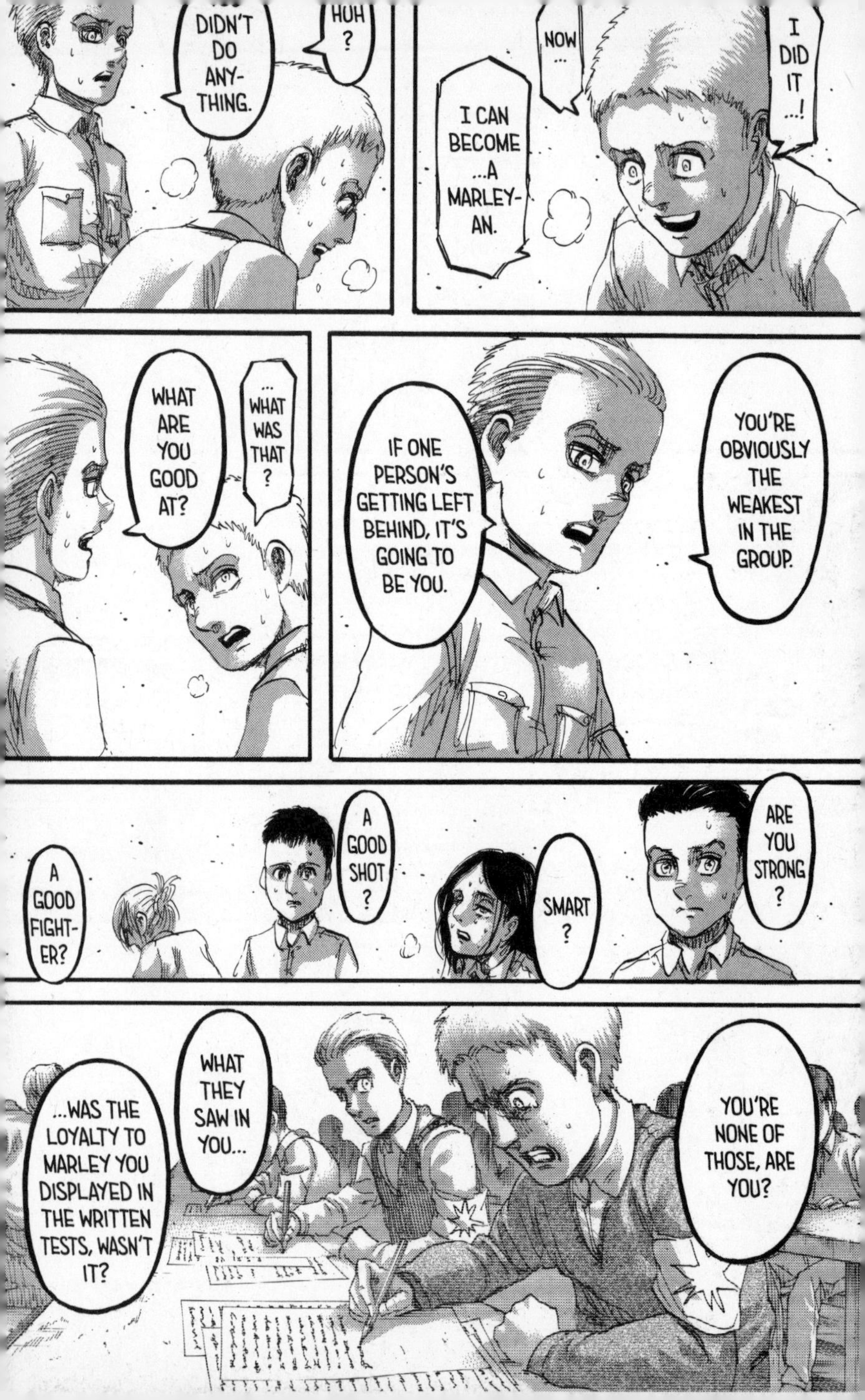
I DID IT ...!
NOW ...
I CAN BECOME ...A MARLEY-AN.
HUH ?
DIDN'T DO ANY-THING.
YOU'RE OBVIOUSLY THE WEAKEST IN THE GROUP.
IF ONE PERSON'S GETTING LEFT BEHIND, IT'S GOING TO BE YOU.
... WHAT WAS THAT ?
WHAT ARE YOU GOOD AT?
ARE YOU STRONG ?
SMART ?
A GOOD SHOT ?
A GOOD FIGHT-ER?
YOU'RE NONE OF THOSE, ARE YOU?
WHAT THEY SAW IN YOU...
...WAS THE LOYALTY TO MARLEY YOU DISPLAYED IN THE WRITTEN TESTS, WASN'T IT?

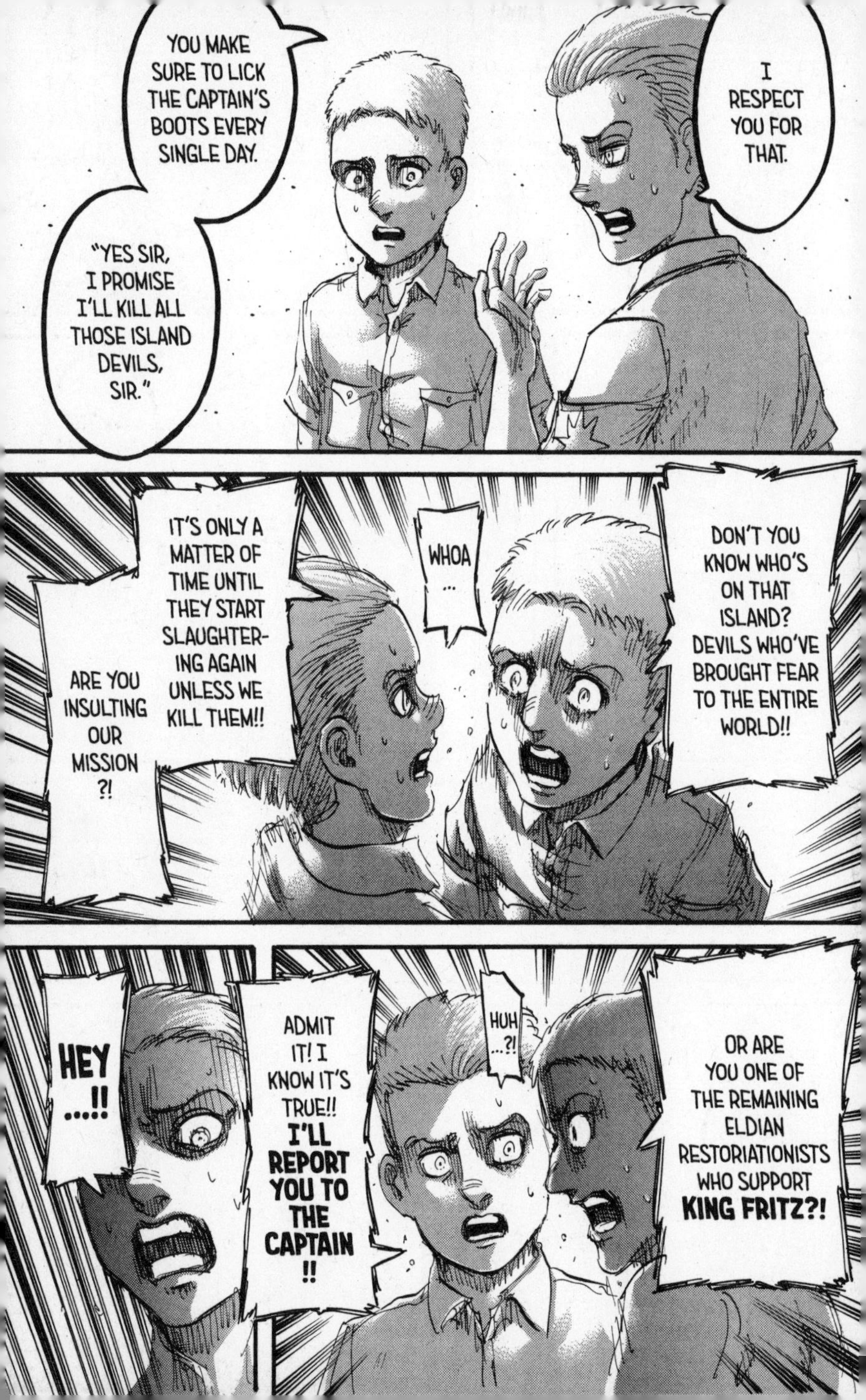
I RESPECT YOU FOR THAT.
YOU MAKE SURE TO LICK THE CAPTAIN'S BOOTS EVERY SINGLE DAY.
"YES SIR, I PROMISE I'LL KILL ALL THOSE ISLAND DEVILS, SIR."
DON'T YOU KNOW WHO'S ON THAT ISLAND? DEVILS WHO'VE BROUGHT FEAR TO THE ENTIRE WORLD!!
WHOA ...
IT'S ONLY A MATTER OF TIME UNTIL THEY START SLAUGHTER-ING AGAIN UNLESS WE KILL THEM!!
ARE YOU INSULTING OUR MISSION ?!
OR ARE YOU ONE OF THE REMAINING ELDIAN RESTORIATIONISTS WHO SUPPORT **KING FRITZ?!**
HUH ...?!
ADMIT IT! I KNOW IT'S TRUE!! **I'LL REPORT YOU TO THE CAPTAIN !!**
**HEY ...!!**

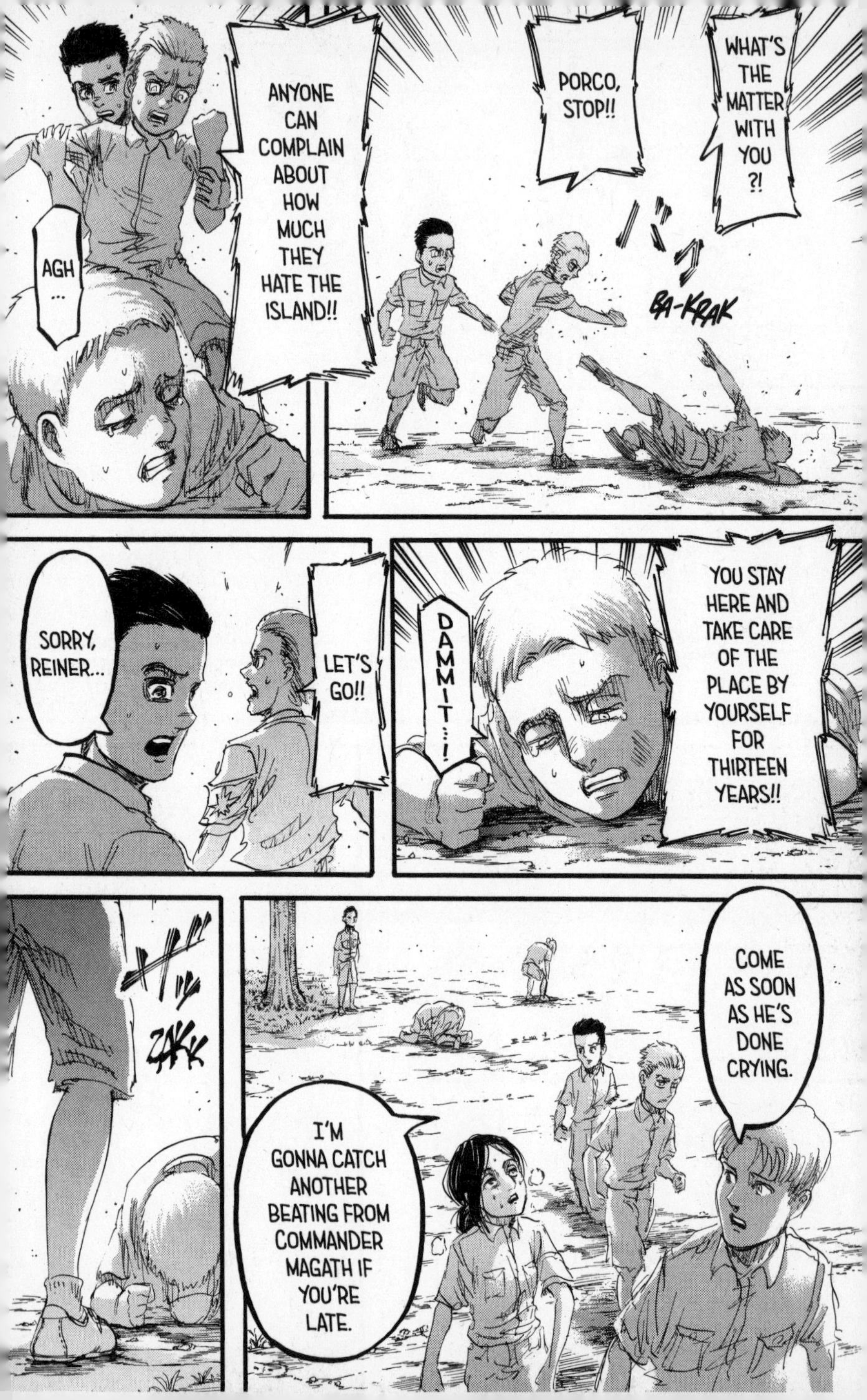
WHAT'S THE MATTER WITH YOU?!
PORCO, STOP!!
BA-KRAK
ANYONE CAN COMPLAIN ABOUT HOW MUCH THEY HATE THE ISLAND!!
AGH ...
YOU STAY HERE AND TAKE CARE OF THE PLACE BY YOURSELF FOR THIRTEEN YEARS!!
DAMMIT...!
LET'S GO!!
SORRY, REINER...
COME AS SOON AS HE'S DONE CRYING.
I'M GONNA CATCH ANOTHER BEATING FROM COMMANDER MAGATH IF YOU'RE LATE.
ZAKK

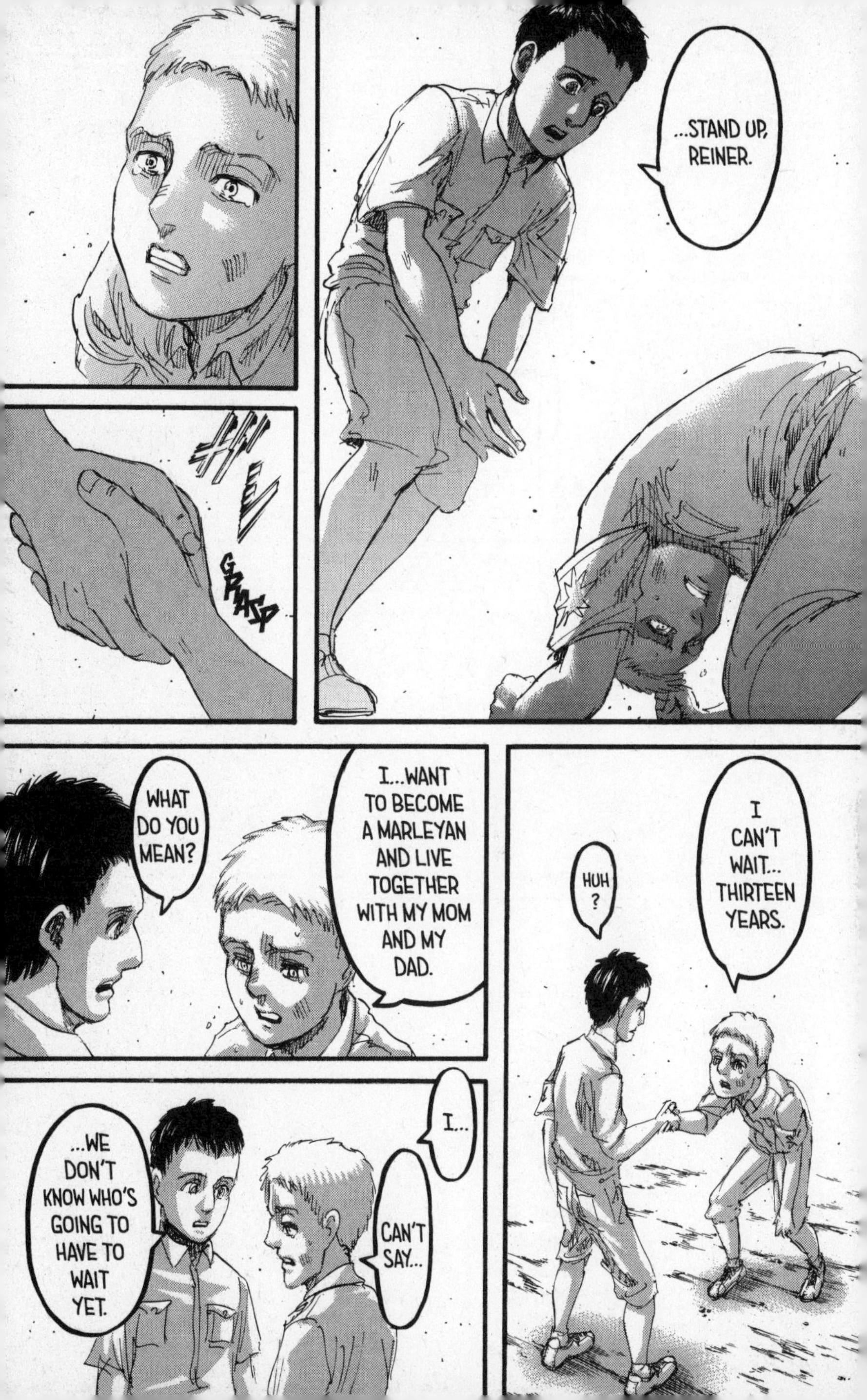
...STAND UP, REINER.
I CAN'T WAIT... THIRTEEN YEARS.
HUH?
I...WANT TO BECOME A MARLEYAN AND LIVE TOGETHER WITH MY MOM AND MY DAD.
WHAT DO YOU MEAN?
I...
CAN'T SAY...
...WE DON'T KNOW WHO'S GOING TO HAVE TO WAIT YET.

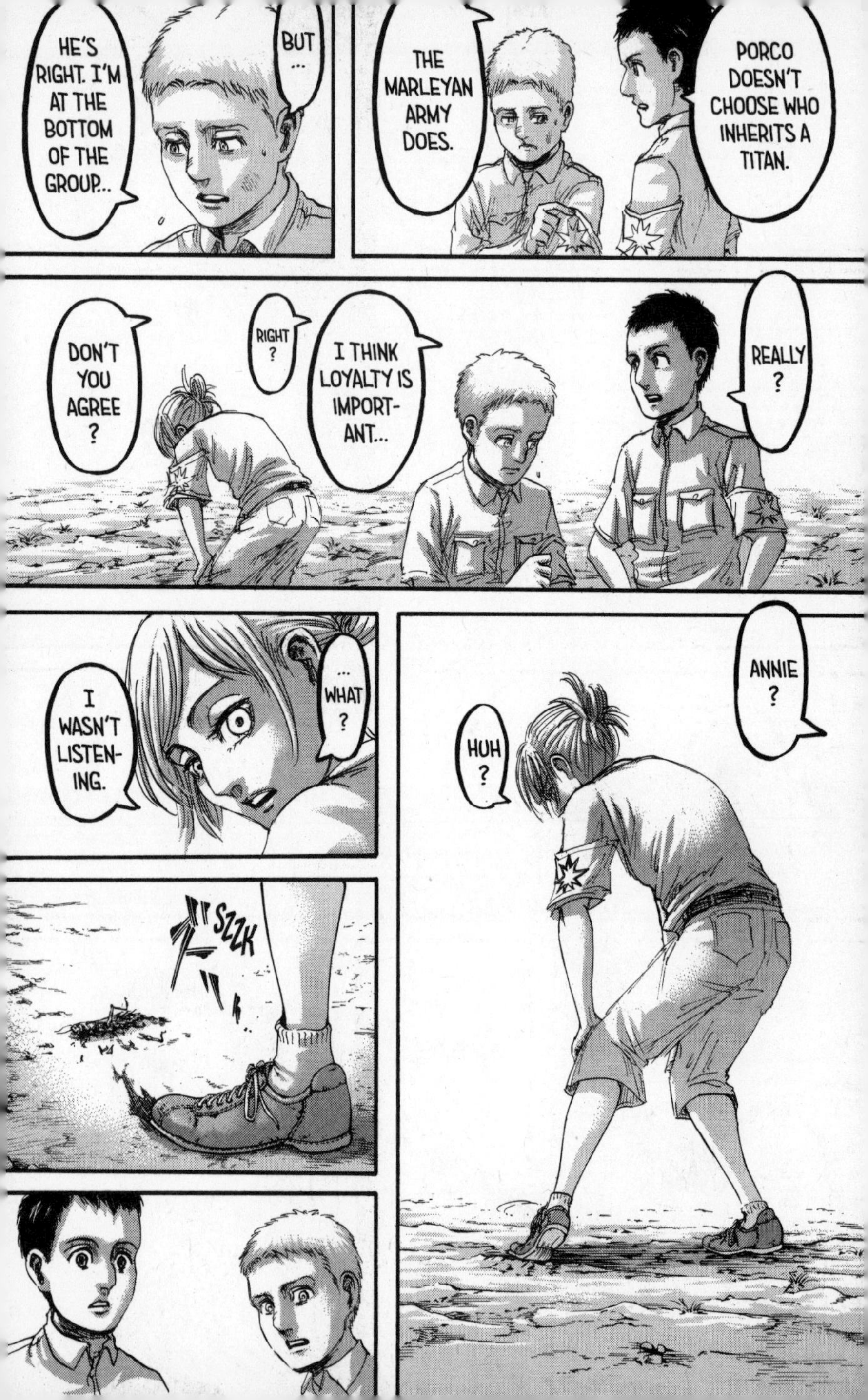
PORCO DOESN'T CHOOSE WHO INHERITS A TITAN.
THE MARLEYAN ARMY DOES.
HE'S RIGHT. I'M AT THE BOTTOM OF THE GROUP...
BUT ...
REALLY ?
I THINK LOYALTY IS IMPORT-ANT...
RIGHT ?
DON'T YOU AGREE ?
ANNIE ?
HUH ?
... WHAT ?
I WASN'T LISTEN-ING.
SZZK

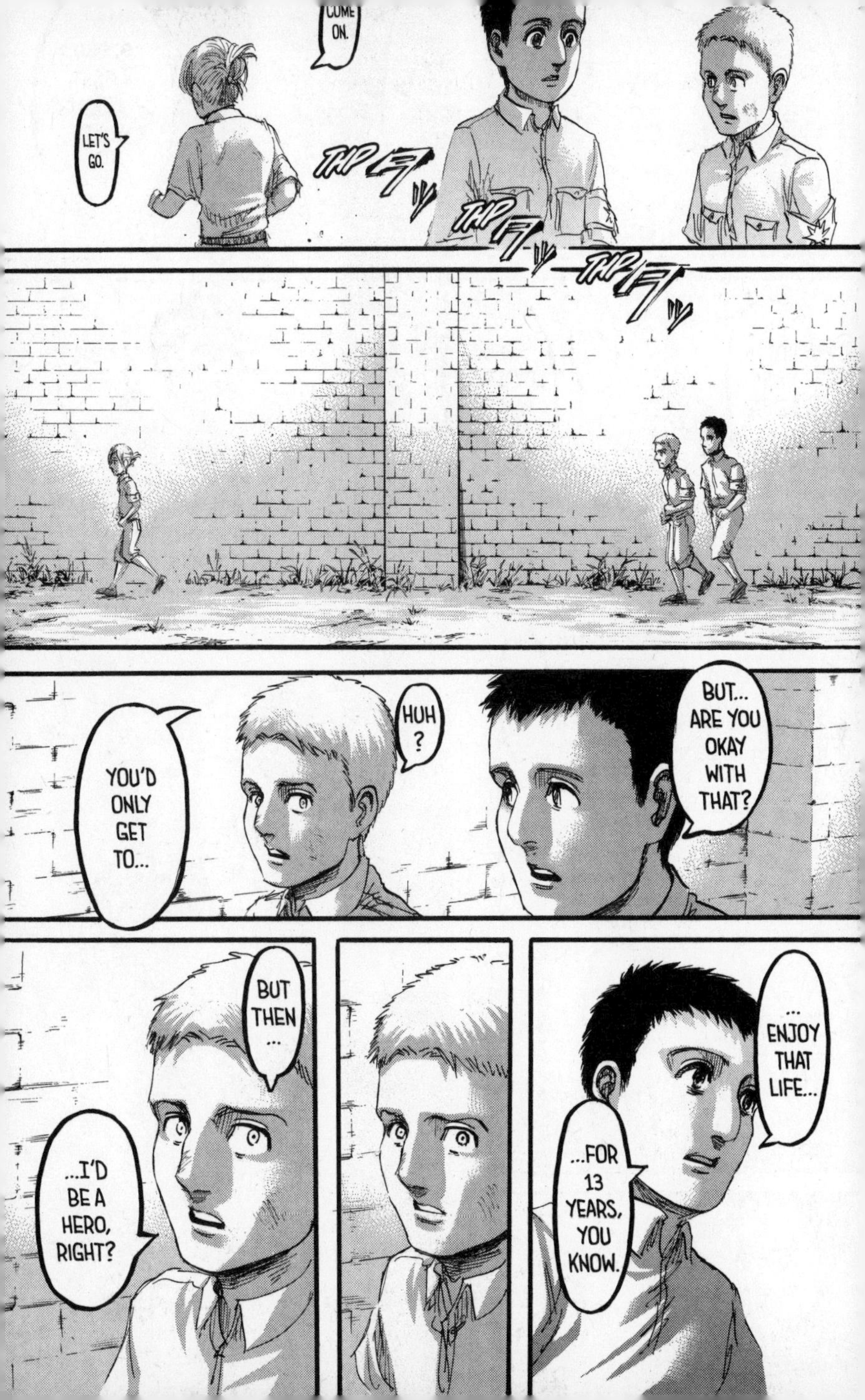
COME ON.
LET'S GO.
THP
THP
THP
BUT... ARE YOU OKAY WITH THAT?
HUH?
YOU'D ONLY GET TO...
... ENJOY THAT LIFE...
...FOR 13 YEARS, YOU KNOW.
BUT THEN ...
...I'D BE A HERO, RIGHT?

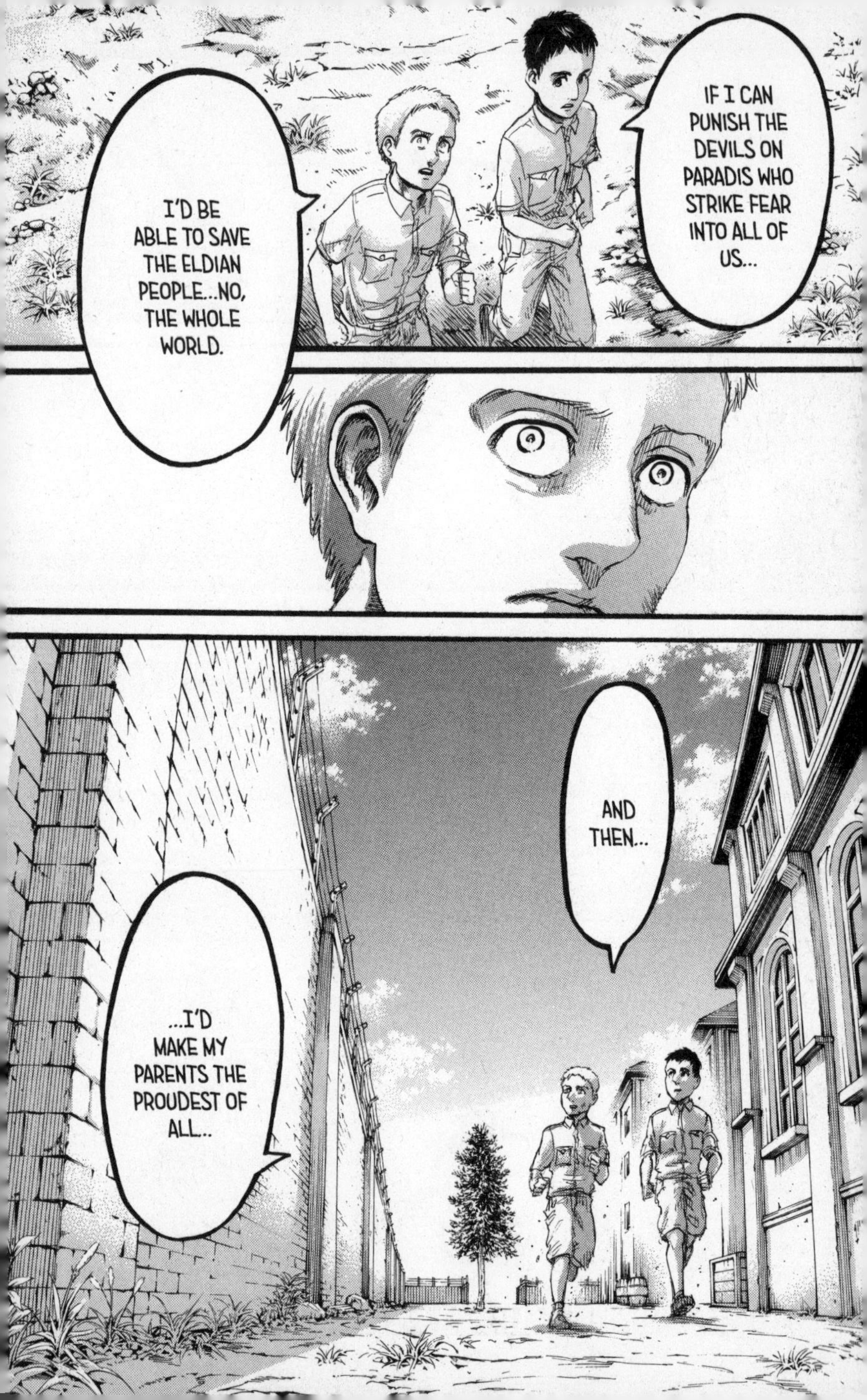
IF I CAN PUNISH THE DEVILS ON PARADIS WHO STRIKE FEAR INTO ALL OF US...
I'D BE ABLE TO SAVE THE ELDIAN PEOPLE...NO, THE WHOLE WORLD.
AND THEN...
...I'D MAKE MY PARENTS THE PROUDEST OF ALL...

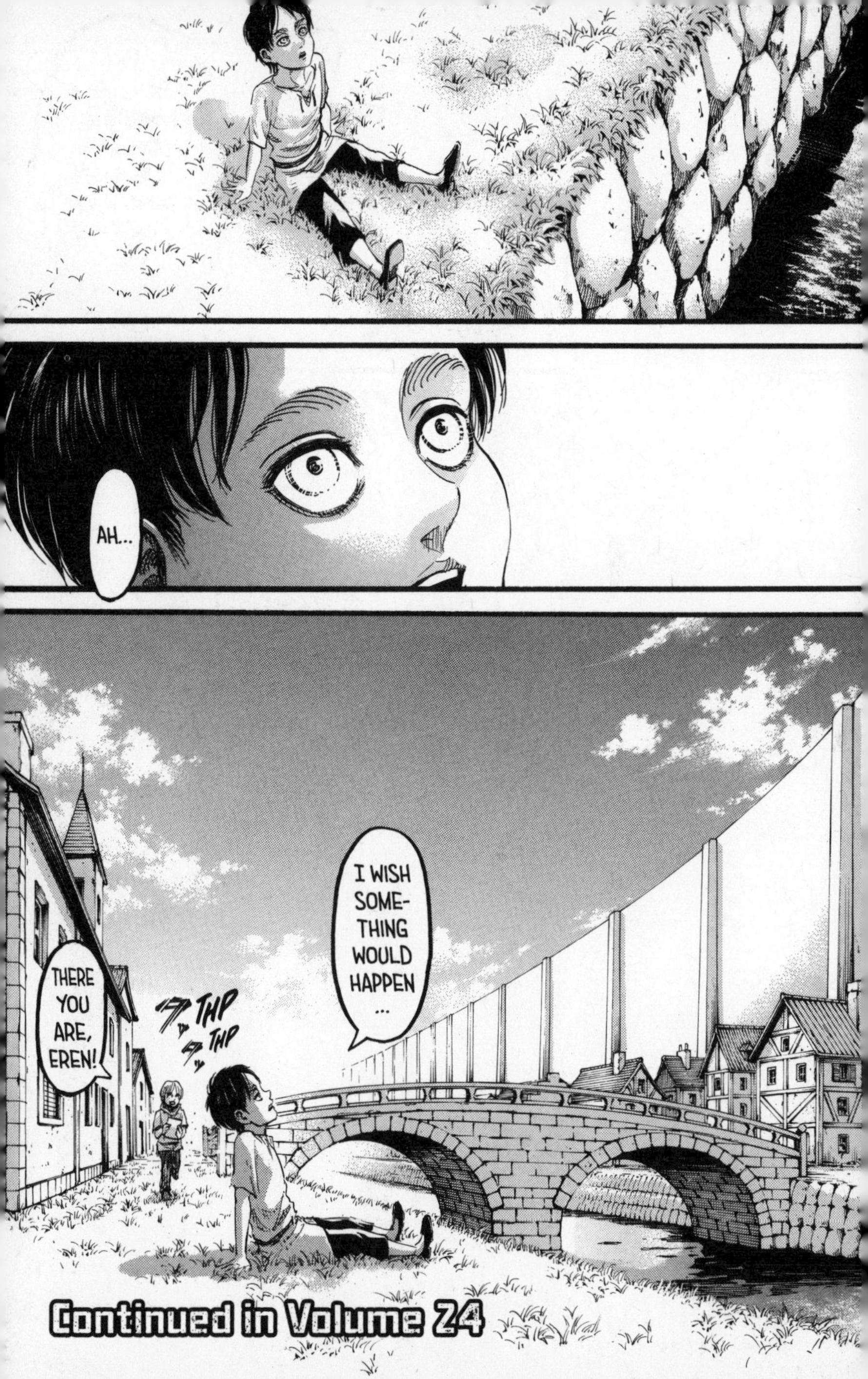
AH...
I WISH SOMETHING WOULD HAPPEN ...
THP THP
THERE YOU ARE, EREN!

Continued in Volume 24

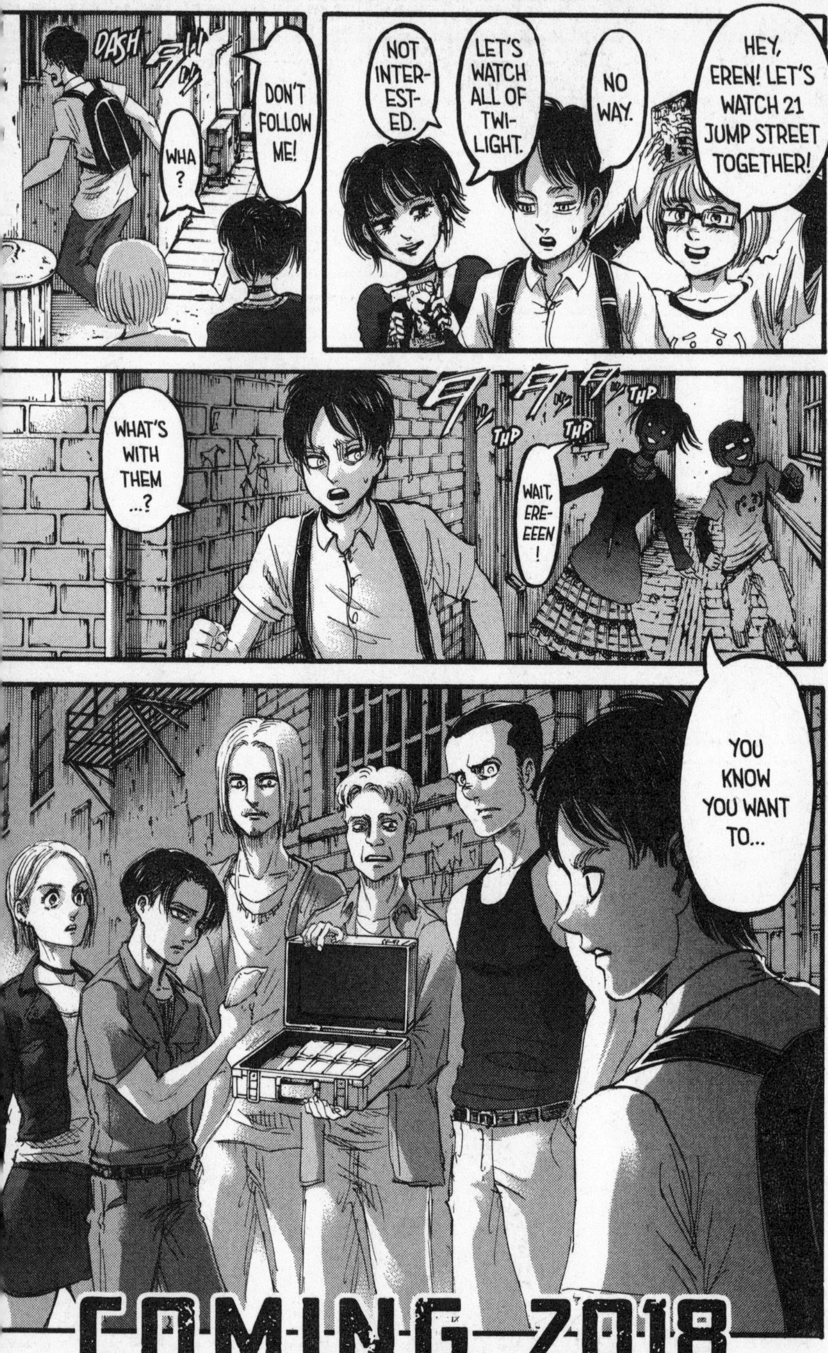
HEY, EREN! LET'S WATCH 21 JUMP STREET TOGETHER!
NO WAY.
LET'S WATCH ALL OF TWILIGHT.
NOT INTER-EST-ED.
DON'T FOLLOW ME!
DASH
WHA?
THP THP THP
WAIT, ERE-EEEN!
WHAT'S WITH THEM ...?
YOU KNOW YOU WANT TO...
COMING 2018

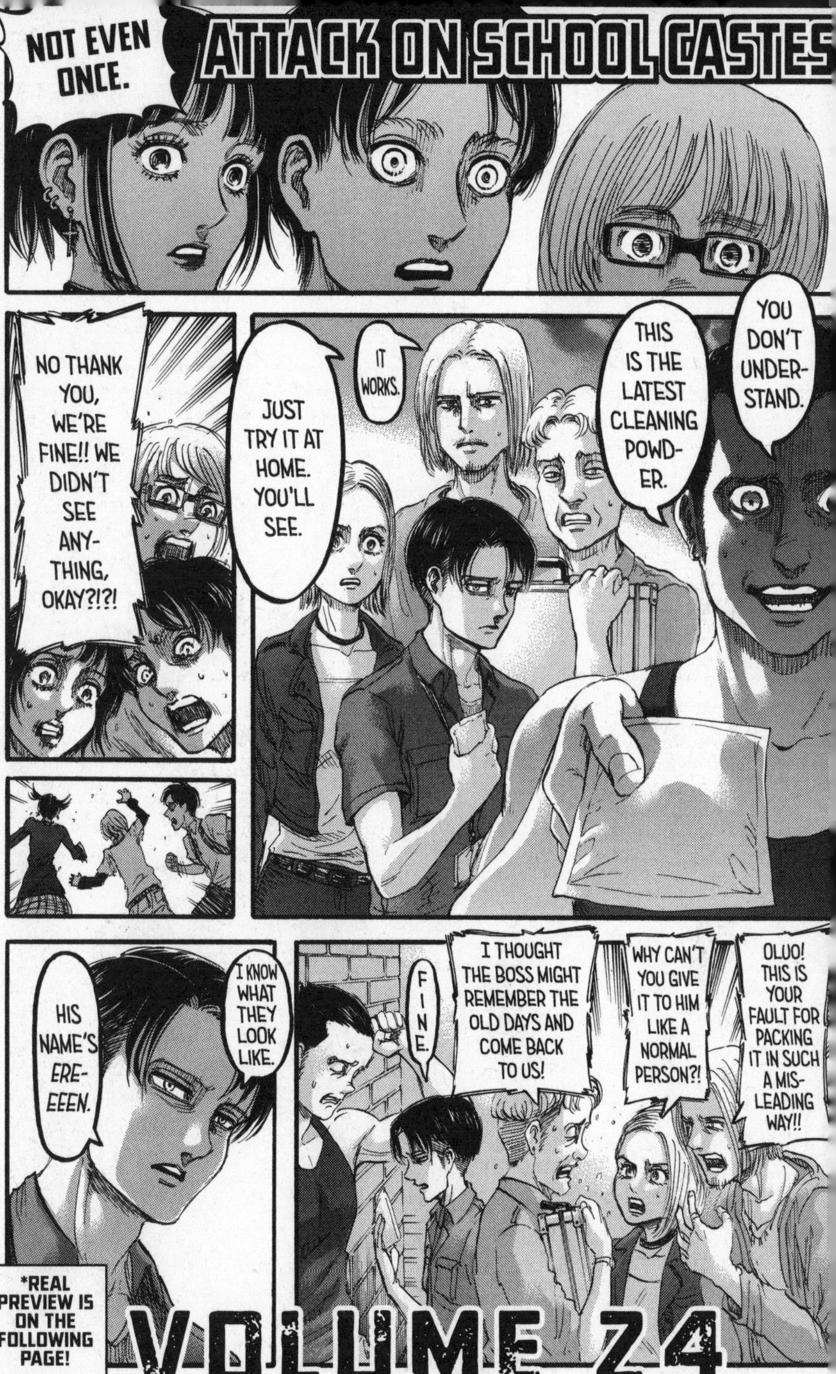
ATTACK ON SCHOOL CASTES
NOT EVEN ONCE.
YOU DON'T UNDER-STAND.
THIS IS THE LATEST CLEANING POWD-ER.
IT WORKS.
JUST TRY IT AT HOME. YOU'LL SEE.
NO THANK YOU, WE'RE FINE!! WE DIDN'T SEE ANY-THING, OKAY?!?!
OLUO! THIS IS YOUR FAULT FOR PACKING IT IN SUCH A MIS-LEADING WAY!!
WHY CAN'T YOU GIVE IT TO HIM LIKE A NORMAL PERSON?!
I THOUGHT THE BOSS MIGHT REMEMBER THE OLD DAYS AND COME BACK TO US!
FINE.
I KNOW WHAT THEY LOOK LIKE.
HIS NAME'S *EREEEEN.*
VOLUME 24
*REAL PREVIEW IS ON THE FOLLOWING PAGE!

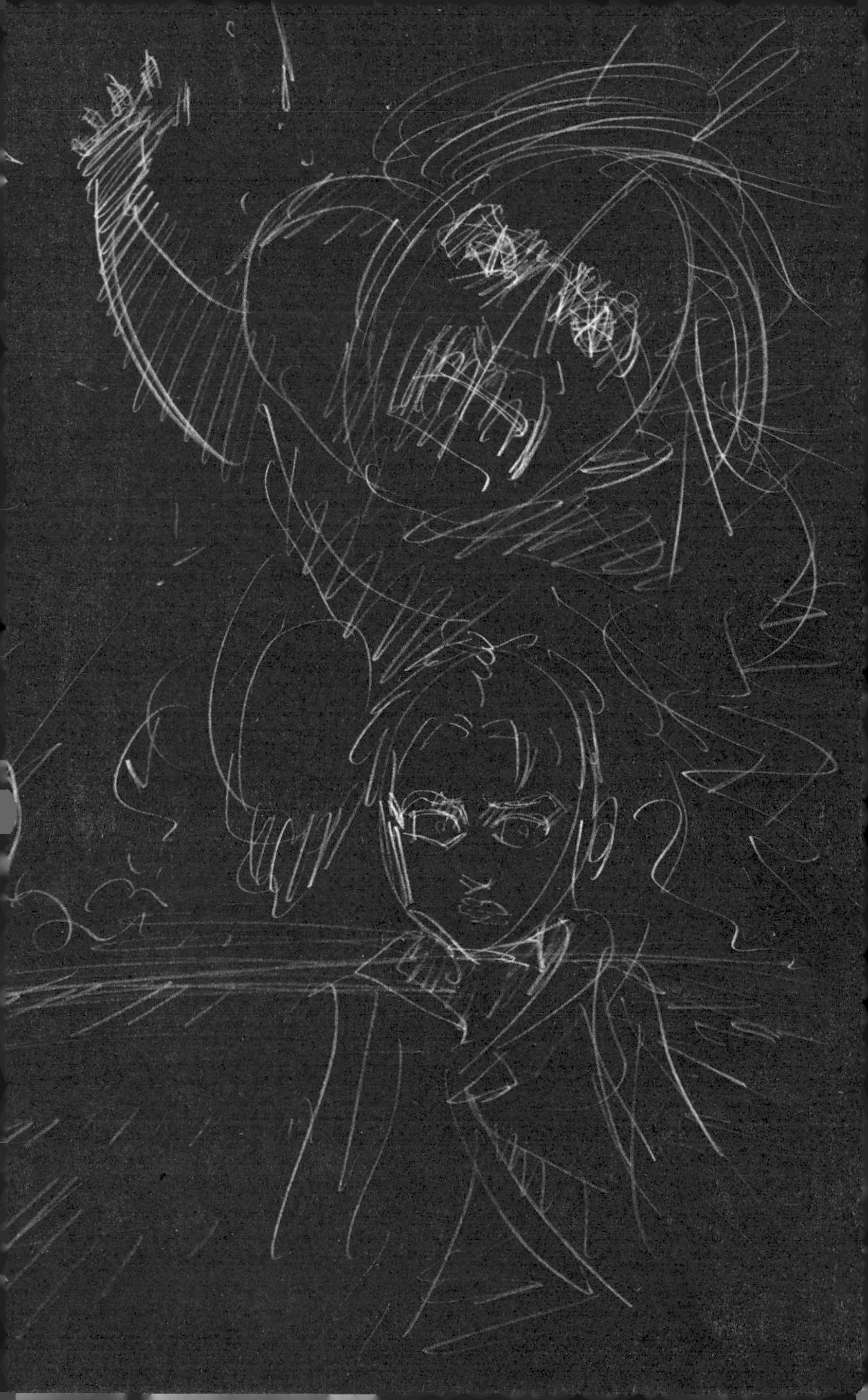

VOLUME 24 COMING 2018!

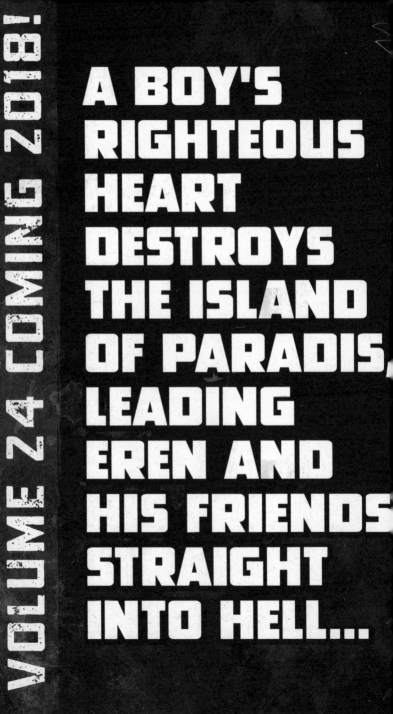

A BOY'S RIGHTEOUS HEART DESTROYS THE ISLAND OF PARADIS, LEADING EREN AND HIS FRIENDS STRAIGHT INTO HELL...

*Attack on Titan* volume 23 is a work of fiction. Names, characters, places, and incidents are the products of the author's imagination or are used fictitiously. Any resemblance to actual events, locales, or persons, living or dead, is entirely coincidental.

A Kodansha Comics Trade Paperback Original
*Attack on Titan* volume 23 copyright © 2017 Hajime Isayama
English translation copyright © 2017 Hajime Isayama

Published in the United States by Kodansha Comics, an imprint of Kodansha USA Publishing, LLC, New York.

Publication rights for this English edition arranged through Kodansha Ltd, Tokyo.

First published in Japan in 2017 by Kodansha Ltd., Tokyo as *Shingeki no kyojin*, volume 23.

ISBN 978-1-63236-463-0

Original cover design by Takashi Shimoyama (Red Rooster)

Printed in the United States of America.

www.kodanshacomics.com

9 8 7 6 5 4 3 2 1
Translation: Ko Ransom
Lettering: Steve Wands
Editing: Ben Applegate
Kodansha Comics edition cover design by Phil Balsman